MULTIUNIT ORGANIZATION AND MULTIMARKET STRATEGY

ADVANCES IN STRATEGIC MANAGEMENT

Series Editor: Joel A. C. Baum

Recent Volumes

Volume 15: Disciplinary Roots of Strategic Management Research

Volume 16: Population-Level Learning and Industry Change

Volume 17: Economics Meets Sociology in Strategic Management

ADVANCES IN STRATEGIC MANAGEMENT   VOLUME 18

MULTIUNIT ORGANIZATION AND MULTIMARKET STRATEGY

EDITED BY

JOEL A. C. BAUM
Rotman School of Management,
University of Toronto, Ontario, Canada

HENRICH R. GREVE
Institute of Policy and Planning Science,
University of Tsukuba, Ibaraki, Japan

2001

JAI
An Imprint of Elsevier Science
Amsterdam – London – New York – Oxford – Paris – Shannon – Tokyo

ELSEVIER SCIENCE Ltd
The Boulevard, Langford Lane
Kidlington, Oxford OX5 1GB, UK

First edition 2001

Library of Congress Cataloging in Publication Data

Multiunit organization and multimarket strategy/edited Joel Baum, Henrich R. Greve.
    p. cm. – (Advances in strategic management; v. 18)
    ISBN 0-7623-0721-8
    1. Strategic planning. 2. Organizational learning. 3. Organizational behavior.
    4. Industrial management. I. Baum, Joel A. C. II. Greve, Henrich R. III. Series.

    HD30.28 .M845 2001
    658.8'02–dc21   2001029425

British Library Cataloguing in Publication Data
A catalogue record from the British Library has been applied for.

ISBN: 0-7623-0721-8
ISSN: 0742-3322 (Series)

♾ The paper used in this publication meets the requirements of ANSI/NISO Z39.48-1992 (Permanence of Paper).
Printed in The Netherlands.

CONTENTS

LIST OF CONTRIBUTORS   *ix*

INTRODUCTION: A MULTIUNIT,
MULTIMARKET WORLD
    Henrich R. Greve and Joel A. C. Baum   *1*

PART ONE: ENTRY

ETHNIC LINKS, LOCATION CHOICE AND
PERFORMANCE: A TEST OF THE RURAL
MOTEL INDUSTRY
    Arturs Kalnins and Wilbur Chung   *31*

BEYOND MULTIMARKET CONTACT TO
MUTUAL FORBEARANCE: PURSUIT OF
MULTIMARKET STRATEGY
    Helaine J. Korn and Terence T. Rock   *53*

TRADEOFFS IN THE ORGANIZATION OF
PRODUCTION: MULTIUNIT FIRMS, GEOGRAPHIC
DISPERSION AND ORGANIZATIONAL LEARNING
    Pino G. Audia, Olav Sorenson and Jerald Hage   *75*

PART TWO: PRODUCTION AND INNOVATION BEHAVIOR

INTERORGANIZATIONAL LEARNING AND
THE DYNAMICS OF CHAIN RELATIONSHIPS
    Paul Ingram and Joel A. C. Baum   *109*

DYNAMICS OF KNOWLEDGE TRANSFER
AMONG MULTIMARKET COMPETITORS
    Christopher M. Cassidy and David Loree   *141*

DESIGNING MULTIMARKET-CONTACT
HYPOTHESIS TESTS: PATENT CITATIONS
AND MULTIMARKET CONTACT IN THE
PRODUCT AND INNOVATION MARKETS OF
THE CHEMICALS INDUSTRY
  John T. Scott   *175*

PART THREE: MARKET BEHAVIOR

COLLUSION IN HORIZONTALLY CONNECTED
MARKETS: MULTIMARKET PRODUCERS AS
CONDUITS FOR LEARNING
  Owen R. Phillips and Charles F. Mason   *205*

GETTING TO MULTIMARKET COMPETITION:
HOW MULTIMARKET CONTACT AFFECTS
FIRMS' MARKET ENTRY DECISIONS
  John Stephan and Warren Boeker   *229*

STRATEGIC MANAGEMENT IN THE NEW
ECONOMY: MODERN INFORMATION
TECHNOLOGIES AND MULTICHANNEL
CONTACT STRATEGIES
  Marc van Wegberg and Arjen van Witteloostuijn   *263*

MARKETS AND MULTIUNIT FIRMS FROM AN
AMERICAN HISTORICAL PERSPECTIVE
  Sukkoo Kim   *305*

PART FOUR: OUTCOMES

RACING FOR MARKET SHARE: HYPERCOMPETITION
AND THE PERFORMANCE OF MULTIUNIT-MULTIMARKET
FIRMS
  Stan X. Li and You-Ta Chuang   *329*

MULTIMARKET CONTACT: MEANING AND
MEASUREMENT AT MULTIPLE LEVELS OF
ANALYSIS
Javier Gimeno and Eui Jeong   *357*

LIST OF CONTRIBUTORS

Pino G. Audia	London Business School
Joel A. C. Baum	Rotman School of Management, University of Toronto
Warren Boeker	Business School, University of Washington
Christopher M. Cassidy	Department of Management, Texas A&M University
You-Ta Chuang	Rotman School of Management, University of Toronto
Wilbur Chung	Stern School of Business, New York University
Javier Gimeno	INSEAD
Henrich R. Greve	Institute of Policy and Planning Science, University of Tsukuba
Jerald Hage	Department of Sociology, University of Maryland
Paul Ingram	Graduate School of Business, Columbia University
Eui Jeong	Department of Management, Texas A&M University
Arturs Kalnins	Marshall School of Business, University of Southern California
Sukkoo Kim	Washington University in St. Louis and NBER
Helaine J. Korn	Zicklin School of Business, Baruch College, City University of New York
Stan X. Li	Rotman School of Management, University of Toronto

David Loree

Ivey Business School,
University of Western Ontario

Charles F. Mason

Department of Economics and Finance,
University of Wyoming

Owen R. Phillips

Department of Economics and Finance,
University of Wyoming

Terrence T. Rock

Tractionworks

John T. Scott

Department of Economics,
Dartmouth College

Olav Sorenson

Anderson School of Management,
University of California – Los Angeles

John Stephan

School of Management,
University at Buffalo – State University of
New York

Marc van Wegberg

Faculty of Economics and Business
Administration, University of Maastricht

Arjen van Witteloostuijn

Faculty of Economics and Business
Administration, University of Groningen

INTRODUCTION: A MULTIUNIT, MULTIMARKET WORLD

Henrich R. Greve and Joel A. C. Baum

A conspicuous feature of the modern economy is the proliferation of multiunit organizations that operate in several markets, often making considerable effort to standardize and coordinate the behavior of their units. The prominence of these multiunit-multimarket (MUMM) organizations in the economy can be seen through their share of the total employment. The National Longitudinal Survey of Youth 1979 panel study revealed that in 1994, 60% of working respondents were employed by large MUMM employers with more than 1,000 workers outside the establishment at which the respondent worked (up from 56% in 1990).[1] The National Organizations Study found that in 1991, 55% of surveyed establishments were affiliated with a MUMM organization, and that these organizations were usually large – the median size was 3,750 employees; the mean was 40,000 (Marsden, Cook & Knoke, 1996).

Table 1 compares the basic characteristics of MUMM organizations with the related multidivisional or 'M-form' organizational form and with singleunit organizations. MUMM organizations differ from the M-form in their greater degree of strategic relatedness of activities and coordination of units. There are different forms of MUMM organizations, with highest degree of relatedness and coordination found in the nearly identical and highly scripted units of service chains, and weaker degrees of relatedness and coordination found in the manufacture of multiple related products. An intermediate form is the multiplant manufacturer, which has plants that are coordinated and functionally highly related, but often add local adaptations to market or production behaviors.

Multiunit Organization and Multimarket Strategy, Volume 18, pages 1–28.
Copyright © 2001 by Elsevier Science Ltd.
All rights of reproduction in any form reserved.
ISBN: 0-7623-0721-8

Table 1.   Characteristics of MUMM and Related Organizational Forms.

Organizational Form	Examples	Production	Units	Markets	Strategy
Singleunit	Singleproduct-singleplant manufacturer or service provider	Geographically concentrated	One	Single or by export	Specialization; adaptation to local demand
MUMM	Multiplant manufacturer; Service chain	Geographically dispersed	Alike	Geographic	Efficient location; standardization
	Multiproduct	Geographically concentrated or dispersed	Dissimilar; related	Product and geographic	Scope economies; Leverage core competence
Multidivisional (M-form)	Conglomerate; Vertically integrated manufacturer	Geographically concentrated or dispersed	Dissimilar; related or unrelated	Product and/or geographic	Control; Scale economies; efficient resource allocation

MUMM organizations are perhaps best known in the guise of multiplant industrial firms, and they are indeed frequent in the manufacturing sector. Dunne et al. (1988) found that multiunit entrants accounted for 45% of all new establishments in the U.S. manufacturing sector, and were larger on average than singleunit entrants. New plants of multiunit organizations entered at 90% of the size of establishments already operating in the same industry, while new singleunit organizations were less than one-third of incumbents' size (31%). Plants of multiunit firms were also much less likely to fail than singleunit organizations, so multiunit organizations' share increased as each cohort of firms aged. MUMM organizations have also penetrated deeply into the retail sector, where one-third of all U.S. sales are done by multiunit organizations (including franchises) (Bradach, 1997). MUMM organizations are now coming to dominate virtually every service industry – from food and travel accommodations to health and human services – at the same time that service industries are increasingly important to economies around the world (Ingram & Baum, 1997a).

The growth of the MUMM organizational form has drawn the attention of academics, and seems at least indirectly responsible for some recent trends in the theory of the firm. Organizations that replicate a set of routines in multiple locations invite discussion of the firm as a bundle of routines (Nelson & Winter, 1982), where firms that have especially valuable routines leverage these by spawning identical units in multiple geographical markets. Firms extending their reach across multiple related product-markets reinforce this concern and add questions of how firms augment their knowledge base when entering new markets. Thus, firms as collections of routines, as sets of competencies, or as knowledge collectors are frequently used metaphors in current theory (Barney, 1991; Starbuck, 1992; Teece, Pisano & Shuen, 1997; Wernerfeldt, 1984).

The rise of the MUMM organizational form during the 20th Century is a transformation in the structure of business equal – perhaps even greater – in scale to the rise of the multidivisional form (Chandler, 1969; Fligstein, 1991; Williamson, 1975). The behavioral consequences of this change are far greater, however, because modern MUMM firms – whether multilocation or multi-product – endeavor to coordinate their production and market behaviors across units more closely than multidivisional firms did in the era of portfolio planning. It is one of the goals of this volume to stimulate research on the effects of MUMM coordination on the firm, its consumers, and the economy and society as a whole.

MUMM ORGANIZATION RESEARCH

Research on the MUMM organizational form has been done from the 'multi-unit organization' perspective, which has used learning and knowledge transfer theory, and the 'multimarket strategy' perspective, which has used commitment and mutual forbearance theory. Both perspectives are extensions of theories of singleunit firms. The multiunit organization perspective is based on research on experiential learning within organizations and in the market (Levitt & March, 1988). The multimarket strategy perspective is an extension of oligopoly and entry deterrence theory (Scherer & Ross, 1990). Both have quickly outgrown their origins, however, and now clearly demonstrate that MUMM organizations differ from singleunit organizations not only quantitatively in scale, but also qualitatively in how they learn and compete.

Multiunit Organization Research

Work on learning in multiunit organizations draws on ideas from learning curves (Yelle, 1979), diffusion of innovations (Coleman, Katz & Menzel, 1966), and competency traps (Levitt & March, 1988). A multiunit organization can improve its routines through transfer learning among its different units (Argote, 1999; Darr, Argote & Epple, 1995), resulting in individual learning curves within each unit and "spillover" learning among the units. Although such spillover also occurs among organizations not connected through ownership (Ghemawat & Spence, 1985; Jarmin, 1994), it is stronger within multiunit systems (Baum & Ingram, 1998; Darr, Argote & Epple, 1995). Thus, learning spillover is a potential source of competitive advantage for multiunit organizations; a fact clearly recognized by the managers of large franchise systems (Bradach, 1997), and corroborated in recent empirical work. Banaszak-Holl and colleagues (2000), for example, have shown how post-acquisition capability transfers from U.S. nursing home chains improves their new components' operating performance (e.g. efficiency of operations) and quality of care (e.g. resident pressure ulcers).

A multiunit organization can also be a conduit for the diffusion of innovations (Greve, 1995, 1996; Levin, Levin & Meisel, 1992). Diffusion within multiunit organizations is a special case of the general finding that diffusion follows social ties among organizations (Chaves, 1996; Davis, 1991; Kraatz, 1998), but again shared ownership is a strong conduit of knowledge transfer that will make diffusion comparably rapid. Diffusion within multiunit organizations make their units prone to early adoption of innovations both because innovations spread rapidly within the multiunit firm and because their representation in several markets allows early detection of innovations (Greve, 1996, 1998).

Thus far, learning theory seems to favor multiunit over singleunit organizations, but complications arise from competency traps. An organization is in a competency trap if it executes some routines so efficiently that it experiences a (short-term) loss in performance if it changes to a more valuable set of routines (Levitt & March, 1988). Because of constraints on organizational attention and change capability (Cyert & March, 1963), organizational learning is fundamentally about tradeoffs between exploiting routines that the organization executes well and exploring whether superior routines exist (March, 1991). Learning by doing improves competencies in the organization's current activity but draws resources away from innovations (Christensen & Bower, 1996; Levinthal & March, 1981; March, 1991). Diffusion can suppress innovations by creating cost structures that favor practices adopted early on and substituting the judgment of others for private information (Arthur, 1989; Bikhchandani, Hirshleifer & Welch, 1992). These tradeoffs occur also in singleunit organizations, but the added information flow of multiunit organizations makes them especially prone to substitute learning done elsewhere for local innovation. Multiunit organizations also confront greater variation in competitive environments, which creates a risk of transferring routines from environments in which they are beneficial to environments where they are neutral or even harmful.

Combining ideas of learning-by-doing, diffusion, and competency traps has yielded several fruitful research initiatives. The most direct application has been research exploring how experience differentially affects the performance and survival of single and multiunit organizations. Ingram and Baum (1997a) found that the experience of hotel chains within a geographic market – Manhattan – was always beneficial for its units in that market, but when chains accumulated experience in other locations it was detrimental, suggesting diffusion of routines into environments where they were detrimental. In a study of U.S. radio stations, Greve (1999) found that experience in a given market reduced the variation in market shares but did not affect the market share level, while experience outside that market increased the variation in market shares and decreased the level. This suggests inappropriate transfer of routines, but does not indicate whether the competency traps are caused by routines being transferred within the corporation or imitated from competitors observed in other markets.

Learning theory has also been applied to market entry as a result of diffusion and learning from experience. Since these processes do not require the organization to have a multiunit form – though it may become one as a result of entering new markets – much of this research is not explicitly multiunit; nevertheless, the findings are clearly relevant. Diffusion studies show that organizations are likely to enter markets that other organizations have entered, and are especially likely to do so when the other organizations are large or high-performing (Greve, 1996; Haveman, 1993; Kraatz, 1998). Studies of organizational learning from experience show that organizations that have recently changed their market position are likely to do so again, either to reinforce their position or adjust it (Amburgey, Kelly & Barnett, 1993; Amburgey & Miner, 1992; Kelly & Amburgey, 1991).

Several recent studies have applied these experiential learning and diffusion ideas to market entry processes. Korn and Baum (1999) found that imitation predicted entry into commuter airline city-pair markets in California. Greve (2000) found that diffusion from large firms and momentum from past decisions predicted branch entry decisions of Tokyo banks. Baum, Li and Usher (2000) found that local search, momentum, and diffusion from similar chains influenced the locations of Ontario nursing home chains' acquisitions. The tendency towards spatial agglomeration found in several studies is also suggestive of a diffusion of market entry decisions (Baum & Haveman, 1997; Caplin & Leahy, 1998; Sorensen & Audia, 2000), but attraction to immobile resources remains an alternative explanation (Kim, 1995).

Multimarket Strategy Research

Work on multimarket strategies has close links with oligopoly and entry deterrence theory (Caves & Porter, 1977), as it treats the key issues of market collusion and entry deterrence with added theory on how firm interdependence in multiple markets affect their strategic and competitive behavior in a given market. The multimarket version of mutual forbearance theory argues that collusive strategies are more likely to emerge when firms face each other in multiple markets because multiple markets give greater scope for firms to respond to their competitors' behaviors (Edwards, 1955). Firms can counterattack in markets where their potential losses are small relative to the aggressor's, forcing the aggressor to bear a higher cost for its initial rivalrous action (Karnani & Wernerfelt, 1985). Market or firm differences allow construction of asymmetric punishments that make forbearance more effective (Bernheim & Whinston, 1990), but are not required for mutual forbearance (Spagnolo, 1999; Scott, this volume).

These arguments yield straightforward predictions for market behavior and outcomes: multimarket contact will lead to higher prices, lower production volume, higher profits, and lower failure rates of the incumbent firms. The evidence is clearly in favor of these predictions. Multimarket contact has been shown to result in higher prices (Barros, 1999; Evans & Kessides, 1994; Feinberg, 1985; Fernandez & Marin, 1998; Gimeno, 1999; Gimeno & Woo, 1996; Jans & Rosenbaum, 1996; Parker & Roller, 1997; Singal, 1996), higher profits (Barnett, Greve & Park, 1994; Phillips & Mason, 1992; Piloff, 1999), higher growth (Haveman & Nonnemaker, 2000), and lower rates of market exit among incumbents (Barnett, 1993; Baum, 1999; Baum & Korn, 1996, 1999; Boeker, Goodstein, Stephan & Murmann, 1997).

The benefits of having multimarket contact suggest that firms will enter markets where such contacts can be established. Indeed, early systematic evidence for the importance of multimarket structures in the economy includes the finding that conglomerate firms have levels of multimarket contact significantly greater than those they would get by following independent diversification strategies (Scott, 1989, 1991). The finding that firms with multimarket contact are more likely to collaborate on R&D and other activities also suggests intent to collude, since such collaboration offers easy and nontransparent communication among firms (Scott, 1988; Scott & Pascoe, 1987; van Wegberg, van Witteloostuijn & Abbing, 1994; Vonortas, 2000). Research on entry into geographical markets supports the idea that firms seek out multimarket contact, but adds a caveat. There is an apparent tendency for firms to seek out multimarket competitors when the level of contact is low to moderate, but not when it is high (Baum, 1999; Baum & Korn, 1999; Baum, Li & Usher, 2000; Greve, 2000; Haveman & Nonnemaker, 2000), perhaps in fear of destabilizing competitive relationships. This suggests that quite moderate levels of multimarket contact may be sufficient to establish forbearance.[2]

SETTING MUMM ORGANIZATIONS APART

Unlike much of management and economic theory, theories of multiunit organization and multimarket strategy are oriented towards a specific organizational form, so they have a narrower focus. As we noted at the outset, organizations with multiple establishments or markets have become a substantial part of the economy. Although there may be justification for separate theory for them on that basis alone, it still is worthwhile asking why separate theories are needed. Are MUMM organizations really so special that standard strategic management and organizational theory is insufficient? To ask this question is the same as asking whether multiunit organizations are qualitatively different from singleunit organizations (of the same size), and whether multiple markets are qualitatively different from a single market (of the same size).

The difference between singleunit and multiunit organizations is most clearly seen at the interface of the organization and its environment. Multiunit organizations face not one environment but many, and seek to solve a difficult problem of identifying and adapting to the common and unique features of these environments. This learning process is distinctive because the different parts of the organization have different experiences. Although this can facilitate learning by permitting comparison of information across units and use of 'quasi-experiments' (Audia, Sorenson & Hage, this volume), it also raises the problem of how to integrate experiences from different units and draw correct implications for the management of the organization as a whole. Multimarket organizations adapt to each of their markets, but also consider strategic links across markets. This complicates interpretation of competitor behavior, since a multimarket competitor's action in a given market may be motivated by a concern for a different market.

Thus, the classic organizational problem of coordination gains an additional dimension from the multiunit structure; the classic economic problem of optimization gains an additional dimension from the multimarket structure. The learning problem can be simplified by full decentralization, but this would disregard the economic justification for the MUMM organizational form: Since a fully decentralized MUMM organization is behaviorally equivalent to a set of singleunit organizations, the common ownership would be a wasteful bundling of assets. The optimization problem is also easier to solve by full decentralization, and such a solution is often desirable since some forms of optimization across markets are anticompetitive (e.g. mutual forbearance). The incentives to behave as if markets are linked suggest that researchers cannot assume decentralization; nor can they assume that any multimarket optimization that occurs is benign. Coordination and optimization across markets and units comes hand in glove with the MUMM organizational form.

Although multiple environments characterize the multiunit organization, they are not unique to the MUMM organizational form. Even singleunit organizations face multiple environments and the problem of integrating their experiences. A singleunit organization facing demands from suppliers, customers, government, and interest organizations can benefit from recognizing the common and unique features of these demands, and since different functional units typically address each of these environments, it has to integrate knowledge from different units just as the multiunit organization does. To put it more strongly, when strategic management and organization theorists write about 'the environment,' it should be understood as a simplifying abstraction that hides considerable differences in the interests and behaviors of the constituent actors. It is natural for theories of multiunit organizations to face these issues head on, and thus to resurrect the problem of environmental differentiation identified so clearly in the behavioral theory of the firm (Cyert & March, 1963), contingency theory (Lawrence & Lorsch, 1967), and resource dependence theory (Pfeffer & Salancik, 1978). Thus, studying multiunit organizations helps advance the mainstream of strategic management and organizational theory by fostering a return to one of the core problems of the field.

Similarly, multimarket theory addresses a more general problem of strategic management and economic theory, where 'the market' is a simplifying abstraction that hides considerable differences in the interests and behaviors of the constituent actors. Defining markets has been a source of great difficulty for empirical economists (Scherer & Ross, 1990: 73–79), and modern consumer societies have such a proliferation of more or less substitutable goods that neatly bounded markets have become exceedingly rare. Substitution on the consumer side is not the only link between markets, however, as strategic linkages on the producer side must also be considered. Strategic linkages are even more difficult to handle because they are unrelated to consumer preferences and can be created or dissolved by organizational fiat.

Any time an organization establishes itself in multiple markets and behaves as if they are linked, its behavior becomes part of the strategic environment of the other organizations in those markets, and ultimately affects consumers. Organizations that meet in multiple markets can raise the level of rivalry from the market to the organization, feeling free to respond to challenges in one market by reactions in another or to offer soft competition in one market as a reward for soft competition in another. Multimarket research focuses on markets with strategic links but weak substitution links, which isolates the rivalry portion of the linked markets problem. As such, it is a step toward resolving the general problem of linked markets in the economy that helps advance the mainstream of economic theory, but is not a complete solution.

Based on sheer frequency of mention, a novice student of strategic management, organization theory, and economics might assume that 'environment' and 'market' are well-defined concepts. This is not so; important conceptual issues have been left unsolved in order to tackle problems in which they are believed to be inconsequential. Research on MUMM organizations clearly shows that the definitions of these concepts are frayed at the edges and require further work. Researchers are currently drawn to MUMM organizations not only because of their strategic and economic importance, but also because they offer a chance to revisit and renew the foundations of the field.

THE CHALLENGE OF MUMM ORGANIZATION RESEARCH

Theoretical perspectives on multiunit organization and multimarket strategy are interdisciplinary, with contributions from management, economics and sociology in each one, but little interaction between the perspectives. Moreover, although the organizations studied are typically both multiunit structures and participants in multiple markets, most studies focus on one aspect – multiunit or multimarket – only. This division of labor has offered researchers efficiencies that have been useful for the early development of these perspectives, but it is now time that they face each other and several recalcitrant facts that call for further theory development and integration.

First, the coordination of units necessary to forbear or transfer skills is a dynamic capability that varies across organizations. Capabilities for mutual forbearance or knowledge transfer cannot be assumed to equal actual conduct, making development of theory on how multiunit organizations learn to use such opportunities an important item on the research agenda (Chandler, 1977; Kim, 1999). There is progress on these issues in both areas. Multimarket research has seen work on how organizations establish channels of communication that can be used for later coordination (Scott, 1993; van Wegberg, van Witteloostuijn & Abbing, 1994; Vonortas, 2000), and learn about mutual forbearance and multimarket competitive behavior through experience (Korn & Baum, 1999; Stephan & Boeker, this volume). Recent multiunit research includes work on organizational mechanisms to facilitate learning across units (Bradach, 1997; Hansen, 1999).

Second, the use of different theories for markets and organizations seems artificial. Learning and knowledge transfer ideas also apply to market behaviors, since knowledge about the market can be transferred among units. Organizational market strategies can be refined through experience (Burgelman, 1991; Noda & Bower, 1996), and strategies for entering markets or maximizing profits in extant markets can be repeated across the different units of an organization (Amburgey & Miner, 1992; Baum, Li & Usher, 2000; Kelly & Amburgey, 1991). Organizational strategies can be learnt from other organizations that are easily observable because of their size (Haveman, 1993) or market contact with the focal organization (Baum & Haveman, 1997; Greve, 1996).

Third, the continued coexistence of multiunit and singleunit organizations creates difficulty for the simplest kinds of forbearance and learning theories. Theories specifying that multiunit organizations have main-effect advantages, or that singleunit organizations do, need to account for their failure to drive each other out of the market. One possible explanation is a division of markets into a core served by the more standardized multiunit organizations and a periphery served by singleunit organizations (Carroll, 1985; Freeman & Lomi, 1994). Such segmentation is likely to be a part of the story, but does not explain markets where both organizational forms are found in the core. This task requires developing more contingent conceptualizations of when MUMM organizations have advantages over single unit organizations (such as Audia et al., this volume; Baum & Ingram, 1997a, b; Greve, 1999).

Lastly, explanations of high performance through forbearance need to deal with how multiunit organizations can forbear against singleunit organizations, since forbearance based on multimarket links is ineffective against organizations that lack such links. This is problematic in markets where multimarket and singlemarket organizations coexist, since it is not clear how some actors in the market can forbear when other actors do not. One resolution is market friction in the form of capacity constraints on singleunit organizations or brand reputations of the multiunit organizations (Baum, 1999; Ingram, 1996). Another is that singleunit organizations decide to 'go along' with the soft competition, preferring to avoid the risk of competition with larger MUMM organizations – at least until they have developed a sufficient competitive strength of their own (Chen & Hambrick, 1995). A third is the suggestion that firms can find behaviors that selectively attack some of their competitors (Barnett, Greve & Park, 1994; Chen & Hambrick, 1995). Finally, multiunit firms may transfer weak competition from markets where they forbear with multimarket firms to markets where they meet only singlemarket firms (see Philips & Mason, this volume).

The recent growth of research on multiunit organization and multimarket strategy is very impressive, and suggests that these problems will soon be tackled. Our aim in this volume is to bring together research from multiunit and multimarket perspectives grounded in management, economics and sociology traditions and to hasten this process by fostering an interchange of ideas and findings among contributors and with readers.

TOWARD AN INTEGRATED THEORY OF MUMM STRATEGIC ORGANIZATION

A long-term goal of this volume is to move the study areas of multiunit and multimarket research towards greater disciplinary, theoretical and empirical integration. The chapters clearly move in this direction, and we believe that further progress will be made. To show why such integration is important, we outline a possible structure for an integrated theory of MUMM strategic organization. Figure 1 summarizes the organizational components of study, the outcomes of interest, and the causal links among them. For simplicity, the figure omits some of the causal relations that can be studied (including some that appear in this volume). Below we describe the framework components and briefly mention some possible extensions. Then we consider the papers in this volume, locating each of their contributions within the framework – and beyond it.

Organizational Subsystems

We divide the figure into production and market subsystems to reflect that these are major domains of organizational learning and strategy, and that MUMM organizations often decouple them so that separate production and market decisions are made. The traditional one-plant one-market correspondence holds only in on-premises service industries such as hotels and restaurants, and even there only as an approximation (e.g. business and leisure travelers are effectively different markets even though they are served by the same production facility). Additional subsystems could be considered. Scott (this volume) finds that innovations are affected by multimarket considerations, suggesting that the innovation subsystem of the organization should also be considered. Also, as van Wegberg and van Witteloostuijn (this volume) point out, different organizational areas of action, such as alliances, can be considered channels of contact among organizations.

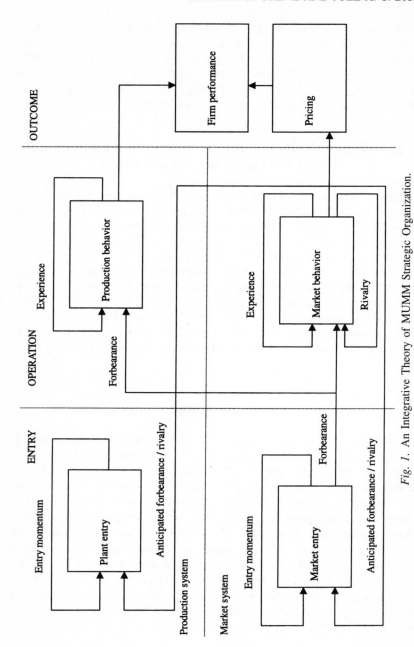

Fig. 1. An Integrative Theory of MUMM Strategic Organization.

Behaviors and Outcomes

Following most treatments of MUMM organizations, we separate entry behaviors, such as establishing a new plant or entering a new market, and operating behaviors, such as running the plant and competing in the market. We also consider outcomes – pricing and performance – that result from the operating behaviors of the firm and its competitors as a third category, thus yielding a division much like the standard structure-conduct-performance paradigm of industrial organization (Scherer & Ross, 1990). This division is not meant as a temporal or causal order – while many causal arrows go from left to right, there are also feedback processes from past behaviors in the same subsystem (mainly from learning theory) and strategic decision making based on anticipated behaviors (mainly from mutual forbearance theory).

Causal Links

The causal links diagrammed here should be familiar to MUMM researchers, but we will give a brief introduction for readers new to the area. First, note four feedback processes from one subsystem to itself, labeled 'entry momentum' and 'experience.' These capture the effects of experiential learning in one domain of action on the same domain, and usually result in self-reinforcement. Organizational attention, interpretation, and routinization processes increase the propensity to repeat a recent action and the competence to perform it (Levinthal & March, 1981).

One variant of this process is when routinization of information collection and decision making leads organizations to repeat strategic actions such as market entry even when their performance consequences are uncertain (Amburgey & Miner, 1992; March, Sproull & Tamuz, 1991). Such decision-making momentum can result in repeated market entries in or near the current market, or repeated plant entries in the same area (Baum, Li, & Usher, 2000; Greve, 2000). Another variant is the well-known learning curve, where the cumulative experience in manufacturing a good decreases unit costs (Argote, 1999; Day & Montgomery, 1983; Yelle, 1979). Extensions of this learning curve to a multiunit context includes work on the costs and benefits of transferring knowledge learned in one unit to other units (Baum & Ingram, 1998; Darr, Argote & Epple, 1995; Greve, 1999; Ingram & Baum, 1997b). A third variant is experiential learning in pricing and volume decisions, where organizations use trial-and-error learning to search for the locally optimal place in differentiated markets (Leifer & White, 1987; White, 1981).

Next, note the links marked 'forbearance' going from market entry to market and production behaviors. These links capture the standard mutual forbearance hypothesis in which a market structure with multimarket linkages among firms leads to weaker competition through raised prices and lowered production volume (Edwards, 1955; Evans & Kessides, 1994; Fernandez & Marin, 1998). A related idea is captured in the feedback loop labeled 'rivalry' linking market behavior to itself. This loop captures a variety of dynamic strategies in market competition, such as building up and exploiting reputations (Borenstein, 1991; Kreps & Wilson, 1982) and monitoring and responding to competitor behavior (Chen & Hambrick, 1995; Chen & Miller, 1994). Some of these arguments apply with greater force in multimarket contexts since such contexts have greater frequency of interaction and range of possible actions (including punitive actions), both of which hold collaborative dynamic equilibria in place (Green & Porter, 1984; van Wegberg & van Witteloostujin, this volume).

Next, note the links labeled 'anticipated forbearance/rivalry' going back from market behavior to the entry of markets and plants. These links capture the strategic entry into markets to create new multimarket contact or benefit from existing multimarket contact, and the anticipated behavior of multimarket competitors is an important factor in this entry decision. Here there are two competing hypotheses. One is that firms enter markets where multimarket competitors are present because they expect such markets to be less competitive (the 'forbear from competing' hypothesis) (Scott, 1989, 1991). The second is that firms avoid markets where multimarket competitors are present as a way of dividing the total market into spheres of influence (the 'forbear from entering' hypothesis) (Baum & Korn, 1996; Gimeno, 1999). Which of these patterns of behaviors will prevail depends on multimarket competitors' conjectured future behavior, and thus is linked with issues of reputation and tacit understandings among competitors. In practice, empirical research cannot measure firm conjectures or tacit agreements. Consequently, work on market entry typically links the observed multimarket structure to the observed market entry behavior, bypassing unobserved conjectures about future market behaviors (Baum & Korn, 1996, 1999; Greve, 2000; Korn & Baum, 1999).

Finally, the obvious links from market behavior to rivalry, and from production (both volume and cost) and rivalry to firm performance and survival are entered. These links are straightforward, but serve to highlight the length of the implicit causal chain in some studies of MUMM behavior. When the multimarket structure is linked to organizational performance, the mediating links to market behaviors, pricing, and performance go unmodeled. Some of these bypassed steps in the causal chain contain important processes such as production efficiency, rivalry and experience in the market. Studies linking market behaviors to pricing are one link shorter and thus lessen the influence from production processes (and experimental studies can eliminate such influence, e.g. Phillips & Mason, this volume). Similarly, studies linking production experience with performance or survival leave the long causal chain involving market behaviors unmodeled, and are thus vulnerable to confounding influence from multimarket behaviors.

It should now be clear why an integration of multiunit and multimarket research is both desirable and difficult. The organizational and strategic processes outlined in Fig. 1 concern a common organizational form and affect the same dependent variables. Even if the processes do not interact with each other or with unobserved variables, each can be a confounding cause in studies of the other.

There is, moreover, some evidence that the processes do interact. Since organizations acquire skills through competitive interactions in the market, weak competition may reduce the speed of learning (Barnett, Greve & Park, 1994). Thus, MUMM organizations that achieve mutual forbearance may be less well adapted to market demands than organizations that do not. As a result, the higher prices from mutual forbearance may be accompanied by high cost structures and/or poor product selection. Consistent with this idea, analysis of performance of singleunit and branch banks showed that singleunit banks benefited from learning but branch banks did not, while branch banks benefited from multimarket contacts (Barnett, Greve & Park, 1994). A related idea is that MUMM organizations are insulated from unit-level selection processes, which will cause them to have weaker competitive strength unless they can construct internal selection processes that mimic those of the market (Barnett, 1997).

Learning and forbearance may also interact with organizational size. Entry momentum results from a sequence of successes (or at least, no obvious failures), which becomes increasingly unlikely as an organization grows. It should thus be weaker for large organizations, as Greve (2000) has found. Mutual forbearance relies on capability and intention to punish MUMM organizations that do not forbear, both of which may increase as MUMM organizations grow and gain experience. It should thus be stronger for larger firms, as Baum and Korn (1999) have shown. Since some measures of multimarket contact are highly collinear with size (Gimeno & Jeong, this volume), they may inadvertently capture an interaction of firm size and forbearance.

ORGANIZATION AND CONTRIBUTIONS
OF VOLUME 18

The contributions of this volume span the entire range of MUMM theory and research, as Fig. 2 shows. Here the theoretical framework of Fig. 1 is reproduced

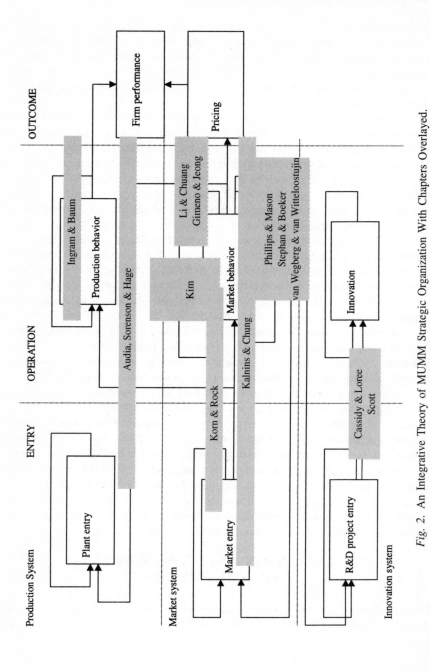

Fig. 2. An Integrative Theory of MUMM Strategic Organization With Chapters Overlayed.

with the chapters of this volume overlaid roughly according to their theme. This requires adding a third domain of behavior, as two chapters – Cassidy and Loree, and Scott – concern the innovation behavior of firms. It also involves taking the main thrust of each paper rather than its full range, as there is enough crossover work in the volume to cover the figure with shading. To avoid this we have not marked that some of these papers have multiple themes, such as the multimarket behavior investigated by Audia et al. or the learning processes studied by Korn and Rock. The figure still shows that the chapters of this volume cover a wide range of themes and theoretical approaches. In addition to this, each chapter has a depth of coverage only seen in top-level research.

Part One: Entry

In "Ethnic links, location choice and performance: A test of the rural motel industry," Arturs Kalnins and Wilbur Chung examine whether multimarket behaviors can be triggered by other mechanisms than joint ownership of establishments. Taking ethnic links as one possible mechanism for multimarket behaviors, they explore whether hotel owners with the surname Patel (frequent in the state of Gujarat in western India) are likely to locate hotels near each other and to have higher room prices when they are near other Patel-owned hotels. They find that Patel-owned hotels co-locate at the regional level, but not at the zip code level, suggesting that the location pattern is not for the purpose of controlling pricing but perhaps for other forms of mutual aid. The analysis of pricing likewise does not show an effect of being near other Patel-owned hotels. Thus, ethnic ties are not a strong enough link to provoke the kind of multimarket behavior exhibited by establishments with shared ownership.

In "Beyond multimarket contact to mutual forbearance: Pursuit of multimarket strategy," Helaine Korn and Terry Rock analyze the organizational decision making process behind the establishment and strategic use of multimarket contact. They argue that the market-based logic behind multimarket strategies is different from and to some degree in conflict with the capability-based logic followed by some firms, so it is not given that firms will seek out multimarket contacts or use them strategically once they are established. They use the theory of managerial cognition to give predictions on the market conditions and organizational forms that give rise to firms behaving as multimarket strategists, multimarket pacifists, or multimarket opportunists. These predictions modify the link from multimarket contact to multimarket behavior posited by standard mutual forbearance theory.

In "Tradeoffs in the organization of production: Multiunit firms, geographic dispersion, and organizational learning," Pino Audia, Olav Sorenson, and Jerald

Hage use multiunit and multimarket theory to explore how different plant locations affect the survival of plants and firms. They suggest that the choice of plant dispersal or concentration is a tradeoff where concentration of plants offers economies of scale and learning advantages while dispersion gives lower transportation costs and greater opportunities for forbearance. Their analysis gives clear evidence of these tradeoffs, as dispersion is beneficial overall but reduces the benefits of experiential learning. They also show that multimarket contact is beneficial. Finally, they find that large size and multiplant structure reduce the ability to adapt to environmental change, so singleunit organizations have advantages over multiunit organizations in dynamic environments.

Part Two: Production and Innovation Behavior

In "Interorganizational learning and the dynamics of chain relationships," Paul Ingram and Joel Baum extend prior work on learning across organizations by studying the role of learning in the formation and dissolution of chain relationships in the Manhattan hotel industry. Drawing on theory on the dynamic advantages and disadvantages of multiunit learning relative to singleunit learning, they explore which kinds of hotels will prefer chain ownerships and which will prefer a singleunit form. The results show that just as little experience can weaken independent hotels, so can too much experience or the wrong kind of experience lead a chain into a competency trap. A singleunit hotel with insufficient experience might be driven into the arms of a chain, but a chain with insufficient experience in the local market cannot retain its components. Highly experienced hotels were likely to enter chains, but long-lasting component relationships were likely to be broken. The results suggest why single and multiunit organizations' components thrive side by side – these forms are strong under different conditions, and so it is unlikely for one or the other of them to gain the upper hand completely.

In "Dynamics of knowledge transfer among multimarket competitors," Chris Cassidy and David Loree develop theory on how the MUMM organizational form learns from other organizations it is in contact with. Extending the theories of interfirm rivalry and knowledge transfer from a singleunit to a multiunit context, they argue that the weaker rivalry and stronger overlap of activities between firms with high multimarket contact increases the motivation and capability for knowledge transfers. This creates a tendency for knowledge transfers among firms with a high degree of multimarket contact, and this tendency will be strengthened if these firms are viewed as a strategic group. Using data on cross-citations of patents in the integrated circuit industry, they show that cross-citations are more likely when firms have a high degree of geographic multimarket contact and are of similar size and age. Thus, both multimarket contact and social similarity of firms drive knowledge transfers among them.

In "Designing multimarket-contact hypothesis tests: Patent citations and multimarket contact in the product and innovation markets of the chemicals industry," John Scott examines how multimarket contacts in the chemicals industry affect the innovation behaviors of its firms. He shows that prior multimarket contact in either product markets or patenting predicts patent cross-citations, suggesting that firms are prone to deepen pre-existing multimarket relations through their innovation behavior. These results add a new kind of multimarket behavior to the literature, and suggest that the role of innovation in changing the competitiveness of markets is not as clear-cut as many have thought. The pattern of innovating in markets shared with multimarket competitors is surely a strategic behavior, and suggests that multimarket firms use innovations not as weapons to defeat rival firms, but as levers for increased profits in markets where weak competition is expected. The results appear to be contrary to Schumpeterian theory of innovations upsetting the balance of markets.

Part Three: Market Behavior

In "Collusion in horizontally connected markets: Multimarket producers as conduits for learning," Owen Phillips and Charles Mason conduct a version of their classic multimarket experiment with an important new variation. In this experimental game, one MUMM firm plays against two single-market firms, so there is no multimarket contact. In such a "learning only" game, there is no market interdependence of the kind that should trigger mutual forbearance among firms, but the multimarket firm still plays as if the markets were interdependent. This remarkable result suggests that weak competition in markets where multimarket firms participate can occur spontaneously through transfer of learning across markets, and does not need any real deterrents. It also suggests that strong competition in some markets where a multimarket firm participates can cause it to behave more competitively in its other markets. Phillips and Mason also find that competitive learning transfers more easily through the MUMM conduit than cooperative learning. Overall, duopoly markets are more competitive with the MUMM conduit.

In "Getting to multimarket competition: How multimarket contact affects firms' market entry decisions," John Stephan and Warren Boeker address the theoretical problem of how much multimarket contact is necessary to deter competitors against competitive behaviors. They suggest that firms move from being in multimarket contact to exhibiting forbearing behaviors when their managers become aware of the competitive interdependence, and that this gap between actual contact and awareness accounts for the fact that levels of multimarket contact between firms often seem higher than would be necessary to deter against strong competition. This theoretical analysis is an important step toward studies that integrate learning and mutual forbearance theory in market entry and market behavior.

In "Strategic management in the New Economy: Information technologies and multichannel contact strategies," Marc van Wegberg and Arjen van Witteloostuijn review current theories of multimarket contacts as learning and forbearance devices and develop new propositions on how such contacts are used by firms. These propositions are applied to business opportunities created by the Internet, yielding the conclusion that this rapid technological change creates competitive uncertainty that encourages high use of alliances and other non-market channels of contacts. Firms that establish such a structure will experience a proliferation of learning and retaliation opportunities, so increased firm coordination and a shift from multimarket contact to alliance contact are likely consequences of the New Economy. They illustrate this process by showing that the diffusion of the Java programming language was influenced both by multimarket and alliance contact among pioneering firms, but that alliance contacts explained the diffusion process best.

In "Markets and multiunit firms from an American historical perspective," Sukkoo Kim analyzes the early growth of the MUMM organizational form in the U.S. economy. He finds that MUMM organizations grew strongly during a period of increased trade in goods that were complex and difficult for the consumer to evaluate, and that MUMM organizations were distinct from single-unit organizations in having branded goods and routines for quality control. This suggests that the MUMM organizational form solved the consumer's problem of evaluating the quality of goods, thus reducing transaction costs in the economy. This thesis is strengthened by analyses showing a shift from multi-unit retail firms to multiunit manufacturing firms just as mass media advertising became cost-effective, and also analyses showing that the establishments of multiunit manufacturers were not larger than singleunit firms in the same industry. Thus, the early multiunit industrial firms appeared less concerned with economies of scale than Chandler's (1977) analysis would suggest.

Part Four: Outcomes

In "Racing for market share: Hypercompetition and the performance of multi-unit-multimarket firms," Stan Li and You-Ta Chuang examine the performance consequences of strategic moves in the insurance industry. The focus is on rivalry rather than collusion, and they examine how the frequency and complexity of strategic moves by one firm relative to other firms in the market affect its market share. They find that frequent and simple strategic actions are most beneficial, suggesting that strategic moves affect performance in a way suggestive of learning from the market rather than strategizing against rival firms: viewed as samples from an uncertain world, simple and frequent strategic moves appear to benefit the firm by providing a high number of observations with easily interpretable effects.

In the final chapter, "Multimarket contact: Meaning and measurement at multiple levels of analysis," Javier Gimeno and Eui Jeong take on the important task of analyzing the current stock of measures of multimarket contact to assess their validity and reliability. This work is essential for developing a truly cumulative empirical tradition, as multimarket measures have proliferated in the work done so far. They use both theoretical and empirical analysis to assess the content validity, reliability, discriminant validity, and predictive validity of measures. They note that there are two broad families of measures: count-based measures and scaled measures, and count-based measures do not seem to differ much from measures of the size of the firm. They also warn against measures that incorporate too many theoretical assumptions into weighting schemes, as these can have low reliability. Finally, they show that the measures perform differently depending on whether they are used on cross-sectional or panel data.

CURRENT TRENDS IN MUMM RESEARCH

Although current research on MUMM organizations is so diverse that it defies easy characterization, some trends are becoming apparent. Along with a steady expansion in the volume of work, both the multimarket and multiunit perspectives are experiencing some changes of emphasis and some integrative work. These trends are partly a consequence of a natural expansion of the domain of research, and partly in response to findings suggesting that new routes will be fruitful.[3]

The multimarket perspective has seen an expansion of the behaviors that can be studied as a consequence of multimarket contact and the introduction of more complex models of the causal relations. Empirical studies still emphasize showing anticompetitive consequences of multimarket contacts through changes in prices or profits, but also examine alliance behavior, innovative behavior, and market entry behavior. This shift is clearly reflected in the chapters of this book. Also, theoretical and empirical treatments have made the link from multimarket contact to mutual forbearance more dependent on the context. Asymmetric contacts, experienced firms, inter-firm communication channels, and transfer of learning are conditions posited to make mutual forbearance more likely among a given set of multimarket competitors, and testing of these hypotheses is well underway. This trend is also apparent in several chapters of this volume.

Models of multiunit firms have reached a much higher level of formalization than before, and have started exploring issues of spatial or temporal learning gradients and of tradeoffs in learning. Transfers of learning across space and across time are approximately equally active research questions, which are both represented in this book. Concurrent with a focus of learning transfers is a more critical view of the consequences of learning than before. Organizations have limited attention and resources, so strengthening one type of learning process often weakens others. The many papers on competency traps, including some in this volume, bear witness to an interest in discovering the conditions under which a given type of learning is helpful or harmful, rather than a simple search for main effects.

Perhaps most exciting is the expansion in the volume of research on MUMM organizations and the high quality of the contributions. It should be obvious from the dates of the references of this review that many contributions are very recent; and a strong bent for cumulative work has led to a steady increase in the quality of research designs. Again, the trend is clearly shown in these chapters. This volume was conceived as a marker of this expansion, which to us appears to have continued during its development. Perhaps most promising is the recent influx of studies that combine insights from multiunit and multimarket perspectives for a more complete theory of MUMM organizations. We have sought to encourage this trend in this volume, and were pleased to see it appear in so many of its papers, but the communication across perspectives was manifest in the literature before work on this volume started. We hope this volume both contributes to and gives further impetus to these trends of expansion and integration.

NOTES

1. Summary statistics from the NLSY CD-ROM 1996 edition.
2. Alternatively, very large organizations may not need to seek out multimarket contacts since they will tend to create them regardless of where they enter (Korn & Baum, 1999).
3. Since these are trends, the examples are so numerous that citing all would be tedious and citing selected examples would be unfair. We refrain from making citations in this section.

REFERENCES

Amburgey, T. L., Kelly, D., & Barnett, W. P. (1993). Resetting the clock: The dynamics of orga-
nizational change and failure. *Administrative Science Quarterly, 38*, 51–73.
Amburgey, T. L., & Miner, A. S. (1992). Strategic Momentum: The effects of repetitive, positional
and contextual momentum on merger activity. *Strategic Management Journal, 13*, 335–348.
Argote, L. (1999). *Organizational Learning: Creating, Retaining, and Transferring Knowledge.*
Boston: Kluwer Academic Publishers.
Arthur, W. B. (1989). Competing technologies, increasing returns, and lock-in by historical events.
The Economic Journal, 99, 116–131.
Audia, P. G., Sorensen, O., & Hage, J. (2001). Geography and the multiunit firm. In: J. A. C.
Baum & H. R. Greve (Eds), *Multiunit Organization and Multimarket Strategy: Advances
in Strategic Management* (Vol. 18) (pp. 75–105). Oxford, UK: JAI Press.
Banaszak-Holl, J., Berta, W. B., Bowman, D., Baum, J. A. C., & Mitchell, W. (2000). *Causes of
chain acquisition of U.S. nursing homes and their consequences for resident health outcomes
and facility operating strategy.* Presented at the Academy of Management Meetings: Toronto,
Canada.
Barnett, W. P. (1993). Strategic deterrence among multipoint competitors. *Industrial and Corporate
Change, 2*, 249–278.
Barnett, W. P. (1997). The dynamics of competitive intensity. *Administrative Science Quarterly,
42*, 128–160.
Barnett, W. P., Greve, H. R., & Park, D. Y. (1994). An evolutionary model of organizational perfor-
mance. *Strategic Management Journal, 15*, 11–28.
Barney, J. (1991). Firm resources and sustained competitive advantage. *Journal of Management,
17*, 99–120.
Barros, P. P. (1999). Multimarket competition in banking, with an example from the Portuguese
market. *International Journal of Industrial Organization, 17*, 335–352.
Baum, J. A. C. (1999). The rise of chain nursing homes in Ontario, 1971–1996. *Social Forces, 78*,
543–584.
Baum, J. A. C., & Haveman, H. A. (1997). Love thy neighbor? Differentiation and agglomera-
tion in the Manhattan hotel industry, 1898–1990. *Administrative Science Quarterly, 42*,
304–338.
Baum, J. A. C., & Ingram, P. (1998). Survival-enhancing learning in the Manhattan hotel industry,
1898–1980. *Management Science, 44*, 996–1016.
Baum, J. A. C., & Korn, H. J. (1996). Competitive dynamics of interfirm rivalry. *Academy of
Management Journal, 39*, 255–291.
Baum, J. A. C., & Korn, H. J. (1999). Dynamics of dyadic competitive interaction. *Strategic
Management Journal, 20*, 251–278.
Baum, J. A. C., Li, S. X., & Usher, J. M. (2000). Making the next move: How experiential and
vicarious learning shape the locations of chains' acquisitions. *Administrative Science
Quarterly, 45*, 766–801.
Bernheim, B. D., & Whinston, M. D. (1990). Multimarket contact and collusive behavior. *RAND
Journal of Economics, 21*, 1–26.
Bikhchandani, S., Hirshleifer, D., & Welch, I. (1992). A theory of fads, fashion, custom, and
cultural change as informational cascades. *Journal of Political Economy, 100*, 992–1026.
Boeker, W., Goodstein, J., Stephan, J., & Murmann, J. P. (1997). Competition in a multimarket
environment: The case of market exit. *Organization Science, 8*, 126–142.

Borenstein, S. (1991). The dominant–firm advantage in multiproduct industries: Evidence from the U.S. airlines. *Quarterly Journal of Economics, 106,* 1237–1266.

Bradach, J. L. (1997). Using the plural form in the management of restaurant chains. *Administrative Science Quarterly, 42,* 276–303.

Burgelman, R. A. (1991). Intraorganizational ecology of strategy making and organizational adaptation: Theory and field research. *Organization Science, 2,* 239–262.

Caplin, A., & Leahy, J. (1998). Miracle on Sixth Avenue: Information externalities and search. *Economic Journal, 108,* 60–74.

Carroll, G. R. (1985). Concentration and specialization: Dynamics of niche width in populations of organizations. *American Journal of Sociology, 90,* 1262–1283.

Caves, R. E., & Porter, M. E. (1977). From entry barriers to mobility barriers: Conjectural decisions and contrived deterrence to new competition. *Quarterly Journal of Economics, 91,* 241–262.

Chandler, A. D. (1969). *Strategy and Structure :Chapters in the History of the Industrial Enterprise.* Cambridge, Mass.: M.I.T. Press.

Chandler, A. D. (1977). *The Visible Hand: The Managerial Revolution in American Business.* Cambridge, Mass.: Belknap Press.

Chaves, M. (1996). Ordaining women: The diffusion of an organizational innovation. *American Journal of Sociology, 101,* 840–873.

Chen, M.-J., & Hambrick, D. C. (1995). Speed, stealth, and selective attack: How small firms differ from large firms in competitive behavior. *Academy of Management Journal, 38,* 453–482.

Chen, M.-J., & Miller, D. (1994). Competitive attack, retaliation and performance: An expectancy-valence framework. *Strategic Management Journal, 15,* 85–102.

Christensen, C. M., & Bower, J. L. (1996). Customer power, strategic investment, and the failure of leading firms. *Strategic Management Journal, 17,* 197–218.

Coleman, J. S., Katz, E., & Menzel, H. (1966). *Medical Innovation: A Diffusion Study.* New York: Bobbs-Merrill.

Cyert, R. M., & March, J. G. (1963). *A Behavioral Theory of the Firm.* Englewood Cliffs, NJ: Prentice–Hall.

Darr, E. D., Argote, L., & Epple, D. (1995). The acquisition, transfer, and depreciation of knowledge in service organizations: Productivity in franchises. *Management Science, 41,* 1750–1762.

Davis, G. F. (1991). Agents without principles? The spread of the poison pill through the intercorporate network. *Administrative Science Quarterly, 36,* 583–613.

Day, G. S., & Montgomery, D. B. (1983). Diagnosing the Experience Curve. *Journal of Marketing, 47,* 44–58.

Dunne, T., Roberts, M. J., & Samuelson, L. (1988). Patterns of entry and exit in U.S. manufacturing industries. *RAND Journal of Economics, 19,* 495–515.

Edwards, C. D. (1955). Conglomerate bigness as a source of power. In: *NBER conference report Business Concentration and Economic Policy.* Princeton: Princeton University Press.

Evans, W. N., & Kessides, I. N. (1994). Living by the "Golden Rule": Multimarket contact in the U.S. airline industry. *Quarterly Journal of Economics, 109,* 341–366.

Fama, E. F. (1980). Agency problems and the theory of the firm. *Journal of Political Economy, 88,* 288–307.

Feinberg, R. M. (1985). 'Sales at risk': A test of the mutual forbearance theory of corporate behavior. *Journal of Business, 58,* 225–241.

Fernandez, N., & Marin, P. L. (1998). Market power and multimarket contact: Some evidence from the Spanish hotel industry. *Journal of Industrial Economics, 46,* 301–316.

Fligstein, N. (1991). The structural transformation of American industry: An institutional account of the causes of diversification in the largest firms, 1919–1979. In: W. W. Powell & P. J. DiMaggio (Eds), *The New Institutionalism in Organizational Analysis* (pp. 311–336). Chicago: The University of Chicago Press.

Freeman, J. H., & Lomi, A. (1994). Resource partitioning and foundings of banking cooperatives in Italy. In: J. A. C. Baum & J. V. Singh (Eds), *Evolutionary Dynamics of Organizations* (pp. 269–310). New York: Oxford.

Ghemawat, P., & Spence, A. M. (1985). Learning curve spillovers and market performance. *Quarterly Journal of Economics, 100*, 839–852.

Gimeno, J. (1999). Reciprocal threats in multimarket rivalry: Staking out 'spheres of influence' in the U.S. airline industry. *Strategic Management Journal, 20*, 101–128.

Gimeno, J., & Jeong, E. (2001). Multimarket contact: Meaning and measurement at multiple levels of analysis. In: J. A. C. Baum & H. R. Greve (Eds), *Multiunit Organization and Multimarket Strategy: Advances in Strategic Management* (vol. 18) (pp. 359–410). Oxford, UK: JAI Press.

Gimeno, J., & Woo, C. Y. (1996). Hypercompetition in a multimarket environment: The role of strategic similarity and multimarket contact in competitive de-escalation. *Organization Science, 7*, 322–341.

Green, E., & Porter, R. (1984). Non-cooperative collusion under imperfect price information. *Econometrica, 59*, 975–994.

Greve, H. R. (1995). Jumping ship: The diffusion of strategy abandonment. *Administrative Science Quarterly, 40*, 444–473.

Greve, H. R. (1996). Patterns of competition: The diffusion of a market position in radio broadcasting. *Administrative Science Quarterly, 41*, 29–60.

Greve, H. R. (1998). Managerial cognition and the mimetic adoption of market positions: What you see is what you do. *Strategic Management Journal, 19*, 967–988.

Greve, H. R. (1999). Branch systems and nonlocal learning in populations. In: A. Miner & P. Anderson (Eds), *Population-Level Learning and Industry Change: Advances in Strategic Management* (Vol. 17) (pp. 57–80). Greenwich, CT: JAI Press.

Greve, H. R. (2000). Market niche entry decisions: Competition, learning, and strategy in Tokyo banking, 1894–1936. *Academy of Management Journal, 43*, 816–836.

Hansen, M. T. (1999). The search-transfer problem: The role of weak ties in sharing knowledge across organization subunits. *Administrative Science Quarterly, 44*, 82–111.

Haveman, H. A. (1993). Follow the leader: Mimetic isomorphism and entry into new markets. *Administrative Science Quarterly, 38*, 593–627.

Haveman, H. A., & Nonnemaker, L. (2000). Competition in multiple geographic markets: The impact on growth and market entry. *Administrative Science Quarterly, 45*, 232–267.

Holmstrom, B. (1990). Agency costs and innovation. *Journal of Economic Behavior and Organization, 12*, 305–327.

Ingram, P. (1996). Organizational form as a solution to the problem of credible commitment: The evolution of naming strategies among U.S. hotel chains, 1896–1980. *Strategic Management Journal, 17*, 85–98.

Ingram, P., & Baum, J. A. C. (1997a). Chain affiliation and the failure of Manhattan hotels, 1898–1980. *Administrative Science Quarterly, 42*, 68–102.

Ingram, P., & Baum, J. A. C. (1997b). Opportunity and constraint: Organizations' learning from the operating and competitive experience of industries. *Strategic Management Journal, 18*, 75–98.

Jans, I., & Rosenbaum, D. I. (1996). Multimarket contact and pricing: Evidence from the US cement industry. *International Journal of Industrial Organization, 15*, 391–412.

Jarmin, R. S. (1994). Learning by doing and competition in the early rayon industry. *RAND Journal of Economics*, *25*, 441–454.

Karnani, A., & Wernerfelt, B. (1985). Multiple point competition. *Strategic Management Journal*, *6*, 87–96.

Kelly, D., & Amburgey, T. L. (1991). Organizational inertia and momentum: A dynamic model of strategic change. *Academy of Management Journal*, *34*, 591–612.

Kim, S. (1995). Expansion of markets and the geographic distribution of economic activities: The trends in U.S. regional manufacturing structure, 1860–1987. *Quarterly Journal of Economics*, *110*, 881–908.

Kim, S. (1999). The rise of multiunit firms in U.S. manufacturing. *Explorations in Economic History*, *36*, 360–386.

Korn, H. J., & Baum, J. A. C. (1999). Chance, imitative, and strategic antecedents of multimarket contact. *Academy of Management Journal*, *42*, 171–193.

Kraatz, M. S. (1998). Learning by association? Interorganizational networks and adaptation to environmental change. *Academy of Management Journal*, *41*, 621–643.

Kreps, D. M., & Wilson, R. (1982). Reputation and imperfect information. *Journal of Economic Theory*, *27*, 253–279.

Lawrence, P. R., & Lorsch, J. W. (1967). *Organization and Environment*. Boston, MA: Harvard Business School Press.

Leifer, E. M., & White, H. C. (1987). A structural approach to markets. In: M. S. Mizruchi & M. Schwartz (Eds), *Intercorporate Relations: The Structural Analysis of Business* (pp. 85–108). Cambridge: Cambridge University Press.

Levin, S. G., Levin, S. L., & Meisel, J. B. (1992). Market Structure, Uncertainty, and Intrafirm Diffusion: The Case of Optical Scanners in Grocery Stores. *The Review of Economics and Statistics*, *74*, 345–350.

Levinthal, D. A., & March, J. G. (1981). A model of adaptive organizational search. *Journal of Economic Behavior and Organization*, *2*, 307–333.

Levitt, B., & March, J. G. (1988). Organizational learning. In: W. R. Scott & J. Blake (Eds), *Annual Review of Sociology* (pp. 319–340). Palo Alto, CA: Annual Reviews.

March, J. G. (1981). Footnotes to organizational change. *Administrative Science Quarterly*, *26*, 563–577.

March, J. G. (1991). Exploration and exploitation in organizational learning. *Organization Science*, *2*, 71–87.

March, J. G., Sproull, L. S., & Tamuz, M. (1991). Learning from samples of one or fewer. *Organization Science*, *2*, 1–13.

Marsden, P. V., Cook, C. R., & Knoke, D. (1996). American organizations in their environments: A descriptive overview. In: A. L. Kalleberg, D. Knoke, P. V. Marsden & J. L. Spaeth (Eds), *Organizations in America: Analyzing Their Structures and Human Resource Practices* (pp. 45–66). Thousand Oaks: Sage.

Nelson, R. R., & Winter, S. G. (1982). An Evolutionary Theory of Economic Change. Boston: Belknap.

Noda, T., & Bower, J. L. (1996). Strategy making as iterated processes of resource allocation. *Strategic Management Journal*, *17*, 159–192.

Parker, P. M., & Roller, L.-H. (1997). Collusive contact in duopolies: Multimarket contact and cross-ownership in the mobile telephone industry. *RAND Journal of Economics*, *28*, 304–322.

Pfeffer, J., & Salancik, G. R. (1978). *The External Control of Organizations*. New York: Harper and Row.

Phillips, O. R., & Mason, C. F. (1992). An experimental investigation of mutual forbearance in conglomerate markets. *RAND Journal of Economics, 23*, 395–414.

Phillips, O. R., & Mason, C. F. (2001). Collusion in horizontally connected markets: Multimarket producers as conduits for learning. In: J. A. C. Baum & H. R. Greve (Eds), *Multiunit Organization and Multimarket Strategy: Advances in Strategic Behavior* (Vol. 18) (pp. 207–229). Oxford, UK: JAI Press.

Piloff, S. J. (1999). Multimarket contact in banking. *Review of Industrial Organization, 14*, 163–182.

Scherer, F. M., & Ross, D. (1990). *Industrial Market Structure and Economic Performance*. Boston: Houghton Mifflin.

Scott, J. T. (1988). Diversification versus co-operation in R&D investment. *Managerial and Decision Economics, 9*, 173–186.

Scott, J. T. (1989). Purposive diversification as a motive for merger. *International Journal of Industrial Organization, 7*, 35–47.

Scott, J. T. (1991). Multimarket contact among diversified oligopolists. *International Journal of Industrial Organization, 9*, 225–238.

Scott, J. T. (1993). *Purposive Diversification and Economic Performance*. Cambridge, UK: Cambridge University Press.

Scott, J. T. (2001). Products, patenting and licensing in diversification and innovation markets. In: J. A. C. Baum & H. R. Greve (Eds), *Multiunit Organization and Multimarket Strategy: Advances in Strategic Management* (Vol. 18) (pp. 175–203). Greenwich, CT: JAI Press.

Scott, J. T., & Pascoe, G. (1987). Purposive Diversification of R&D in Manufacturing. *Journal of Industrial Economics, 9*, 225–238.

Singal, V. (1996). Airline mergers and multimarket contact. *Managerial and Decision Economics, 17*, 559–574.

Sorensen, O., & Audia, P. G. (2000). The social structure of entrepreneurial activity: Geographic concentration of footwear production in the U.S., 1940–1989. *American Journal of Sociology, 106*, 424–462.

Spagnolo, G. (1999). On Interdependent Supergames: Multimarket Contact, Concavity and Collusion. *Journal of Economic Theory, 89*, 127–139.

Starbuck, W. H. (1992). Learning by knowledge-intensive firms. *Journal of Management Studies, 29*.

Stephan, J., & Boeker, W. (2001). Getting to multimarket competition: How multimarket contact affects firms' market entry decisions. In: J. A. C. Baum & H. R. Greve (Eds), *Multiunit Organization and Multimarket Strategy: Advances in Strategic Management* (Vol. 18) (pp. 231–263). Greenwich, CT: JAI Press.

Teece, D. J., Pisano, G., & Shuen, A. (1997). Dynamic capabilities and strategic management. *Strategic Management Journal, 18*, 509–533.

Vonortas, N. S. (2000). Multimarket contact and inter–firm cooperation in R&D. *Journal of Evolutionary Economics, 10*, 243–271.

Wegberg, M. van., & Witteloostuijn, A. van. (2001). Strategic management in the New Economy: Information technology and multicontact competition. In: J. A. C. Baum & H. R. Greve (Eds), *Multiunit Organization and Multimarket Strategy: Advances in Strategic Management* (Vol. 18) (pp. 265–306). Oxford, UK: JAI Press.

Wegberg, M. van, Witteloostuijn, A. van, & Abbing, M. R. (1994). Multimarket and multiproject collusion: Why European integration may reduce intra-community competition. *De Economist, 142*, 253–285.

Wernerfeldt, B. (1984). A resource based view of the firm. *Strategic Management Journal, 5*, 171–180.

White, H. C. (1981). Where do markets come from? *American Journal of Sociology*, *87*, 517–547.
Williamson, O. E. (1975). *Markets and Hierarchies: Analysis and Antitrust Implications*. New York: Free Press.
Yelle, L. E. (1979). The learning curve: Historical review and comprehensive survey. *Decision Science*, *10*, 302–328.

Part One:
ENTRY

ETHNIC LINKS, LOCATION CHOICE AND PERFORMANCE: A TEST OF THE RURAL MOTEL INDUSTRY

Arturs Kalnins and Wilbur Chung

ABSTRACT

This paper explores whether membership in ethnically based groups influences conduct and performance in a spatially dispersed industry. We test two propositions. First, when group members own several units in a given market, prices and revenues might be similar to when just one person owned these units. Second, if group membership provides such performance benefits, members may locate their units to obtain these benefits. Using over a thousand hotels located in rural Texas, we test the role of ethnic group membership by examining hotels owned by individuals with the surname "Patel". This surname is common in the hotel industry, with some estimates of Patels owning one in four U.S. motels. Though most are not directly related, much anecdotal evidence suggests that Patels try to lessen the competition among their units. Interestingly, we find that for Patel-owned hotels, proximity of other Patels confers no performance gains. While collocating at a regional level, Patels do not collocate at the finer zip code level, which prevents them from coordinating to enhance performance.

Multiunit Organization and Multimarket Strategy, Volume 18, pages 31–51.
ISBN: 0-7623-0721-8

I. INTRODUCTION

Firms that own multiple units within a market or that repeatedly contact other firms across multiple markets may coordinate prices in such a way as to enjoy performance higher than if the firms were active competitors. Typically, such coordination requires the multiple units to be owned by the same firm. Yet, recent research suggests that informal relationships can also sometimes influence firms' performance. For example, Ingram and Roberts (2000) show that luxury hotels in Sydney Australia experience greater revenues per room when their top managers are friends – when they admire each other and have repeated informal exchanges. Beyond formal links via common ownership, Ingram and Roberts demonstrate that informal relationships provide the basis for firms to achieve performance differences.

We extend this inquiry of the importance of informal relationships within an ethnic business network. Past studies on networks of expatriate Chinese entrepreneurs have concluded that trust (Wong, 1988) and organization flexibility resulting from network membership (Redding, 1996) have yielded superior performance outcomes for network members. In this study, we examine whether informal links via ethnic group membership among multiple collocated firms cause conduct and performance outcomes similar to those of a single firm that enjoys market power. Group membership and informal relationships provide channels for members to coordinate their actions and mechanisms to discipline members who deviate from the coordinated activity. Group membership provides informal governance – the more important the group membership, the stronger the governance. Two propositions emerge. First, when several firms in a given market are owned by group members, we expect pricing and performance to be similar to a market where all those firms are owned by the same owner. Second, if group membership confers performance benefits, we expect members of the group to locate their firms in configurations to obtain and increase these benefits.

Our empirical setting is the rural Texas hotel industry for the period 1991 through 1998. In this context, we study one specific ethnically based group: hotel owners with the surname "Patel". We focus on Patels since they currently play an important role in this industry – as a group they own a significant percent of non-luxury hotels in the U.S. Asian Indian Americans own over 30% of the American hotel-motel business, according to Mike Patel, chairman of the Asian American Hotel Owners Association.[1] And among Asian Indian American hoteliers, "Patel" is the most common surname. A main reason why the Patels have come to play a key role in the hotel industry is their sheer numbers; the name is very common in the Gujarat state of India where most Asian American hotel owners emigrate from, more so than Smith or Jones in the United States.

Given the name's commonness, the likelihood that two Patels in disparate locations are directly related is low. Consistent with this, sources often include quotes like: "It gets so confusing," states Pushpa Patel, owner of a Howard Johnson's in Paramus, NJ. "Guests are constantly saying to me, 'We stayed at a hotel and the manager was so-and-so Patel. Is he your cousin or your brother?' "[2] While not originating from the same nuclear family across states, anecdotal evidence suggests that Patels typically collaborate with each other in the management of their hotels. Other anecdotes suggest that those Patels in close proximity often are direct relations, which would enhance informal governance beyond just ethnic group membership.

Overall, while expecting Patel-owned units to experience enhanced financial performance when surrounded by other units also owned by Patels and therefore for Patels to collocate; we find that proximity of other Patels confers no performance benefit. Further investigating the lack of performance we find that while Patels locate regionally proximate to one another, they do not locate in close proximity; they locate in the same regions, but not the same zip codes. Likely the lack of close proximity permits non-Patel owned hotels to locate intermediately, which reduces the Patels' ability to coordinate among themselves and thus achieve enhanced financial performance.

The structure of the paper is as follows. First, we present information about the phenomenon of Patel-owned hotels, both from other sources and from our data set. We describe the nature of the ties within the community of Patels, as well as some explanations for the evolution of the dominance of Patels in the hotel industry. Second, we present simple hypotheses regarding the pricing decisions and revenue performance of the Patel hotels. Third, we present hypotheses regarding the location of the Patels and present results of a full-information nested logit model. The fourth section concludes.

II. PATEL HOTELS

Patels are Asian Indian Americans, coming mostly from the western coastal state of Gujarat in India. They represent a surprisingly high percent of owners among non-luxury hotels and motels in the United States. The Asian American Hotel Owners Association reports that "nearly all of the trade group's 4,000 members are named Patel."[3] Consistent with pervasiveness of Patel-owned hotels, our data for the rural Texas hotel industry shows that 59 of 741 hotels (8.0%) first opened after 1990, were opened as sole proprietorships by Patels or by corporations where one owner is a Patel. We define as rural the units that lie outside the six largest counties in Texas, those that contain Dallas, Fort Worth, Houston, San Antonio, Austin, and El Paso. At the end of 1998, 310

of 2057 rural Texas hotels/motels (15.1%) with 15 rooms or more were operated as sole proprietorships by Patels or by corporations where at least one
owner is a Patel.

India Abroad, a publication for Indian expatriates, believes the first Patel to
go into the hotel business was Nagiihhai Patel, who bought his first motel in
Sacramento in 1933.[4] From there, Millman (1997) chronicles the rise of the
Patel-owned hotels. When India was a British colony, Patels wound up in
England or in African colonies such as Malawi, Zambia and Uganda. Many
Patels were expelled from Uganda during the brutal reign of dictator Idi Amin
in the 1970s, who also confiscated their businesses. Fleeing with limited savings,
these Indian expatriates searched for suitable destinations.

These Indian expatriates and subsequent Indian immigrants found non-luxury
hotels in the U.S. an attractive business opportunity for several reasons. First,
entry barriers are low. With an investment of $40,000, the displaced could
secure immigrant status in the United States. The question became "What to
invest in?" With a $40,000 investment, choice was limited to small establish-
ments such as diners or roadside motels. Versus other choices, rural hotels
provide both a business opportunity and a place of residence. Brothers C. Z.
and D. Z. Patel own the Villa Inn, a 1960s-vintage 40-room motel. "It's like
a home business," said D. Z. Patel, 45, who was a mechanical engineer in India
before he came to the United States 10 years ago. "You live on the premises
and save money." D. Z. Patel moved to Colorado City with his wife and two
children in 1997. They live at the Villa Inn with his brother's family. The only
non-family member who works at the motel is a part-time housekeeper.[5]
Choosing to operate a hotel provides Asian Indian immigrants both a livelihood
and lodging. Finally, their East Indian cultural background limits their choices.
Operating restaurants was not palatable since as Hindus, they were uncomfort-
able handling meat. And being foreigners, they found difficult the face-to-face
interactions restaurant work requires, such as seating the customer, taking the
order, serving, revisiting the customer, bringing a check and bringing change.
Therefore, the Patels developed the Indian motel plan, renting rooms for $25
to $50 a night, with minimal customer interaction. The plan was once half-
jokingly described as: "Here is your room. Here is your key. Goodbye."

Contagion further increased the size of the Patel hotel community. Much like
the format adoption of radio stations described in Greve (1995), the Patels'
likelihood of choosing to operate a hotel in the low-price market niche was
higher than other potential owners due to contagion, in this case based on their
ethnic background. Millman reports that the well-maintained but no-frills "Patel
motel" not only created a new market, but was so successful that it forced full-
service hotel chains such as Marriott to respond with "economy" lodgings.

Not initially having the resources to afford more expensive hotels, Patel-owned hotels often lie in rural areas and along highways. For example in Texas, Pankaj Patel, Mahesh Patel, Hasmukh Patel and Pravin Patel own motels in the Midland-Odessa area. At least four Patels own motels in Lubbock. Both of these towns are over 300 miles from any large Texan city. Other articles in the popular press confirm similar trends across the United States.

Once in the U.S., initial immigrants attracted a profusion of followers through family and friendship ties, enabling the contagion to take place. One sibling would help find a suitable hotel for their siblings and other relations. One article from Oregon describes how one family's location choice planted the seed for an entire community. Nick Patel, the article states, and several dozen other Patels have carved a niche in the metro Portland area's economy lodging industry.[6] The article discusses how Nick's move to Portland in 1978 made the area more attractive for other Hindu immigrants. Nick became a leader of the local Hindu community, almost all of whom are innkeepers. These familial ties increase the likelihood of a new arrival's success by providing managerial knowledge, emotional support, and financial assistance.

However, such assistance was not limited to just nuclear families. "Whenever one of our countrymen runs into trouble, we are always there to help him out," says Deepak Bhayani, a 49-year-old Indian-born franchisee with two Dunkin' Donuts shops in Illinois. When Mr. Bhayani was unable to work for two months because of heart-bypass surgery, he says other immigrant franchisees stepped in to supervise his stores – including Amrit Patel. "They are my friends," Mr. Patel says. "When friends need help, I always go for it."[7] Such behavior is consistent with Granovetter's (1995) argument that informal links can provide advantage when entities are simultaneously "coupled" and "decoupled". Entities upon whom reciprocal claims can be made are coupled to each other, but being coupled to many others can be detrimental – too many potential claims can lead to claims going unanswered. Immigrant business owners as minorities are coupled to each other through their ethnicity but are also simultaneously decoupled ethnically from the majority (they are also geographically decoupled from others of their same ethnicity in their home country).

"In India, everybody thinks like a family," Bob Patel, owner of a Red Carpet Inn in North Carolina, said. "We try to help each other." People from India looking to own a business might logically choose the lodging industry, he said, because so many of their friends own hotels and motels. Established innkeepers can advise and support newcomers. Further, these immigrant communities maintain close and regular contact. For example, fifty Hindu families meet weekly for religious observances in the Portland area. Bob Patel states further "The Indian immigrants will share information with each other about which banks offer the lowest rates on mortgages. They'll spread among themselves the names of customers who have stiffed them on a room bill. To save money, they'll join forces to buy televisions and other motel equipment in bulk. When times are tight, they'll loan each other money."

The proliferation of hotels owned by East Indians might heighten competition among them, especially if they are proximately located. The location of Patels proximately to one another is a likely outcome since existing immigrant hoteliers often assist subsequent entrants by identifying suitable properties. Such a search for suitable properties is likely bounded by distance – an existing hotelier can ill afford to travel far from their own hotel. This heightened competition might outweigh the benefits that accrue through family and ethnic ties. Aldrich and Waldinger (1990) argue that while offering benefits, ethnic groups are also their own most likely competition. For example, when asked why he was forced to go back to accepting business from prostitutes, Dallas motel-owner Chandrakant Patel said, "After awhile, you say, 'I can't survive, I've got to go back to hourly rates.' Competition among the various Patels is the biggest problem we have."[8]

While some note the heightened competition, surprisingly, many Indian hoteliers say they don't mind the added competition. The benefits of numbers apparently outweigh the costs. Suresh Gupta, an Indian hotelier who owns a Holiday Inn near Orlando, states that he would help any Indian asking for advice on a hotel location. Gupta claims he would even loan such a person the money to start, even if that person would end up a competitor.[9] The Indian hotel and motel owners are banding together to achieve monopsony power when buying supplies or insurance, which may outweigh the problems of competition. "If you're one person, who cares . . . they'll drop you like that," said Tulsi Dhanani, who has been in the lodging business since 1983. "But if you have a crowd of ten, you have power. When you're a group, you have strength."[10]

The initial displacement of Indian expatriates combined with the presence of managerial knowledge, emotional support, and financial assistance accruing through ethnic ties helps explains how the Patel hotel phenomenon grew to its present proportions. Further, the ethnic ties mean that Patel hoteliers need to choose locations trading off heightened competition versus managerial, emotional, and financial assistance. Both result from proximity. Baum and Haveman (1997) emphasize such trade-offs of losses and gains from proximity, which provides many dilemmas for hotel owners in general. They find that new hotels establish themselves at similar prices but of different sizes to those around them in order to reduce the competition but gain from lucrative locations. The Patels have an even more complex set of issues due to proximity than most due to their ethnic ties.

Given the prominence of such a social, ethnic group in the rural hotel industry, we develop propositions as to how group membership affects financial performance and location choice.

III. PRICING CONDUCT AND REVENUE PERFORMANCE

Theory and Hypotheses

Given the prevalence of Patels in Texas and the ethnic links influencing their location patterns, proximity among Patel-owned units is inevitable. We ask how this proximity affects the performance of Patel-operated hotels.

Industrial economists such as Levy and Reitzes (1992) and Werden and Froeb (1994) have studied the effects on price of mergers in a spatial setting. Their theoretical work shows that ownership of multiple nearby outlets allows an owner to charge higher prices relative to what would be charged with the same configuration of outlets under separate ownership due to the spatial market power they enjoy. Consistent with such hypotheses, Conlin (1999) presents evidence that hotel room prices are higher when the same owners own multiple units in a city. Even if spatially dispersed outlets are owned by different owners, they may collude on price under certain conditions, yielding price and performance outcomes similar to those of the spatial market power case. In the standard game theoretic arguments (e.g. Fudenberg & Tirole, 1991) and specifically in a geographic multimarket context (Bernheim & Whinston, 1990), firms can maintain a collusive agreement if each firm can construct a punishment for the other that outweighs the benefit of reneging on the agreement.

Williamson (1993, 1996) emphasizes the role of such calculative behavior in the trust that allows firms to maintain collusive agreements. While the punishments available to firms are typically restricted to lowering price in future periods, economists have pointed out that loss of reputation within a group can also serve as a type of punishment that would prevent an individual from reneging on an agreement (e.g. Ellickson, 1989). Sociologists have argued that the mechanism through which agreements are more likely to be respected when a party is part of a group may not be a calculated response to a threat of punishment. Uzzi (1996) discusses a heuristic character of trust that appears inconsistent with rational calculation, yet facilitates the exchange of assets that benefit both parties. Regardless of which of these approaches is preferable to the reader, both suggest that members of a group are more likely to cooperate than those who share no group membership.

In our empirical context, Patels who belong to the same social and ethnic group may have such punishments available – they may not be allowed to participate when other Patels group purchase from suppliers or they might be made to feel unwelcome at community gatherings. Given such potential penalties, we expect Patels who operated hotels that are proximate to each other will be able to coordinate their pricing policies. Assuming the Patels jointly optimize prices along with occupancy, then they would also experience increased revenues. More formally, we propose:

Hypothesis 1: If agglomeration by Patels is likely due to maintenance of pricing agreements, Patels should be able to charge higher prices than their equivalent non-Patel competition.

Hypothesis 2: If agglomeration by Patels is likely due to maintenance of pricing agreements, Patels should enjoy higher revenues than their equivalent non-Patel competition.

Data

Our data were provided to us by the Texas State government and includes all establishments operating as hotels or motels in Texas for the quarters between the years of 1991 and 1998 inclusive. The data provides a hotel's name, opening date, street address, owner name, owner location, size in rooms, and revenues. In the original data, often hotel owners are listed as corporations and Patels might own some of these corporations. Therefore, to identify Patel-owned corporations, we used the Texas State incorporation-listing file and compared the list of all corporations owned by Patels with the corporations that owned hotels. Any hotel that has an owner with or that is incorporated and has a partner with the surname "Patel" we identify as a Patel owned hotel.

While primarily hotels and motels, this data also includes many bed and breakfasts, rental rooms in private residences, and time-share condos. We purposefully want to exclude such occurrences, which do not operate in the same segment as hotels and motels; bed & breakfasts are often destinations themselves, while hotels and motels are temporary housing on the way to or proximate to travelers' end destinations. To remove such observations, we examine an establishment's reported number of rooms and remove the observation if the number of rooms is below fifteen. After applying the greater than fifteen rooms cutoff, on average 1,600 establishments remain in each quarter of data.

We use zip codes to define market locations, which is the finest level of geographic gradation available in our data. In rural Texas, typically a zip code only contains one if any freeway exits. Since the likelihood of a hotel being in a zip code but not at a freeway exit is small, we say hotels are agglomerated when they are in the same zip code. Therefore, any hotels in the same zip code, we assume to be agglomerated – or collocated around the freeway exit.

From the original Texas government data, we obtain one dependent variable: revenues per room, which is an industry standard measure of performance. Revenues can increase through greater occupancy, higher prices, or a combination of both. All these possibilities increase revenues. Instead of just total revenues, we scale a hotel's revenues by its number of rooms since we are interested in an establishment's performance relative to its size. Large hotels are clearly going to have higher revenues than smaller hotels; we ask if a hotel performs better than other hotels, given its size.

To obtain our second dependent variable, room prices, we conducted a phone survey. Between May 15 and May 20, 1999, we conducted a price survey of all rural hotels with current telephone listings in the Yellow Pages. We were able to contact 1097 active telephone listings and asked these hotels for their price including tax for one room for one person on weekdays and weekends.[11] The results presented below are based on the weekday prices, which in most cases, do not vary from the weekend prices. Of these 1097 hotels, Patels owned 171.

Given our price data is only for early 1999, we use revenue per room data from the Texas government for the closest comparable period available, the 4th quarter of 1998. To explain differences in revenue per room and prices, our variables of theoretical interest are: (1) a dummy variable indicating whether a given hotel is owned by a Patel, (2) the percentage of hotel rooms in a zip code owned by Patels, not counting the current hotel, and (3) an interaction term of these two variables.[12]

Other variables are included as controls. These include hotel-specific measures such as size in rooms of the hotel, an incorporation dummy, the number of stars that AAA has assigned to the hotel, and multimarket contact at an owner and chain level. The multimarket measures are the typical count measures of total markets of overlap (Evans & Kessides, 1994; Gimeno, 1999); as mentioned above, we define a market at the zip code level. The other variables are zip code level controls including population, average income, aggregate number of hotel rooms, whether an interstate runs through the zip code, and a Herfindahl index of concentration. This index can be written as $\sum_k (\text{share})^2$ where share the percentage of rooms in zip code owned by owner k. This variable ranges from zero to one, with zero indicating the case of perfect competition and one indicating a monopoly. These measures are constructed from the Texas State data or obtained from the 1990 U.S. Census of Population.

Method and Results

We test the financial performance hypotheses using a two-dimensional fixed-effects ordinary least squares model, with price and revenues per room as the dependent variables. Fixed effects are included for each chain and each county. Prices and revenues certainly vary by chain and by location. Holiday Inns will on average earn more than Red Roof Inns. Similarly, some hotels might be located in counties home to important rural attractions like the state fairgrounds. To prevent such variation from being attributed to our variables of interest, we include the fixed effects. Thus, the coefficients of all our other variables reflect within-chain and within-county variation. Independent hotels are lumped together as the base case. Note a hotel might both be chain affiliated and operated by a Patel; in such a case both the particular chain dummy variable and the Patel dummy variable would be coded as "1".[13]

The price and revenue per room regressions both contain the same sets of independent variables. The interaction term between: (1) the dummy variable indicating whether a given hotel is owned by a Patel and (2) the percentage of hotel rooms in a zip code owned by Patels should have a positive effect on prices and revenues if Hypotheses 1 and 2 are corroborated. The interaction term indicates that a given Patel can charge higher prices because a high percentage of other rooms are owned by Patels, giving them the ability to collude on price.

As Table 1 shows, none of the coefficients of the Patel-related variables are significantly different from zero. Both the main effects and the interaction between the main effects are insignificant. Patels do not charge higher prices than anyone does in high-Patel areas, nor do they enjoy higher revenues per room.

While the variables of theoretical interest are non-significant, several controls are significantly different from zero. The controls for hotel traits are signed as expected. Owner level multimarket contact is significantly positive, which suggests that multi-unit owners who encounter each other repeatedly across markets can price higher and thus enjoy higher revenues. Whether a hotel is incorporated significantly increase both measures of financial performance, which likely indicates the relative quality of the hotel – owners of higher quality hotels incorporate. Larger hotels (as measured by room size) charge more; larger hotels have more features that allow them to price higher. And higher quality hotels, as indicated by AAA star ratings, also charge more and earn higher revenues per room.

Most control variables for market conditions within the zip code are also signed as expected. While population and average income are related, together

Table 1. Determinants of Hotel Financial Performance
Ordinary Least Squares (OLS) with 2-way Fixed Effects.

	Dependent Variable: Room Price		Dependent Variable: Revenue/Room	
	Coefficient	Std. Error	Coefficient	Std. Error
Patel-owned hotel	0.168	2.005	−0.021	0.111
Pct Patel hotels in zip code	4.227	4.342	−0.085	0.239
Interaction of Patel-owned and pct Patel	−2.795	8.274	−0.598	0.456
Multimarket contact, owner level	0.255**	0.052	0.017**	0.003
Multimarket contact, chain level	−0.068	0.053	−0.005	0.003
Incorporated hotel	3.771**	1.348	0.377**	0.074
Room count in hotel	0.154**	0.013	0.002*	0.001
AAA stars (if listed)	1.590**	0.572	0.150**	0.032
1990 Zip population	−0.276**	0.056	0.002	0.003
1990 Average income	0.330*	0.142	0.011	0.008
Hotels in zip code	0.854**	0.132	0.003	0.007
Interstate in zip code	−7.193**	2.072	−0.228*	0.114
Herfindahl index	5.039*	2.093	0.145	0.115
Chain & county dummies	Yes**		Yes**	
R^2	0.691		0.648	
N	1097		1097	

** $p < 0.01$; * $p < 0.05$

they suggest that hotels set higher prices in wealthier zip codes. Surprisingly, the presence of an interstate in the zip code has negative effects, likely resulting from higher competition in these areas. Presence of an interstate in a zip code needs to be considered together with hotels in a zip code since an interstate will increase demand by providing a conduit for travelers, but such a conduit will then attract more competitors.[14] The significance of the Herfindahl index indicates that hotel owners raise price when all hotels in a market are owned by a smaller number of total owners, confirming the results of Conlin's study of hotels (1999). We note, however, that concentration of ownership as measured by the Herfindahl has no revenue performance benefit.

Given that most control variables conform to expectations, the lack of effect for the three Patel variables is curious. Given that we expect Patels to informally coordinate over prices, such coordination requires physical proximity. Therefore, to better understand the non-significant results, we investigate further and examine location choice.

IV. THE CHOICE OF LOCATION OF NEW HOTELS

Theory and Hypotheses

As a starting point, we ask "are Patels likely to agglomerate in their location choices in particular areas?" All anecdotes suggest that they will. However, an interesting subsequent question is "what is the reason for the agglomeration?" Is agglomeration merely to be close to other Patels for social and religious purposes? Or is it to be close enough so that information is meaningful and can be effectively exchanged? Finally, is it to be close enough to coordinate pricing decisions for market power purposes? Not surprisingly since such behavior is illegal, none of the Patels quoted in the popular press mention pricing agreements as a way in which the Patels could help each other. While not mentioned, such behavior is possible. These questions suggest that we examine location behavior to see how closely Patels physically locate their hotels to each other.

If maintaining market power is the primary reason for agglomerating, this would require closer proximity because the hotels would have to be seen as close substitutes by potential customers. While the Patels might locate their hotels further apart to reduce supply and thus maintain market power; the low barriers to entry in the hotel industry likely preclude this possibility – a non-Patel owned hotel might choose an intermediate location that would reduce the Patel's likelihood of coordinating on price. More likely is the possibility that Patels encourage other Patels to locate nearby in order to pre-empt competition, that is, to make the location less appealing for potential non-Patel competition.[15]

On the other hand, information transfer or social reasons may be the cause of any collocation. Audia, Sorensen, and Hage (this volume) for example find that among geographically dispersed firms, those that are more spatially concentrated learn more quickly than those more dispersed. Patels may be able to enjoy similar learning benefits if they locate proximately to each other.

Proximity for community and religious activities, or for coordinating purchases, may also be the primary reason for any agglomeration among Patels. In any of these case, the close proximity required for any pricing coordination purposes is not needed. As long as the choice of a particular location allowed the Patels to meet on weekends for religious observances, for example, it would be acceptable. Thus, Patels could build hotels reasonably far apart, even upwards of a hundred miles apart.

Thus, intent should be consistent with the level of agglomeration; agglomeration at a broad level is consistent with social activities, while agglomeration at a fine level is consistent with economic activities. Or stated more formally:

Hypothesis 3: If agglomeration by Patels is likely due to maintenance of pricing agreements or for pre-emption purposes, Patels are likely to agglomerate at a narrow market level.

Hypothesis 4: If agglomeration by Patels is likely due to maintenance of social and religious ties, Patels are likely to agglomerate at a broad regional level.

The Nested Logit Method

To test these two hypotheses, we model the choice of location for new hotels using the random utility framework. In this model, we treat zip codes in Texas that contain hotels as the elemental alternatives for each choice of hotel location. In the random utility framework, all actors making the choice are assumed to value fundamental attributes of an alternative (such as number of existing hotels in a zip code) equally. We expect to observe different choices of location for two reasons. First, the levels of the attributes for the same alternative are not identical across different actors. For example, as the different actors make their choice at different times, the number of existing hotels in a zip code will change. Second, an error term is also included for each choice for each actor, leading to some variation even if all values of the observable attributes are equal across all actors.

Some of the primary alternatives (the zip codes) in our choice set are likely to share unobserved characteristics due to geographical proximity. Therefore, the error terms of such zip codes are likely to be correlated, and we estimate a nested conditional logit model. McFadden (1978) proves that the nested logit model is consistent with the random utility model of choice preference. Use of nested logit models requires the researcher to choose a nesting structure for the random utility model, that is, to make assumptions regarding the correlation between alternatives. In our case, all zip codes that are within driving distance of a location where the Indian community may hold social or religious events would exhibit a positive unobservable correlation in their probability of being chosen as a hotel site by a Patel. Thus, we split Texas into 25 regions in the first level of our nesting structure. The second level choice set consists of three zip codes per region: the zip code actually chosen and two others that are drawn randomly.[16] For the regional and zip code levels, we introduce sets of independent variables. Choice among the zip codes tests Hypothesis 3 by assessing the significance of X_{ij}, the zip code level variables. Choice among these regions tests Hypothesis 4 by assessing the significance of Z_i, the regional level variables. This nested logit technique with multiple levels and choice sampling is a standard technique used commonly among transportation alternative and brand selection studies in economics and marketing.

In our random utility model, we define an underlying latent variable V_{ijk} to represent the utility to each new hotel owner k of opening a hotel in zip code j within Region i. i=1 to 25 are the 25 regions, each containing N_i zip codes. j=1 to Ni are the zip codes within each region i that contain at least one hotel. Then the observed variable Y_{ijk} is such that:

$$Y_{ijk} = 1 \text{ if } V_{ijk} > V_{mnk} \text{ for } m = 1 \text{ to } 25 \text{ and } n = 1 \text{ to } Nm,$$
$$\text{but n is not equal to j, and } Y_{ijk} = 0 \text{ otherwise.}$$

In other words, we observe the owner k locating a hotel in zip code j within region i if the utility of such a choice exceeds all other choices.

The utility for each owner V_{ijk} is given by observable characteristics Z_{ik} and X_{ijk}. Assuming a linear relationship between observables and the latent variable, we can write:

$$V_{ijk} = b_1' Z_{ik} + b_2' X_{ijk} + e_{ijk}, \text{ where } Z_{ik} \text{ only varies by region i}$$
$$\text{and the hotel owner k and the } X_{ijk} \text{ vary by zip code j as well.}$$

Due to the disturbance term e_{ijk}, consisting of variables unobservable to the researcher, in the calculation of V_{ijk} the utility takes on a random form. Within this random utility framework, the probability of an owner choosing a particular zip code for a new hotel can be viewed as the product of a marginal and conditional probability.

The probability of Y_{ijk} being 1 is equivalent to the probability of observing a new hotel opening in that zip code, which occurs when that location offers a higher utility versus all other options; or $P(Y_{ijk} = 1) = P(\text{Zip Code}_{ij})$ $= P(V_{ijk} > V_{mnk})$.

$$P(\text{Zip Code}_{ij}) = P(\text{Zip Code}_{ij} \mid \text{Region}_i) * P(\text{Region}_i), \text{ where}$$
$$P(\text{Zip Code}_{ij} \mid \text{Region}_i) \text{ is the probability of choosing Zip Code}_j$$
$$\text{conditional on the choice of Region}_i.$$

If the residuals are drawn from an extreme value (Gumbel) distribution, then we can write:

$P(\text{Zip Code}_{ij} \mid \text{Region}_i) = \exp(\mathbf{b}_2'\mathbf{X}_{ij}) / \exp(\mathbf{I}_i)$ where $\mathbf{I}_i = \log(\sum_j \exp(\mathbf{b}_2'\mathbf{X}_{ij}))$, and $P(\text{Region}_i) = \exp(\mathbf{b}_1'\mathbf{Z}_i + \mathbf{b}_3\mathbf{I}_i) / \sum_m \exp(\mathbf{b}_1'\mathbf{Z}_m + \mathbf{b}_3\mathbf{I}_m)$ where m = 1 to 25.

These two equations can be estimated simultaneously via full information maximum likelihood (FIML). While a sequential method would be less data intensive, in this case the full information method is particularly important because we are trying to tease apart the relative importance of variables at two levels of agglomeration (the regional and zip code level). Sequential methods cannot evaluate both levels simultaneously.

The $\mathbf{I}_i$ are called "inclusive values" and are a measure of the sum of the utilities for all zip codes within a region. The coefficients on the inclusive values, the variables $\mathbf{b}_3$, measure the degree of correlation across error terms of alternatives. This correlation should be positive for zip codes within the same region since these zip codes' error terms should contain common unobservable influences. This positive correlation should exist for all zip codes in a region and for a random sample of zip codes in a region.

We note that a nested logit is a variation of McFadden's conditional logit model. In a conditional logit formulation, the investigator estimates how attributes of the choices themselves influence their likelihood of being chosen. In the case of a multinomial logit, the investigator estimates how attributes of the choosers influence what is chosen. For example, whether a person drives a BMW, a Volkswagen, or a Ford is both a function of the drivers' characteristics and the cars' characteristics. While the traditional multinomial logit focuses on the drivers' characteristics, the conditional logit focuses on the cars' characteristics. The conditional logit yields one coefficient per variable regardless of number of choices, while the multinomial logit yields $N-1$ coefficients per variable for a model with N choices. To continue the car example, a conditional model would yield a single coefficient for the independent variable "miles per gallon", while the variable "consumer's income" in a multinomial setting would yield one coefficient for its effect on the choice of a BMW relative to the baseline choice of a Ford, and one for the Volkswagen, again relative to the choice of a Ford. For a comprehensive presentation of the nested logit model the reader is referred to McFadden (1978), Ben-Akiva and Lerman (1985), and Maddala (1983).

The Data and Results

The dependent variable is where new hotels were built – in which zip code within which region. Independent variables are characteristics of the locations where these hotels were built versus those where they were not. Using our data from the Texas State Government we include an observation for all 741 new hotels built in Texas between 1991–1998, including 59 owned by Patels.[17]

The independent variables of theoretical interest are the counts of existing Patel hotels in each zip code and region at the time the decision is made by owner k to open the new hotel. An interaction term is added that equals the count of existing Patel hotels if the owner choosing the location is a Patel and zero otherwise. We include the choices of non-Patel hoteliers to determine whether the Patels behavior is any different from that of the other hotel owners.

The other variables are included as control variables. At the zip code level, we include population and average income to reflect demand. For the nature of supply, we include the counts of chain hotels and incorporated non-chain hotels at both the zip code and regional levels. As Patels are more likely to be non-incorporated than the general population of hotel owners, the incorporated counts must be included to prevent significance from being attributed to membership in the Patel group. The inclusion of the chain variable has similar rationale, because the chain membership is negatively correlated with Patel ownership.

Results are shown as Table 2. Regional level variables are grouped above zip code level variables.

Before interpreting the coefficient estimates, we need to assess the suitability of our nested structure using the coefficients attracted by the "inclusive values" – the estimate of the sum of the utilities for all zip codes within a region. The coefficients on the inclusive values measure the degree of correlation across error terms or alternatives and therefore should range from zero to one. But a large number of inclusive values greater than one indicates that the alternatives in different nests are actually more correlated than those within the given nest, implying that the analyst has not chosen a valid nesting structure. To determine our nesting structure, we initially group zip codes into regions based upon contiguity, common access to the same interstate highway, and proximity to potential regional centers. With our 25 regions, 24 of the inclusive values are in the range from zero to one. The one remaining is negative, but statistically not different from zero. Further, in our model, 15 of the values are statistically different from one at a 5% level or better, implying that the nesting structure is preferable to a simple single-level choice model at the zip code level. This indicates that our model is correctly specified; that is, we have chosen an appropriate nesting structure.

In Table 2, looking at the group of regional variables on the top half of the table, we see that Patels do agglomerate at the regional level, based on the positive and significant coefficient of the interaction of Patel count for Patels.

Table 2. Determinants of Hotel Location Choice
Full Information Maximum Likelihood (FIML) Nested Logit.

	Dependent Variable: Choice of Zip Code	
	Coefficient	Std. Error
Regional level variables (b_3)		
Count of hotels owned by chooser	0.734**	0.118
Count of chain hotels	–0.068**	0.021
Count of Patel-owned hotels	–0.033	0.050
Count of incorporated non-chain hotels	0.032	0.025
Interaction of chain count for chain	0.008	0.015
Interaction of Patel count for Patels	0.174*	0.073
Zip code level variables (b_2)		
Population of zip code (1990)	0.006	0.004
Avg income of zip code (1990)	0.014*	0.006
Count of chain hotels	–0.001	0.052
Count of Patel-owned hotels	–0.107	0.127
Count of incorporated non-chain hotels	0.250**	0.067
Interaction of chain count for chain	0.472**	0.082
Interaction of Patel count for Patels	0.181	0.354
Inclusive values	Yes**	
Log Likelihood	–3033**	

** $p < 0.01$; * $p < 0.05$

In other words, Patels are more likely to choose regions of Texas that have more existing Patel hotels. Turning to the zip code level variables on the bottom half of the table, we see that this trend does not persist at this more refined geographic level. The likelihood of Patels locating in zip codes that already contain Patels does not increase or decrease in a statistically significant way. Thus, Patels agglomerate at a regional but not a zip code level.

Several control variables attract statistically significant coefficients. The coefficients for "interaction of chain count for chain" indicate that while not co-locating on a regional level, chain hotels do co-locate with other chain units at the finer zip-code level. While suggestive of chains distinctly seeking each other out, these estimates might also reflect chains being attracted by similar unobserved location traits. Interestingly, the count of incorporated non-chain variable at the zip code attracts a significant positive coefficient indicating that hoteliers are more likely to choose zip codes with non-chain hotels.

Hoteliers may see such hotels as weaker competition and be drawn to such locations.

V. CONCLUSION

Recent research highlights the importance of informal links for firms' performance. We extend the inquiry into the importance of informal links by examining whether social and ethnic group membership alters a firm's financial performance. Group membership and informal relationships provide possible channels for members to coordinate their actions and mechanisms to discipline members who deviate from the coordinated activity. Using the rural hotel industry of Texas, we focus on hotel owners with the surname of "Patel". These Patel-owned hotels compose 15% of rural hotels in Texas and anecdotal evidence suggests that Patels have extensive informal contact and cooperate with each other in the management of their hotels.

We investigated two propositions. First, whether Patel-owned hotels experience enhanced financial performance when surrounded by other units also owned by Patels. Second, whether Patels tend to collocate their hotels. Our results indicate that the proximity of other Patels confers no financial performance gains; two-way fixed-effect regressions show that the prices and revenues per rooms of Patel owned hotels are not significantly different when other Patels are located close by.

To better understand this non-significant finding for financial performance, we investigate location choices by Patel-owned hotels. The Patel hotels may geographically locate in such a way that makes colluding on price difficult. Using a nested logit model, we find that Patels do cluster in broad geographical areas in Texas, but not at a finer geographic level; they collocate on a regional level, but not at a zip code level. This provides a likely explanation for why the performance results showed no effect on price or revenue per room at the zip code level. They locate close enough to obtain social and cultural benefits, but not close enough for coordination on pricing. Potentially, we never observe great enough concentration of Patels at a zip code level for them to coordinate and achieve enhanced financial performance. Indeed, this suggests coordination of another type – recognizing that price maintenance with each other might be difficult, they purposefully locate far enough apart not to have to compete on price. Another potential explanation is that since the Patels fill a low-price niche, even when coordination among themselves would otherwise be possible, they are unable to charge higher prices.

Because of the lack of significance for Patel owned hotels on price or revenue performance at a local level, we do not explore whether Patels are able to behave as a single multimarket owner when dealing with other firms. Without any apparent ability to collude on price among themselves, it is very unlikely that they could act as a single owner in achieving mutual forbearance with competitors.

The non-significant findings for price and revenue performance do not preclude the importance of informal links. Cooperation of the Patels likely cannot be captured by price and revenue performance alone. Most of the anecdotal evidence of cooperation discussed cost-saving activities, not price heightening issues. Cooperation among the Patels in the sphere of obtaining financing, buying in bulk, or sharing information would most likely reduce costs and increase the probability of survival. If cost structures of the hotels were available, this presents a fruitful avenue for future research.

Overall, this study helps define the limits of informal links. Ingram and Roberts note that one of the main discipline mechanisms among luxury hotels is referrals – overbooking by luxury hotels is common and when hoteliers are friends they will reciprocally refer surplus customers to each other. Not being considered for such referrals is a significant punishment. Such pecuniary punishment may be unavailable among Patel owned hotels, which decreases the likelihood of coordination. Future research might distinguish between direct family members and just owners with the same surname. Versus ethnic group membership, membership in the same nuclear family likely provides much stronger coordination and discipline mechanisms. Finally, since this study provides an interesting set of findings and non-findings for members of informal groups, this suggests further investigation of who agglomerates and how location choice affects performance for other groups such as chain versus non-chain hotels, single owner versus multi-unit owner hotels, and in-state versus out-of-state owned hotels.

NOTES

1. "Indians Find Niche in Hotel Industy," New Orleans Times-Picayne, September 24, 1998, p. 4A1.
2. Ibid, p. B1.
3. "What's in a Surname? A passel of Patels: Indian Moniker is Big in Motel Biz," The Record – Northern New Jersey, August 10, 1995, p. B1.
4. India abroad, Summer, 1989.
5. All quotes from this paragraph taken from "Where the East meets West. Texas Indian immigrants' 'Patel motels' thrive," The Dallas Morning News, April 25, 1999.
6. All quotes in this paragraph taken from "Immigrants Find Sweet Success in Lodgings," Portland Oregonian, April 22, 1999.
7. Quotes taken from "Spreading the Dough Around," The Wall Street Journal, February 22, 1999.

8. "Indian Entrepreneurs: Immigrant Patels cashing in on Dallas' sexually oriented motels," The Dallas Morning News, June 14, 1987.

9. "Hands Across the Water: Close-knit Indian Community Strong Force in Economy Hotels," Orlando Business Journal, June 12, 1998, p. 23.

10. "Passage From India Immigrants Work Together To Make A Mark In N.O. Area," The New Orleans Times-Picayune, July 28, 1992.

11. Use of prices in the AAA guides was not useful because under 20% of hotels in our sample were listed in AAA.

12. All tests were also conducted changing the percentage of hotel rooms in a zip code owned by Patels to a case including the current hotel. None of the results changed in any way.

13. Chains in the hotel industry are often franchised. As a result, they are often made up of many small local owners such as the Patels. See Chung and Kalnins (2000) for more details of ownership structures within chains.

14. While initially expecting a negative sign for hotels in zip code and a positive sign for interstate in zip code, the positive sign for hotels in zip code suggests heighten demand results when hotels agglomerate. When multiple hotels are present in one location, this offers travelers greater breadth and depth of selection; this increased selection would increase visitation by travelers, which increases demand and thus the price that hotels could charge. The coefficient estimates suggest that this potential agglomeration gain though heightened demand occurs in zip codes where interstates pass through that have more than 8.4 hotels ($8.4 * 0.854 > -7.193$).

15. For the basic pre-emption argument, please see Dixit (1980). For the case of pre-emption via multiple locations in geographic or product space, please see Judd (1985) and Hadfield (1991).

16. The selection of 25 regions and 3 zip codes within a region is driven by software constraints. The Limdep 7.0 software package limits the user to 75 elemental alternatives.

17. While having some data for hotels founded before 1991, we do not have full information on the competitive landscape since for those hotels established before 1991, the data set only includes surviving hotels. We only observe survivors. Therefore, we limit our panel to 1991 and after.

REFERENCES

Aldrich, H. E., & Waldinger, R. (1990). Ethnicity and Entrepreneurship. *Annual Review of Sociology, 16*, 111–135.

Audia, P. G., Sorensen, O., & Hage, J. (2001). Tradeoffs in the Organization of Production: Multi-Unit Firms, Geographic Dispersion and Organizational Learning. In: J. A. C. Baum & H. R. Greve (Eds), *Multiunit Organization and Multimarket Strategy; Advances in Strategic Management,* Vol. 18 (pp. 75–105). Oxford, U.K.: JAI Press.

Baum, J. A. C., & Haveman, H. (1997). Love Thy Neighbor? Differentiation and Agglomeration in the Manhattan Hotel Industry, 1898–1990. *Administrative Science Quarterly, 42*(2), 304–339.

Ben-Akiva, M., & Lerman, S. R. (1985). *Discrete Choice Analysis.* MIT Press; Cambridge, MA.

Bernheim, B. D., & Whinston, M. D. (1990). Multimarket Contact and Collusive Behavior. *RAND Journal of Economics, 21*(1), 1–27.

Chung, W., & Kalnins, A. (2000). Localized Agglomeration Spillovers and Firm Performance: A Test of the Texas Lodging industry. Unpublished Working Paper – Stern School of Business, New York University.

Conlin, M. (1999). An Empirical Analysis of the Effect of Divisionalization and Franchising On Competition. Unpublished Working Paper – Department of Economics, Cornell University.

Dixit, A. (1980). The Role of Investment in Entry Deterrence. *Economic Journal, 90*(March). 95–106.

Ellickson, R. (1989). A Hypothesis of Wealth-Maximizing Norms: Evidence From the Whaling industry, Journal of Law. *Economics and Organization, 5,* 83–97.

Evans, W. N., & Kessides, I. N. (1994). Living by the Golden Rule: Multimarket Contact in the U.S. Airline industry. *Quarterly Journal of Economics, 109,* 341–366.

Fudenberg, D., & Tirole, J. (1991). *Game Theory.* MIT Press, Cambridge, MA.

Gimeno, J. (1999). Reciprocal Threats in Multimarket Rivalry: Staking Out Spheres of influence in the U.S. Airline industry. *Strategic Management Journal, 20,* 101–128.

Granovetter, M. (1995). The Economic Sociology of Firms and Entrepreneurs. In: A. Portes (Ed.), *The Economic Sociology of Immigration: Essays On Networks, Ethnicity, and Entrepreneurship.* Russell Sage Foundation, New York, NY.

Greve, H. R. (1995). Jumping Ship: The Diffusion of Strategy Abandonment. *Administrative Science Quarterly, 40*(3), 444–474.

Hadfield, G. (1991). Credible Spatial Pre-Emption Through Franchising. *RAND Journal of Economics, 22*(4), 531–543.

Ingram, P., & Roberts, P. W. (2000). Friendship Among Competitors in the Sydney Hotel industry. *American Journal of Sociology,* Forthcoming.

Judd, K. L. (1985). Credible Spatial Preemption. *RAND Journal of Economics, 16*(Summer), 153–166.

Levy, D. T., & Reitzes, J. (1992). Anticompetitive Effects of Mergers in Markets with Localized Competition. *Journal of Law, Economics and Organization, 8,* 427–440.

Maddala, G. S. (1983). *Limited Dependent and Qualitative Variables in Econometrics.* Cambridge: Cambridge University Press.

McFadden, D. (1978). Modeling the Choice of Residential Location. In: P. Karlqvist et al. (Eds), *Spatial Interaction Theory and Planning Models.* North Holland: Amsterdam.

Millman, J. (1997). *The Other Americans: How Immigrants Renew Our Country, Our Economy, and Our Values.* New York: Viking.

Redding, S. G. (1996). Weak Organizations and Strong Linkages: Managerial Ideology and Chinese Family Business Networks. In: G. G. Hamilton (Ed.), *Asian Business Networks.* Berlin: Degruyter.

Uzzi, B. (1996). The Sources and Consequences of Embeddedness for the Economic Performance of Organizations: The Network Effect. *American Sociological Review, 61,* 674–698.

Werden, G. J., & Froeb, L. (1994). The Effects of Mergers in Differentiated Products Industries: Logit Demand and Merger Policy. *Journal of Law, Economics and Organization, 10,* 407–422.

Williamson, O. (1993). Calculativeness, Trust, and Economic Organization. *Journal of Law and Economics, 34,* 453–502.

Williamson, O. (1996). Economic Organization: The Case for Candor. *The Academy of Management Review, 21,* 48–57.

Wong, S.-L. (1988). *Emigrant Entrepreneurs: Shanghai Industrialists in Hong Kong.* Hong Kong:Oxford University Press.

BEYOND MULTIMARKET CONTACT TO MUTUAL FORBEARANCE: PURSUIT OF MULTIMARKET STRATEGY

Helaine J. Korn and Terence T. Rock

ABSTRACT

In this paper we differentiate between the creation and subsequent exploitation of multimarket contact. We examine specific factors that influence the likelihood that a firm will seek to develop a purposive set of overlapping markets with specific competitors, as opposed to developing naïve contacts based on an internally derived logic. We suggest that competitor identification, organization structure, ease of competitive response and industry structure (including the presence of network externalities, barriers to entry, and industry growth rate) all play important roles in determining the ability of managers to seek rivalry-reduction that has been found to follow the development of market overlap. We offer several propositions that serve to define the boundaries of research into mutual forbearance and multimarket competition, and that may help to explain empirical results obtained to date.

Multiunit Organization and Multimarket Strategy, Volume 18, pages 53–74
Copyright © 2001 by Elsevier Science Ltd.
All rights of reproduction in any form reserved.
ISBN: 0-7623-0721-8

INTRODUCTION

Fundamental to defining a business is choosing the products a firm will offer and the markets in which it will compete (Abell, 1980). Consequently, product-market choices are key among the strategic decisions a firm makes. The pattern reflected by firms' choices is of great interest to organizational and strategic management scholars (Greve, 2000; Haveman, 1993; Porter, 1980, 1985). In particular, the extent to which firms' product-market choices overlap with one another and the causes and consequences of such overlaps have been the concern of recent attention to the phenomena of multimarket contact and mutual forbearance (Baum & Korn, 1996, 1999; Boeker et al., 1997; Gimeno & Woo, 1999; Korn & Baum, 1999).

The aim of much of this research has been to explore whether or not multi-market contact leads to mutual forbearance and a consequent reduction in rivalry (see Jayachandran, Gimeno & Varadarajan, 1999 and Korn & Baum, 1999 for recent summaries of this literature). However, the issues of *why* and *how* firms navigate the transition from multimarket contact to mutual forbearance, thus pursuing a multimarket strategy, are unresolved, leaving two important research questions under-explored. First, what factors lead to the initial establishment and the subsequent expansion of multimarket contact, necessary precursors to firms mutually forbearing from competing against one another? Do these happen by chance, with the possibility that firms may or may not even notice the situation, or do firms intentionally seek out such contact, perhaps with hopes of later reducing rivalry? Second, what determines whether firms successfully bridge the gap between the occurrence of multimarket contact and the potential outcome of mutual forbearance, i.e. why and how do firms pursue a multi-market strategy, the aim of which is to generate and sustain a pattern of multimarket relationships characterized by reduced rivalry? In other words, if we can establish whether firms recognize their interdependence and intentionally and strategically act to benefit from it by reducing the intensity of rivalry they experience with competitors, what will determine if they are able to achieve their desired outcome?

Only when we understand these issues regarding the derivation and pursuit of multimarket strategy can strategic management scholars more adequately comment about the conditions under which multimarket contact and mutual forbearance are likely to be operating. Thus, in the remainder of this paper, we develop propositions regarding factors that lead firms to pursue multimarket strategies by creating and exploiting multimarket contact that may generate mutual forbearance. In developing these propositions, we attempt to delineate the boundary conditions within which multimarket strategies will be consciously and effectively employed. We conclude with a discussion regarding managerial implications of this framework and some guidelines for future empirical testing.

BEYOND MULTIMARKET CONTACT TO MUTUAL FORBEARANCE

There are two important distinctions to be made when characterizing firms' patterns of multimarket contact. First, it is important to differentiate between the dynamics of managerial attempts to *create* multimarket contact on the one hand, and the dynamics of managerial attempts to *exploit* established contact on the other, by withholding from engaging in price warfare or successive new product introductions, for example. In previous studies, this distinction often has not been made explicit. For example, when Baum and Korn (1999) discuss the reduction of rivalry due to multimarket contact, they are talking about the reduction of market entry/exit behavior, a strategic action that directly impacts the level of multimarket contact or market overlap. Hence, it is difficult to separate here the motivations firms have for establishing multimarket contact from those they have for exploiting multimarket contact. Gimeno's (1999) study, by contrast, examines the impact of established market contact (and the qualitative differences among types of contact) on an outcome (i.e. revenue or yield) more directly associated with firm performance. Consequently, we learn about why firms might react in particular ways to the multimarket contact they experience, but we do not learn why they experience this contact in the first place. Thus, although this distinction between the creation and exploitation of multimarket contact does not imply that the two activities cannot happen concurrently, it does imply that there may well be different underlying causal mechanisms operating for each.

Consequently, it is also important to differentiate the possible motives firms have for generating initial and subsequent multimarket contact and to try to separate out those instances when mutual forbearance is the ultimate goal from those in which potential reduced rivalry is not a primary consideration in firms' decisions about which markets to enter. Although empirical research on the effects of multimarket contact and policy suggestions on the effects of such contact hinge on the assumption that the contacts are deliberate, firms' explicit attempts to create a particular set of multimarket contacts to reap benefits from mutual forbearance appear to account for only a portion of the observed multimarket contact and mutual forbearance (Korn & Baum, 1999; Scott, 1989). Moreover, some recent evidence about the relationship between multimarket contact and the outcome of mutual forbearance raises questions about whether managers are necessarily insightful and whether they intentionally strive to achieve multimarket contact to receive benefits of mutual forbearance (e.g. Greve, 2000; Korn & Baum, 1999). In his study of the role of multimarket contact in market niche entry decisions in Tokyo banking, for example, Greve (2000: 330) concluded that "forward looking strategies will be de-emphasized, as past experience and current opportunities are more salient and certain than future actions of competitors, and decision makers tend to favor salient and certain information." Similarly, building on Scott's (1982, 1989, 1991) work regarding the motivations for establishing multiple market contacts, Korn and Baum (1999) explored chance, imitative, and strategic antecedents to multi-market contact. They found that "multimarket contact may arise more as a result of chance contacts among competitors pursuing uncoordinated strategies and trait-based imitation unrelated to multimarket contact than as a result of strategic attempts to develop multimarket contact and mutual forbearance" (Korn & Baum, 1999: 188).

Once firms find themselves positioned in complex networks of inter-relationships with other firms, however, they may or may not actively nurture such relationships in order to enjoy potential benefits from reduced rivalry. Although firms may not seek out purposively all multimarket relationships they experience, they still may recognize the benefits of their competitive context and work to keep it at equilibrium. So, although mutual forbearance is frequently assumed to be a natural outcome of multimarket contact and it is possible that this behavior results from multimarket contact, some evidence indicates that under conditions of identical firms and demand functions in multiple markets, multimarket contact alone is not enough to generate mutual forbearance (Bernheim & Whinston, 1990). Indeed, managers' cognitive limitations may render it too difficult to anticipate the likely moves of several other competitors and their competitive behaviors over time, and thus make it too difficult to construct forward-looking strategies about which markets to enter or about how intensely to compete (Clark & Montgomery, 1999; Porac, Thomas & Baden-Fuller, 1989).

Therefore, it seems important to elaborate upon the possible sources of firms' multimarket contact and their possible goals of engaging in multimarket strategies. For example, is it necessary to conclude that a firm creates purposive multimarket contact with a competitor with the long-term goal of mutual forbearance in mind? Certainly such goals are *possible*, and much of the empirical and anecdotal evidence gathered in support of the rivalry-lowering impact of multimarket contact ascribes this type of rationality to firms. However, an alternative model, in which naïve multimarket contact arises as a result of decisions based solely on internally derived knowledge and imitation of competitor moves unrelated to multimarket contact can make just as much sense. For instance, Jayachandran et al. (1999), offer the example of a pattern of competition in the pet food industry in which firms engaged in a series of product-market entries and in which market overlap was established. Once market entry slowed, prices rose and firms began a process of brand extension in the markets in which they were dominant. There is no reason to believe, however, that market entry behavior necessarily was an intentional strategy with the long run goal of lowering competitive rivalry. Rather, the initial entry moves could have been due to the pursuit of economies of scope (production of different types of pet food seems to be a strong area of potential synergy), with any further moves not making economic sense (i.e. they would have resulted in diminishing returns). Once one firm "shows" others that it is possible to achieve economies of scope, it is only natural that other firms would follow (DiMaggio & Powell, 1983; Miner & Haunschild, 1995). The next set of moves, higher prices and brand extension, primarily could be due to these competitors' familiarity with each other. They have established a homogeneous macroculture and enjoy high barriers to entry, both shown to lower rivalry for reasons not related to multimarket contact (Abrahamson & Fombrun, 1994; Porter, 1980; Scherer & Ross, 1990). Imitation of competitive moves would be expected in such an environment as it is quite clear who the competitors are; thus, innovations in a firm's strategy repertoire would rapidly diffuse to other competitors in the industry (Abrahamson & Fombrun, 1994; Greve, 1998).

The previous discussion thus poses two problems with which theorists must contend. First, does the fact that the firms discussed above do not compete intensely with one another *necessarily* imply that mutual forbearance is taking place, i.e. that they recognize their mutual interdependence and purposively compete less intensely toward each other as a result? Or, is it possible that the firms are simply attending to what seem to be more lucrative opportunities for the present time, based on their particular resource endowments? This distinction is important, since without *recognition* of *mutual interdependence by both actors*, it is difficult to conceive of a situation in which a manager will be able to employ the optimal multimarket strategy. Being clear about firm-specific, efficiency- or value-based reasons for competitive action and the possible outcomes therefore is important. Current thinking in multimarket competition tends not to recognize the possibility that firms' competitive moves may be differently motivated. Rather, this line of research assumes from the outset or at least gives primacy to the idea that firms' competitive moves are determined by a motivation primarily based on provoking and/or responding to the moves of competitors (Chen & MacMillan, 1992; Chen & Miller, 1994). If two firms are seen to be competitors because they operate in common markets, but don't actually engage in rivalrous behaviors with one another (e.g. price wars, brand extensions, entering more of, and not exiting, each others' markets), the extant multimarket contact literature almost always would consider them to be forbearing (Barnett, 1993; Baum & Korn, 1996, 1999; Boeker et al., 1997; Gimeno & Woo, 1996, 1999). As described briefly above, however, firms' motivations for creating multimarket contact and for exploiting that which they experience, irrespective of how the contact came to exist, may be related or unrelated to their understanding of and desire to achieve potential rivalry-lowering benefits of multimarket contact. Firms' competitive moves might be based on an assessment of how their competitors are likely to react or, instead, they might be based on an internal analysis that suggests potential sources of rent for the resources a firm currently employs or plans to invest in (Barney, 1990). Since firms represent unique bundles of competencies and resources, managers in different firms may have different expectations about the value they will receive from pursuing similar opportunities (Barney, 1990). An internally based motive of competitive action suggests that competitive moves directed away from an apparent rival are not necessarily indications of forbearance, but rather differential pursuit of opportunity.

Earlier, we identified contacts that arise from internally derived motivations for competitive action in a multimarket environment as *naïve*, in that the action that generates them occurs absent recognition of mutual interdependence. We call contacts that arise from motivations deriving from recognition of mutual interdependence (or the possibility of it) *purposive*. These two motives appear to reflect a differing emphasis on strategic similarity versus market common-ality (Chen, 1996; Gimeno & Woo, 1996). Creation, and further exploitation, of naïve multimarket contact appears to be driven primarily by strategic similarity that leads firms to pursue similar opportunities independent of their possible recognition of their similarities with one another. Firms may be so engrossed and single minded in pursuing competitive advantage based upon their capabilities, that even once multimarket contact does arise, it barely even might be noticed and certainly not given a prominent role in the development of future strategic moves. Once firms have multimarket contact with other firms, if they remain unaware of these contacts, they may fail to exploit them, contin-uing to determine pricing and brand extension decisions upon internally based criteria. (So, in actuality, exploitation of naïve contacts really is not even exploitation at all.) A recognition that market commonality has potential benefits in moderating the intensity of a rivalrous relationship, perhaps because of past experience with such a situation, however, may lead firms to create purposive multimarket contacts and then further exploit them. Thus, if firms recognize the multimarket contacts they have developed, regardless of how they came about, exploitation of such contacts would seem to be based upon some understanding and goal to achieve influence in their rivalrous behaviors.

To this point we have identified two important issues that need to be considered in a complete theory of multimarket competition. First, when discussing the process of competition, we must distinguish between the *creation* of multimarket contact and the *exploitation* of such contact. Second, we must understand the motivation underlying competitive action by focal actors: is it driven by recognition of mutual interdependence or by some other internally derived goals? We need to more clearly understand and control for market structure-based explanations for the lowering of market entry behavior (when establishing contact) and for the less intense nature of the subsequent competitive behavior under conditions of market overlap. There are several factors that will influence (and be influenced by) the competitive motive underlying competitive actions to create and/or exploit multimarket contact. We consider the following factors: whether or not competitors are identified or identifiable, and when this identification occurs; the ease of undertaking a chosen strategy (how much learning is necessary?); organization structure; and industry structure. By clearly understanding the role of these critical factors that influence strategic multimarket behaviors, we move closer to understanding under what organizational conditions and in what types of industries successfully employing multimarket strategies is viable. Having identified these possible patterns of multimarket competition, we proceed to examine different influences on their unfolding. Though these influences will not be operating in isolation, for ease of exposition we consider them separately.

FACTORS UNDERLYING PURSUIT OF MULTIMARKET STRATEGY

Competitor Identification

Because most firms tend not to operate as monopolists and must contend with the presence of other competitors in their markets, the outcomes of firms' competitive moves affect other firms and their destinies are mutually dependent (Porter, 1980). "Firms feel the effects of each other's moves and are prone to respond to them" (Porter, 1980: 88). But, what determines which potential competitors' moves a firm will feel and respond to? Much of the extant multimarket contact research has tended to take for granted that firms are aware of whom their multimarket competitors are, merely describing how competitive de-escalation may evolve among them. However, we believe that explicit attention to how firms make this determination about which others comprise their competitive set is crucial to understanding how multimarket strategies may evolve (Clark & Montgomery, 1999; Lant & Baum, 1995). According to Chen (1996), one of three drivers of firms' competitive behavior that merit consideration is awareness of actual or potential rivals (the others are motivation and capability to act). Thus, a necessary, although not sufficient, condition for managers to create and exploit purposive multimarket contact in order to receive benefits from mutual forbearance would be that they first identify each other as (potential) multimarket competitors.

In the broader context of competitor identification, research on strategic groups and managerial cognition has contributed much to our understanding of how firms decide what other firms' behaviors to pay attention to. These streams of research suggest that firms similar along dimensions of price, location, size, and competitive strategy recognize and respond to each others' competitive behaviors (Abrahamson & Fombrun, 1994; Baum & Mezias, 1992; Clark & Montgomery, 1999; Gimeno & Woo, 1996; Greve, 1998; Lant & Baum, 1995; Porac & Thomas, 1990; Porac et al., 1995; Reger & Huff, 1993). Thus, firms with greater strategic similarity are likely to identify each other as members of their competitive sets. Moreover, only once firms identify other firms' as competitors at all might they view them as multimarket competitors. To make this transition from recognizing another firm as a competitor whose moves merit attention because of interactions in a single market to recognizing it as one who is significant across multiple contexts, however, is potentially a more complex and difficult process than is required to notice in the first place simple similarities along a few attributes.

When potential multimarket competitors cannot be mutually identified due to dissimilar value chains, naïve multimarket contacts may be created until market commonality has been established (Abrahamson & Fombrun, 1994; Chen, 1996; Gimeno & Woo, 1996). Even if this market commonality develops, potential multimarket competitors may never be mutually identified if market commonality is not the intended outcome and firms' value chains and general patterns of interaction actually may diverge (Korn & Baum, 1999; Porac et al., 1995). In this scenario, any patterns that appear to be the consequence of mutual forbearance, in which firms are not competing intensely against one another, most likely, are really reflections of firms' differing activities.

When firms have similar value chains and share some suppliers (Abrahamson & Fombrun, 1994; Gimeno & Woo, 1996), cues exist that make the identity of potential multimarket competitors more readily available, even though the firms share no downstream markets. The existence of upstream structural equivalence is likely to cause managers operating in the same environment to make similar evaluations regarding the potential uses of their technologies and capabilities. Spender (1989) refers to this as the development of recipes that are sets of heuristics shared by industry participants.

Once market commonality has been established, there are a number of factors that make it likely that managers will recognize each other as competitors (even if the initial contact was naïve). First, the social networks of the managers will be more highly interconnected (Porac et al., 1995) due to such mechanisms as industry associations, common customers, and some of the same employees (a consequence of turnover and rehiring). Moreover, informal links among managers may play a significant role in the competitive behavior of firms towards one another, as suggested by Kalnins and Chung (this volume) in their exploration of location choices of Patel owned hotels in rural Texas. Second, industry publications and other sources of information tend to be market-based (as opposed to input-based), increasing the likelihood that managers will become aware of competitive moves through third party sources. Third, and perhaps most important, in a situation of direct competition, managers will clearly notice the impact of competitive moves that reduce their market share, such as pricing or advertising decisions. All of these conditions will lead to the identifiability of multimarket competitors increasing as market overlap increases (Baum & Oliver, 1996) and a greater possibility that firms will exploit such contact actively.

P1: Pursuit of internally driven competitive advantage lowers the likelihood that firms will conceptualize or identify each other as multimarket competitors, increasing the creation of naïve multimarket contact; pursuit of externally driven competitive advantage raises the likelihood that firms will conceptualize or identify each other as multimarket competitors, increasing the creation of purposive multimarket contact.

P2: Pursuit of internally driven competitive advantage lowers the likelihood that firms will conceptualize or identify each other as multimarket competitors, decreasing the exploitation of multimarket contact; pursuit of externally driven competitive advantage raises the likelihood that firms will conceptualize or identify each other as multimarket competitors, increasing the exploitation of multimarket contact.

We have thus far primarily discussed the cognitive bases for the identification or lack of identification of multimarket competitors. However, there may also be internal organization structure factors, as well as industry structural characteristics, that facilitate or limit a firm's ability to notice potential multimarket competitors. Moreover, if and when firms do recognize and seek to act upon their mutual interdependence, the ease with which they can generate a competitive response will also influence their competitive behaviors. We next consider these three broad factors separately, though they may have joint effects on patterns of multimarket competition.

Organization Structure

Of critical importance when discussing organization structure as it relates to competing in multiple markets is the type and scope of decisions that are made at different levels of the firm. We are particularly concerned about the outcomes of two types of decisions: in which product-markets do firms compete and how do they initiate and respond to tactical moves (such as pricing or advertising) in these markets? The first question is central to creating multimarket contact, while the latter reflects exploitation of multimarket contact. Both kinds of decisions can be centralized or decentralized, easily or not easily communicated throughout the firm.

Firms that compete in multiple markets adopt a variety of mechanisms for how to plan their activities in each market in which they compete and then coordinate their activities across these markets within the firm. Some set up distinct divisions based upon geographic location that may span several product lines; others set up distinct divisions for each product line that may span several geographic regions. Still others do not coordinate activities across product or geographic boundaries at all, with each unit operating in a distinct product-geographic market combination acting independently of all others. Chain organizations, for example, are a type of multiunit firm that reflect a set of assumptions about how to transfer knowledge from one market to another and appropriate coordinating mechanisms for doing so (Greve, 2000, 1998; Ingram & Baum, 1997a, b). Multidivisional firms, another example of multi-unit organizations, have been observed to adopt a variety of structures for coordinating decisions across strategic business units based upon their extent of related versus unrelated diversification (Markides & Williamson, 1996; Hill, 1988; Hill, Hitt & Hoskisson, 1992).

The choices that a firm makes along these lines of differentiation and integration of its activities are likely to influence which other firms it notices in its competitive landscape and how it responds to their presence in common markets (Golden & Ma, 1995; Jayachandran et al., 1999). Audia, Sorenson and Hage (this volume), for example, observed that although multiunit firms operating in multiple markets benefited from more multifaceted interactions with other competitors by being less likely to get involved in competitive escalation, due to increased rigidity, they also faced increased risks of failure in the presence of environmental instability. The extent to which firms' decisions and actions are coordinated across markets thus influences its likelihood of creating and exploiting multimarket contact. As has been noted elsewhere (e.g. Jayachandran et al., 1999), it is difficult to conceive of an effective multimarket strategy being employed without at least the decisions regarding market entries and exits being highly centralized.

P3:   Greater decentralization of strategic decision making increases the creation of naïve multimarket contact; greater centralization of strategic decision making increases the creation of purposive multimarket contact.

P4:   Greater decentralization of strategic decision making decreases the exploitation of multimarket contact; greater centralization of strategic decision making increases the exploitation of multimarket contact.

Ease of Competitive Response

Multimarket strategy involves integrating actions across markets so that a firm may respond to a competitor's move not only in the market in which it was initiated, but perhaps also in another market that they may have in common. Thus, a central feature of multimarket strategy is posing a credible threat to a competitor in a variety of markets in which the two interact. One indication that a firm will be able to pose a credible threat to a competitor is its ability to quickly and decisively respond to a competitive provocation (Chen & MacMillan, 1992; Chen & Miller, 1994; Porter, 1980). If a firm has already demonstrated its ability to respond to a given challenge (i.e. it "knows how" to implement the move), competitors must presume that it has the ability to repeat this move in the future. For example, airlines "know how" to open gates at new airports. There is minimal new learning that has to take place to accomplish this competitive action. In a sense, they are simply replicating their system in a new location. Moreover, research about firms' strategic choices has demonstrated that they exhibit strategic momentum, i.e. "the tendency to maintain or expand the emphasis and direction of prior strategic actions in current strategic behavior" (Amburgey & Miner, 1992). This implies that if a firm has entered a market requiring a specific set of routines, it is likely to enter other markets in which it could exploit that same set of routines (Greve, 2000; March, 1991). When competitors visibly demonstrate the ability and motivation to pose a credible threat of retaliation, it would behoove firms to factor this in to their decisions about which markets to enter. Thus, market entry choices that generate multimarket contact would most likely reflect an understanding of mutual interdependence and be part of attempts to generate purposive multimarket contact.

On the other extreme, however, is the case of a firm entering a new product market by greenfield startup. In this case, the entire system has to be built from scratch and there is tremendous learning that must take place. Consequently, future competitive implications are quite low. The variation and randomness associated with startup organizations would lower the deterrent nature of a new startup. Thus, it is unlikely that such market entries would result from firms' trying to create purposive multimarket contact to demonstrate their ability to respond to competitors' moves in other markets.

P5: Market entry based on developing new routines increases the creation of naïve multimarket contact; market entry based on replicating routines that are widely known among competing firms increases the creation of purposive multimarket contact.

Somewhere between these two extremes lies entering a new market by product line extension or merger/acquisition activity. In the former case, firms that are attempting to gain economies of scope presumably know much of the value chain, so while there will be some learning involved, it still serves as a threat to do it in the future. In a highly related industry (or within a broad industry), a merger may only involve a small amount of learning about the new products/ markets, but there may be much learning about how to effectively manage this firm. These risks are only magnified as the merger/acquisition becomes less related. Depending on the industry and the prevalence of this mode of market entry, it may provide a strong source of threat to continue subsequent market entries. In the networking equipment industry, for example, Cisco, Nortel and Lucent all have exhibited well-developed capabilities to undertake acquisitions.

P6: Unrelated mergers/acquisitions increase the creation of naïve multimarket contact; related mergers/acquisitions increase the creation of purposive multimarket contact.

Industry Structure

There are a few considerations regarding industry structure that we must examine, including the role of network externalities, barriers to entry, industry concentration, and industry growth rates. Network externalities are generally found in situations where "the utility that a user derives from consumption of the good increases with the number of other agents consuming the good" (Katz & Shapiro, 1985; p. 424). We expect to find the impact of these network effects in (among others) industries in which a product is not just a product, but is also an entry point to a broader set of products and benefits.[1] A clear example is a city-pair market (route) for an airline. By linking two cities, a firm doesn't just give customers access to those cities, but also to all of the other cities that are linked in some manner to each end of the route. In this case then, dominance of every geographic market is not necessary, nor even efficient. As long as customers are presented with an entrypoint to the network, a very broad set of needs may be met. Gimeno (1999) notes that in the airline industry, strong nodes in a network (hubs) play a major role in the ensuing competitive forbearance. In these types of industries, the establishment of a network, which may include several weak nodes (as simple entrypoints) and a few strong nodes (hubs), appears to be a key success factor for long-term survival. Thus, we would expect firms competing in industries in which network externalities are important to be very aware of the network patterns of their competitors, and hence the pattern of overlap between the two networks. Adding to this argument is the fact that network-based industries will also by nature employ market-entry modes based on the replication of existing routines in a new setting making it easier to respond to competitive provocation.

P7: Competing in network-based industries decreases the creation of naïve multimarket contact; competing in network-based industries increases the creation of purposive multimarket contact.

P8: Competing in network-based industries increases the exploitation of multimarket contact.

Another characteristic of network externalities is that they can provide high barriers to entry (Farrell & Saloner, 1986). A new entrant faces the prospect of having to establish a network that offers different benefits than those of the incumbents. Depending on the industry, significant investment may be required to develop enough nodes that the network is valuable. In addition to this investment cost, there is the added hurdle of overcoming inertia associated with consumption externalities of existing networks (Farrell & Saloner, 1986). Porter (1980) talks about several other important barriers to entry that all serve to lower rivalry independent of multimarket contact. In industries with high barriers to entry, competitor identification will be easier due to the stability of the identities of the major players in the industry. This stability makes understanding mutual interdependencies much more probable (as in the development of an industry macroculture [Abrahamson & Fombrun, 1994] or industry recipe [Spender, 1989]), and exploitation more likely.

P9: High barriers to entry to an industry in which competition takes place in multiple markets raises the likelihood that firms will conceptualize or identify each other as multimarket competitors, increasing the exploitation of multimarket contact.

Jayachandran et al. (1999) summarize the role of industry concentration in the reduction of rivalry, concluding that moderately concentrated industries are most likely to see large benefits in terms of rivalry reduction due to multimarket contact. In high-concentration industries, decision makers, due to the ease of competitor identification, likely will also consider the benefits of creating multiple market contacts. Even though Jayachandran et al. (1999) note that oligopolies themselves reduce rivalry to the point that the impact of multimarket contact will be marginal, it is important to note that multimarket contact likely will still be prominent in the strategic decision-making of firms in high-concentration industries. In low-concentration industries, competitor identification is much more difficult and there is much to gain by competing intensely for market share; thus rivalry is less likely to be reduced due to multimarket contact.

P10: Lower industry concentration increases the creation of naïve multimarket contacts; greater industry concentration increases the creation of purposive multimarket contact.

P11: Lower industry concentration decreases the exploitation of multimarket contact; greater industry concentration increases the exploitation of multimarket contact.

A final consideration regarding industry structure is that of industry growth rate (or the stage in the industry life cycle) (Bernheim & Whinston, 1990). In a high growth industry, firms will tend to be more concerned with meeting the growth in primary demand and less concerned with battles over secondary demand. This implies more internally focused strategy and paying less attention to competitors' behaviors. Firms that overlap in two high-growth markets may focus their efforts away from each other not due to forbearance, but rather due to the desire to meet the rapid growth in demand they see in their "own back yard." Thus, if they do happen to experience market overlaps with other firms, these are unlikely to be the consequence of purposive attempts to forbear.

P12: Greater industry growth rate increases the creation of naïve multimarket contact; lower industry growth rate increases the creation of purposive multimarket contact.

P13: Greater industry growth rate decreases the exploitation of multimarket contact; lower industry growth rate increases the exploitation of multimarket contact.

ELABORATION OF MULTIMARKET STRATEGY SCENARIOS

Having described various influences on motivations for firms to create and exploit multimarket contact, we are left with putting these influences together in an attempt to understand where and when they might manifest themselves, and from that, determining the implications for research into the topic and for managers competing in multimarket environments. Below we describe each scenario reflecting the creation and exploitation of multimarket contact in greater detail (see Table 1 for a summary).

The Multimarket Strategist: Creating and Exploiting Purposive Contact

In the scenario in which firms create purposive multimarket contact, as well as exploit such purposive multimarket contact, it appears that firms' competitive actions are driven largely by efforts to influence the nature of interaction with other firms with whom they come into contact (Chen & MacMillan, 1992; Porter, 1980). Firms that seek to create purposive multimarket contact seem to understand the multimarket nature of competition in their industry. Network effects will be important, and firms will react to new opportunities by racing to establish spheres of influence or markets that will be recognized by their competitors as being of significant importance (Gimeno, 1999). In other words, their choices of which markets to enter are guided by their desire to establish dominance in some markets that may be used as a deterrent to discourage multi-market rivals from competing aggressively in other markets. Once spheres of influence are established, tactical rivalry subsides due to the recognition of mutual interdependence (Edwards, 1955).

Under this multimarket strategy scenario, market entry will not require much learning. There will be tried-and-true methods of competing, with competitive routines easily replicated in new product markets. In the vast majority of cases of creating and exploiting purposive multimarket contact, "market entry" will refer to new geographic markets. Though it is possible that entry into new product markets could be guided by this kind of multimarket strategy, the amount of learning necessary (and thus the lack of credible threats), the relative rarity of this type of action, and the organization structures necessary to facilitate coordination across product lines all conspire against it.

P14: Multimarket Strategists will predominate in geographic market entry situations.

Table 1.   Elaboration of Multimarket Strategy Scenarios.

| Underlying Factors | Type of Multimarket Strategy | | | Propositions |
	Multimarket Strategist	Multimarket Opportunist	Multimarket Pacifist	
Competitive Motive	Managers understand the multimarket nature of competition in their industry, and react to new opportunities by "racing" to establish spheres of influence. Once spheres of influence are established, tactical rivalry subsides due to recognition of mutual interdependence.	Managers are driven primarily to improve the efficiency of their overall operations. This leads to a search for economies of scope, which may result in related diversification. Technological capabilities will tend to drive these moves, making it likely that firms will establish multiple market overlaps with other firms. Once a competitive relationship is established, tactical rivalry will eventually subside once competitors recognize their mutual interdependence.	Again, Managers are driven primarily to improve the efficiency of their overall operations. This leads to a search for economies of scope, which may result in related diversification. Technological capabilities will tend to drive these moves, making it likely that firms will establish multiple market overlaps with other firms. However, once the relationship is established, tactical rivalry may be low due to reasons other than the realization of mutual interdependence. Rather, firms may not compete intensely with each other because they are each simply pursuing different opportunities.	
Competitor Identification	Potential multimarket competitors will be readily identifiable, as they will have generally identical value-chains, and may share some suppliers. They will already be competitors in the industry in general. They may be already involved in multimarket relationships with other competitors, and the social networks of the managers will already be highly interconnected.	Potential multimarket competitors will not likely be mutually identified until market commonality is established. Competitors are unlikely to have identical value-chains, though they may be similar. Value-chains will tend to converge over time and managers' social networks will intersect once market commonality is established, making exploitation of the multimarket strategy easier.	Potential multimarket competitors may never be mutually identified for the reasons noted in the multimarket strategy scenario 2. In pursuing different opportunities, firms' value-chains and general interaction will diverge.	P1, P2
Organization Structure	Decisions regarding market entry *and* tactical maneuvers such as pricing and advertising will be highly centralized.	Both centralized and decentralized organization structures will be found. More centralized structures will lead to a longer period of equilibrium in the relationship.	Decentralized organization structures will be most common, preventing the ability to identify opportunities to exploit multimarket contact.	P3, P4

***Table 1*.** Continued.

	Type of Multimarket Strategy			
Underlying Factors	Multimarket Strategist	Multimarket Opportunist	Multimarket Pacifist	Propositions
Ease of Competitive Response (Role of Learning)	Market entry will not require much learning, in that it will essentially be replicating the basic operational activities the firm in a new market.	There will be significant learning necessary to enter a new market. The firm will have to develop new competencies in order to compete. This makes it difficult to rationally plan to establish a multimarket strategy, as there will be uncertainty surrounding a competitor's ability to "keep up."	Significant learning will be required to enter a new market. Firms will tend to be internally focused on exploiting efficiencies and searching for new sources of value to provide their customers.	P5, P6
Industry Structure	Network effects play a strong role in the industry, explaining the race to establish spheres of influence. The product offered to the customer is more than "just" a product, it is an entry to a network. Firms will be heavily invested in some nodes of their network and only maintaining other nodes. Market entry from outside competitors will be difficult. Markets will experience only incremental growth.	Likely to be a moderately concentrated industry (Jayachandran et al, 1999) in which there are a few established major competitors. Markets will be populated by competitors with interests in more than one industry (relatedly diversified). Network effects not necessary.	Fragmented structures with many possible competitors. Market entry is possible from numerous related industries or startups, thus the industry will continually be in transition. Markets likely to be characterized by high growth, which makes direct competition less important and the development of internal competitive capabilities more important.	P7, P8, P9, P10, P11, P12, P13
Prevalence	Likely to be rare. Will be found when established industries expand or readjust to external shocks (such as deregulation).	Likely to be quite common, but difficult to detect as it may be transitive since the original search for economies of scope may continue, destroying the equilibrium. Will be more stable, and thus detectable, if firms are highly centralized.	Moderate frequency. Due to the development of industry macrocultures (Abrahamson & Fombrun, 1994), only very volatile industries with highly decentralized firms will prevent competitors from identifying their mutual interdependence.	P14, P15, P16
Likely industries	Passenger airline, banking, hotel chains, retail e-commerce	Consumer packaged goods, franchise restaurants, many other candidates.	Computer software, Small food processors, many candidates	

The Multimarket Opportunist: Exploiting Naïvely Created Multimarket Contact

When firms create naïve multimarket contact, their market entry decisions are guided primarily by a desire to improve the efficiency of their overall operations. This leads to a search for economies of scope, which may result in related diversification (Panzar & Willig, 1981). Technological capabilities will tend to drive these moves, so although not as a result of their explicit attempts to do so, it is likely that firms will establish multimarket overlaps with other firms that have similar capabilities (Chen, 1996; Gimeno & Woo, 1999). Once a competitive relationship is established, however, firms may or may not recognize their mutual interdependence. The structure of the industry and the structure of the organization will play major roles in determining whether or not firms are able to recognize their mutual interdependence. For example, firms in moderately or highly concentrated industries may have organization structures that prevent the communication and coordination necessary to facilitate competitor recognition. However, once firms do recognize their mutual interdependence, tactical rivalry will subside as competitors purposively seek to exploit their multimarket contact.

For this multimarket strategy scenario, however, there generally will be significant learning necessary to enter a new market. The firm will have to develop new competencies in order to compete. This makes it difficult to rationally plan to establish multimarket contact, as there will be uncertainty surrounding a competitor's ability to keep up. In addition, once recognition of mutual interdependence occurs, there likely will have to be changes in organization structure in order to facilitate more coordination of tactical competitive moves such as advertising and pricing policies.

P15: Multimarket Opportunists will predominate in product-market entry situations.

The Multimarket Pacifist: Ignoring Naïvely Created Multimarket Contact

Under this multimarket strategy scenario, the development of multimarket contact proceeds as described above in the second multimarket strategy scenario. However, once multimarket contact is created, firms still may not recognize their mutual interdependence and therefore may not compete intensely with one another simply because they are pursuing different opportunities that each deems appropriate for exploiting its own distinctive competencies and product-market choices (hence, "pacifists"-they choose not to fight). For this multimarket strategy scenario, significant learning will be required to enter a new market. Firms will tend to be internally focused on exploiting efficiencies and searching for new sources of value to provide their customers.

In addition, organization structures will tend to be highly decentralized, while industry structures will be fragmented with high growth rates. These are general characteristics of emerging industries. Thus, when market overlaps are created, they are likely to be low in number, and thus difficult to notice. Even if the overlaps are noticed, firms will be more preoccupied with taking advantage of market growth than with lowering rivalry with their competitors.

P16: Multimarket Pacifists will predominate in emerging industries.

CONCLUSION

This paper was motivated by dissatisfaction with the theoretical status of multi-market contact and the mutual forbearance that has been shown to result from it. We know that forbearance happens, but we do not know to what extent this strategy can be employed purposively by managers. In order to understand better the empirical results that already exist, and to guide future research, we have attempted to develop a more fully specified theory. In doing so, we have differentiated between the motivations and mechanisms behind the creation and the exploitation of multimarket contact.

In the propositions outlined above, we have shown that a number of conditions exist in which the creation and exploitation of naïve multimarket contact are plausible. In these cases, we argue that outcomes that *look like* mutual forbearance are probably not, making it difficult to develop managerial prescriptions in such situations. We also identify industry and organizational factors that make the implementation of multimarket strategies more difficult. Thus, our framework allows researchers to focus effort on industries in which the payoffs from multimarket strategy will be significant. In Table 1, we suggest industries in which each multimarket strategy scenario is likely to play out and the relative prevalence of each scenario. We implore researchers in this area to consider examining the phenomena of multimarket contact and mutual forbearance in some of these settings to facilitate comparing and contrasting results obtained from the narrower set of industries most typically studied (e.g. airlines, banking).

Clearly, in order to move multimarket theory forward, empirical work must begin to penetrate the "black box" of managerial decision-making in multi-market environments. We have postulated factors that will motivate and enable managers to purposively undertake multimarket strategies. However, it remains to be seen whether or not these factors do influence decisions, if there are other factors we have not included, or if mutual forbearance is nothing more than a chance outcome about which managers remain unaware.

NOTE

1. Note that Katz and Shapiro (1985) and Farrell and Soloner (1986) are concerned primarily (if not exclusively) with "consumption externalities" arising from networks. In the argument presented here, we are postulating the existence of what might be termed "production externalities" that arise from the network-based nature of the product/service. In the final analysis, however, as we argue, it appears that network-based products/ services also lead to consumption externalities.

REFERENCES

Abell, D. F. (1980). *Defining the business: The starting point of strategic planning.* Englewood Cliffs, NJ: Prentice-Hall.

Abrahamson, E., & Fombrun, C. J. (1994). Macrocultures: Determinants and consequences. *Academy of Management Review, 19,* 728–755.

Amburgey, T., & Miner, A. S. (1992). Strategic momentum: The effects of repetitive, positional, and contextual momentum on merger activity. *Strategic Management Journal, 13,* 335–348.

Audia, G. P., Sorenson, O., & Hage, G. (2001). Geography and the Multiunit Firm. In: J. A. C. Baum & H. R. Greve (Eds), *Multiunit Organization and Multimarket Strategy; Advances in Strategic Management, 18,* (pp. 75–105). Oxford, UK: JAI Press.

Barnett, W. P. (1993). Strategic deterrence among multipoint competitors. *Industrial and Corporate Change, 2,* 249–278.

Barney, J. B. (1990). *Gaining and sustaining competitive advantage.* Reading, MA: Addison-Wesley.

Baum, J. A. C., & Korn, H. J. (1996). Competitive dynamics of interfirm rivalry. *Academy of Management Journal, 39,* 255–291.

Baum, J. A. C., & Korn, H. J. (1999). Dynamics of dyadic competitive interaction. *Strategic Management Journal, 20,* 251–278.

Baum, J. A. C., & Mezias, S. (1992). Localized competition and organizational failure in the Manhattan hotel industry, 1898–1990. *Administrative Science Quarterly, 37,* 580–604.

Baum, J. A. C., & Oliver, C. (1996). Toward an institutional ecology of organizational founding. *Academy of Management Journal, 39,* 1378–1427.

Bernheim, B. D., & Whinston, M. D. (1990). Multimarket contact and collusive behavior. *RAND Journal of Economics, 21,* 1–26.

Boeker, W., Goodstein, J., Stephan, J., & Murmann, J. P. (1997). Competition in a multimarket environment: The case of market exit. *Organization Science, 8,* 126–142.

Chen, M.-J. (1996). Competitor analysis and interfirm rivalry: Toward a theoretical integration. *Academy of Management Review, 21,* 100–134.

Chen, M.-J., & MacMillan, I. C. (1992). Non-response and delayed response to competitive moves: The roles of competitor dependence and action irreversibility. *Academy of Management Journal, 35,* 539–570.

Chen, M.-J., & Miller, D. (1994). Competitive attack, retaliation, and performance: An expectancy-valence framework. *Strategic Management Journal, 15,* 85–102.

Clark, B. H., & Montgomery, D. B. (1999). Managerial identification of competitors. *Journal of Marketing, 63,* 67–83.

DiMaggio, P. J., & Powell, W. W. (1983). The iron cage revisited: Institutional isomorphism and collective rationality in organizational fields. *American Sociological Review, 48,* 147–160.

Edwards, C. D. (1955). Conglomerate bigness as a source of power. In: the National Bureau Committee for Economic Research conference report, *Business Concentration and Price Policy* (pp. 331–352). Princeton, NJ: Princeton University Press.

Farrell, J. & Saloner, G. (1986). Installed based and compatibility: Innovation, product preannouncements and predation. *American Economic Review, 76,* 940–955.

Gimeno, J. (1999). Reciprocal threats in multimarket rivalry: Staking out "spheres of influence" in the U.S. airline industry. *Strategic Management Journal, 20,* 101–128.

Gimeno, J., & Woo, C. Y. (1996). Hypercompetition in a multimarket environment: The role of strategic similarity and multimarket contact in competitive de-escalation. *Organization Science, 7,* 322–341.

Gimeno, J., & Woo, C. Y. (1999). Multimarket contact, economies of scope, and firm performance. *Academy of Management Journal, 43,* 239–259.

Golden, B. R., & Ma, H. (1995). The role of intra-firm integration and rewards in the implementation of multiple point competitive strategies. Unpublished manuscript.

Greve, H. R. (1998). Managerial cognition and the mimetic adoption of market positions: What you see is what you do. *Strategic Management Journal, 19,* 967–988.

Greve, H. R. (1999). Branch systems and nonlocal learning in populations. In: A. Miner & P. Anderson (Eds), *Population-Level Learning and Industry Change: Advances in Strategic Management, 16* (pp. 57–80). Stamford, CT: JAI Press.

Greve, H. R. (2000). Market niche entry decisions: Competition, learning and strategy in Tokyo banking, 1894–1936. *Academy of Management Journal, 43,* 816–836.

Haveman, H. (1993). Follow the leader: Mimetic isomorphism and entry into new markets. *Administrative Science Quarterly, 38,* 593–627.

Hill, C. W. (1988). Internal capital market controls and financial performance in multidivisional firms. *The Journal of Industrial Economics, 37,* 67–83.

Hill, C. W., Hitt, M. A., & Hoskisson, R. E. (1992). Cooperative versus competitive structures in related and unrelated diversified firms. *Organization Science, 3,* 501–521.

Jayachandran, S., Gimeno, J., & Varadarajan, P. R. (1999). The theory of multimarket competition: A synthesis and implications for marketing strategy. *Journal of Marketing, 63,* 49–66.

Ingram, P., & Baum, J. A. C. (1997a). Chain affiliation and the failure of Manhattan hotels, 1898–1980. *Administrative Science Quarterly, 42,* 68–102.

Ingram, P., & Baum, J. A. C. (1997b). Opportunity and constraint: Organizations' learning from the operating and competitive experience of industries. *Strategic Management Journal, 18,* 75–98 (Summer Special Issue).

Kalnins, A., & Chung, W. (2001). Ethnic links and multimarket outcomes: A test of the rural motel industry. In: J. A. C. Baum & H. R. Greve (Eds), *Multiunit Organization and Multimarket Strategy; Advances in Strategic Management, 18,* (pp. 31–51). Oxford, UK: JAI Press.

Katz, M., & Shapiro, C. (1985). Network externalities, competition and compatibility. *American Economic Review, 75,* 424–440.

Korn, H. J., & Baum, J. A. C. (1999). Chance, imitative, and strategic antecedents of multimarket contact. *Academy of Management Journal, 42,* 171–193.

Lant, T. K., & Baum, J. A. C. (1995). Cognitive sources of socially constructed competitive groups: Examples from the Manhattan hotel industry. In: W. R. Scott & S. Christensen (Eds),

The Institutional Construction of Organizations (pp. 15–38). Thousand Oaks, CA: Sage Publications.

March, J. G. (1991). Exploration and exploitation in organizational learning. *Organization Science, 2*, 71–87.

Markides, C. C., & Williamson, P. J. (1996). Corporate diversification and organizational structure: A resource-based view. *Academy of Management Journal, 39*, 340–367.

Miner, A. S., & Haunschild, P. R. (1995). Population level learning. In: B. M. Staw & L. L. Cummings (Eds), *Research in organizational behavior*, Vol 17 (pp. 115–166). Greenwich, CT: JAI Press.

Panzar, J. C., & Willig, R. D. (1981). Economies of scope. *American Economic Review, 71*, 268–272.

Porac, J. F., & Thomas, H. (1990). Taxonomic mental models in competitor definition. *Academy of Management Review, 15*, 224–240.

Porac, J. F., Thomas, H., & Baden-Fuller, C. (1989). Competitive groups as cognitive communities: The case of Scottish knitwear manufacturers. *Journal of Management Studies, 26*, 397–416.

Porac, J. F., Thomas, H., Wilson, F., Paton, D., & Kanfer, A. (1995). Rivalry and the industry model of Scottish knitwear producers. *Administrative Science Quarterly, 40*, 203–227.

Porter, M. E. (1980). *Competitive Strategy: Techniques for Analyzing Industries and Competitors*. New York, NY: The Free Press.

Porter, M. E. (1985). *Competitive Advantage: Creating and Sustaining Superior Performance*. New York, NY: The Free Press.

Reger, R. K., & Huff, A. S. (1993). Strategic groups: A cognitive perspective. *Strategic Management Journal, 14*, 103–124.

Scherer, F. M., & Ross, S. (1990). *Industrial Market Structure and Economic Performance* (3rd ed.). Boston: Houghton Mifflin.

Scott, J. T. (1982). Multimarket contact and economic performance. *The Review of Economics and Statistics, 64*, 368–375.

Scott, J. T. (1989). Purposive diversification as a motive for merger. *International Journal of Industrial Organization, 7*, 35–47.

Scott, J. T. (1991). Multimarket contact among diversified oligopolists. *International Journal of Industrial Organization, 9*, 225–238.

Spender, J.-C. (1989). *Industry recipes: An inquiry in the nature and sources of managerial judgment*. Cambridge, MA: Basil-Blackwood, Inc.

TRADEOFFS IN THE ORGANIZATION OF PRODUCTION: MULTIUNIT FIRMS, GEOGRAPHIC DISPERSION AND ORGANIZATIONAL LEARNING

Pino G. Audia, Olav Sorenson and Jerald Hage

ABSTRACT

Firms face a choice in the organization of production. By concentrating production at one site, they can enjoy economies of scale. Or, by dispersing production across multiple facilities, firms can benefit from product-specific efficiencies and enhanced organizational learning. When choosing to organize in multiple units, firms must also decide where to locate these units. Concentrating production geographically can enhance economies of scale and facilitate organizational learning. On the other hand, dispersing facilities might allow the firm to lower transportation costs, reduce risks, and forbear competition. To examine these tradeoffs, we compare exit rates of single-unit organizations to multiunit organizations and their constituent plants in the U.S. footwear industry between 1940 and 1989. Our results suggest that, multiunit organizations benefit primarily from enhanced organizational learning, competitive forbearance and the diversification of risk. Nevertheless, these benefits appear to come at the expense of organizational adaptability.

Multiunit Organization and Multimarket Strategy, Volume 18, pages 75–105
2001 by Elsevier Science Ltd.
ISBN: 0-7623-0721-8

INTRODUCTION

In the last two centuries, the organization of production has shifted from small, single-unit firms toward large, multiunit organizations. Much debate surrounds the interpretation of this profound shift. Some view the rise of the multiunit organization as an inevitable stage in the natural progression of economic evolution (Chandler, 1977; Galbraith, 1956). In sharp contrast, others, calling attention to the failure of many large corporations and the persistence of small firms in most industries, suggest that the prevalence of the multiunit organization stems from a recent, yet ephemeral, configuration of economic and social conditions (Acs & Audretsch, 1990; Piore & Sabel, 1984).

Both economists and organization theorists offer explanations for the rise of the multiunit form. Economists and business historians tout the superiority of multiunit firms by pointing to their ability to reach higher efficiency levels, (Chandler, 1977; Sherer et al., 1975). They argue that multiunit firms can realize product-specific economies not available to single-unit organizations through the efficient allocation of production across their multiple units. Meanwhile, organization theorists contend that multiunit firms benefit from more effective incremental learning through the accumulation and transfer of knowledge across establishments (Argote, Beckman & Epple, 1990; Greve, 1999; Ingram & Baum, 1997a).

When firms do choose to organize production into multiple production units, managers face the additional task of deciding where to locate these facilities. Concentrating establishments geographically can facilitate organizational learning both by improving information transfer across units and by increasing the likelihood that knowledge generated at one plant applies to another (Ingram & Baum, 1997b). On the other hand, dispersing operations can allow multiunit firms to reduce transportation costs (Greenhut, 1956) and to diversify the economic risks associated with operating in a particular location (Ingram & Baum, 1997a, 1997b). Managers might also wish to consider the degree to which they avoid or seek contact with rivals in their choice of locations, as research shows that meeting competitors in multiple markets improves the firm's ability to forbear competition (Bernheim & Whinston, 1990; Edwards, 1955; Simmel, 1950).

Although the multiunit form offers many benefits, these advantages may come at a cost. To coordinate the operations of multiple units and maintain consistency across establishments, multiunit organizations add layers of managerial staff for coordination and control (Chandler, 1977). These complex bureaucratic structures allow multiunit firms to operate effectively, but they can also inhibit the organization's ability to adapt to shifts in environmental conditions (Hannan & Freeman, 1984).

We investigate these tradeoffs in the U.S. footwear industry from 1940 to 1989. Since these issues ultimately weigh on the success of the firm, we analyze the effects of these strategic choices on firm performance (organization survival). However, because previous studies on multiunit organizations often examine the outcomes of the constituent units (e.g. Ingram & Baum, 1997a), we also analyze this issue at the plant level. Our results suggest that multiunit organizations benefit primarily from organizational learning. Nevertheless, the bureaucracy necessary to maintain this structure impedes the organization's response to rapid environmental change. Multiunit firms also appear to face a tradeoff between dispersing to benefit from multi-local organization and concentrating to enable organizational learning. From a methodological point of view, our study suggests that plant level analyses may not translate well to organization level outcomes. Let us begin by reviewing the tradeoffs inherent in the organization of production.

THEORY AND HYPOTHESES

Multiunit Advantages: Product-Specific Economies

Production systems can benefit from both technology-specific and product-specific economies of scale. Efficiencies that accrue when the increased size of a single operating unit reduces the unit cost of production fall into the first category. Both single-unit and multiunit organizations can realize these economies depending on the size of their plants. In contrast, product-specific economies arise from the efficient use of multiple productive units. Thus, these economies of production represent a unique source of advantage for multiunit organizations.

Multiunit firms achieve these efficiencies through product specialization. According to Sherer et al. (1975: p. 295) "Product specialization exists when plants belonging to the same organization produce for a broad geographic market some narrow segment of the product line normally encompassed within an industry's definition." Product specialization allows longer production runs that facilitate worker productivity, increase product quality and simplify production planning. For example, according to Pratten and Dean (1965), shoe manufacturers can reduce labor and overhead costs by roughly 10 to 15% by increasing average production run lengths from 200 pairs to between 1,000 and 6,000 pairs. A second benefit of product specialization arises from centralizing inventories. By concentrating special raw material stocks and finished good inventories in one place, firms can reduce inventories as a percentage of production because random variations in consumption tend to offset each other (Kekre, 1987).

Can single-unit firms benefit from these product-specific economies? In principle, single-unit firms can achieve production economies by focusing on specialty lines such as work shoes or high-quality men's shoes. Nonetheless, they operate at a disadvantage even then because, not offering a broad product line, they cannot provide frequent replacement of stock without incurring exorbitant shipping costs. Hansen's (1959) study reports that single-plant firms that specialized their production to a single type of shoe felt considerable pressure from retailers to offer a broader product line and to replace stock more frequently. Though inefficient in terms of production costs,[1] broad product lines allow single-unit firms to meet retailer demands and to reduce risk by adjusting their production mix to frequent fluctuations in the demand for specific products (Sorenson, 2000). Thus, it should not surprise us that research on the shoe industry reports that single-unit firms typically offer a wide array of products (Hansen, 1959; Szenberg, Lombardi & Lee, 1977). This leads us to our first expectation: To the extent that product-specific economies exist, firms that distribute their production across several specialized plants should outperform those that manufacture all of their products within a single facility.

Hypothesis 1. Dividing operations among a larger number of plants increases organizational performance.

Multiunit Geography: Multi-local Production

When a firm organizes into multiple units, the geographic distribution of its facilities can importantly affect the firm's performance. Multi-local firms – those operating in many dispersed locations – can realize competitive advantages from several sources (Greenhut, 1956). First, multi-local firms can minimize transportation costs by locating plants in close proximity to important markets and by adapting production to local tastes. Theoretical models of spatial competition show that firms should space themselves maximally when transportation costs affect the price of providing goods to customers (Lösch, 1954; Smithies, 1941). Although most consider the footwear industry to operate at a national (OECD, 1976), rather than local or regional, level, manufacturers supplying multiple distribution channels might reduce the transportation costs associated with delivering goods to distributors by maintaining geographically dispersed production.

A type of statistical economy of scale offers a more likely source of multi-local advantage. At a general level, units that belong to larger collectives can often avoid selection pressures (Barnett, 1997). Ingram and Baum (1997a,

1997b) extend this argument to cover multiple geographically distinct units that tie their fates together through common ownership. They argue that the operation of multiple units allows the firm to weather idiosyncratic risks associated with particular locations. For example, if the labor market tightens in one location, a multiunit firm can shift some portion of production to plants operating in areas where wages remain low. Similarly, the operation of multiple plants probably gives the firm leverage against union activity because employees may find it difficult to engage in collective action across geographically dispersed facilities. Regardless of whether they actually do, firms clearly *could* engage in this redistribution of labor, as plants in this industry typically operate substantially below capacity.[2] Together these factors suggest that firms might benefit from spreading production geographically.

Hypothesis 2. Dispersing operations geographically increases organizational performance.

Additionally, operating in multiple geographic markets might allow firms to forbear competition with their rivals. Two rationales suggest that competing with rivals across multiple markets might increase the likelihood of cooperative behavior (Baum & Korn, 1999). Economists focus on the ability to retaliate credibly should a rival decide to compete too vigorously in the focal firm's primary market (Bernheim & Whinston, 1990; Edwards, 1955). Meanwhile, sociologists highlight the notion that firms might understand the benefits of tacit cooperative behavior, allowing a rival to dominate one market in exchange for acquiescence in another (Simmel, 1950). These complementary views both suggest that firms might benefit from multi-point competition. Indeed, a growing body of research finds evidence of this benefit in the form of increasing margins (Evans & Kessides, 1994; Gimeno & Woo, 1996; Scott, 1982, 1991) and decreasing market exit rates (Barnett, 1993; Baum & Korn, 1996; Boeker et al., 1997) when firms engage in multi-point competition.

Hypothesis 3. Meeting rivals in multiple geographic markets increases organizational performance.

Multiunit Advantages: Organizational Learning

Organization theorists point instead to the ability to learn incrementally and transfer that knowledge across units as a chief advantage of the multiunit form (Argote, Beckman & Epple, 1990; Greve, 1999; Ingram & Baum, 1997a). To benefit from the transfer of knowledge across units, constituent plants must perform similar tasks, as one sees in the footwear industry. Unlike vertically organized firms in which constituent plants produce different components that other facilities assemble, plants belonging to multiunit organizations in the footwear industry typically make similar products and tend to employ the same production processes.[3]

Under parallel production conditions, even random variation across sites allows multiple plant organizations to garner comparative information regarding the best means of production (Teece, 1977). Savvy managers can take further advantage by engaging in systematic strategic experimentation and the implementation of best practices. Organizations with only one site can also experiment strategically, but multi-plant organizations enjoy an advantage when engaging in experimentation: While single plant organizations must experiment sequentially, organizations with multiple sites can participate in several experiments at once.

Parallel experimentation offers at least two advantages over sequential experimentation. First, parallel experimentation allows learning to occur at a faster pace. Experiments take place in chronological time. Parallel processing allows the firm to reduce substantially the time required to investigate the potential benefits of a change in operating procedures. When experiments reveal opportunities to improve performance, firms benefit by adopting these changes sooner. Second, parallel experimentation increases the internal validity of the conclusions garnered from the experiment. Sequential experimentation suffers from an inability to control for several threats to internal validity that parallel experimentation, presumably with a control group, covers (Cook & Campbell, 1979). For example, maturation can bias sequential tests. In the U.S. footwear industry, both employee-level learning and equipment wear could impact the perceived results of a strategic experiment. One experimental condition might appear to outperform another simply due to the order of testing the conditions. When run sequentially, managers cannot decompose the effects of these maturation factors from the effect of the experimental condition. Essentially, this confounding of factors introduces noise into the learning process. Thus, sequential experimentation increases the risk that the organization learns superstitiously (March, 1988).

Empirical research suggests that organizational learning benefits multiunit firms (for a review, see Argote, 1999). For instance, Ingram and Baum (1997a) find that chains with greater operating experience offer stronger survival advantages to their component hotels. Moreover, knowledge transfer appears to offer additional improvements in firm performance. For example, Darr, Argote and Epple (1995) find that organizations operating multiple fast food restaurants lower production costs by transferring best practices. And Banaszack-Holl et al. (2000) find that chains that acquire poorly performing nursing homes appear able to raise the performance of these acquisitions toward the level of the other units in the chain.

Unlike economies of scale that result from the contemporaneous organization of production, learning accrues through the accumulation of experience over time. Thus, the literature on learning curves in manufacturing and services focuses on cumulative output as a measure of economies of experience (Argote, 1999). Alternatively, one might consider the cumulative years of operating experience embodied in an organization as an indicator of learning (e.g. Greve, 1999; Ingram & Baum, 1997a). These studies often incorporate some discounting factor to account for the fact that old experience, forgotten or irrelevant, might no longer improve firm performance (e.g. Argote, Beckman & Epple, 1990; Ingram & Baum, 1997a). Regardless, we expect learning to enhance the viability of multiunit organizations and their constituent plants. Moreover, more plants provide more points at which strategic experiments can occur.

Hypothesis 4. Greater cumulative operating experience increases organizational performance.

Multiunit Geography: Dispersion and Learning

Though largely absent from the research on organizational learning, the geographic dispersion of the organization likely influences the efficiency of knowledge transfer (Argote, 1999). The transfer of tacit knowledge can prove difficult even with face-to-face contact – without it, nearly impossible. Thus, knowledge tends to diffuse slowly through space (Jaffe, Trajtenberg & Henderson, 1993). Though organizations provide conduits for the transfer of this knowledge (Argote, Beckman & Epple, 1990; Greve, 1996), even within these institutions face-to-face contact seems less likely when employees must travel long distances to learn from their colleagues. Indeed, Jaffe and Adams (1996) find that spillovers within an organization decline rapidly with distance and several other studies suggest that organizations learn best within tight geographic boundaries (Argote, Beckman & Epple, 1990; Epple, Argote & Murphy, 1996; Greve, 1999). Thus, we expect geographic dispersion to reduce the efficiency of knowledge transfer in the organization, thereby limiting the returns to learning across units.

A second issue regarding geographic dispersion and organizational learning relates to the usefulness of the knowledge being transferred. As the similarity of two components declines, it becomes increasingly likely that routines learned at one unit would not improve the performance of the other unit. For example, Banaszak-Holl et al. (2000) find that chains acquiring nursing homes unlike their existing units encounter more difficulties improving performance at these newly acquired sites. Units that reside in geographically distant locations often face different factor markets, product markets and distribution channels. These differences can limit the usefulness of (or perhaps even make harmful) trans-ferring routines from one constituent unit to another. Both Ingram and Baum (1997b and this volume) and Greve (1999) find evidence that geographically distant experience benefits chain components less than local experience. Thus, we expect dispersed organizations to generate knowledge with less applicability on average to all of their constituent units.

Hypothesis 5. Geographically dispersed firms benefit less from cumulative operating experience than geographically concentrated organizations.

Multiunit Disadvantage: Bureaucratization

Although organizing into multiple units might improve the organization's ability to realize product-specific economies and to improve efficiency through incre-mental learning, the multiunit form also has its drawbacks. Chandler (1977, 1990) persuasively argues that the number of operating units, rather than the total assets or the size of the workforce, determines the number of middle and top managers, the nature of their tasks, and the complexity of the institution they manage. Based on his historical analysis, Chandler observes that:

> Each unit has its own administrative office, its own managers and staff, its own set of books, as well as its own physical facilities and personnel. The activities of the managers of these units (lower level managers) are monitored and coordinated by a full-time top-level exec-utive, or a team of such executives, who plan and allocate resources for the operating units and the enterprise as a whole (1990: p. 15).

Although these administrative structures critically allow multiunit organizations to achieve product-specific economies and to generate and transfer knowledge across units through their coordinating activities, this bureaucratization also constrains organizations' ability to adapt to changing environments (Hannan & Freeman, 1984). Decisions become farther removed from the locus of execution, which can lead to frequent delays and mistakes as the complexity of the decision-making process increases. Operating procedures that ensure individuals perform tasks in an efficient manner across establishments can generate additional inflexibility because adaptation requires managers to overrule well-established control systems. When change does occur, it often fails to account adequately for shifts in environmental conditions because long-term planning and time consuming compromises between conflicting departments introduce political interests into the decision-making process (March & Olsen, 1976). Lending support to this account, Sherer et al. (1975) in their study of multiunit firms report virtual unanimity among the people they interviewed that decision making slows in large multi-plant firms and that top executives became more isolated from operational problems, potentially degrading the quality of managerial decisions. This organizational rigidity becomes most pronounced when changes in environmental conditions invalidate the old way of doing things.

Hypothesis 6. Dividing production across a larger number of facilities decreases performance when the environment shifts.

DATA AND METHODS

To test these hypotheses, we analyzed the evolution of the U.S. footwear industry from 1940 to 1989. Some historical background on the industry may prove useful.

History of the Shoe Manufacturing

In his study of shoemaking from 1649 to 1895, Commons (1909) provides a fascinating and detailed account of the evolution of production arrangements in the industry. At first, itinerant shoemakers traveled with their tools from house to house making shoes to customers' specifications. Craftsmen, who worked in their own shops, began to replace these itinerant shoemakers at the end of the 17th century. Then, during the 18th century, the increased concentration of people in space created markets for standard shoe sizes and shapes, spurring additional changes in the organization of shoe production. Although the technology of shoe production remained largely unchanged, this movement away from bespoke shoe manufacturing generated economies of scale that led craftsmen to specialize in their production activities (Commons, 1909).

The McKay sole-sewing machine, introduced in 1862, dramatically changed the business of making shoes. By reducing eighty hours of work, using traditional production methods, to just one hour, using the McKay machine, it justified the centralization of production, facilitating the transition from a craft system to a mass production system (Commons, 1909; Hansen, 1959). Nevertheless, until the 1920s, single plant firms accounted for nearly all production. Two factors aided the dominance of small single-unit organizations: First, the production process allowed efficient manufacturing in plants of varying size (Hoover, 1937; Szenberg, Lombardi & Lee, 1977). Second, the widespread practice of leasing machinery minimized the need for startup capital (Davis, 1940; OECD, 1976).

Beginning in the 1920s, single-unit firms began to face a new type of competitor: the multiunit firm.[4] Two features distinguished this form: it comprised a number of distinct units and a hierarchy of full-time salaried executives managed it (Chandler, 1977). Despite the low barriers to entry that characterized the industry, multiunit firms grew rapidly to become important players. In 1957, the four largest firms, Endicott Johnson, Brown Shoe, General Shoe, and International Shoe, respectively operated 25, 27, 31, and 45 plants, and together accounted for 23% of domestic production (Hansen, 1959).

The U.S. footwear industry remained relatively stable from the advent of mass production until the 1960s. Starting in the sixties, several external changes began altering the competitive landscape. Synthetics, which required new production technology, started to replace leather (OECD, 1976) and auxiliary industries introduced several new procedures for manufacturing leather shoes (Boon, 1980). Moreover, markets became more and more fashion oriented – increasingly requiring manufacturers to monitor and adapt to fickle consumer preferences instead of producing classic styles for years on end (OECD, 1976). Footwear manufacturers in the United States found it difficult to adapt to these radical changes (Duchesneau, Cohn & Dutton, 1979; OECD, 1976; USITC, 1984).

A flood of imports swamped the U.S. footwear industry, growing from 26.6 million pairs in 1960 to 241.6 million in 1970 (Footwear Industries of America, various years). Easy access to raw material, cheap labor, and low barriers to entry allowed countries such as South Korea and Taiwan to develop export capabilities quickly (OECD, 1976). Strong political pressure led the U.S. to establish import quotas for South Korea and Taiwan in 1977, but the government terminated all import relief following the expiration of these quotas; President Reagan vetoed a Senate Commission's proposal to extend them. In the 1980s, imports exploded – led this time by Brazil and China – peaking at 940.8 million pairs, 82% of the U.S. market (Footwear Industries of America, various years).

This radical change in the competitive landscape prompted a variety of strategic responses by American manufacturers in the 1980s. Many of the larger firms adopted automation to compete on time, capitalizing on growing retail channel demand for just-in-time delivery (Freeman & Kleiner, 1998; Hazeldine, 1986; Warrock, 1985). Lacking the scale to justify and the resources to implement these improvements, many smaller manufacturers retreated to high quality niches (Bahls, 1989; Freeman & Kleiner, 1998). Some companies acted as middlemen, selling imported shoes through their distribution channels, but few manufacturers moved their own production abroad (Warrock, 1985). Although these changes improved the competitiveness of American shoe manufacturers, for many firms, it proved too little, too late; between 1968 and 1989, the number of plants operating in the U.S. fell from 1330 to 632.

Sample and Data Sources

The data incorporated the histories of all American shoes manufacturing plants from 1940 to 1989. The *Annual Shoemaking Directory of Shoe Manufacturers*, a comprehensive listing of footwear manufacturers published by the Shoe Traders Publishing Company, provided most of the data. For each plant, this publication contains a rich array of information including the year of its founding, the year of its closure, daily output, and the plant's owner. Annual data from *Moody's* and *Footwear News* supplemented the information in the *Shoemaking Directory*. Data on international trade tracing the imports of footwear came from publications of the Footwear Industries of America.

The data included information on 5119 distinct shoe manufacturing plants. During the study period, 4116 new plants opened, while 1003 plants opened prior to 1940. Using editions of the *Shoemaking Directory* that date back to 1921, we determined the founding dates for 758 of these left-censored plants. The remaining 245 plants with unknown founding dates received a founding year of 1921 and a dummy variable marking them as left-censored observations. Of the plants in the data set, 4395 ceased operations by the end of 1989. The cessation of plant operations defined a failure event at the plant level. Changes in name or ownership did not indicate plant failure because the plant continues to produce shoes. Nevertheless, this information did allow us to track changes in multiunit organizations. Often a change in ownership implied shrinkage or expansion of a multiunit organization. For single-unit organizations, plant founding and failure coincided with organization founding and failure. For multiunit organizations, founding occurred with entry of its first plant; failure occurred when the last plant closed. Figure 1 depicts the density of the population, average plant output and imports over time.

Model

To test our propositions, we estimated organization and plant exit rates as a function of industry, plant and organization level characteristics. Although one could use other measures of performance, exit provided a particularly useful

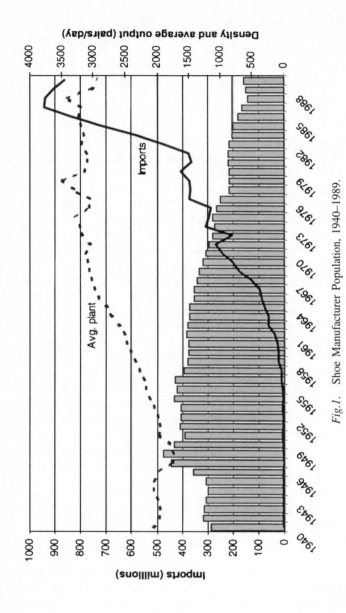

Fig.1. Shoe Manufacturer Population, 1940–1989.

measure in these data for two reasons. First, the preponderance of private firms (> 90% of firm-years) precludes the use of profit information. Exit provided an observable outcome for every firm in the industry. Second, relatively few organizations exited through acquisition. Therefore, exit likely represented an unsatisfactory outcome for both the managers and investors involved. We estimated all models as instantaneous hazard rates of market exit:

$$\mu_i(t) \lim_{\Delta t \to 0} \frac{\Pr(t < T \le t + \Delta t \mid T > t)}{\Delta t}$$

where T is a random variable for the time of firm exit, t is the time that organization i has spent in the shoe industry, $\Pr(.)$ is the probability of firm exit over the interval $[t,\ t + \Delta t$ given that the organization belonged to the risk set at the beginning of the interval, and the rate can vary as a function of organization age. We implemented these models using TDA (Rohwer, 1995).

Use of the instantaneous hazard rate allowed us to estimate the risk of market failure while explicitly controlling for age dependence (Tuma & Hannan, 1984). Researchers have found a variety of relationships between age and failure rates. Early research typically found that failure rates declined as organizations aged (e.g. Carroll, 1983). However, subsequent studies find nearly every conceivable relationship between age and mortality rates (for a review, see Baum, 1996). To control for age dependence and avoid the possibility of misspecification, we employed the piece-wise exponential model, which does not require one to assume a functional form for time dependence. The piece-wise exponential splits time into pieces (dummy variables) according to the age of the organization. The base failure rate remains constant within each piece, but base rates vary freely across age pieces. We selected age intervals of 0–3 years, 3–10 years, 11–20 years, and over 20 years. As an additional benefit, left censoring, which exists in these data, does not bias estimation of the piece-wise exponential (Guo, 1993). Nonetheless, we included a dummy variable to account for any systematic differences across the left-censored cases introduced by the downward bias in our age measures for these cases.

Measures

Plant count indicated the number of plants, in excess of one, commonly owned by the same company.[5] We expected the number of plants to reduce both organization and plant failure rates (Hypothesis 1). To test the effect of multiple plants under changing environmental conditions (Hypothesis 6), we interacted this variable with imports and expected the interacted term to increase plant and organization failure rates.

Geographic dispersion captured the average distance between manufacturing facilities in hundreds of miles. To generate this variable, we located each plant in space using the longitude and latitude of the town in which the plant resided. Then, we calculated the distance between each dyad (i.e. pair of plants) using spherical geometry, logged these dyadic distances, and averaged them across all possible dyads within the firm (an analogue to the weighted density term in Sorenson & Audia, 2000).[6] Larger values on this variable indicate greater degrees of dispersion. For the plant-level analyses, we constructed this variable individually for each plant. We anticipated decreasing failure rates with dispersion due to the benefits of multi-local production (Hypothesis 2).

Multi-market contact allowed us to estimate the potential benefits of meeting competitors in multiple markets. To create this measure, we simply counted, for each multiunit firm, the number of geographic markets (defined as towns) in which they met each other multiunit firm. We then averaged this count across all multiunit organizations that the focal firm met in local markets. For example, if firm A met firm B in 3 markets and firm C in 4 markets, then it would receive a multi-market contact score of 3.5 [= (3 + 4)/2]. High levels of this measure indicated a higher degree of multi-market contract.[7] Therefore, we expected multi-market contact to decrease failure rates (Hypothesis 3).

Experience provided our measure for the effects of organizational learning. Following Ingram and Baum (1997a, b) and Greve (1999), we cumulated years of operating experience to form an indicator of organizational learning.[8] We logged the experience measure to account for decreasing returns. In the plant-level models, we separated out experience in the focal plant from experience at other plants that belong to the same owner. We expected experience to decrease both organization and plant exit rates (Hypothesis 4).

To test the limits that dispersion placed on organizational learning, we created two interaction terms between operating experience and dispersion. For the organization models, we multiplied the average distance between plants by the number of plants in operation before cumulating these experience figures over time. Thus, a positive effect for this interaction suggests that dispersed firms learn more slowly than concentrated firms (Hypothesis 5). The plant-level models used a slightly different measure. Here, we weighted the experience associated with all plants other than the focal plant by the inverse of their distance from the focal plant. The two measures differed because the plant-level models had an obvious reference point – the focal plant – while the organization-level models did not.

Imports in billions of pairs of shoes in a given year provided an indicator of environmental change in the shoe industry. Although the rise of imports marked a clear change in the competitive landscape for the industry, we remained agnostic as to whether the rise of imports itself changed the industry or whether imports arose from several interrelated changes in production technology, materials and consumer preferences. Regardless, we expected firms with multiple plants to adjust more slowly to these changes, and therefore to suffer declining performance (Hypothesis 6).

Control Variables

Plant size controlled for plant-level economies of scale. The technology of production might require that organizations operate at multiples of some discrete size to minimize per unit costs – often referred to as the minimal efficient scale, or MES (e.g. Scherer & Ross, 1990). Various studies of shoe manufacturing estimate that plants producing more than 2500 shoes per day generate 15% to 28% higher gross profits than smaller facilities[9] (Bain, 1956; Szenberg, Lombardi & Lee, 1977). Plant size measured the number of pairs of shoes manufactured each day. Unfortunately, roughly 70% of cases did not report output information in any given year. To increase the number of usable cases, we used straight-line interpolation to estimate production information for plants with gaps in their reported size information. Interpolation increased the percentage of usable cases in the plant level models from 30% to 92% and in the organization level models from 26% to 91%.[10] Since we considered size an important control variable, only those cases with size information available entered the analyses. In the organization-level exit models, we included only organization size because this variable together with the number of plants already captures the impact of plant-level (technology-specific) economies of scale.

Organization size captured many types of production economies stemming from the ability to amortize certain costs (e.g. administrative) over a large number of units. Since scale economies operate as a function of size, these effects could spuriously affect the plant count measure without a control for organization size. This variable also accounted for the fact that large organizations might experience advantages beyond those captured by plant size and the number of facilities as a result of their power relative to buyers and suppliers (Pfeffer & Salancik, 1978) or their stock of slack resources (Cyert & March, 1963). Organizational size summed the shoes manufactured per day by all plants in a common ownership group.

We also controlled for the effects of fundamental variables influencing the carrying capacity of the industry, such as density and population. A large body of research in organizational ecology demonstrates that the number of firms in an industry crucially affects the mortality rates of organizations (for a review, see Baum, 1996). This theory posits a U-shaped relationship between the number of organizations and mortality rates (Hannan & Freeman, 1989; Hannan & Carroll, 1992) for populations of organizations observed since their birth. Nevertheless, our left-censored sample cannot actually test density-dependence because late low density – when legitimacy might not decline – rather than low density at the population's emergence drives the linear term (Baum & Powell, 1995). Regardless, we included organization and plant density as control variables. **Density** counted the number of firms in the industry. **Plant density** tallied the number of plants operating in a given year. Although ecology studies typically use organization density, those studies that analyze site-level data commonly use site density (e.g. Baum & Mezias, 1992). **Population**, a proxy for domestic demand, counted the number of people in millions living in the United States in a given year. **Year**, which tracked the number of calendar years since the beginning of our observation period, captured other factors that vary systematically with the passage of time. Table 1 displays the descriptive statistics for these variables. Table 2 reports estimates for Models 1 through 5.

Table 1. Descriptive statistics for organization-level characteristics (4,341 firms for 51,581 firm-years).

Variable	Mean	Std. Dev.	Minimum	Maximum
Organization age	11.83	11.13	0	49
Density	1,134.47	301.53	438	1,656
Plant density	1,358.75	321.82	566	1,893
Imports	1.42	2.28	0.002	9.41
Population	1,770.44	395.37	1,321	2,504
Organization size	3,903.03	16,922.69	1	1,897,500
Plant count	0.21	1.77	0	52
Dispersion	0.34	0.77	0	3.30
Multi-market contact	0.24	1.23	0	8
Experience	18.94	45.89	0	1,179
Avg. plant size	2,689.06	4,170.69	1	110,000
Left-censoring	0.00	0.06	0	1

RESULTS

Model 1 provided a baseline for our hypothesis tests. The control variables behave sensibly in the baseline. Population increases, which expand the potential domestic market and presumably ease competition, decrease failure rates. Moreover, the declining failure rates with size correspond to our notions of the advantages that these firms hold in terms of economies of scale, power and buffering mechanisms.

Model 2 included the plant count to test Hypothesis 1. The addition of this variable significantly improved the model ($\chi^2 = 40.0$, 1 d.f.). Multi-plant firms appear to enjoy an advantage relative to single-unit organizations even after controlling for scale.

In Model 3, we added measures of geographic dispersion and multi-market contacts to test Hypotheses 2 and 3. Firms that locate their plants such that they meet other multiunit firms in several markets appear able to obtain a reduction in competition. As the degree of multi-market contact increases, the likelihood of firm exit declines, supporting Hypothesis 3. This competitive forbearance apparently offers substantial benefits to the firm as organizations exhibiting the maximum degree of multi-market contact enjoy a 42% reduction in exit rates relative to their single market rivals. However, mutual forbearance alone does not explain the multi-local advantage. Even after explicitly accounting for multi-market contact, results indicate that firms with geographically dispersed production outperform those that concentrate production, in support of Hypothesis 2. The inclusion of these spatial configuration measures not only improved the model ($\chi^2 = 39.7$, 2 d.f.), but also appears to explain much of the multi-plant advantage, as the number of plants has no independent effect following the inclusion of these variables. We interpret this pattern as suggesting that multiunit firms benefit from their spatial configurations rather than from the reduction of line setup costs and inventories through plant specialization, leading us to reject Hypothesis 1.

Model 4 included the experience terms to account for organizational learning and test Hypotheses 4 and 5. Model 4 dramatically improves the model ($\chi^2 = 343.7$, 2 d.f.) and provides substantial evidence that multiunit firms benefit from enhanced organizational learning. As organizations accumulate operating experience, their failure rates decline, supporting Hypothesis 4. The interplay between experience and dispersion lends further credence to this interpretation. As expected in Hypothesis 5, firms that disperse their units geographically benefit less from the accumulation of operating experience.

Model 5 added interaction terms between imports and plant count and organizational size to test Hypothesis 6. These additions built significantly on Model

Table 2.   Organization level exit models.[†]

	Model 1	Model 2	Model 3	Model 4	Model 5
Age 0–3 years	0.899	0.908	0.890	1.516	1.779•
	(0.791)	(0.790)	(0.790)	(0.790)	(0.788)
Age 3–10 years	1.308	1.318	1.299	2.575••	2.844••
	(0.792)	(0.791)	(0.791	(0.792)	(0.790)
Age 11–20 years	0.836	0.845	0.836	2.537••	2.816••
	(0.791)	(0.790)	(0.790)	(0.794)	(0.792)
Age 20+ years	0.879	0.902	0.900	2.905••	3.129••
	(0.794)	(0.794)	(0.794)	(0.798)	(0.796)
Year	0.040••	0.040••	0.040••	0.031••	0.033••
	(0.006)	(0.006)	(0.006)	(0.006)	(0.006)
Density/100	1.865••	1.859••	1.845••	1.624••	1.683••
	(0.240)	(0.240)	(0.240)	(0.240)	(0.241)
Density^2/10,000	−0.070••	−0.070••	−0.069••	−0.056••	−0.056••
	(0.013)	(0.013)	(0.013)	(0.013)	(0.013)
Plant density	−2.102••	−2.100••	−2.087••	−1.905••	−1.962••
	(0.269)	(0.269)	(0.269)	(0.269)	(0.269)
Plant density^2/1000	0.072••	0.072••	0.071••	0.061••	0.061••
	(0.013)	(0.013)	(0.013)	(0.013)	(0.013)
Imports	0.446	0.443	0.430	0.449	−0.284
	(0.318)	(0.318)	(0.318)	(0.318)	(0.331)
Population	−0.005••	−0.005••	−0.005••	−0.005••	−0.005••
	(0.001)	(0.001)	(0.001)	(0.001)	(0.001)
Ln (organization size)	−0.094••	−0.089••	−0.085••	−0.080••	−0.115••
	(0.006)	(0.006)	(0.006)	(0.006)	(0.007)
Plant count		−0.181••	−0.029	−0.027	−0.037
		(0.040)	(0.032)	(0.033)	(0.075)
Geographic dispersion			−0.501•	−1.028•	−1.581•
			(0.195)	(0.559)	(0.791)
Multi-market contact			−0.159••	−0.136••	−0.122••
			(0.037)	(0.037)	(0.037)
Ln (experience)				−0.487••	−0.489••
				(0.025)	(0.025)
Ln (experience) X geographic dispersion				0.241•	0.384•
				(0.121)	(0.200)
Imports X plant count					0.240•
					(0.099)
Imports X ln (org. size)					0.119••
					(0.015)
Left censored	−1.776	−1.761	−1.751	−0.811	−0.767
	(1.003)	(1.003)	(1.003)	(1.004)	(1.005)
Log-likelihood	−14,292.11	−14,272.12	−14,252.29	−14,080.46	−14,042.85
χ^2 (d.f.)		40.0 (1)	39.7 (2)	343.7 (2)	75.2 (2)

[†] 4,341 firms; 3,836 exit events.   • $p < 0.05$ •• $p < 0.01$

4 ($\chi^2 = 75.2$, 2 d.f.) revealing strong evidence for the rigidity of multiunit firms. Although multiunit firms generally enjoy performance advantages relative to their single-unit rivals, this advantage erodes when the environment shifts substantially (in this case, in the form of rising imports). Thus, dividing production into multiple facilities does impose a cost on the organization, in the form of lost adaptability. By controlling for the interaction between organizational size and imports, Model 5 rules out the possibility that this disadvantage captures some type of resource partitioning that large organizations might experience by competing in market segments more vulnerable to international competition (Carroll, 1985).

Though these results appear robust, the experience measure reported in Models 1 through 5 does not incorporate discounting. Nevertheless, previous studies typically find that discounted measures of experience provide better estimates of learning because these measures account for the fact that old routines likely benefit the firm's operations less than more recently acquired knowledge (Argote, 1999; Greve, 1999; Ingram & Baum, 1997a). Therefore, we re-estimated model 5 using the various discount factors suggested by Ingram and Baum (1997a). Specifically, we generated three measures that weight prior learning according to the age of that learning in years. One measure divides previous learning by the square root of the number of years since the learning occurred; another divides it by the simple age of the experience; the final one divides experience by the square of its age. Because the models do not nest, we use the change in the Bayesian Information Criterion (BIC) to compare the models (Raftery, 1995). Model 5 provides the baseline for ΔBIC. Therefore, positive values for the difference indicate that model 5 provides a better fit to the data, while negative values signify the inferiority of model 5 to the model being compared to it. When the magnitude of ΔBIC exceeds 10, Raftery (1995) suggests that we should strongly prefer the model with the lower BIC. Table 3 shows the results of these estimates.

Unlike previous research, the model without discounting provides the best fit to our data. Model fit actually declines with the sharpness of the discounting of prior experience. This pattern points to a problem with using discounting on multiunit experience measures. For example, note that discounting according to the square of knowledge age weights recent experience so heavily that it nearly collapses to a count of the number of plants ($r = 0.98$). Thus, independent of the plant count, this discounted measure primarily picks up changes in the number of plants. As such, it captures the impact of opening and closing plants, rather than cumulated experience. Regardless, the models do illustrate the robustness of our other findings with respect to alternative specifications.

Table 3. Estimates of learning decay parameters.[†]

	Model 5	Model 6	Model 7	Model 8
Ln (organization size)	−0.115••	−0.115••	−0.117••	−0.120••
	(0.007)	(0.007)	(0.007)	(0.007)
Plant count	−0.037	−0.063	−0.111	−0.354••
	(0.075)	(0.092)	(0.099)	(0.110)
Geographic dispersion	−1.581•	−1.610•	−0.060	−1.191•
	(0.791)	(0.742)	(0.552)	(0.562)
Multi-market contact	−0.122••	−0.115••	−0.119••	−0.136••
	(0.037)	(0.037)	(0.037)	(0.038)
Ln (experience)	−0.489••			
	(0.025)			
Ln (experience) X geographic dispersion	0.384•			
	(0.200)			
Ln (experience)/$\sqrt{\text{age}}$		−0.919••		
		(0.058)		
Ln (experience)/$\sqrt{\text{age}}$ X geographic dispersion		0.807•		
		(0.397)		
Ln (experience)/age			−0.480••	
			(0.074)	
Ln (experience)/age X geographic dispersion			−0.089	
			(0.231)	
Ln (experience)/age^2				0.769••
				(0.100)
Ln (experience)/age^2 X geographic dispersion				0.224
				(0.295)
Imports X plant count	0.240•	1.891•	2.519•	2.965••
	(0.099)	(0.091)	(0.105)	(0.115)
Imports X ln (org. size)	0.119••	0.132••	0.122••	0.115••
	(0.015)	(0.015)	(0.015)	(0.015)
Left censored	−0.767	−1.989	−1.883	−1.379
	(1.005)	(1.003)	(1.003)	(1.004)
Log-liklihood	−14,042.85	−14,094.53	−14,194.15	−14,182.53
Δ BIC (vs. model 5)		103.4	305.6	279.4

[†]4,341 firms; 3,836 exit events, estimates of control variables not shown
• p < 0.05   •• p < 0.01

The data also allowed us to verify whether organization level results hold at the plant level of analysis – an interesting test since most studies of multiunit organizations have analyzed data on productive units rather than organizations. Table 4 presents the results of these investigations. Model 9 essentially replicates Model 5 using plant exit, rather than organization exit, as the dependent variable. To create a model consistent with much of the existing research on constituent

Table 4. Plant level exit models.

	Model 9 Plant Exit	Model 10 Plant Exit Single plants	Model 11 Plant Exit Mult-plants
Age 0–3 years	−3.773••	−4.319••	−3.362
	(1.153)	(1.253)	(3.173)
Age 3–10 years	−2.660••	−3.222•	−1.850
	(1.158)	(1.259)	(3.175)
Age 11–20 years	−2.978••	−3.545•	−2.066
	(1.161)	(1.263)	(3.185)
Age 20+ years	−2.964••	−3.534••	−2.080
	(1.163)	(1.264)	(3.187)
Year	0.031	0.017	0.114
	(0.025)	(0.027)	(0.069)
Plant density/10	0.009	0.008	0.023
	(0.008)	(0.009)	(0.020)
Plant density^2/1000	0.002	0.002	−0.003
	(0.003)	(0.003)	(0.007)
Imports	1.229••	1.428••	−0.291
	(0.293)	(0.324)	(1.083)
Population	−0.003••	0.002	0.002
	(0.001)	(0.010)	(0.003)
Plant count	−0.063••		−0.038••
	(0.011)		(0.012)
Ln (plant size)	−0.100••	−0.101••	−0.121••
	(0.006)	(0.006)	(0.016)
Ln (other organization size)	−0.067••		−0.091•
	(0.012)		(0.037)
Weighted distance	0.0032		0.003
	(0.003)		(0.002)
Multi-market contact	−0.007••		0.012••
	(0.003)		(0.005)
Ln (plant experience)	−0.369••	−0.373••	−0.323••
	(0.035)	(0.038)	(0.111)
Other organization experience	0.006••		0.005••
	(0.001)		(0.001)
Other organization experience/ distance	−0.006••		−0.006••
	(0.001)		(0.001)
Imports X plant count	−0.104••		−0.085••
	(0.025)		(0.029)
Imports X ln (organization size)	0.108••	−0.170	0.218••
	(0.023)	(0.149)	(0.094)
Left censored	−1.143	−1.070	−0.988•
	(9.146)	(6.577)	(17.84)
Log-liklihood	−15181.0	−13130.9	−2034.9
Plants	5127	4410	717
Exits	4609	4018	591

units (e.g. Ingram & Baum, 1997a), we included plant density and calculated organizational measures, such as experience, with respect to the focal plant. We also split the population into two groups[11] – independent plants and plants that belong to multiunit organizations. Model 10 reports the results for plants that operate independently, while Model 11 provides the estimates for plants that belong to a larger collective. Although these models differ significantly in a statistical sense $((\chi^2 = 30.4, 13$ d.f.), the two models bear remarkable similarity to each other, though notably, while imports primarily hurt the larger multi-plant manufacturers, they appear to affect all single-plant organizations equally.

Comparing the plant level models to the organization level analyses reveals interesting disjunctions. First, the interaction between imports and plant count suggests that whereas multi-plant firms experience higher failure rates when imports rise their constituent units appear less likely to close with the influx of imports. Second, the weighted distance variable indicates that, although geographic dispersion improves firm performance, plants located distant from the company's other operations do not enjoy lower exit rates. Third, despite the beneficial effects of multi-market contact, plants that substantially expand the firm's exposure to multi-market contact appear most likely to close.

DISCUSSION

This study demonstrates that – holding constant organizational size – different configurations of production activities influence the effectiveness of the entire organization and of its components. More precisely, our study demonstrates that having multiple sites offers both benefits and liabilities to the firm. During the relatively stable environment of the U.S. footwear industry prior to the 1960s, operating multiple establishments increased the viability of multiunit organizations and their plants through enhanced organizational learning and advantageous spatial configurations. This competitive advantage, however, depended crucially on the environment. To operate effectively, multiunit firms developed complex bureaucratic structures that stifled their ability to adapt to radical external changes (Chandler, 1977; Hannan & Freeman, 1984). Thus, when the environment changed, beginning in the 1960s, multiunit organizations became disadvantaged relative to independent plants.

Our results contribute interesting data to the study of organizational learning. Consistent with evidence on service and retail chains (Argote, 1999), we find that operating experience lowers the failure rate of multiunit producers and their units. The diffusion of incremental process improvements across the firm's facilities appears to increase its productive efficiency over time. However, the fact that the number of plant-years of experience, our measure of organizational learning, generates strong effects on organization performance raises interesting theoretical and measurement issues for research on organizational learning. Our analyses suggest that organizing production into a larger number of smaller plants increases the organization's capacity for learning. Nevertheless, studies that measure experience in terms of cumulative output – the typical metric used to capture organizational learning effects (e.g. Darr, Argote & Epple, 1995) – miss the impact of the structure of production on learning because producing the same number of units in one plant or ten yields the same measure of experience. That approach overlooks the fact that managers may find it difficult to evaluate information derived from a single site. Multiunit firms may also benefit from the ability to observe and learn from a larger number of rivals (Loree & Cassidy, this volume). Thus, even holding constant aggregate output, firms might learn more when production occurs across several facilities. Elaborating this relationship between organizational structure and learning strikes us as a rich topic for future research.

This study also presents strong evidence that multiunit producers enjoy an advantage relative to single-unit firms as a result of their spatial configurations. Geographic dispersion lowers organizational failure rates. Holding other factors constant, a one standard deviation increase in the degree of geographic dispersion in plant locations (an increase in the average distance between plants of 77 miles) predicts a 70% decline in the likelihood of firm exit. Theories of location suggest that these dispersion effects might stem either from a reduction in the transportation costs required to ship products to buyers or from the diversification of location specific risks. In this particular case, diversification of risk may play a stronger role since studies reveal that shipping accounts for only a small percentage of total production costs in the footwear industry (Hoover, 1939; Raehse & Sharpley, 1991). Thus, one might expect even stronger advantages to geographic dispersion in industries with high costs for transporting goods to the consumer. Firms with a higher degree of multi-market contact also exhibited lower failure rates, presumably because multi-faceted interaction with competitors allows these firms to avoid competitive escalation.

Though spatial configuration can benefit the multiunit firm, managers of these organizations face tradeoffs in their decisions. The multiunit firm's learning advantage depends critically on geographic dispersion, with concentrated firms benefiting the most from the accumulation of operating experience. Learning in the multiunit organization involves both the generation of new knowledge and the diffusion of knowledge across units. Not only does the difficulty of transferring knowledge across facilities increase with distance, but also the likely usefulness of that knowledge declines across space. In our study, when the average distance between facilities exceeds 127 miles (roughly one quarter of the multiunit firms), additional operating experience actually *increases* the likelihood of organizational failure, a result that matches Ingram and Baum's (1997a, b, this volume) finding that non-local operating experience degrades unit performance. Only recently have researchers begun to explore how organizational processes unfold in space, for example with studies of interlocking directorates (Kono et al., 1998) and ecological work on the spatial range of competition and legitimacy (Carroll & Wade, 1991; Hannan et al., 1995). This research proves further evidence of the need for continued investigation of this issue.

Managers should note: The benefits of the multiunit firm do not come free. In the face of changing environmental conditions, multiunit firms appear unable to adapt. Though we attribute this rigidity to bureaucratization, inertia might also arise from investments in inflexible production technologies. The volume-driven pursuit of efficiency leads managers of multiunit organizations to favor incremental improvements in the production process over the introduction of radical innovations and/or the launch of new products (Utterback & Abernathy, 1975). This narrow focus on efficiency can result in the development of rigid technologies that impair the ability of multiunit organizations to adjust their product mix to environmental changes. In contrast, lacking the expertise and the resources to invest in sophisticated production techniques, single-unit firms may focus their efforts on finding the right market segment. By doing so, they develop the ability to switch from niche to niche in response to fluctuations in demand. Regardless, the expectations associated with the adoption of rigid technologies differ little from those generated by bureaucratic rigidity.

The discrepancies between the organization-level and plant-level analyses strike us as interesting for two reasons. First, they clearly demonstrate that analyzing the results at the level of the constituent unit can miss important factors in organizational performance. For example, using only the plant-level analyses, one would likely conclude that geographic dispersion does not impact firm performance and might think that multi-market contact actually produces detrimental outcomes, though the organization-level analyses reveal the fallacy of these conclusions. The problem stems from the fact that plant-level exit models confound internal managerial decisions with environmental selection (i.e. performance). This confound brings us to the interesting theoretical implications of these discrepancies: They show that managers fail to reconfigure their organizations in a manner that maximizes firm performance (regardless of their intentions). For example, though closing the most distant plants reduces the dispersion of the organization as a whole and closing the plants with the highest exposure to multi-market contact reduces the opportunities for mutual forbearance – both actions that hurt organizational performance – managers show no propensity to avoid these actions.

Our results contribute to the organizational research in several ways. First, by linking organizational learning to the literature on experimental design, we provide a strong argument and evidence for why multiunit firms might enjoy accelerated organizational learning. Second, the presence of multiunit advantage in the shoe industry extends the evidence for the advantages of this organizational structure beyond industries with local markets, such as hotels and banks, to an industry with a national market. Third, our paper considers explicitly the role of geographic dispersion in the multiunit firm, a factor particularly relevant to these national markets. Fourth, we argue and demonstrate that the multiunit advantage might only exist during periods of environmental stability. Fifth, our results demonstrate that the results of analyses carried out at the organization- versus the plant-level may yield very different accounts and managerial prescriptions.

This study also suggests interesting new directions for future research on multiunit organizations. Future studies might delve more deeply into those factors that make certain multiunit firms more effective than others. For example, some multiunit firms might reduce the negative impact of dispersion on learning by adopting new technologies that widen and accelerate communication channels (e.g. intranets), or limit bureaucratic inertia by outsourcing less critical stages of their production activities. The direct examination of the factors underlying the multiunit effect – for example, knowledge transfer across units and bureaucratization – strikes us as another interesting line of investigation. Although an in-depth understanding of how multiunit firms function offers clear benefits, the difficulty of this approach lies in obtaining direct measures of these underlying processes. Unlike our study, which covers an entire industry for a period of fifty years, the need for such data would probably confine the investigation to a shorter period of time and a much smaller sample.

For managers, the results call attention to two important tradeoffs faced when designing the organization of production. The first tradeoff concerns the tension between maximizing efficiency and optimizing flexibility. Although splitting the firm's operations into a large number of units can generate efficiency gains through accelerated organizational learning, the bureaucracy necessary to manage these operations introduces substantial inertia that can hurt the firm in the face of radical environmental change. Moreover, growth through the opening of new facilities rather than the expansion of existing plants limits the firm's ability to realize plant-level economies of scale.

A less obvious tradeoff faces the managers of multiunit firms: Where should they locate these facilities? Geographic concentration facilitates the transfer of knowledge, but this centralization conflicts with the need to reduce transportation costs and diversify risk. The ideal balance between these two contrasting needs probably depends on the specifics of the industry. For example, in industries where proximity to customers seems key, like the dairy industry, managers might opt for dispersion to minimize transportation costs and diversify risk. By dedicating resources to the transfer of knowledge across sites, perhaps they can avoid the detrimental learning consequences of this configuration. In industries less affected by transportation costs – for example, computer hardware – managers may prefer geographic concentration hoping that the advantages to learning outweigh those of dispersion.

We introduced this paper asking whether the multiunit organization offered a new dominant mode of organization or whether it simply arose as a response to transient environmental conditions. Our study sheds new light on the understanding of these two fundamental organizational forms by drawing on both economics and organization theory. From our analyses of the footwear industry, we can say that neither multiunit organizations nor single-unit organizations hold a position of absolute superiority. Rather, the optimal form shifts over time with changes in the underlying economics of production and in the dynamics of competition.

NOTES

1. Although automated production techniques introduced in the 1980s somewhat reduced the inefficiency of producing in small batches (Hazeldine, 1986), only the largest single plant firms could afford these new technologies (Freeman & Kleiner, 1998).

2. The Federal Reserve Board's statistical information on capacity utilization (available at http://www.bog.frb.fed.us/releases/) indicates that from 1967 to 1989, plants operated at roughly 80% of capacity, on average. Davis reports similar utilization rates before World War II (1940).

3. Unfortunately the data do not provide complete information about the production methods used in multiunit organizations. Nonetheless, 8% of our organization–years include production process information. The mean Herfindal index for production technologies in multiunit firms of 0.85 (SD = 0.22) indicates an extremely high degree of parallel production, as 1 corresponds to all plants using the same technology. Even firms with a large number of plants rarely use more than two production technologies.

4. Caves (1982) identifies three kinds of multiunit organizations: (1) those in which plants make similar goods (horizontal multiunit organizations); (2) those in which the products of some plants serve as inputs to other plants (vertical multiunit organizations); and, (3) those in which plants' outputs have no relation (diversified multiunit organization). We use 'multiunit' to refer to the first of these: horizontal multiunit organizations.

5. We also tested dichotomous (i.e. single-unit vs. multiunit) and non-linear specifications, but the linear count of productive units provided the best functional form for multiunit effects.

6. Logging the distance accounted for the fact that substitution between modes of transportation and communication typically prevents distance from relating to either the time or the expense of these activities in a linear fashion (Sorenson & Stuart, 2001).

7. Though Gimeno and Jeong (this volume) note that count measures of multi-market contact sometimes correlate highly with size, these data exhibit only a weak relationship between this measure and firm size ($r = 0.27$).

8. Some researchers suggest that cumulative output provides a better proxy for learning (Darr, Argote & Epple, 1995; Lieberman, 1984; Rapping, 1965). Using cumulative output yields did not change our models qualitatively. However, we feel more comfortable reporting the models using operating experience as our size measure relies heavily on interpolation.

9. Some of these studies (Bain, 1956; Simon & Bonini, 1958; Szenberg, Lombardi & Lee, 1977) find diseconomies of scale at production levels above 6000 pairs of shoes per day. Our data showed decreasing returns to plant scale; however we did not see evidence for actual diseconomies of scale. We simply logged plant size to account for the decreasing returns.

10. In unreported models, we included a dummy variable to denote cases with interpolated size measures. These models did not indicate any significant difference between the cases using interpolated data and the cases with observed size data.

11. Splitting the groups equates mathematically to interacting all terms in Model 6 with a dummy variable indicating membership in a larger organization.

ACKNOWLEDGMENTS

Financial support from the University of Maryland and the University of Chicago Graduate School of Business made this research possible. We thank Jesper Sørensen, Jan Rivkin, Paul Ingram, and especially Joel Baum and Henrich Greve for comments on earlier versions of this paper. We accept responsibility for any remaining deficiencies.

REFERENCES

Acs, Z. J., & Audretsch, D. B. (1990). *Innovation and small firms*. Cambridge, MA: MIT Press.

American shoemaking directory of shoe manufacturers (various years). Boston: Shoe Traders Publishing Company.

Argote, L. (1999). *Organizational learning: Creating, retaining and transferring knowledge*. Boston: Kluwer Academic Publishers.

Argote, L., Beckman, S. L., & Epple, D. (1990). The persistence and transfer of learning in industrial settings. *Management Science, 36*, 140–154.

Bahls, J. E. (1989, February). U.S. Shoe firms thrive in high-quality market. *Nation's Business, 77*, 38–40.

Bain, J. S. (1956). *Barriers to new competition*. Cambridge, MA: Harvard University Press.

Banaszak-Holl, J., Berta, W. B., Bowman, D., Baum, J. A. C., & Mitchell, W. (2000). Causes and consequences of chain acquisitions: Health performance and operating strategy of U.S. nursing homes, 1991–1997. Working paper, University of Michigan.

Barnett, W. P. (1993). Strategic deterrence among multipoint competitors. *Industrial and Corporate Change, 2*, 249–278.

Barnett, W. P. (1997). The dynamics of competitive intensity. *Administrative Science Quarterly, 42*, 128–160.

Baum, J. A. C. (1996). Organizational ecology. In: S. R. Clegg, C. Hardy & W. Nord (Eds), *Handbook of Organization Studies* (pp. 77–114). London: Sage.

Baum, J. A. C., & Korn, H. J. (1996). Competitive dynamics of interfirm rivalry. *Academy of Management Journal, 39*, 255–291.

Baum, J. A. C., & Korn, H. J. (1999). Dynamics of dyadic competitive interaction. *Strategic Management Journal, 20*, 251–278.

Baum, J. A. C., & Mezias, S. J. (1992). Localized competition and organizational failure in the Manhattan hotel industry. *Administrative Science Quarterly, 37*, 580–604.

Baum, J. A. C., & Powell, W. W. (1995). Cultivating an institutional ecology of organizations: Comment on Hannan, Carroll, Dundon, and Torres. *American Sociological Review, 60*, 529–538.

Bernheim, B. D., & Whinston, M. D. (1990). Multi-market contact and collusive behavior. *RAND Journal of Economics, 21*, 1–26.

Boeker, W., Goodstein, J., Stephan, J., & Murmann, J. P. (1997). Competition in a multimarket environment. *Organization Science, 8*, 126–142.

Boon, G. K. (1980). *Technology and employment in footwear manufacturing*. Aphen aan den Rijn: Sijthoff & Noordhoff.

Carroll, G. R. (1983). A stochastic model of organizational mortality: Review and reanalysis. *Social Science Research, 12*, 303–329.

Carroll, G. R. (1985). Concentration and specialization: Dynamics of niche width in populations of organizations. *American Journal of Sociology, 90*, 1262–1283.

Carroll, G. R., & Wade, J. B. (1991). Density dependence in the organizational evolution of the American brewing industry across different levels of analysis. *Social Science Research, 20*, 271–302.

Cassidy, C., & Loree, D. (2001). Knowledge transfer between multimarket organizations: Whom do they borrow from? In: J. A. C. Baum & H. R. Greve (Eds), *Multiunit Organization and Multimarket Strategy; Advances in Strategic Management* (Vol. 18, pp. 141–174). Oxford, U.K.: JAI Press.

Caves, R. E. (1982). *Multinational enterprise and economic analysis*. Cambridge, MA: Cambridge University Press.

Chandler, A. D. Jr. (1977). *The visible hand: The managerial revolution in American business*. Cambridge, MA: Belknap Press.

Chandler, A. D. Jr. (1990). *Scale and scope: The dynamics of industrial capitalism*. Cambridge, MA: Belknap Press.

Commons, J. R. (1909). American shoemakers, 1645–1895: A sketch of industrial evolution. *Quarterly Journal of Economics, 26*, 39–63.

Cook, T. D., & Campbell, D. T. (1979). *Quasi-experimentation: Design and analysis issues for field settings*. Boston: Houghton-Mifflin Company.

Cyert, R. M., & March, J. G. (1963). *A behavioral theory of the firm*. Englewood Cliffs, NJ: Prentice-Hall.

Darr, E., Argote, L., & Epple, D. (1995). The acquisition, transfer, and depreciation of knowledge in service organizations. *Management Science, 41*, 1750–1762.

Davis, H. B. (1940). *Shoes: The workers and the industry*. New York: International Publishers.

Duchesneau, T. D., Cohn, S. F., & Dutton, J. E. (1979). *Case studies of innovation decision making in the U.S. footwear industry*. Orono, ME: Social Science Research Institute, University of Maine.

Edwards, C. D. (1955). Conglomerate bigness as a source of power. In NBER conference report, *Business concentration and price policy*. Princeton, NJ: Princeton University Press.

Epple, D., Argote, L., & Murphy, K. (1996). An empirical investigation of the micro structure of knowledge acquisition and transfer through learning by doing. *Operations Research, 44,* 77–86.

Evans, W. N., & Kessides, I. N. (1994). Living by the 'golden rule': Multi-market contact in the U.S. airline industry. *Quarterly Journal of Economics, 109,* 341–366.

Footwear Industries of America (various years). *Current highlights of the non-rubber footwear industry.* Washington, DC: Footwear Industries of America.

Freeman, R. B., & Kleiner, M. M. (1998). The last American shoe manufacturers: Changing the method of pay to survive foreign competition. Working paper No. 6750, National Bureau for Economic Research.

Galbraith, J. K. (1956). *American capitalism: The concept of countervailing power.* Boston: Houghton Mifflin.

Gimeno, J., & Jeong, E. (2001). The meaning and measurement of multimarket contact: Towards consistence and validity in empirical research. In: J. A. C. Baum & H. R. Greve (Eds), *Multiunit Organization and Multimarket Strategy; Advances in Strategic Management* (Vol. 18, pp. 359–410). Oxford, U.K.: JAI Press.

Gimeno, J., & Woo, C. Y. (1996). Hypercompetition in a multimarket environment: The role of strategic similarity and multimarket contact in competitive de-escalation. *Organization Science, 7,* 322–341.

Greenhut, M. L. (1956). *Plant location in theory and practice.* Chapel Hill, NC: University of North Carolina Press.

Greve, H. R. (1996). Patterns of competition: The diffusion of market position in radio broadcasting. *Administrative Science Quarterly, 41,* 29–60.

Greve, H. R. (1999). Branch systems and nonlocal learning in populations. In: A. Miner & P. C. Anderson (Eds), *Population-Level Learning and Industry Change: Advances in Strategic Management* (Vol. 16, pp. 57–80). Greenwich, CT: JAI Press.

Guo, G. (1993). Event history analysis for left truncated data. *Sociological Methodology, 23,* 217–243.

Hannan, M. T., & Carroll, G. R. (1992). *Dynamics of organizational populations.* New York: Oxford University Press.

Hannan, M. T., Carroll, G. R., Dundon, E. A., & Torres, J. C. (1995). Organizational evolution in a multinational context: Entries of automobile manufacturers in Belgium, Britain, France, Germany, and Italy. *American Sociological Review, 60,* 509–528.

Hannan, M. T., & Freeman, J. (1984). Structural inertia and organizational change. *American Sociological Review, 49,* 149–164.

Hannan, M. T., & Freeman, J. (1989). *Organizational ecology.* Cambridge, MA: Harvard University Press.

Hansen, H. (1959). *A study of competition and management in the shoe manufacturing industry.* Washington, DC: National Shoe Manufacturers Association.

Hazeldine, S. J. (1986). Implementing FMS. *Data Processing, 28,* 146–150.

Hoover, E. M. (1937). *Location theory and the shoe and leather industries.* Cambridge, MA: Harvard University Press.

Ingram, P., & Baum, J. A. C. (1997a). Chain affiliation and the failure of Manhattan hotels, 1898–1980. *Administrative Science Quarterly, 42,* 68–102.

Ingram, P., & Baum, J. A. C. (1997b). Opportunity and constraint: Organizations' learning from the operating and competitive experience of industries. *Strategic Management Journal,18,* 75–98.

Ingram, P., & Baum, J. A. C. (2001). Interorganizational learning and the dynamics of chain relationships. In: J. A. C. Baum & H. R. Greve (Eds), *Multiunit Organization and Multimarket Strategy; Advances in Strategic Management* (Vol. 18, pp. 109–139). Oxford, U.K.: JAI Press.

Jaffe, A. B., & Adams, J. D. (1996). Bounding the effects of R&D: An investigation using matched establishment-firm data. *RAND Journal of Economics, 27,* 700–721.

Jaffe, A. B., Trajtenberg, M., & Henderson, R. (1993). Geographic localization of knowledge spillovers, as evidenced by patent citations. *Quarterly Journal of Economics, 108,* 577–598.

Kekre, S. (1987). Performance of a manufacturing cell with increased product mix. *IIE Transactions, 19,* 329–339.

Kono, C., Palmer, D., Friedland, R., & Zafonte, M. (1998). Lost in space: The geography of inter-locking directorates. *American Journal of Sociology, 103,* 863–911.

Lieberman, M. B. (1984). The learning curve and pricing in the chemical processing industries. *RAND Journal of Economics, 15,* 213–228.

Lösch, A. (1954). *The economics of location.* New Haven, CT: Yale University Press.

March, J. G. (1988). *Decisions and organizations.* Oxford: Basil Blackwell.

March, J. G., & Olsen, J. P. (1976). *Ambiguity and choice in organizations.* Bergen: Universitetsforlaget.

OECD (Organisation for Economic Cooperation and Development). (1976). *The footwear industry: Structure and governmental policies.* Paris: OECD.

Pfeffer, J., & Salancik, G. R. (1978). *The external control of organizations.* New York: Harper & Row.

Piore, M. J., & Sabel, C. F. (1984). *The second industrial divide: Possibilities for prosperity.* New York: Basic Books.

Pratten, C., & Dean, R. M. (1965). *The economics of large scale production in British industry.* Cambridge: Cambridge University Press.

Raehse, S. L., & Sharpley, M. F. (1991). *Footwear (men's, women's, boys' and girls').* New York: Fairchild Fashion and Merchandising Group.

Raftery, A. E. (1995). Bayesian model selection in social research. In: P. V. Marsden (Ed.), *Sociological Methodology 1995* (pp. 111–196). Oxford: Blackwell.

Rapping, L. (1965). Learning and World War II production functions. *Review of Economics and Statistics, 47,* 81–86.

Rohwer, G. (1995). *TDA (transitional data analysis) 5.7.* Florence: European University Institute.

Scherer, F. M., Beckenstein, A., Kaufer, E., & Murphy, R. D. (1975). *The economics of multi-plant operation: An international comparison study.* Cambridge, MA: Harvard University Press.

Scherer, F. M., & Ross, D. (1990). *Industrial market structure and economic performance* (3rd ed.). Boston: Houghton Mifflin Company.

Scott, J. T. (1982). Multimarket contact and economic performance. *Review of Economics and Statistics, 64,* 368–375.

Scott, J. T. (1991). Multimarket contact among diversified oligopolists. *International Journal of Industrial Organization, 9,* 225–238.

Simmel, G. (1950 trans.). *The sociology of Georg Simmel.* New York: Free Press.

Simon, H. A., & Bonini, C. (1958). The size distribution of firms. *American Economic Review, 48,* 607–617.

Smithies, A. F. (1941). Optimum location in spatial competition. *Journal of Political Economy, 49,* 423–439.

Sorenson, O. (2000). Letting the market work for you: An evolutionary perspective on product strategy. *Strategic Management Journal, 21,* 577–592.

Sorenson, O., & Audia, P. G. (2000). The social structure of entrepreneurial activity: Geographic concentration of footwear production in the U.S., 1940–1989. *American Journal of Sociology, 106,* 324–362.

Sorenson, O., & Stuart, T. E. (2001). Syndication networks and the spatial distribution of venture capital investment. *American Journal of Sociology, 106*, forthcoming.

Szenberg, M., Lombardi, J. W., & Lee, E. Y. (1977). *Welfare effects of trade restrictions: A case study of the U.S. footwear industry.* New York: Academic Press.

Teece, D. J. (1977). Technology transfer by multinational firms: The resource costs of transferring technological know-how. *The Economic Journal, 87*, 242–261.

Tuma, N. B., & Hannan, M. T. (1984). *Social dynamics: Models and methods.* New York: Academic Press.

U.S.ITC (United States International Trade Commission). (1984). *Nonrubber footwear.* Washington, DC: U.S.ITC.

Utterback, J. M., & Abernathy, W. J. (1975). A dynamic model of process and product innovation. *OMEGA: The International Journal of Management Science, 6*, 639–656.

Warrock, A. M. (1985, October 21). Shoemakers feel the pinch. *New England Business, 7*, 62–66.

Part Two:
PRODUCTION AND INNOVATION BEHAVIOR

INTERORGANIZATIONAL LEARNING AND THE DYNAMICS OF CHAIN RELATIONSHIPS

Paul Ingram and Joel A. C. Baum

ABSTRACT

Interorganizatonal relationships in general and chain relationships in particular are a critical channel for interorganizational learning. Learning may not only be a result of interorganizational relationships, however; it may also be a primary cause of them. We examine this idea in the empirical context of Manhattan hotels and their relationships with hotel chains. Our analysis shows that hotels are likely to form relationships when they have very low, or very high levels of their own operating experience. The relationship between hotel and chain is less likely to dissolve when the chain has more operating experience in the hotel's local market, and more likely to dissolve when the chain has more operating experience in non-local markets. The duration of a chain relationship has a ∩-shaped effect on its dissolution, indicating that relationships go through a honeymoon period, and that the parties to a relationship learn to better collaborate over time.

Multiunit Organization and Multimarket Strategy, Volume 18, pages 109–139
2001 by Elsevier Science Ltd.
ISBN: 0-7623-0721-8

Theories of organizational learning have embraced the idea that learning can come not just from an organization's own experience, but from the experience of others (Huber, 1991). Such 'interorganizational learning' is facilitated by interorganizational relationships that provide the common language, interaction opportunities and motivation for the extensive sharing of experience that is necessary for interorganizational learning. This claim is supported by learning curve studies, which show that organizations benefit more from the experience of others they are related to than from the experience of unrelated others (Darr, Argote & Epple, 1995; Baum & Ingram, 1998; Darr & Kurtzburg, 2000). As evidence showing that relationships facilitate interorganizational learning builds, however, the reciprocal question, "what role does potential and realized learning play in the establishment and dissolution of relationships between organizations?" has not been answered. In this paper we address that question by studying the role of learning in the formation and dissolution of chain relationships in the Manhattan hotel industry.

This study aims to contribute to theories of organizational learning by determining whether learning through relationships is by default or design. Kogut (1988) and Mitchell (1994) have argued that relationships are formed and dissolved partly because of their implications for interorganizational learning, but it is fully possible that the potential for learning plays no role in the formation and dissolution of relationships, either because non-learning implications of the relationships are more important, or because decision makers are not aware that such relationships facilitate interorganizational learning. Qualitative studies of relationship formation, such as Grindley, Mowery and Silverman's (1994) account of the formation of SEMATECH, Stuart and Podolny's (1996:34) observations on the role of alliances in technological innovation among Japanese semiconductor firms, and Inkpen and Dinur's (1998) longitudinal exploration of five joint ventures between U.S. automotive industry suppliers and Japanese automobile manufacturers, provide some evidence for the idea that the learning implications of relationships affect their formation and dissolution, but to our knowledge there have been no systematic empirical tests. Further, the results of this study will be useful for translating research on interorganizational learning into advice for practicing managers. If relationships facilitate learning, then the processes of establishing and dissolving relationships are important to managers who want to improve their organization's learning capacity. Framed more generally, this study can be seen as addressing an overlooked question in organization science: we know much more about the consequences of relationships between organizations than about the processes by which those relationships are determined. For learning, we will clarify the link between the consequences and the determinants of interorganizational relationships. Our analysis also includes non-learning variables, and therefore contributes to a broad understanding of the processes by which relationships are formed and dissolved.

There are many conceptualizations of 'organizational learning.' Following the extensive learning curve literature, we define learning as an improvement in performance or the capacity to perform from (own or others') experience. This definition is narrower than some organizational researchers use, but it allows us to link to a robust empirical literature with well-established findings of the effect of experience on important performance variables such as cost, time to produce, profitability, and risk of failure (see Argote & Epple, 1990 and Argote, 1993 for reviews). Our main focus is on the implications of organizations' *operating* experience. By operating experience we mean the cumulative history of core operations (production or service provision) of the organization. The benefits to organizations of operating experience are both internal and external. Internally, organizations benefit from operating experience through efficiencies of production or providing service (Yelle, 1979). Externally, organizations benefit from operating experience by improving their models of the external environment, particularly about consumers' preferences (Cyert, Kumar & Williams, 1993). Through producing products or services and offering them to the market, organizations learn what consumers want.

The chain relationships we consider are horizontal, between organizations of the same type. Hawley (1950) called these relationships commensalistic, and they are in contrast to vertical (or symbiotic) relationships between organizations of different types (e.g. customers and suppliers). Commensalistic relationships are particularly suited for interorganizational learning from operating experience because that experience will be most useful to organizations that have the same production process, and face the same external environment, as the organization generating the experience. Interorganizational learning is one of the most frequently cited benefits of, and implicit motivations for, relationships among commensals (e.g. Kogut, Shan & Walker, 1992; Grindley et al., 1994; Shan, Walker & Kogut, 1994; Stuart & Podolny, 1996). Among commensalistic relationships, the ownership, incentive and control structures of chain relationships seem particularly likely to facilitate the transfer of operating experience, and learning-curve research has indicated that individual units benefit from the operating experience of others in their chains (Darr, Argote & Epple, 1995; Baum & Ingram, 1998; Greve, 1999; Darr & Kurtzburg, 2000; Audia, Sorenson & Hage, this volume).

Our basic approach to explaining the role of learning in the dynamics of chain relationships is borrowed from Mitchell's (1994) study of divestiture in American medical sector product markets. For our study, Mitchell's key insight is that the sale of a business is likely to occur when there is an alignment of the interests of a buyer and seller. This position clarifies the tension in the status of a hotel as independent or chain-affiliated. For a chain relationship to form the owner of an independent hotel must be willing to sell it at a given price and a chain must be willing to buy it at that price.[1] Similarly, for a chain relationship to dissolve, the chain must be willing to sell the hotel at a given price, and an independent operator willing to buy it at that price. The likelihood of a chain and an independent operator agreeing on a price depends on their perceptions of the relative profitability of the hotel as independent or chain affiliated. If an independent hotel would be more profitable as part of a chain, for example because it would benefit from the operating experience of the chain, then a sale to a chain (at the right price) would be in the interests of both buyer and seller (Nelson & Winter, 1982). Likewise, if a chain-affiliated hotel is suffering from its chain affiliation, sale to an independent operator could benefit both buyer and seller (Williamson, 1985).

Our overarching view of the dynamics of chain relationships, then, is that the likelihood of relationships forming is higher when the characteristics of the hotel are such that it could be more effectively operated as part of a chain. The likelihood of an existing relationship dissolving is higher when the characteristics of the hotel or the chain are such that the hotel could be more effectively operated independent of the chain. The trick, of course, is to determine what features of hotels and chains make relationships more or less advantageous. We undertake that task next as we develop hypotheses.

We present three sets of hypotheses. First, we consider the effect of the hotel's *own* operating experience. We argue that chain relationships will be *formed* and *maintained* when a hotel's own operating experience is lacking. An organization's own operating experience is lacking when there is either so little of it that significant learning has not taken place, or so much of it that the organization becomes myopic and falls into a competency trap. Second, we examine the operating experience of the chain and argue that relationships will be maintained when the chain's operating experience is *local*, and therefore most useful to the component hotel, and that relationships will be dissolved when the chain's operating experience is *non-local*, and therefore less useful and potentially harmful to the hotel. Third, we consider the effect of *collaborative experience*, which refers to partners learning to work together as their relationship endures. The basic effect of collaborative experience is to make relationships more robust, but relationships also have an initial "honeymoon period" (Levinthal & Fichman, 1988) either because of goodwill, or because of unrealized learning potential. The effect of collaborative experience combines with the honeymoon period to justify a prediction that the duration of a relationship will have a ∩-shaped effect on its likelihood of dissolution.

Hotel Operating Experience

A number of learning curve studies indicate that chain relationships facilitate the transfer of operating experience (Darr, 1994; Darr, Argote & Epple, 1995; Baum & Ingram, 1998; Greve, 1999, Audia et al., this volume). The value of transferred operating experience to an organization, however, should depend on the amount of operating experience the organization itself has accumulated. The incremental value of successive units of operating experience declines (Argote, 1993), which suggests that relationships and the promise of transferred experience will be more valuable to organizations with lower levels of their own experience. The core idea here, that firms become less likely to enter into and sustain relationships as they gain experience, is consistent with literature that considers the transfer of experience in foreign environments. The fundamental assertion of that literature is that firms form relationships to enter foreign markets where they lack experience, but after they have accumulated or acquired their own experience, they are more likely to make subsequent investments without a partner (e.g. Johanson & Vahline, 1977, 1990; Kogut & Singh, 1988; Mitchell, Shaver & Yeung, 1994; Pennings, Barkema & Douma, 1994; Chang, 1995; Li, 1995; Barkema, Bell & Pennings, 1996; Barkema & Vermeulen, 1998).

Complicating the matter, managers' effort to try to learn from experience is not an unbiased activity; rather it is myopic (March, 1991; Levinthal & March, 1993). Managers attribute outcomes to the events that preceded them. But these events are chosen from a small set of possibilities that is constrained by selective attention and prior beliefs (Levinthal & March, 1993). So when outcomes are positive, managers attribute them to internal acts they had already focused on, validating their prior beliefs and lowering the likelihood that they will experiment and discover evidence of any strategic errors. When managers mistakenly credit a practice or skill for good performance, they rarely receive any information that might reveal their error. In this way myopic learning induces managers to give more and more credence to the policies and practices (correct or not) they previously exploited – especially if there are few negative results to broaden managers' range of concerns – and the more likely it becomes that any false or superstitious beliefs they hold will be reinforced. Managers' attributions of success to their own abilities and policies can lead them to become complacent and to fall into competency traps in which they favor the exploitation of their own past experiences over the exploration of new ones

(Miller, 1990; Levinthal & March, 1993). Increasing myopia and risk of competency traps indicate an effect of operating experience on positive outcomes that is ∩-shaped, first increasing as the organization gains valuable experience, but then decreasing as high levels of experience lead the organization into competency traps (Baum & Ingram, 1998; Ingram & Baum, 1997; Ingram & Simons, 1997).[2]

Considering this theoretical argument and supporting empirical evidence, we predict that chain experience will be the most benefit to hotels with low levels of their own experience, or with high levels of their own experience, and of least benefit to hotels with moderate levels of their own experience. Chains can transfer vital experience to hotels lacking their own experience, and help hotels with too much of their own experience to break out of competency traps. If the hotels that are most in need of chain experience are most likely to form and least likely to dissolve relationships with chains (and this will occur despite myopia at the hotel level, as long as managers at the chain recognize the value of breaking out of the competency trap), we expect the hotel's operating experience to have ∪-shaped relationship to the likelihood of forming, and a ∩-shaped relationship to the likelihood of dissolving a chain relationship.

Hypothesis 1a: The likelihood of forming a chain relationship is a ∪-shaped function of the hotel's operating experience.

Hypothesis 1b: The likelihood of dissolving an existing chain relationship is a ∩-shaped function of the hotel's operating experience.

The specific nature of the learning through experience that stands behind the above hypotheses can be seen in a review of effective operating practices discovered by Manhattan hotels in one year, 1907 (examples taken from the *Hotel Monthly*, 1907, January: 22–37, March: 43, November: 18–35, December: 42–43). For internal efficiencies, hotels discovered through their experience: a recipe for wood polish; improved mechanics for door hinges; the advantage of outsourcing the cleaning of glass; color-coded menu cards for waiters (menu items in black, descriptions in red); wooden shoes for kitchen cleaners; best practices for moving pianos; tricks to attach carpet to stairs; leather covers to prevent maids' keys from rattling; the effectiveness of aluminum for transferring heat on restaurant service tables; ways to assign tasks to waiters (and to prevent shirking); and the taxi meter (first used in taxis operated by the Plaza Hotel). For the external benefit of operating experience (market knowledge), Manhattan hotels in 1907 discovered the value of offering both smoking and non-smoking dinning rooms, wheelchairs and public baths on every floor, and they received feedback on the right price for breakfast and the relative attractiveness of the

European (including meals) vs. American plans of accommodation. All of these things were learned from hotels' operating experience, and through a chain relationship, they could be transferred to other hotels.

Examples of competency traps are also available. Perhaps the most compelling competency trap in the history of American hospitality concerns hotels' response to the automobile, which caused the grand hotels that dominated in the late nineteenth and early twentieth centuries to stumble (Belasco, 1979). Those hotels had fluourished by providing service that we would now describe as formal and stuffy. This style of service was their competency, and they exploited it even after the demands of the market changed. Early auto-tourists, fresh from the road in their dirty clothes, received contemptuous glares from doormen who had perfected those glares in an era when they were integral to protecting the ambiance of the hotel. Auto-tourists felt dirty and awkward as they were made to walk through an ornate and formal hotel lobby. Many of the grand hotels were too slow to adjust to changes in the way Americans used hotels, and they became unprofitable and even failed, while newer hotels, and newer organizational forms like motels, responded with new practices like check-in at the garage.

Chain Operating Experience

By the nature of a chain, its operating experience is generated in different locations. The most useful operating experience for a given component is that which comes from its local market, while non-local operating experience may be useless, or even harmful. Market conditions vary between geographic locations, so for non-local experience the external benefit of creating knowledge about the environment is limited.[3] Similarly, as market conditions vary the product of an organization, broadly defined, may also vary, limiting the internal benefit (production efficiencies) from non-local experience.

The Manhattan hotel industry is an ideal one to illustrate the problem of non-local experience. At professional meetings, hoteliers discussed the vast difference between the experience of small-market and large-market hoteliers (*Hotel Monthly*, April, 1940: 31–32). Market conditions in Manhattan reflect a unique set of attractions, and were more closely tied to European tourism than those in any other American city, large or small. The product offered by Manhattan hotels includes larger, more luxurious hotels, with higher levels of service than almost all other American cities, and differed on specific dimensions such as the mode of transport by which a guest would arrive, and the length of time the guest was likely to stay. All these differences indicate that a hotel related to a chain will benefit more from the chain's experience in

Manhattan than from experience elsewhere. Non-local experience could even harm the hotel because chains often use standardization, applying successful operating practices throughout the chain with little or no consideration of the appropriateness of the practice for a specific market. Consistent with these arguments, Baum and Ingram (1998) found that the failure rate of Manhattan hotels that were parts of chains was lower as a function of their chain's local experience, but *higher* as a function of their chain's non-local experience.

That result is reinforced by the findings in Greve's (1999) analysis of learning within branch systems (chains) in the U.S. radio-broadcasting industry. He found that branch unit performance (audience share) declined as the branch systems to which the unit belonged accumulated operating experience outside the branch unit's local market. Consistent with the argument above, Greve suggested that the experience of the system in other markets impeded adaptation by preventing the unit from locally adaptive learning or by causing it to adopt inappropriate routines or behaviors. These theoretical arguments and empirical results combine with our assertion that chain relationships will persist when they benefit the component and dissolve when they harm it, to generate the following hypotheses:

> *Hypothesis 2a*: Components belonging to chains with high levels of local experience are less likely to dissolve chain relationships.

> *Hypothesis 2b*: Components belonging to chains with high levels of non-local experience are more likely to dissolve chain relationships.

Relationship Duration and Collaborative Experience

A necessary feature of an examination of the role of learning in the dynamics of relationships is the idea that parties to relationships learn to manage the relationship. Therefore, for the final hypothesis, we broaden the concept of experience to include *collaborative experience*, which we define at the relationship level, and see as accruing with the duration of an active relationship. This relational definition of collaborative experience should be distinguished from conceptualizations of collaborative experience at the organizational level, which we consider in the discussion (Lyles, 1988; Simonin & Helleloid, 1993; Simonin, 1997; Barkema, Shenkar, Vermeulen & Bell, 1997; Inkpen & Dinar, 1998).

Just as every organization is different, every relational pairing of organizations creates unique issues surrounding communication, integration and control. Lyles (1988) showed how collaborative experience is critical in creating know-how that is tailored to specific firms, changing their approach to collaboration on the basis of their ongoing experiences. Inkpen and Dinur (1998) described how, over time, "strategic integration" led joint ventures between U.S. automotive industry suppliers and Japanese automobile producers to function as if they were *divisions* of the ventures' parent firms. Levinthal and Fichman (1988) also argue that with time, parties to a relationship "learn to work together." They link the accretion of collaborative experience to a decrease in the risk that a relationship will dissolve. Levinthal and Fichman realize, however, that the increase of collaborative experience is not the only thing that changes over the duration of a relationship. They argue that relationships begin with a honeymoon period during which the relationship is likely to persist – even when early outcomes are unfavorable – due to an initial endowment of goodwill and other assets. The relationship is at maximum risk when it is not brand new, but relatively new, so the initial endowment has been exhausted but collaborative experience is still low. After that point, if the relationship survives (because, for example, necessary routines were established and/or sufficient resources were generated), it grows stronger with time as collaborative experience increases. This "liability of adolescence" argument predicts a ∩-shaped effect of relationship duration on the likelihood of dissolution.

Evidence in support of the liability of adolescence argument comes from two contexts, auditor-client relationships (Levinthal & Fichman, 1988) and joint ventures in the electronics industry (Park & Russo, 1996). Chain-hotel relationships are different in many ways from those two relationships, but we believe that they involve some initial goodwill and that they benefit from the collaborative experience of the hotel and the chain interacting together, which are the two features necessary for a liability of adolescence. Collaborative experience in the context of hotel-chain relationships could result in increased familiarity and friendship between the staffs of the hotel and chain; awareness at the hotel level of the reporting and strategic requirements of the chain, and of the other components in the chain; and awareness at the chain level of the hotel's local environment and its unique characteristics.

Research on 'learning alliances' provides an alternative, complementary, rationale for the initial honeymoon period in the liability of adolescence argument. This research stream shares our central premise, that interorganizational alliances among commensals are sources of up-to-date information and knowledge critical to competitive success (e.g. Liebeskind et al., 1996; Khanna, Gulati & Nohria, 1998). It explicitly addresses the strategic implications of interorganizational learning, recognizing that competitive success may come from 'outlearning' the organization's partners (thus winning the learning race, Hamel, 1991; Khanna et al., 1998). From this perspective, organizations may strategically manage the duration of the relationship – maintaining it while there is more to learn, but breaking it when the race has been won. By this account, the initial 'honeymoon period' occurs because chains or components (or both) have not yet learned all they want to from the relationship. Once they do, however, the rate at which relationships dissolve rises, until diminishing learning benefits are offset by increasing collaborative experience.

Hypothesis 3:   The rate of dissolution of a chain relationship will have an ∩-shaped relationship to the duration of the relationship.

DATA DESCRIPTION

The data used in this study include life history information on all 558 transient hotels that operated in Manhattan at any time between 1898 and 1980 (Baum & Ingram, 1998; Baum & Mezias, 1992). Four archival sources were used to construct the life histories of Manhattan hotels: (1) the *Hotel Redbook*, published annually since 1887, contains detailed information on the name, number of rooms, location, and room rates of hotels; (2) the *Manhattan Classified Directory/Yellow Pages*, published since 1929; (3) the *Annual Directory of the Hotel Association of New York City*, published since 1940; and (4) the *Hotel and Travel Index*, published since 1951. The hotel data was supplemented by data on hotel chains, and the relationships between chains and hotels. The primary source for this data was the *Directory of Hotel and Motel Systems*, published since 1931. The secondary data source (and the primary source for 1898–1930) was the *Hotel Redbook*. We use the industry definition of chains as organizations operating at least three hotels. Most U.S. hotel chains owned and operated all their units, but there were alternative ownership arrangements, such as franchising. Rates of forming and dissolving chain relationships may depend on the type of relationship, but franchising was extremely uncommon in the Manhattan hotel industry during the period we studied (less than 1% of chain relationships), so we don't differentiate between types of relationships in the analysis.[4] The formation of a chain relationship occurred when a previously independent hotel became part of a chain. Dissolution occurred when a chain-affiliated hotel became independent while both the hotel and chain persisted. Consistent with our theoretical position that relationship formation and dissolution arises from a congruence of interests between buyer and seller, instances where the hotel or the chain failed were not treated as dissolutions.

   A total of 189 hotels (35.2% of the hotels in the sample) were at one point part of a chain. Seventeen hotels had two chain affiliations over their lives, and five hotels had three affiliations, resulting in a total of 216 chain affiliations. Twenty-six of the affiliations resulted from a chain founding a hotel, and 190 from a pre-existing hotel forming a relationship with a chain. Seventy-one components failed, and there were 110 instances where a component saw its chain relationship dissolve. In seven of those 110 instances, a hotel left one chain to immediately join another.[5]

Variables

Variables, operationalizations, and predictions are summarized in Table 1. The operationalizations for the operating-experience variables need some explanation. Typically, the experience of organizations is operationalized as an accumulation of production over time (Argote, 1993). Reflecting past research, we operationalize experience as an accumulation of the past levels of operation of hotels and chains. For hotels we use the number of rooms of the hotel to reflect its experience in a year. This approach is consistent with evidence that both success and failure lead to learning (Miner et al., 1999). Even rooms that are not occupied provide an opportunity for learning, particularly since the external component of the learning from operating experience is information about consumer preferences. We conducted a supplementary analysis, which showed that, for a shorter period when occupancy rates were available, operationalizations of hotel experience by occupied rooms yielded comparable results for relational dynamics. For chain experience, we use the number of hotels in the chain during the year – Manhattan hotels to operationalize local experience, and non-Manhattan hotels to operationalize non-local experience (total rooms operated by the chain were not available for our whole sample).

We investigated the appropriateness of discounting older values of experience as a response to the possibility that organizational knowledge depreciates. This approach is consistent with Argote and Epple's (1990: 924) observation that "although cumulative output is typically used as the measure of knowledge acquired through learning by doing, measures that put relatively greater weight on recent output than on output in the distant past are appropriate if depreciation occurs." Why might knowledge acquired from operating experience depreciate? Perhaps because individual employees forget the lessons of experience; because organizational records of experience (such as manuals) physically decay or get lost; and because of changes in products or the business environment (Argote & Epple, 1990; Epple, Argote & Devadas, 1991). Particularly relevant to the hotel industry, depreciation is also likely to come about from employee turnover (Darr, Argote & Epple, 1995).

Table 1.   Variable Operationalizations and Predictions.

Independent Variables	Operationalization	Effect on Formation Rate	Effect on Dissolution Rate
Hotel experience	$\sum_{t-founding}^{t-1} \dfrac{Number\ of\ rooms}{Age\ of\ experience}$	∪ (hypothesis 1a)	∩ (hypothesis 1b)
Chain's local (Manhattan) experience	$\sum_{t-joining}^{t-1} \dfrac{Manhatton\ components}{Age\ of\ experience}$	not in models*	− (hypothesis 2a)
Chain's non-local (non-Manhattan) experience	$\sum_{t-joining}^{t-1} \dfrac{Non\text{-}Manhattan\ components}{Age\ of\ experience}$	not in models	+ (hypothesis 2b)
Duration of chain relationship	Number of years since the chain component joined	not in models	∩ (hypothesis 3)

Control Variables	Operationalization		
Shared names	% of the components other components that have the same name as the focal component	not in models	no prediction
Distance	Euclidian geographic distance between Manhattan and chain's headquarters	not in models	no prediction
Number of past chain relationships	Count of the hotel's number of past chain relationships	no prediction	no prediction
Hotel size	ln(number of rooms in hotel)	no prediction	no prediction
Hotel price	ln(hotel price)	no prediction	no prediction
Chain's local mass	ln(total rooms of the chain's other Manhattan hotels)	not in models	no prediction
Chain age	Chain age in years	not in models	no prediction
Chain size	Number of components the chain operatesoutside of Manhattan	not in models	no prediction
Hotel age	Hotel age in years	no prediction	no prediction
Left censored	1 if hotel founded before 1898	no prediction	no prediction
Founded by chain	1 if hotel was founded by a chain	no prediction	no prediction
Size-localized competition	Sum of Euclidean size distances between focal hotel and all others within a range of ±1/2 the focal hotel's size	no prediction	no prediction
Chain's Manhattan components	Number of Manhattan components in the chain	no prediction	no prediction

Table 1. Continued.

Control Variables	Operationalization		
Visits	Number of visitors to New York City	no prediction	no prediction
GNP growth	GNP growth rate	no prediction	no prediction
Number of independent hotels	Number of independent hotels in Manhattan	no prediction	no prediction
Number of component hotels	Number of component hotels in Manhattan	no prediction	no prediction
Chain relationship formations (t−1)	Number of chain relationships formed in the prior year	no prediction	no prediction
Chain relationship dissolutions (t−1)	Number of chain relationships dissolved in the prior year	no prediction	no prediction
Calendar year	Calendar year	no prediction	no prediction

* Chain and chain-component relationship variables cannot be included in the relationship formation models because before a hotel joins a chain, the set of chains it may join is unbounded.

To investigate the need to discount, we estimated models using four discount rates based on the age of the experience: (1) no discount, (2) square root of age of experience, (3) age of experience, and (4) age of experience squared. The different discounts represent different rates of decay of the experience, with the squared age of experience producing the fastest rate of decay. Models that discounted experience fit the data better than models with no discounting (as indicated by a comparison of log-likelihood ratios). In the results presented here, we employed a discounting of experience by its age, so a unit of experience from ten years ago provides one-half the benefit of a unit of experience from five years ago. We used this discount because, overall, it provided the best fit to our data, but all the discounts yielded results that were comparable on all substantive issues. Therefore, the interpretation of our results is not sensitive to the choice of discount rate, although we do find support for the claim that experience depreciates in the Manhattan hotel industry.

Our models also include a number of control variables for which we do not have hypotheses, but may nevertheless affect rates of forming and dissolving chain relationships. In all models, at the hotel level, we include the age, size and price of the hotel, the number of chain relationships it has had in the past, whether it is left censored (founded before 1898), its potential for size-localized competition (a measure of competition based on the proximity of the hotel's size to the sizes of other hotels (Baum & Mezias, 1992) and whether it was part of a chain when it was founded. The size variable is particularly important because of the necessity of controlling for economies of scale in models that include operating experience (Argote & Epple, 1990).

In models of dissolution, at the chain level, we include the number of hotels the chain operates in Manhattan and the mass (the aggregate of the rooms) of those hotels. We also include the size and age of the chain. At the relationship level we include the geographic distance of the component from the chain's headquarters and the percentage of the chain's components that have the same name as the component.

In all analyses, at the level of the industry, we include the number of independent hotels, the number of chain components, the number of relationships formed and dissolved in the prior year, the GNP growth rate, the number of visitors to Manhattan, and calendar time. For GNP growth rate and the number of visitors to Manhattan we investigated various lags based on the suspicion that the effects of these macro-economic variables would not be immediate. We found a lag of two years to be most effective for these variables, so we used that lag in the models we report below.

Tables 2a, 2b and 2c present basic statistics and correlations for all variables. The sample for the dissolution analysis included 3,349 yearly spells for hotels that were affiliated with a chain at the start of a given year; for the forming analysis, the sample included 16,995 yearly spells for hotels that were *not* affiliated with a chain at the start of a given year. The correlations among the study variables are generally small to moderate, although there are some higher correlations, in the 0.7 to 0.8 range (49–64% shared variance), between experience variables and the contemporaneous measures of their base (e.g. between hotel size and organizational experience; chain's number of Manhattan components and chain's Manhattan experience). Overall, however, the moderate correlations in do not suggest that multicollinearity poses a serious estimation problem, but it may result in imprecise parameter estimates (i.e., larger standard errors) making hypothesis testing less efficient (Kennedy, 1992). In response to this possibility, in a preliminary analysis we followed a strategy of estimating hierarchically-nested models and testing for the overall significance of sets of added theoretical variables. These tests confirmed all the conclusions we reach below in our discussion of results.

Method

The dependent variables we are studying are the likelihoods at any point in the life of a hotel of: (1) forming a chain relationship, or if it is already part of a

Table 2a. Descripitve Statistics.*

Variable	Dissolving Sample (N = 3,349)		Forming Sample (N = 16,995)	
	Mean	Std.Dev.	Mean	Std.Dev.
Hotel Characteristics				
Age	29.061	16.665	28.145	20.112
ln(size)	6.031	0.719	5.544	0.719
ln(price)	1.697	0.601	1.490	0.559
left-censored	0.025	0.155	0.058	0.234
(Hotel Experience) $\times$ 10^{-4}	0.861	0.749	2.803	3.053
Founded by chain	0.119	0.324	0.024	0.155
Number of past chain relationships	0.985	0.120	0.492	0.500
Relationship Characteristics				
Relation duration	14.433	13.265	–	–
% share same name	0.179	0.178	–	–
HQ Distance from Manhattan	0.181	0.808	–	–
Chain Characteristics				
Age	15.088	12.321	–	–
No. Manhattan components	5.971	5.342	–	–
No. Manhattan rooms	6.798	2.919	–	–
No. non-Manhattan components	29.224	136.282	–	–
Local (Manhattan) experience	8.567	9.064	–	–
Non-local (non-Manhattan) experience	60.950	232.270	–	–
Environmental Characteristics				
Calendar time	156.251	15.973	148.140	21.146
Visitors to NYC	55.242	11.364	50.063	14.383
GNP growth	3.558	6.287	3.276	6.459
Size-localized competition	11.963	8.075	10.908	7.715
Manhattan component density	59.044	17.077	47.292	25.983
Manhattan independent density	238.635	42.211	222.185	54.789
Chain relationships formed (t−1)	3.306	3.233	2.554	2.684
Chain relationships dissolved (t−1)	2.145	2.115	1.502	1.442

Chain and chain-component relationship variables cannot be included in the relationship formation models because before a hotel joins a chain, its chain is unknown.

chain, (2) dissolving a chain relationship. Event-history models estimate over time the instantaneous risk of an event occurring, and are therefore the appropriate method for this analysis. Almost all of the independent variables we are interested in change over time. Time-varying covariates are incorporated into event history models by splitting the observations (in this case, the life histories of hotels) into spells, and updating covariates in each spell (Blossfeld & Rohwer, 1995). We applied this approach by splitting the life histories of hotels into one-year spells, and for each spell setting covariates to their value at the beginning of the year.

Table 2b. Correlation Matrix, Forming Sample ($N = 16{,}995$)*.

	1	2	3	4	5	6	7	8	9	10	11	12	13	14	15
Hotel Characteristics															
1. Age	1.000														
2. ln(size)	0.050	1.000													
3. ln(price)	0.024	0.275	1.000												
4. Left-censored	0.339	0.014	−0.090	1.000											
5. (Hotel experience) $\times 10^{-4}$	0.454	0.701	0.194	0.133	1.000										
6. Number of past chain relationships	0.050	0.351	0.155	−0.118	0.239	1.000									
7. Founded by chain	−0.020	0.055	0.033	−0.039	0.039	0.162	1.000								
Environmental Characteristics															
8. Calendar time	0.623	0.057	0.193	−0.217	0.343	0.140	0.082	1.000							
9. Visitors to NYC	0.528	0.044	0.071	−0.216	0.294	0.128	0.078	0.879	1.000						
10. GNP growth	0.036	0.000	0.002	0.021	0.029	−0.014	−0.004	0.015	−0.095	1.000					
11. Component hotel density	0.250	0.029	−0.095	−0.219	0.169	0.112	0.053	0.639	0.609	0.080	1.000				
12. Independent hotel density	−0.021	0.015	−0.171	−0.216	0.020	0.096	0.026	0.318	0.335	−0.108	0.788	1.000			
13. Size-localized competition	−0.028	0.022	0.045	−0.019	−0.006	0.008	−0.026	0.051	0.054	0.000	0.050	0.034	1.000		
14. No. joining events $(t-1)$	−0.101	0.015	−0.096	−0.107	−0.027	0.055	0.004	0.079	0.085	−0.233	0.335	0.595	0.013	1.000	
15. No. dropping $(t-1)$ events	0.060	0.023	−0.072	−0.136	0.061	0.074	0.019	0.304	0.303	−0.154	0.649	0.592	0.028	0.350	1.000

*The experience discount was set to the square-root of the age of the experience.

Table 2c. Correlation Matrix, Dissolving Sample. (N = 3,349)*

	1	2	3	4	5	6	7	8	9	10	11	12	13	14	15	16	17	18	19	20	21	22	23	24
Hotel and Relationship Characteristics																								
1. Relation duration (collaborative experience)	1.000																							
2. Age	0.533	1.000																						
3. ln(size)	0.282	0.098	1.000																					
4. ln(price)	0.214	0.120	0.237	1.000																				
5. Left-censored	-0.043	0.274	-0.043	-0.222	1.000																			
6. (Hotel experience) × 10^-4	0.291	0.101	0.895	0.190	-0.059	1.000																		
7. Founded by chain	0.068	-0.239	0.038	0.036	-0.058	-0.001	1.000																	
8. % share same name	0.096	-0.032	0.155	0.056	-0.035	0.175	-0.027	1.000																
9. Number of past chain relationships	0.114	0.093	0.102	-0.057	0.005	0.086	0.044	0.060	1.000															
10. HQ distance from	0.045	0.054	0.032	0.128	0.010	0.030	0.044	-0.015	0.027	1.000														
Manhattan Chain Characteristics																								
11. Age	0.477	0.294	0.199	0.268	-0.046	0.203	0.028	0.063	0.020	0.058	1.000													
12. No. Manhattan components	-0.048	-0.134	-0.158	-0.139	0.052	-0.145	0.020	-0.257	0.047	-0.153	0.195	1.000												
13. No. Manhattan rooms	0.311	-0.006	0.155	0.069	0.007	0.140	0.058	0.178	0.137	-0.023	0.386	0.546	1.000											
14. No. non-Manhattan components	0.030	0.016	0.027	0.189	0.002	0.022	0.011	-0.110	0.023	0.553	0.110	-0.078	0.016	1.000										
15. Local (Manhattan) experience	0.081	-0.048	-0.117	-0.113	0.047	-0.101	-0.088	-0.219	0.036	-0.140	0.320	0.833	0.471	-0.064	1.000									
16. Non-local (non-Manhattan) experience	0.086	0.044	0.038	0.187	0.002	0.037	0.030	-0.127	0.027	0.449	0.216	-0.017	0.056	0.861	0.026	1.000								
Environmental Characteristics																								
17. Calendar time	0.514	0.533	0.202	0.531	-0.166	0.179	0.022	0.034	0.100	0.209	0.418	-0.261	0.044	0.234	-0.154	0.235	1.000							
18. Visitors to NYC	0.378	0.417	0.139	0.278	-0.109	0.123	0.021	0.059	0.074	0.155	0.298	-0.256	0.024	0.180	-0.127	0.200	0.770	1.000						
19. GNP growth	0.011	0.008	-0.025	-0.044	-0.011	-0.022	-0.027	0.001	-0.006	-0.009	0.012	0.032	0.037	-0.014	0.086	-0.010	0.011	-0.130	1.000					
20. Size-localized competition	0.085	-0.009	-0.080	-0.006	0.065	-0.129	0.151	-0.012	0.048	0.020	0.095	0.004	0.028	-0.004	0.029	-0.012	0.042	0.026	0.003	1.000				
21. Component hotel density	0.011	-0.017	-0.069	-0.207	-0.105	-0.069	-0.045	-0.082	0.103	-0.116	0.052	0.208	0.136	-0.125	0.214	-0.108	0.102	0.167	0.191	0.014	1.000			
22. Independent hotel density	-0.216	-0.246	-0.119	-0.368	-0.129	-0.015	-0.024	-0.100	0.075	-0.194	-0.144	0.250	0.046	-0.223	0.194	-0.216	-0.335	-0.242	-0.078	0.014	0.660	1.000		
23. Chain relationships formed (t - 1)	-0.240	-0.192	-0.094	-0.178	0.020	-0.085	-0.009	-0.121	-0.025	-0.105	-0.172	0.104	-0.185	-0.085	0.065	-0.082	-0.296	-0.243	-0.181	-0.006	0.065	0.451	1.000	
24. Chain relationship dissolved (t - 1)	-0.088	-0.120	-0.065	-0.128	-0.040	-0.069	-0.010	-0.067	0.025	-0.072	-0.037	0.162	0.049	-0.076	0.109	-0.068	-0.111	-0.020	-0.137	0.001	0.419	0.387	0.162	1.000

*The experience discount was set to the square of the age of the experience.

A second issue for using event history models concerns parameterizing time-dependence – different models are used depending on assumptions regarding the functional form of the relationship between the rate and time. It is particularly difficult to make these assumptions in studies like ours, where there is no past research, so we use the piecewise exponential model, which allows for a flexible specification of time dependence (Blossfeld & Rohwer, 1995). Using the piecewise exponential model requires prespecifying a set of time ranges, and the model allows the risk of the event to vary independently for each range. This is analogous to using dummy variables for time periods. The time scale for the relationship-formation models was the age of the hotel, and for the relationship-dissolution models, the duration of the chain relationship. Based on preliminary analysis where we began with fine-grained time ranges, and collapsed consecutive ranges with no statistical differences between their coefficients, we chose three time-ranges for both sets of models. The piecewise exponential model we estimated was of the form:

$$r(t) = e^{\beta \chi} e^{\alpha_t} t$$

where $r(t)$ is the instantaneous risk of an event occurring, χ is a vector of covariates, β a vector of coefficients, and α_t is the coefficient associated with the time range, t. We obtained maximum likelihood estimates for piecewise exponential models using the statistical package TDA 5.7 (Rohwer, 1995).

A final issue for the dissolution model is the problem of interdependence between observations. The data from each chain's multiple components are pooled. Consequently, if chain i makes decisions regarding several components simultaneously, our modeling approach treats these interactions as independent. Fortunately, this problem, also known as the "common actor effect," can be understood as one of model misspecification (Lincoln, 1984). If the statistical model incorporates all essential chain-level characteristics that influence decisions to drop components, no unobserved effects of cross-sectional interdependence would remain. Our models include a number of important chain-level variables, including the age, size inside and outside Manhattan, and experience of the chain. Although our empirical models are richly specified, they may suffer from some degree of omitted variable bias. Therefore, in a preliminary analysis, we estimated exponential models that account for unobserved heterogeneity implemented in TDA 5.7 to adjust for systematic biases resulting from model misspecification. Results with those models were comparable to those we report below. Therefore, we concluded that our model was well-specified with regards to chain characteristics, and our results were not likely attributable to interdependence between observations.

RESULTS

The first two columns of Table 3 present estimates for the model of the likelihood of relationship forming for independent hotels. Hypothesis 1a, which predicts a ∪-shaped effect of hotel experience on the likelihood of forming a chain relationship, is supported, as indicated by the negative first-order effect, and positive second-order effect, of that variable. Chain relationships are most likely to form for hotels when they have low, or high levels of their own experience. These are the situations where the hotel is least-well served by its own experience, either because of the lack of own experience, or because of competency traps, and therefore, most likely to benefit from experience of a chain. At moderate levels of experience, where hotels benefit most from their own experience, the likelihood of chain-relationship formation is lowest.

The minimum of the non-monotonic effect of own experience comes at about 5.3 units of experience. That minimum occurs at the right tail of the distribution of experience values for Manhattan hotels, with only five percent ever achieving 5.3 units of experience. If as we argue the upturn occurs because hotels with high levels of experience fall into competency traps, then it is only a small group of hotels with the most experience that turn to chains to help them escape competency traps. This is consistent with analyses of learning from operating experience in three different populations (Manhattan hotels, U.S. hotel chains, and Israeli kibbutzim) which showed that only a small set of the most experienced organizations were harmed by myopic learning and competency traps (Baum & Ingram, 1998; Ingram & Baum, 1997; Ingram & Simons, 1997). Of the hotel-level control variables, the size and price of a hotel increased the likelihood of chain-relationship formation. The effect of hotel age on the formation rate is shown by the coefficients for the three age ranges. Different formation rates for hotels of different ages would be indicated by differences between the coefficients associated with different age ranges. In all of the models, however, there are no significant differences between any of the age-range coefficients. This indicates that the likelihood of chain-relationship formation does not depend on the age of the hotel. The number of chain relationships the hotel had in the past increased the likelihood of forming a new one. Left-censored hotels were not more likely to form chain relationships, so there is no bias created by the fact that some hotels enter our data 'mid-life,' when the observation period begins in 1898. Hotels that were part of a

Table 3. Maximum Likelihood Estimates of Manhattan Hotels and U.S. Hotel Chains Forming and Dissolving Relationships, 1898-1980.

Hotel Characteristics	Relationship Forming[1]		Relationship Dissolution[2]	
	Coefficient beta	Standard error	Coefficient beta	Standard error
Hotel age <5 years	−9.742	(1.405)	–	–
Hotel age 5–10 years	−9.455	(1.273)		
Hotel age >10 years	−9.394	(1.402)		
Age			0.016*	(0.005)
ln(Size)	0.662*	(0.186)	−0.478*	(0.142)
ln(Price)	0.279	(0.106)	−0.254*	(0.109)
Left-censored	0.174	(0.286)	−0.528	(0.394)
Hotel experience $\times$ 10^{-4}	−0.522*	(0.177)	−0.044	(0.104)
(Hotel experience $\times$ $10^{-4})^2$	0.0491*	(0.0149)	0.004	(0.023)
Founded by hotel chain	−0.121	(0.233)	0.021	(0.188)
Number of past chain relationships	2.893*	(0.247)	0.444	(0.718)
Hotel-Chain Relationship Characteristics				
Relation duration <5 years	–[3]	–	−2.619	(1.517)
Relation duration 5-10 years	–	–	−1.431+	(1.432)
Relation duration >10 years	–	–	−2.159	(1.111)
Percent of other components with same name	–	–	−0.902*	(0.291)
Distance of HQ from Manhattan	–	–	0.158*	(0.053)
Chain Characteristics				
Age	–	–	−0.014*	(0.006)
Number of Manhattan components	–	–	−0.054*	(0.019)
ln(Number of Manhattan rooms)	–	–	0.314*	(0.047)
Number of non-Manhattan components	–	–	−0.0026*	(0.0013)
Local (Manhattan) experience	–	–	−0.0123*	(0.0055)
Non-local (Non-Manhattan) experience	–	–	0.0011*	(0.0005)
Environmental Characteristics				
Calendar time	−0.004	(0.006)	0.018*	(0.007)
Visitors to NYC $\times$ 10^{-6} (t−2)	0.025*	(0.007)	−0.041*	(0.005)
GNP growth (t−2)	0.012	(0.009)	−0.031*	(0.010)
Size-localized competition	0.012*	(0.005)	−0.016*	(0.007)
Manhattan component hotel density	−0.005*	(0.002)	−0.017*	(0.006)
Manhattan independent hotel density	−0.001	(0.005)	−0.004*	(0.002)
Number of chain relationships formed (t−1)	0.131*	(0.011)	0.005	(0.012)
Number of chain relationships dissolved (t−1)	−0.019	(0.015)	0.120*	(0.015)
Log Likelihood	−1565.18		−1220.32	
df	18		27	

[1]. The sample included 16,995 yearly spells and 190 chain relationship formation events.

[2]. The sample included 3,349 yearly spells and 110 chain relationship dissolution events.

[3]. Chain and chain-component relationship variables cannot be included in the relationship formation model because before a hotel joins a chain, its chain is unknown.

* $p < 0.05$; standard errors in parentheses.

+ indicates coefficient for relation duration 5-10 years is significantly greater than the coefficients for duration <5 years ($p < 0.05$) and duration >10 years ($p < 0.10$).

chain when they were founded (but subsequently became independent) are not more likely to form chain relationships.

Turning to the industry-level control variables, the number of component hotels in the industry increases the likelihood of formation, while the number of independent hotels decreases the likelihood. The number of relationships formed in the prior year has a positive effect on the likelihood of formation. Similarly, when the number of visitors to Manhattan is higher, the likelihood of formation is also higher. None of the other industry-level controls were significant.

The final two columns of Table 3 present results for the model of the likelihood of the dissolution of component hotels' relationships with their chains. The hotel-experience prediction, hypothesis 1b, that dissolution will have an ∩-shaped relationship to the hotel's experience, is not supported. In fact, there is no relationship between hotel experience and the dissolution of chain relationships.[6] Hypothesis 2a, that components of chains with high levels of local experience will be less likely to have their relationships dissolve, is supported as shown by the negative coefficient for local experience. The non-local experience of the chain increases the likelihood of dissolution, as predicted by hypothesis 2b. These findings reinforce earlier findings that chain units benefit from the local experience of their chains, but may be harmed by chains' non-local experience (Ingram & Baum, 1996; Greve, 1999).

Hypothesis 3, which predicted an ∩-shaped relationship between the duration of a relationship and its likelihood of dissolution, was tested by comparing the magnitudes of the coefficients of the duration periods. To perform this test, the coefficients of the first two duration periods were constrained to be equal, and the log-likelihood of that model was compared to the unconstrained model using a chi-square test. This process was repeated for the second and third duration periods. This test indicated that the coefficient of the middle duration period (5–10 years) is significantly larger than the coefficients of the previous and subsequent periods. So, the likelihood of dissolution is higher for relationships of moderate duration than it is for new or old relationships. Hypothesis 3 is supported by this ∩-shaped relationship between duration and dissolution.

Of the controls at the hotel level, the age of the component increased the likelihood of dissolution. The size and price of the hotel decreased the likelihood of dissolution. Of the chain level controls, age and size had the effect of reducing the likelihood of dissolution. The chain's Manhattan components also reduced the likelihood of dissolution, while the mass of Manhattan components increased the likelihood. At the relationship level, the distance from chain headquarters increased, and the percentage of other components in the chain with the same name decreased the likelihood that the relationship would dissolve.

Of the industry-level controls, the number of component hotels had a negative effect on the dissolution likelihood, and the number of dissolutions in the prior year had a positive effect. The localized competition variable is a measure of the Euclidian distance, on the dimension of size, so its negative coefficient indicates that the dissolution likelihood is lower for hotels that faced less localized competition (i.e. were farther from competitors). Lastly, increases in the number of visitors to Manhattan and the GNP growth rate decreased the likelihood of dissolution.

DISCUSSION AND CONCLUSION

The results supported four of our five hypotheses. Hotels' operating experience had a U-shaped effect on the likelihood of forming chain relationships, consistent with the claim that chains' experience helps hotels that are lacking in their own experience, or that have become myopic and fallen into competency traps. Once established, relationships were less likely to dissolve if the chain had operating experience from the hotel's local market, and more likely to dissolve if the chain had operating experience from non-local markets. This supports the idea that local experience is most useful, and that sometimes-harmful experience is applied to chain components. The duration dependence of chain relationships had an ∩-shape. This effect is argued to result from the combination of a honeymoon period and collaborative experience that allows parties to the relationship, over time, to learn to work together.

Together, these results give a rich picture of the effects of experience on chain dynamics in one very important hotel market, and provide a baseline for necessary future research regarding the effects of experience on the dynamics of chain relationships, and interorganizational relationships more broadly. There are also notable results of control variables at the level of the hotel, the chain, the relationship, and the industry. Our discussion is in three parts. First we discuss the implications of the experience results for the literature on organizational learning. Then, we consider the results of the control variables, which have important implications for relational dynamics. Finally, we summarize the implications of this research for our understanding of the dynamics of chain and other types of relationships.

The Effects of Experience

The results of operating experience at both hotel and chain levels are exciting because they contribute a new dimension to a well-established literature. The past research showing that relationships facilitate interorganizational learning represented a substantial advance in our understanding of the opportunities for organizations to learn. As we show here, the flipside to the role of interorganizational relationships in learning is that experience is a driver of the formation, persistence and dissolution of interorganizational relationships. Organizations do form and maintain relationships with an eye to the learning implications of those relationships. This finding gives a fuller picture of just how organizations learn from each other. Interorganizational learning is not the fortunate spin-off of relationships formed for other reasons, but instead one of the reasons that relationships are formed in the first place.

The specifics of how chain-components learn from their chains has implications both for management and for understanding market structure. Our results combine with earlier research (Ingram & Baum, 1997; Greve, 1999) to indicate that chain components learn more and perform better when their chain has more local experience and less non-local experience. Such a chain structure is created by limiting the geographic scope of the organization. If managers were to incorporate this idea into their strategic decision making, we would ultimately expect to see a territorial structure of chains that specialize in a limited set of similar geographic markets. Chains would succeed and perhaps dominate a territory then by sharing relevant experience and avoiding the risk of forcing inappropriate experience onto units.

The findings also indicate that operating experience is not the only type of experience relevant to the dynamics of chain relationships. Collaborative experience makes relationships more robust as it accounts for the down side of the ∩-shaped effect of duration on the risk of dissolution. Our finding joins with Levinthal and Fichman's (1988) and Park and Russo's (1996) comparable results to broaden support for the prediction that the duration of interorganizational relationships depends on an initial honeymoon period, which helps relationships to survive when they are new, and collaborative experience which helps relationships to survive when they are old. This evidence should encourage further research into the duration dependence of relationships.

The existence of multiple types of experience raises an interesting question for the application of our findings elsewhere. Other types of experience could be transferred through a relationship. For example, the learning literature has also examined foreign entry experience (Mitchell, Shaver & Yeung, 1994; Pennings et al., 1994; Li, 1995; Barkema et al., 1996) and competitive experience (Barnett, Greve & Park, 1994). It seems likely that these types of experience will be better transferred across relationships, so the possibility that relationships are formed for that purpose exists. Perhaps the most important question is what types of relationships will form? An organization's competitive experience will likely be most useful for similar organizations that face similar competitors, so commensalistic relationships, like those we studied, would seem appropriate mechanisms for transfer. Foreign-entry experience, on the other hand, could be useful to organizations from many industries. Symbiotic relationships, between organizations from different industries, might thus be formed as a mechanism to transfer foreign-entry experience.

The one surprising result was that the hotel's operating experience did not affect the rate of dissolution, as H1b argued it should. One possible explanation for this concerns the salience of hotel operating experience to the decision makers who consider dissolving a chain relationship. Once a component's experience, which depends on its operating and relational history, has been blended with the experience of a chain it may become less observable to decision makers than contemporaneous features of the component such as its size, price, and age. The difficulty of observing experience may mean that after a hotel becomes part of its chain, chain managers who must decide whether to sell the hotel, and independent hoteliers who must decide whether to buy it, simply do not attend to its own experience.

Other Results on the Dynamics of Chain Relationships

Our control variables yield many interesting results that are informative of the dynamics of interorganizational relationships as they are shaped by factors other than learning. We will describe these results by level of analysis.

Hotel-level Controls

Hotel size and price yield consistent results across the formation and dissolution models. Large expensive hotels are more likely to establish and maintain chain relationships. This is indicative of the value of highly visible components to a chain. A marquee hotel in Manhattan can contribute not only operating revenue, but also word-of-mouth advertising to a chain that owns it. Chain operators have historically demonstrated that they view bigger as better, independent of the operating implications of hotel size (*Tavern Talk*, September, 1922; Hilton, 1957: 224). The importance of marquee hotels to chains can be viewed generally as indicative of the value of high-status partners in relationships (Podolny, 1993).

The number of chain relationships the hotel has had in the past increased the likelihood it would form another relationship. This finding is consistent with Gulati's (1995a, b) finding in a broad sample of firms, that the number of past alliances predicted alliance formation. The most obvious interpretation of this result is as an organization-level application of collaborative experience. There is empirical evidence that, through cumulative relationships, firms develop general relational knowhow, which includes skills in identifying potential collaborators, negotiating the form and specifics of collaborative agreements, managing and monitoring the arrangements, knowing when to terminate them, and transferring knowledge (Simonin & Helleloid, 1993; Pennings et al., 1994; Simonin, 1997; Barkema, Shenkar, Vermeulen & Bell, 1997). The logic of organizational-level relational know how can also be turned on its head: It may be that, rather than learning to operate in interorganizational relationships, organizations with many past relationships lose the capacity to operate independently. We have no way to distinguish between these two ideas in our analysis. Finally, a methodological caution on this result: If our models were missing some important variable that affected the likelihood of forming relationships, then the count of past relationships might have a positive coefficient because it is likely to be highly correlated with the unobserved variable. Our models include many variables, and we ran models that statistically controlled for unobserved heterogeneity, but this risk should be kept in mind.

Chain-level Controls
Chain size and age yield results in support of structural inertia arguments that large, old organizations are less likely to change. Both size and age of the chain reduced the likelihood that a chain relationship would be dissolved. The findings for age are important because most evidence for the link between age and inertia has been indirect, with inertia being offered as an explanation for findings that older organizations are more likely to fail (Barron, West & Hannan, 1994).

Relationship-level Controls
The finding that components are more likely to see their chain relationship dissolve when they are more distant from chain headquarters has implications for theories of the transfer of experience, and of control in interorganizational relationships. Directly relevant to the focus of this paper, the transfer of operating experience between organizations should be easier when physical distance between them is smaller (Galbraith, 1990; Epple, Argote & Murphy, 1996). When physical proximity is greater, awareness and contact between the organizations should be greater, and so should the transfer of experience. Physical proximity is also a response to the challenge for chains of monitoring managers and employees in remote locations (Brickley & Dark, 1987).

The other relationship-level control, percentage of other components in the chain with the same name as the focal component, reduced the likelihood of dissolution. This result can also be interpreted as demonstrating a smoother transfer of operating experience. Shared names are indicative that the components are part of the same marketing strategy. Darr (1994) demonstrated that strategic similarity of components facilitated the sharing of experience in English pizza chains. Shared names bring other advantages to a chain and its components, as Ingram (1996) has argued. Shared names allow the chain to engage in repeated interactions with customers, which should bring more business for all components. They also reduce customer uncertainty, particularly when they imply some standardization.

Environmental Controls

A number of the environmental controls suggest that processes of forming and dissolving chain relationships are subject to 'bandwagon' effects. Relationships are more likely to form when there were more formations in the previous year, when there are more components, and when there are fewer independent hotels. Relationships are more likely to dissolve when there were more dissolutions in the previous year, and when there are fewer components. Formations in the previous year inform both chain and independent hotel managers of the opportunity of independent hotels forming chain relationships and suggest that the time may be right for such transitions, while dissolutions in the previous period remind managers that there are costs to chain affiliation, and that it may be a good time to dissolve relationships so that component hotels become independent. Apparently, the absolute numbers of independent and component hotels have a similar effect: the lure of forming relationships and thereby turning independent hotels into components is greater when there are more components and fewer independent hotels, while dissolutions, which convert components into independents, are more likely when there are fewer components. Decision makers may look at the number of component and independent hotels as a signal of the munificence of the environment to each type. The generalizability of this claim is supported by Gulati (1995a) who demonstrated empirically that the total level of alliance activity drove alliance formation in multiple sectors.

The Dynamics of (Chain) Relationships

Perhaps the most important question concerning the implications of our results for theory is what do they say about the role of experience in the formation and dissolution of other types of interorganizational relationships? Kogut (1988) proposed interorganizational learning as an explanation for the formation of joint ventures, which are often vertical relationships. Mitchell's (1994) analysis of business sales in medical equipment industries led him to conclude that sales of business units "provide a mechanism for acquiring innovative capabilities that are embodied in the [acquired businesses] routines" (p. 599).

So, the idea that other types of relationships are formed for the purpose of transferring experience is a significant possibility, worthy of future research. Scott (this volume) and Cassidy and Loree (this volume) both suggest, and provide empirical evidence, that multimarket relationships may also be established in pursuit of learning. Regarding collaborative experience, the range of relationships that have already been found to have similar duration-dependence (chain, auditor-client, and high-tech joint ventures) is suggestive of a broad phenomenon.

When applying this research to other contexts, two features deserve careful consideration. First, the relationships we studied were commensalistic – chains bring together organizations that do essentially the same thing. Vertical relationships have different implications for interorganizatonal learning and may have different processes of relationship formation and dissolution (Mowrey et al., 1996). Operating experience may be less relevant in vertical relationships because the organizations do different things. Vertical relationships may have different dynamics because the parties are not in direct competition (Hamel, 1991; Gomes-Casseres, 1994; Khanna et al., 1998). Second, chain relationships are different than, for example, joint ventures in that the autonomy of the parties is affected by the relationship. Chain hotels can be considered organizations in the sense that they have the capacity to operate independently, but the operational control that chains have over their components is greater than many other interorganizational relationships. This may have both positive (e.g. forced sharing of experience) and negative (e.g. forced adoption of non-local practices) implications for learning, and may imply that our results are most germane to relationships where the organizations do not share power equally.

Regardless of the implications of our results for other types of relationships, the implications for chain relationships seem clear. A number of studies identified the role of chains for interorganizational learning. Overall, the results of those studies supported the idea that chains constituted "integrated learning communities" that provide both chains and their components competitive advantages that aided them in "out-evolving" their independent rivals (Ingram & Baum, 1997). This study expands the scope of that earlier work by examining processes leading to the formation and dissolution of chain relationships, and showing that the learning properties of chains are not accidental, but rather the result of systematic processes of forming and dissolving relationships to improve learning. Although this study is the first to examine the *dynamics* of chain relationships, its results support past research on the *effects* of chain relationships. The accumulation of research at multiple levels illuminates the rise and persistence of an organizational form, the chain, which has come to have a fundamental effect on modern economic life.

NOTES

1. We use "sell" and "buy" because in the Manhattan hotel industry, pure ownership of components accounted for more than ninety-nine percent of chain relationships. There are other types of chain relationships that do not involve ownership. For generality, you could substitute "acquire rights" and "give up rights" for our use of buy and sell.

2. This prediction is conditional on a sufficient level of environmental change. If the environment doesn't change, then organizations can succeed by continuing to apply the routines that made them successful in the past, and competency traps will not arise.

3. Audia et al. (this volume) provide an interesting theoretical contrast to these ideas and findings, in which experience from different locations is proposed to facilitate learning by permitting comparison of information across units and use of 'quasi-experiments.' The problem of how to integrate experiences from different units and draw correct implications for the management of the organization as a whole, nevertheless, remains.

4. The very low instance of franchising in our data is likely the result of two factors: (1) most of the period we study is before franchising became common in the hotel industry; and (2) Manhattan, with its dense population and high marquee value, is exactly the type of city where organizations should own rather than franchise their units (Brickely & Dark, 1987). We conducted a sensitivity analysis that excluded franchised hotels. The results were not different from those reported below.

5. Since our arguments on why a hotel would leave a chain all rely on the absence of benefit in a particular relationship, the destination of exit (to independence or another chain) is unimportant. Therefore it is theoretically correct to include the seven chain-to-chain transfers in our analysis. In any case, the results do not differ from those reported below when those seven transfers are excluded from the analysis.

6. With the squared term for hotel experience removed, the linear term remained insignificant ($\beta = -0.019$, s.e. $= 0.057$) and the model log likelihood (1220.57) was not significantly different from the reported model.

ACKNOWLEDGMENTS

We are grateful to Richard Blackburn, Mark Fichman, Henrich Greve, Bill McEvily, as well as seminar participants at the Australian Graduate School of Management, Tel Aviv University, the 1997 American Sociological Association meetings and the 1998 Academy of Management meetings for helpful comments on earlier versions of this paper. For their data collection and coding efforts we are also grateful to Gretchen Dematera, Corrine Imbert, Bridget Ingram, Colin Ingram, Bill Krause, Alan Mibab, Kiril Okun, and Sheila Peterson.

REFERENCES

Argote, L. (1993). Group and organizational learning curves: Individual, system, and environmental components. *British Journal of Social Psychology, 32*, 31–51.

Argote, L., & Epple. D. (1990). Learning curves in manufacturing *Science, 247,* 920–924.

Audia, P. G., Sorenson, O., & Hage, J. (2001). Tradeoffs in the organization of production: Multiunit firms, geographic dispersion and organizational learning In: J. A. C. Baum & H. R. Greve (Eds), *Multiunit Organization and Multimarket Strategy: Advances in Strategic Management,* Vol. 18, (pp. 75–105). Oxford UK: JAI Press.

Barkema, H. G., Bell, J. H. J., & Pennings, J. M. (1996). Foreign entry, cultural barriers and learning. *Strategic Management Journal, 17,* 151–166.

Barkema, H. G., Shenkar, O., Vermeulen, F., & Bell. J. H. (1997). Working abroad, working with others: How firms learn to operate international joint ventures. *Academy of Management Journal, 40,* 426–442.

Barkema, H. G., & Vermeulen, F. (1998). International expansion through start-up or acquisition: A learning perspective. *Academy of Management Journal, 41,* 7–26.

Barnett, W. P., Henrich, G. R., & Park. D. Y. (1994). An evolutionary model of organizational performance. *Strategic Management Journal, 17,* 139–157.

Barron, D. N., West. E., & Hannan, M. T. (1994). A time to grow and a time to die: Growth and mortality of credit unions in New York City. *American Journal of Sociology, 100,* 381-421.

Baum, J. A. C., & Ingram, P. (1998). Survival-enhancing learning in the Manhattan hotel industry. *Management Science, 44,* 996–1016.

Baum, J. A. C., & Mezias, S. J. (1992). Localized competition and organizational failure in the Manhattan hotel industry, 1898–1990. *Administrative Science Quarterly, 37,* 580–604.

Belasco, W. J. (1979). *Americans on the road.* Cambridge, MA: The MIT Press.

Blossfeld, H., & Rohwer, G. (1995). *Techniques of Event History Modeling: New Approaches to Causal Analysis.* Mahwah, NJ: Lawrence Erlbaum Associates.

Brickley, J. A., & Dark, F. H. (1987). The choice of organizational form: The case of franchising. *Journal of Financial Economics, 18*: 401–420.

Cassidy, C., & Loree. D. (2001). Dynamics of Knowledge Transfer Among Multimarket Competitors, In: J. A. C. Baum & H. R. Greve (Eds), *Multiunit Organization and Multimarket Strategy: Advances in Strategic Management,* Vol. 18, (pp. 141–174). Oxford UK: JAI Press.

Chang, S. (1995). International expansion strategy of Japanese firms: Capability building through sequential entry. *Academy of Management Journal, 38,* 383–407.

Cyert, R. M., Kumar, P., & Williams, J. R. (1993). Information, market imperfections, and strategy. *Strategic Management Journal, 14,* 47–58.

Darr, E. D., & Kurtzburg. T. R. (2000). An investigation of partner similarity dimensions on knowledge transfer. *Organizational Behavior and Human Decision Processes, 82,* 28–44.

Darr, E. D., Argote, L., & Epple,. D. (1995). The Acquisition, Transfer and Depreciation of Knowledge in Service Organizations: Productivity in Franchises. *Management Science, 41,* 1750–1762.

Epple, D., Argote, L., & Devadas, R. (1991). Organizational learning curves: A method for investigating intra-plant transfer of knowledge acquired through learning by doing. *Organization Science, 2,* 58–70.

Epple, D., Argote, L., & Murphy, K. (1996). An empirical investigation of the microstructure of knowledge acquisition and transfer through learning by doing. *Operations Research, 44,* 77–86.

Fichman, M., & Levinthal, D. A. (1991). Honeymoons and the liability of adolescence: A new perspective on duration dependence in social and organizational relationships. *Academy of Management Review, 16,* 442–468.

Galbraith, C. S. (1990). Transferring core manufacturing technologies in high-technology firms. *California Management Review, 32,* 56–70.

Gomes-Casseres, B. (1994). Group versus group: How alliance groups compete. *Harvard Business Review, (July-August)*: 62–74.

Greve, H. R. (1999). Branch systems and non-local learning in populations. In: A S. Miner & P Anderson (Eds), *Population-Level Learning and Industry Change: Advances in Strategic Management*, Vol. 16, (pp. 57–80). Stamford, CT: JAI Press.

Grindley, P., Mowery D. C., & Silverman, B. S. (1994). SEMATECH and collaborative research: Lessons in the design of high-technology consortia. *Journal of Policy analysis and Management, 13*, 723–758.

Gulati, R. (1995a). Social structure and alliance formation patterns: A longitudinal analysis. *Administrative Science Quarterly, 40*, 619–652.

Gulati, R. (1995b). Does familiarity breed trust? The implications of repeated ties for contractual choice in alliances. *Academy of Management Journal, 38*, 85–112.

Hamel, G. (1991). Competition for competence and interpartner learning within international strategic alliances, *Strategic Management Journal, 12*, 83–103.

Hawley, A. (1950). *Human ecology: A theory of community structure*. New York: Ronald Press.

Hilton, C. (1957). *Be My Guest*. Englewood Cliffs, NJ: Prentice Hall.

Huber, G. P. (1991). Organizational learning: The contributing processes and literatures, *Organization Science, 2*, 88–115.

Ingram, P. (1996). Organizational form as a solution to the problem of credible commitment: The evolution of naming strategies among U.S. hotel chains, 1896–1980. Strategic *Management Journal, 17*, Summer Special Issue: 85–98.

Ingram, P., & Baum, J. A. C. (1997). Opportunity and Constraint: Organizations' Learning from the Operating and Competitive Experience of Industries, *Strategic Management Journal (Summer Special Issue), 18*, 75–98.

Ingram, P., & Simons, T. (1997). *Interorganizational relationships and the performance outcomes of experience*. Academy of Management Best Paper Proceedings. CD-Rom.

Inkpen, A. C., & Dinur, A. (1998). Knowledge management processes and international joint ventures. *Organization Science, 9*, 454–468.

Johanson, J., & Vahline, J. E. (1977). The internationalization process of the firm: A model of knowledge development and increasing foreign market commitments. *Journal of International Business Studies, 8*, 23–32.

Kennedy, P. (1992). *A Guide to Econometric Methods (3rd Ed.)*. Cambridge, MA: MIT Press.

Khanna, T., Gulati, R., & Nohria, N. (1998). The dynamics of learning alliances: Competition, cooperation and relative scope. *Strategic Management Journal, 19*, 193–210.

Kogut, B. (1988). Joint ventures: Theoretical and empirical perspectives. *Strategic Management Journal, 9*, 319–332.

Kogut, B., Shan, W., & Walker, G. (1992). The make-or-cooperate decision in the context of an industry network. In: N. Nohria & R. G. Eccles (Eds), *Networks and Organizations: Structure, Form and Action*, (pp 348–365). Boston: HBS Press.

Kogut, B., & Singh, H. (1988). The effect of national culture on choice of entry mode. *Journal of International Business Studies, 19*, 411–432.

Levinthal, D. A., & Fichman, M. (1988). Dynamics of interorganizational attachments: Auditor-client relationships. *Administrative Science Quarterly, 33*, 345–369.

Levinthal, D. A., & March, J. G. (1993). The myopia of learning. *Strategic Management Journal, 14*, 94–112.

Li, J. (1995). Foreign entry and survival: Effects of strategic choices on performance in international markets. *Strategic Management Journal, 16*, 333–351.

Liebeskind, J. P., Oliver, A. L., Zucker, L., & Brewer, M. (1996). Social networks, learning and flexibility: Sourcing scientific knowledge in new biotechnology firms. *Organization Science, 7*, 428-443.

Lincoln, J. R. (1984). Analyzing relations in dyads, *Sociological Methods and Research, 13*, 45–76.

Lyles, M. A. (1988). Learning among joint venture sophisticated firms. *Management International Review, 28* (special issue), 85–98.

March, J. G. (1991). Exploration and exploitation in organizational learning. *Organization Science, 2*, 71–87.

Miller, D. (1990). *The Icarus Paradox*. New York: HarperCollins.

Miner, A. S., Kim, J., Holzinger, I. W., & Haunschild, P. (1999). Fruits of failure: Organizational failure and population-level learning. In: A. S. Miner & P. Anderson (Eds), *Population-Level Learning and Industry Change: Advances in Strategic Mangement*, Vol. 16 (pp. 187–220). Stamford CT: JAI.

Mitchell, W. (1994). The dynamics of evolving markets: The effects of business sales and age on dissolutions and divestitures. *Administrative Science Quarterly, 39*, 575–602.

Mitchell, W., Shaver, M. J., & Yeung, B. (1994). Foreign entrant survival and foreign market share: Canadian companies' experience in the United States medical sector markets. *Strategic Management Journal, 15*, 555–567.

Mowery, D. C., Oxley, J. E., & Silverman. B. (1996). Strategic alliances and interfirm knowledge transfer, *Strategic Management Journal, 17*, (winter special issue), 77–91.

Nelson, R. R., & Winter, S. G. (1982). *An Evolutionary Theory of Economic Change*. Cambridge MA: Harvard University Press.

Park, S. H., & Russo, M. V. (1996). When competition eclipses cooperation: An event history analysis of joint venture failure. *Management Science, 42*, 875–890.

Pennings, J. M., Barkema, H. G., & Douma, S. (1994). Organizational learning and diversification. *Academy of Management Journal, 37*, 608-640.

Podolny, J. M. (1993). A status-based model of market competition. *American Journal of Sociology, 98*, 829–872.

Rohwer, G. (1995). *TDA (Transitional Data Analysis)* 5.2. Florence: European University Institute.

Scott, J. T. (2001). Designing Multimarket-Contact Hypothesis Tests: Patent Citations and Multimarket Contact in the Product and Innovation Markets of the Chemicals Industry, In: J. A. C. Baum & H. R. Greve (Eds), *Multiunit Organization and Multimarket Strategy: Advances in Strategic Management,* Vol. 18, (pp. 175–203). Oxford UK: JAI Press.

Shan, W., Walker, G., & Kogut, B. (1994). Interfirm cooperation and startup innovation in the biotechnology industry. *Strategic Management Journal, 15*, 387–394.

Simonin, B. L. (1997). The importance of collaborative know-how: An empirical test of the learning organization. *Academy of Management Journal, 40*, 1150–1174.

Simonin, B. L., & Helleloid. D. (1993). Do organizations learn? An empirical test of organizational learning in international strategic alliances. In: D. Moore (Ed.), *Academy of Management Best Paper Proceedings*, (pp. 222–226).

Singh, K., & Mitchell, W. (1996). Precarious collaboration: Business survival after partners shut down or form new partnerships. *Strategic Management Journal, 17* (Summer Special Issue), 99–115.

Stuart, T. E., & Podolny, J. M. (1996). Local search and the evolution of technological capabilities. *Strategic Management Journal, 17* (Summer Special Issue), 21–38.

Williamson, O. E. (1985). *The Economic Institutions of Capitalism: Firms, Markets, and Relational Contracting*. New York: Free Press.

DYNAMICS OF KNOWLEDGE TRANSFER AMONG MULTIMARKET COMPETITORS

Christopher M. Cassidy and David Loree

ABSTRACT

This paper addresses the topic of knowledge transfer between firms that meet in multiple markets. Theoretical arguments are developed regarding the issues thought to influence the process of knowledge transfer between multimarket firms, in general, and also regarding the emergence and influence of macrocultures on this process. We use a structural equivalence lens to develop this theory, suggesting that multimarket competitors are likely to share macrocultures to the degree that their markets overlap. The structural equivalence of multimarket competitors influences the direction that they are likely to look for knowledge resources.

Multiunit Organization and Multimarket Strategy, Volume 18, pages 141–174
ISBN: 0-7623-0721-8

INTRODUCTION

The purpose of this chapter is to theoretically examine knowledge transfer dynamics between firms that interact in multiple markets. We focus on the basic question, "How does multimarket contact affect interfirm knowledge transfer?" While the literature streams associated with multimarket interactions (Baum & Korn, 1996; Bernheim & Whinston, 1990; Chen, 1996; Gimeno & Woo, 1996; Phillips & Mason, 1992) and interfirm knowledge transfer (Cohen & Levinthal, 1990; Grant, 1996; Winter, 1987) are strong and growing, the combination of the two streams is under-developed and should benefit from purposeful integration.

The effect of multimarket contact has important implications for knowledge transfer. Previous literature on multimarket contact has primarily concerned itself with the antecedents and consequences of strategic decision making under conditions of competition and mutual forbearance (Baum & Korn, 1996; Gimeno & Woo, 1996; Phillips & Mason, 1992). The literature on knowledge transfer is rooted in the knowledge-based view of organizations and is seen as one way for firms to acquire strategic assets that might be used to create a sustainable competitive advantage (Almeida, 1996; Barney, 1997). Knowledge transfer is thus one way to provide a firm with resources essential for competition with rivals. But while knowledge assets are resources necessary for competition between rivals, these resources are generally transferred between organizations through cooperative processes. The dynamic tension between market competition and cooperative knowledge acquisition has interesting and important implications given the prevalence of multimarket organizations in many industries. If Grant's claim is correct that knowledge is "the critical input in production and primary source of value" (Grant, 1996, 112), this begs the development of theory addressing how knowledge is transferred between multiunit organizations that participate and compete in multiple markets.

Markets And Multimarket Contact

The concept of markets and multimarket contact needs elaboration before discussion of knowledge transfer in such a context. Firms exchange goods and services for their mutual benefit in a variety of markets. Firms also compete for trading partners with their rivals in these same markets.[1] Traditional examples of markets tend to focus on one dimension of the exchange relationship (Scherer & Ross, 1990; Walters, 1993), such as the market for a specific product (Stigler & Sherwin, 1985) or a restricted geographic market (Elzinga & Hogarty, 1978). Traditional thinking on markets would suggest that two firms that sell similar products or operate in the same geographic area operate in the same market. While this traditional definition is conceptually easy to grasp, it is also overly simplistic.

Abell's (1980) discussion of markets provides a more precise definition of and distinction between different types of markets. Specifically, "product markets" are focused on similar products and services, the technology needed to produce these products, and the consumers that use these particular products (Abell, 1980). Abell's definition implies that a product market does not focus solely on "products," but rather all the linkages in the production process or value chain that produces a specific product (Porter, 1985). This includes, for instance, the suppliers of input materials, technology and manufacturing methods, distribution and marketing channels, channels of information, and consumers who will purchase the product. Extrapolating from Abell's (1980) definition of product markets, we can construct definitions for other types of markets focused on additional characteristics of exchange relationships, such as geography, suppliers, distributors, etc. For instance, geographic markets could be conceptualized around the specific regions served, but would also include information on the various products consumed in each region, the consumers inhabiting each region, channels of distribution that serve each region, and the constraints imposed by political and economic regulation within each region. This view of markets can be applied to individual firms, sets of firms, industries and economies, and allows us to aggregate various product markets as a product multimarket. The creation of complete multimarkets centered on the traditional market dimensions will in the aggregate describe the entire market domain (Baum & Korn, 1996). This is a broader conceptualization of markets than is generally used, and is consistent with the conceptualizations of both markets and channels provided by van Wegberg & van Witteloostuijn (this volume). Their distinction between markets and channels reflects the traditional conceptualization of exchange markets as different from the channels through which exchange occurs, but their chapter provides further discussion of this topic.

Multimarket situations provide a valuable concept because they force us to consider the interconnected relationships involved in resource exchange by addressing the question of who wants what, where, when, and how. This emphasizes markets separate from but connected to the markets under primary consideration. Additionally, the aggregate of product (or any other specific dimension) multimarkets will contain all information on all of the other multimarkets because of the overlap contained in each multimarket. Market contact refers to the interactions of firms in a specific market. For instance two firms might have market contact with each other in the market for a product that they both sell. Multimarket contact refers to the situation when firms meet each other in more than one market. More precisely, this refers to the interactions of firms across at least two markets. Firms that produce two similar products have two product markets in common. Firms that service the same geographic regions share geographic markets. Multimarket contact, just like multimarkets, can be conceptualized as a continuous measure of market overlap with another firm. For most discussions and comparisons of multimarket contact we do not need to examine the entire market domain of the firm. We can restrict ourselves to the specific multimarkets in which the two firms interact. While Walters (1993) and other antitrust scholars emphasize the importance of product and geographic markets for most questions concerning firm cooperation and competition, other dimensions may be appropriate to specific inquiries.

CHARACTERISTICS OF MULTIMARKET INTERACTIONS

Up to now we have discussed firm interactions without specifically defining what is meant by the term "interaction." Our use of this term refers to the cooperative or rivalrous behaviors of firms. These two behavioral interactions are distinguished from outcome interdependencies, such as mutualism and competition, which develop through patterns of firm interactions (Hawley, 1950). Intuitively we understand that firms can engage in a number of behavioral interactions that can include varying degrees of cooperation and rivalry. Cooperation will exist when firms perceive mutual benefit in the exchange relationship and interact directly with each other (Axelrod, 1984). Rivalry will exist when essential resources are constrained in shared markets (Chen, 1996; Porter, 1980). As Chen (1996) points out, the degree of rivalry between pairs of firms is both directional and asymmetrical, meaning that two interacting firms might perceive different amounts of rivalry with each other. The same can be said of cooperation.

Cooperation and rivalry are not mutually exclusive behaviors (Chen, 1996), with fierce rivals sometimes cooperating with each other for mutual benefit (Steiner & Steiner, 2000). In 1991, Apple Computer and IBM engaged in a joint venture in an attempt to regain technological and market leadership in the personal computer market (Coale, 1991). Given the intensity of competition between the two firms just one year earlier, a joint venture seemed unlikely (Parker, 1990). Despite this cooperation, each would still compete with the other in the PC industry with new product innovations created in the joint venture. Given that cooperative and rivalrous interactions are not exclusive, rivalry and cooperation should each be conceptualized as distinct constructs. It should be noted that the general use, and distinction between, of the terms rivalry, rivals, competition, and competitors is not standardized. Scott (this volume) addresses what we refer to as rivalry using slightly different terminology, distinguishing between *rivalrous-competition* and *non-rivalrous competition* as conditions that highlight the degree to which one firm's actions directly influence another firm in a market. Van Wegberg and Van Witteloostuijn (this volume) also highlight this idea of direct and indirect market contact in a slightly different way by focusing on the presence or absence of intermediary firms. These views complement our general discussion of multimarket interaction.

Cooperative interactions involve direct exchanges between firms and will be a continuous function of perceived multimarket exchange benefits whereas rivalrous interactions do not necessarily involve direct exchanges. Rivalrous interactions, such as competition for resources and customers, are transmitted through the indirect effects of the market, such as through pricing and production choices. For example, consider two rivals selling similar products, produced with similar technology, marketed in the same region, to similar consumers, and using similar resources. While each is subject to the same constrained markets, their direct interactions will be with suppliers, customers, distributors, and other symbionts with which they have beneficial relationships (Abrahamson & Fombrun, 1994; Hawley, 1950), not specifically with each other. On the other hand, cooperative interactions between firms are direct interactions. Only when two rivals cooperate in a mutually beneficial effort, such as in an exchange of technical information or other form of joint venture, will they directly interact. Competitive versus mutualistic outcome interdependencies will be a function of the continuous measures of rivalry and cooperation (Hawley, 1950).

THE KNOWLEDGE TRANSFER PROCESS

Knowledge creation and knowledge transfer are highly interrelated. Firms that need knowledge either create knowledge or they acquire (or transfer) knowledge from other sources, but most do some combination of both. A firm's ongoing effort to create knowledge resources through research and development activities is expected to both create new knowledge and enable the firm to better acquire knowledge from outside the firm (Cohen & Levinthal, 1990). New knowledge resources are the result of successfully combining or extrapolating from existing knowledge resources. Newly created knowledge resources may provide a bridge to understanding external knowledge resources, in which case the firm can acquire such resources. Acquired knowledge resources can fill in the gaps between existing knowledge, and thus spark the creation of new knowledge within the firm (Cohen & Levinthal, 1990).

An example from the Integrated Circuit (IC) industry illustrates this process. During the 1950s, the manufacturers of semiconductors tried to discover a process to make the integrated circuit commercially viable. Fairchild Semiconductor had previously developed a manufacturing technique called the planar process. Fairchild combined its planar process with acquired knowledge about basic IC technology to create a commercially viable production process the framework of which is still in use today. In short, Fairchild demonstrated that internally developed knowledge could be combined with externally acquired knowledge resources to create new knowledge.

Intent, Opportunity, and Capability

There are three characteristics associated with knowledge acquiring firms that facilitate its transfer: intent, opportunity and capability (Greve, 1996; Hamel, 1991). Intent to acquire knowledge assesses the firm's desire or propensity to discover or seek out and absorb knowledge (Hamel, 1991). Explicit goals or an implicit culture of knowledge acquisition, reinforced by reward systems, create strong organizational incentives to acquire valuable knowledge resources. Without the organizational intent to acquire knowledge, some knowledge might still inadvertently diffuse across organizations, but is unlikely to be put to systematic use for the benefit of the organization. Opportunity is a reflection of a firm's access to available knowledge, and can manifest itself through proximity to and contact with other organizations or access to other sources of knowledge (Audretsch, 1998). Firms that interact across greater distances have a reduced opportunity to transfer knowledge. Firms that operate over a larger geographic scope or cross many different product markets increase the opportunity to acquire knowledge. Firms that erect procedural or institutional barriers that restrict the transfer of knowledge reduce or eliminate opportunity, virtually assuring that knowledge transfer will not take place. Capability to acquire knowledge is an assessment of a firm's ability to perceive, understand, and meaningfully use such a resource. While the contagion and diffusion literature uses the more passive term, susceptibility, we use the more active term, capability (Greve, 1996). Cohen and Levinthal (1990) argue that firms must possess knowledge resources that are sufficiently similar to be capable of knowledge transfer. Inherent in the capability to acquire knowledge is the ability to both 'identify' the specific knowledge resource desired and the ability to 'specify' or distinguish it from other similar types of knowledge resources. This element of capability ensures that firms understand what knowledge resources they are looking for and will recognize those resources when exposed to them. The absence of capability virtually assures that knowledge transfer will not take place.

These characteristics, intent, opportunity, and capability, interact to place limits on the ability of firms to transfer knowledge between each other. Intent directs an organization toward sources of knowledge that are perceived as useful and relevant to its current resource needs while limiting transfer with firms whose knowledge is viewed of little use. Market interaction, whether cooperative or rivalrous, will provide the opportunity to observe the usefulness and relevance of knowledge, and therefore influence the intent to transfer knowledge. Cohen and Levinthal's (1990) observation that common knowledge resources are necessary to enable transfer capability further reduces the pool of firms that will transfer knowledge to those that deal with similar knowledge resources. And similar knowledge resources will tend to be found in firms that share markets using similar technologies and producing similar products. Firms in differing markets, using different technologies and producing different products, will neither have sufficient knowledge overlap to enable transfer knowledge capability nor will they perceive the other firm's knowledge resources to be useful or relevant to their operations.

Market Mechanisms For Knowledge Transfer

Provided a firm has some combination of intent, opportunity, and capability, knowledge transfer can occur. Cooperative knowledge transfer can be accomplished through formal or informal market mechanisms. A formal market transfer of knowledge resources involves mechanisms such as the sale or licensing of knowledge, joint venture development of knowledge by investing partners, and mergers and acquisitions of target firms possessing desired knowledge resources. An informal market transfer of knowledge can occur when the members of various firms transfer knowledge among themselves in professional or social situations under conditions where reciprocal transfers are expected. Both formal and informal market mechanisms are used to capture the economic benefits of knowledge creation and transfer. The failure to adequately capture the economic benefits of knowledge transfer with market mechanisms opens the possibility that firms may act to restrict knowledge transfer to prevent free riding.[2]

MULTIMARKET EFFECTS ON RIVALRY AND COOPERATION

We expect that differing degrees of market overlap should be associated with changing levels in both cooperation and rivalry. When two firms are dependent on constrained resources in a particular market, they are likely to experience rivalry due to resource limitations. When constrained resources exist in multiple markets, rivalry will intensify but only up to a point. At some point market overlap will increase to the degree where further rivalry is harmful to each firm. Further increases in multimarket contact beyond this point decreases rivalry, resulting in an inverted U-shaped relationship between multimarket contact and rivalry.

As the level of multimarket overlap increases, we would expect different degrees of cooperative behavior due to the interaction between multimarket overlap and knowledge transfer. Firms that are separated on geographic or consumer market dimensions but share common technology or products have an incentive to cooperate. As multimarket overlap increases, rivalry increases, and firms will have incentives to decrease cooperation as they struggle to obtain scarce resources and deny resources to their rivals. However, at increasing levels of multimarket contact the marginal benefits of cooperation for knowledge resources exceed the marginal costs of rivalry. At this level of multimarket overlap, firms find cooperation beneficial and engage in mutual forbearance, suggesting an U-shaped relationship between multimarket contact and cooperation. The next section will develop this U-shaped relationship further as it pertains to knowledge transfer in the multimarket context.

Mutual forbearance (Chen, 1996; Gimeno & Woo, 1996) is a tacit cooperative response to high levels of rivalry and is intended to benefit the firms that engage in forbearance. As conceived by antitrust authorities and economists (Friedman, 1983), mutual forbearance may result from direct firm interactions (collusion), or it may result from implicit selection of the Cournot-optimal response given a rival's actions (Scherer & Ross, 1990; Tirole, 1988). For example, firms that observe a decrease in profits associated with increasing rivalry will reduce rivalry and increase mutual forbearance. While such cooperative interactions by multimarket competitors are discouraged by antitrust laws and normative beliefs about the beneficial effects of competition, they will not be completely eliminated if cooperation results in increased profitability (Walters, 1993).

KNOWLEDGE TRANSFER IN
A MULTIMARKET CONTEXT

The preceding discussion of markets, rivalry, and cooperation, provides the necessary elements to develop a perspective of knowledge transfer in a multimarket context. Given that knowledge may be a valuable, inimitable, and rare strategic resource (Barney, 1997; Grant, 1996), we assume that a unique market exists for its exchange (Ekelund & Tollison, 1994). However, unlike other firm inputs that are exchanged directly between symbionts, knowledge is a good transferred between competitors. Cohen and Levinthal's (1990) absorptive capacity argument addresses this process. For one firm to have the capability to acquire knowledge from another firm, the first firm must possess elements of a common body of knowledge with which to interpret the new knowledge. It is more likely that similar firms, such as industry rivals, will possess the knowledge necessary to understand and interpret newly acquired knowledge from each other. Given that similar firms are more likely to speak the same language and therefore are more capable of interfirm knowledge transfer, it seems logical to further explore the role of multimarket contact in moderating this relationship.

Multimarket Interaction And Industry Evolution

When an industry is in its infancy and the number of participating firms is small, we might expect all or most of the firms to interact cooperatively and exchange knowledge, either formally or informally, with each other. In the early years, many members of these firms probably possessed similar educational backgrounds and industry experience. If proximal, they may even worked together or socialize together. Dependency on new knowledge during industry infancy would tend to increase interfirm cooperation, and the common stocks of knowledge held by rivals would make them more capable of transferring the knowledge among themselves. If resource munificence remained high, and demand for industry output exceeded supply, it is likely that rivalry would remain low. Rivalry would remain low until industry growth caused resource scarcity within one of the many developing markets (Hannon & Freeman, 1977).

As an industry grows, the number of firms increases and the network of potential firm interactions becomes increasingly complex. Aside from numerical complexity, product and geographic market expansion and diversification increases the complexity of the network of firm interactions while reducing the knowledge benefits of those interactions. As the industry network becomes more densely packed, rivalry will increase and firms might become less likely to cooperate with each other. These factors contribute to a reduction in the total number of cooperative links with other firms as an industry grows. Those firms that continue to cooperatively interact would likely be those that have dependencies on similar knowledge resources. Just as Chen (1996) pointed out with regard to competitive interactions, cooperation and knowledge transfer between firms does not have to be symmetric. It is possible for one firm to benefit strongly from the actions of a second firm while the second firm is almost unaffected by the first. The small retailer is likely to see the large wholesaler as both a major symbiotic supplier and a major rival, while the large wholesaler is likely to see the small retailer only as a minor symbiotic customer. One firm views its relationship with another firm independently and differently from the way the other firms might view that same relationship.

Rivalrous Interaction And Knowledge Transfer

When rivalry occurs, it has the effect of suppressing both cooperative interaction and intentional knowledge transfer between firms. In addition to rivalry suppressing cooperative interaction on its own, there are normative and legal expectations against cooperation between rivals (Walters, 1993). These expectations against cooperation tend to suppress formal mechanisms for knowledge transfer.

Rivalry also acts to suppress informal market mechanisms of knowledge transfer. Dependency on constrained resources creates situations in which firms will bid up the price of the constrained resources. Firms react by attempting to reduce waste and increase efficiency across the entire firm. One area where firms might perceive excessive waste is in the informal market mechanisms of knowledge transfer. If a firm has previously allowed its rivals access to its costly knowledge resources through non-market mechanisms, and perceives that the exchange is not symmetric or that the exchange subsidizes a rival's operations, the firm may respond by shutting down non-market transfer mechanisms. Plugging the knowledge leaks in a firm is achieved in part by secrecy agreements and restricted access to knowledge resources (Kochen, 1994). Reduction in knowledge transfers is one sided. Specifically, it does not reduce the demand for knowledge resources by other firms, but it does reduce the supply of outgoing knowledge. In markets where the demand for knowledge is high but where firms have taken steps to reduce the supply, conditions may exist where firms seek out surreptitious or accidental knowledge transfers through unrecognized informal channels, the recruitment of rival employees, or industrial espionage (Rufford, 1999).

When firms can be reasonably certain that they will recapture the economic benefits of knowledge, there may be strategic motivations for the intentional spillover of knowledge resources. For instance, if knowledge is, or soon will be, legally protected through patents, it might be in a firm's best interest to encourage its use and assimilation by other firms, who will eventually have to pay royalties for its use. In this case, firms with the intent and capability to acquire knowledge would be provided with the opportunity. The knowledge-spilling firm will be able to capture the economic benefits through the legal protection of the patenting process.

Cooperative Interaction and Knowledge Transfer

When potential rivals are insulated from each other by market separation, they may not perceive each other as a threat, in which case there may be incentives for inter-firm collaboration. The implication of this is that non-competing firms may have an increased incentive for knowledge transfer. They may cooperate in order to reduce the overall cost of knowledge creation and acquisition. This is especially likely if they utilize the same or similar knowledge resources. In the integrated circuit industry, for example, two firms might produce two different products that are purchased by the same consumers (e.g. analog and digital circuits, which are often integrated into complete systems). The two products are complementary in that they are sold in different product markets, and there might be common manufacturing techniques and other IC specific knowledge resources that the two firms can share without the worry that cooperation will be detrimental. They essentially share the costs of knowledge and provide each other with a below market cost advantage. These mutualistic relations can create strong and lasting interactions that allow both firms to deal with rivals more effectively.

Situations may also occur where benefits accrue to only one partner in a cooperative pair. While possible, such a relationship is generally unstable. In such commensalistic relationships, the first firm has strong incentives to find some way to either convert the unidirectional benefit to a bi-directional benefit through some formal or informal market mechanism, or to discontinue cooperation with the second firm (Gibbons, 1992). Commensalism is only stable if the first firm cannot control the knowledge spillovers. An example of uncontrollable spillover benefits occurs in advertising, where larger firms that advertise benefit the smaller firms that do not advertise. In such a case, the spillover benefits might be limited through more selective and controlled advertising, however the costs of more selective advertising might be greater than the spillover losses.

Group Level Factors That Affect Knowledge Transfer

A firm-level lens provides a logical starting point in understanding the interactions between firms that facilitate the transfer of knowledge, but a richer understanding of these dynamics becomes apparent when we switch to a group-level lens. There are two broad and overlapping theoretical perspectives on the development and strength of groups within industries: strategic groups and macrocultures. Both streams of literature attempt to classify industry sub-groupings and the firm interactions that result.

The study of relationships between industry members is inherently a study of the set of dyadic interactions between those members that interact and those that do not (Baum & Korn, 1999). In infant industries, or those with a small number of firms, we might expect every organization to interact with every other organization. This expectation is less likely as the number of firms in the industry increases. Specifically, as the number of firms within an industry increases, only the most valuable interactions will be maintained. This leads to the formation of subgroups of firms, with pockets of intense interaction within the subgroup while interaction with firms outside the subgroup is less likely (Abrahamson & Fombrun, 1994).

Strategic Groups

Originating with Caves and Porter (1977), the concept of strategic groups has been discussed and debated for over two decades (Porter, 1980). Strategic groups are theorized as subgroups within an industry where members are grouped by similar strategies or other similar strategic dimensions (Porter, 1980). Each of these strategic dimensions could be mapped to a resource market providing a conceptual link between strategic groups and multimarkets. Rivalry is expected to be stronger between firms within a strategic group than between firms that cross group boundaries. As originally conceived, strategic groups were thought to result from entry and mobility barriers between the different subgroups in an industry (Caves & Porter, 1977). These barriers divide industries into subsets of firms that could engage in collusive behavior to earn economic rents. Performance differences between various strategic groups might attract new entrants, but the presence of barriers prevents free access. This ability for strategic groups to earn economic rents might also be explained by the cooperative interaction of mutual forbearance in the multimarket context discussed earlier. This early I/O based conceptualization also suggests that performance within strategic groups should be relatively homogeneous. Firm interactions based on this older view of strategic groups tend to emphasize competition and under-emphasize cooperative interactions (Caves & Porter, 1977). Relatively recent developments in I/O and game theory literature identify specific situations where either competitive or cooperative interactions will provide the greatest benefits (Tirole, 1988).

A more recent conceptualization of strategic groups, informed by the managerial cognition literature, suggests that managers focus their attention on industry players that are perceived to be within their group (Reger & Huff, 1993). Managers are likely to view firms that are perceived to be outside their own strategic groups as background effects. Selective perception of competitors allows managers to more effectively scan and process the enormous amount of available environmental information. This conceptualization based on cognitive strategic groups suggests that cooperation and knowledge transfer should be more likely within groups than across groups. Cognitive barriers to entry will serve as barriers to knowledge transfer because firms will ignore others that they perceive to be outside their strategic group, in turn reducing the interactions that might facilitate between group knowledge transfer. In short, organizations will blind themselves to knowledge available outside their perceived group.

Metaphors to social processes have also had a tremendous impact on theories of group formation. Granovetter's (1985) discussion of firms as embedded in social networks that limit completely free action is strongly informed by our own experiences with the constraints of social interaction. For example, while the limits of what is socially acceptable are continuously being pushed back, there are still taboos, such as those against public nudity, swearing, and violence, that constrain our behavior. Institutional theory (DiMaggio & Powell, 1983) and the concept of macrocultures (Abrahamson & Fombrun, 1994) are strongly influenced by this comparison to social networks. The concept of macrocultures also focuses on cognitive processes, but is somewhat different from a strategic groups lens. Strategic groups focuses on inter-organizational similarities based on barriers to entry and strategic dimensions, while macrocultures focuses on systems of perceived inter-organizational similarities based on shared values, frames of reference, philosophies, norms, expectations, rites, rituals and structures (Abrahamson & Fombrun, 1994).

As an illustration of the influence of macrocultures, Abrahamson and Fombrun (1994) cite the example of the failure of U.S. domestic auto producers to perceive Japanese and European producers as viable rivals until many U.S. firms had lost significant market share. Domestic auto producers perceived foreign producers as less similar, operating in different product markets, buying from different suppliers, servicing different customers, and therefore ignored them. Even when the economic barriers between foreign and domestic auto manufacturers decreased and market overlap increased, domestic producers still perceived foreign producers as different enough to cognitively exclude them on the basis of group interdependencies. The lessons of the U.S. domestic auto producers lends credibility to the macrocultural explanation for groups by suggesting that, under certain conditions, social factors may have effects that overpower the economic effects of competition.

A similar example lies in IBM's failure to fully exploit the emerging microcomputer market. IBM had a difficult time developing its first PC due to the firm's slow moving and tight reined bureaucracy. In 1980 William Lowe, the PC project manager, reported to John Opel, soon to become IBM's president, "We can't do this within the culture of IBM." (Chposky & Leonsis, 1988). Opel authorized the unthinkable, giving William Lowe unprecedented autonomy from IBM's internal regulations in order to get a PC to market (Langlois, 1992). Given IBM's technical capability, market power and reputation in the business computing industry, it should have been able to dominate the PC industry, yet it didn't (Kirkpatrick, 1996). Despite its success in standardizing the PC market, IBM under-anticipated demand for its new XT machines by 500% in 1983 and failed to utilize learning curve pricing, actions that left it open to competition by PC clone makers (Langlois, 1992). Its undisputed product failures include the PC Jr. in 1984, the PC portable in 1984, a work station in 1986, and its first laptop in 1986 (Chposky & Leonsis, 1988). Although intended to meet or counter competition, these product missteps demonstrate a myopic misunderstanding of the speed of technological innovation, consumer demand, and the competitive moves of other firms in the PC market (Dickson & Kehoe, 1992; Fitzgerald & Klett, 1994). IBM clearly had the technical capability and resources to dominate the field, yet was unable to do so, in part due to the macrocultural lens developed in and nurtured by its industry (Demarzo, 1993; Haynes, 1994; Zachmann, 1988). While the lessons of both situations could suggest that they correctly judged their respective competitive threats and that their failures were solely in implementation, a strong case can be made that macrocultural blinders prevented accurate perceptions of the competitive threat and that the domestic automobile producers and IBM acted appropriately given their filtered perceptions (Manasian, 1993).

The macroculture explanation of groupings that develop within industries directly addresses the processes of invention and innovation diffusion, arguing that innovations are created in inter-organizational settings that involve symbiotic exchanges between specialized organizations (Abrahamson & Fombrun, 1994; Tushman & Rosenkopf, 1992). Which organizations are involved in these exchange relationships is at least partially a function of the macroculture binding them together. The strength of a macroculture's boundary influences whether or not member organizations will look outside their group for these exchange relationships, with top managers being "less likely to pay attention to the innovative activities of organizations outside their macroculture because they consensually agree that these organizations are different or unrelated" (Abrahamson & Fombrun, 1993, 744). In short, we would expect the knowledge transfer process to be bounded in relation to the strength of the macroculture, with organizations being more likely to exchange knowledge with others that are part of their macroculture and less likely to exchange knowledge with those outside.

A closer look at the competitive-economic model and the macrocultural-social model reveals some interesting differences, especially as they relate to knowledge transfer. Economic competition between firms appears to be a strong force, in that firms that ignore economic forces such as competition are, in general, often punished. Competitive interdependence is a strong force because it compels a firm to react or suffer. The equilibrium models provided by economics tell us that we should expect firms to increase rivalry in proportion to the amount of the increase in competition (Mas-Colell, Whinston & Green, 1995). On the other hand, if competition decreases, we should expect firms to decrease their rivalry. It matters little if competitive interaction is gradually introduced or gradually withdrawn, or quickly introduced or quickly withdrawn. Firms are predicted to modify their response in accordance with the contemporaneous level of economic competition. Economic theory predicts, in short, a symmetrical response. The symmetry lies in the equilibrium assumptions about the firm's rational response to competition (Ekelund & Tollison, 1994). For competitive responses using economic models, we could say that the responses are independent of previous history, or essentially path independent. In short, a specified level of competition should compel an appropriate response in rivalry.

On the other hand, the perceived interdependency effects of macrocultures seem more resistant to change. The domestic auto industry failed to notice foreign auto producers as a threat despite significant economic losses (Abrahamson & Fombrun, 1994). The perception of foreign producers as viable rivals lagged their competitive impact, resulting in a loss of market share. Even in the face of economic impact, the perception that foreign producers were not part of the macroculture prevented domestic producers from action. As a thought experiment, we might imagine that if foreign auto manufacturers decided to withdraw from the U.S. market, it might take several years for domestic producers to recognize their withdrawal from the market and react accordingly to the reduced competition. Both in cases of actual market entry and in hypothetical market withdrawal, we have observed and would expect a lag between action and response due to the social perceptions of perceived group interdependencies. If the perception of interdependencies persists after economic interaction is eliminated, this suggests that history is important in explaining firm and industry outcomes (Arthur, 1989).

The Structural Equivalence of Multimarket Organizations

To this point, we have explained cooperative and rivalrous interactions, and the basic process of knowledge transfer that occurs between organizations in the context of multimarkets. We have also discussed how the emergence and presence of macrocultures within an industry can constrain this dynamic process, but we have yet to address the role of multimarket competitors in the development of macrocultures. As Abrahamson and Fombrun (1994) point out, managers can rank the degree of competition expressed by many of the organizations within their industry along many different dimensions, including geographic proximity, strategic profile, technology, and size. One characteristic that has yet to be explicitly considered in such a conceptualization is the degree of multimarket overlap experienced with other firms in the industry. We propose that the degree of structural equivalence that exists between multimarket competitors contributes to their manager's perceptions of a shared macroculture. While our ideas regarding the structural equivalence of multimarket competitors are applicable to different market dimensions, the line of thought we will develop is centered on firms that compete in multiple international markets.

Burt's structural equivalence theory (1987) argues that firms do not have to directly interact in order to influence each other's behavior. While it is possible that direct interaction will influence each other's behavior (basically a cohesion argument), structural equivalence takes a slightly different path towards the same outcome. Structurally equivalent organizations occupy the same position in the social structure of the industry in which they compete, and so are proximate to the extent that they have the same pattern of relations as other organizations (Burt, 1987). In structural equivalence models, the frame of reference shifts from pair-wise dyadic interactions to a big picture view of the social structure in which firms exist. Within this social structure, organizations can be viewed as more or less similar to each other with respect to their relationships with the various symbionts that comprise the system. This view suggests that organizations are not the source of actions as much as they are the vehicles for structurally induced action (Burt, 1987).

Structural equivalence theory can be easily extended to multimarket situations. The various structures used by multimarket organizations to compete in multiple markets provide linkages with perhaps not identical, but similar, symbionts in each market. While the original definition required two organizations to have exactly the same pattern of relationships as each other in order to be considered structurally equivalent (Lorrain & White, 1971), such a constraint seems unnecessary and unrealistic. Instead, we propose that structural equivalence between two firms can be viewed as a continuous construct. In short, instead of asking, "whether or not two firms are structurally equivalent," we focus on the question of "how structurally equivalent are two firms?" Such a view uses the constructs of multimarket competition (e.g. market overlap, resource similarity, market commonality) in a less "strategic" sense than is typically the case. With a structural equivalence lens we move beyond focusing primarily on firm interactions, and outcome interdependencies, and instead consider other issues such as the development of shared beliefs and macrocultures that bind multimarket competitors.

We can hypothesize a straightforward multimarket situation to help clarify our perspective. Consider an industry experiencing the initial stages of globalization with the appearance of, say, two international markets beyond the initial market of the industry's inception. Figure 1 illustrates both the market overlap and the structural equivalence of Firms X and Y. In this case, we have illustrated a situation of complete market overlap and structural equivalence between these two firms, something referred to as a *position* in the network literature (Burt, 1987). The positions of Firms X and Y are structurally equivalent because of their similar exchange relationships with comparable symbionts, but it's key to point out that these symbiotic relationships within each market do not necessarily have to directly link Firms X and Y together. Specifically, Firm X and Firm Y might actually pursue different customers in Market A such that they do not directly overlap, but it is the comparability of the customers (as symbionts for both firms) that facilitates the structural equivalence argument.

Increasing structural equivalence between two firms is argued to increase competition, similarity in beliefs, and the homogeneity of the macroculture that binds these two organizations (Abrahamson & Fombrun, 1994). As discussed earlier, the stronger the macroculture binding firms together, the less likely managers of these firms are to look outside its boundary for knowledge and innovations. Pulling these perspectives together allows us to comment on the

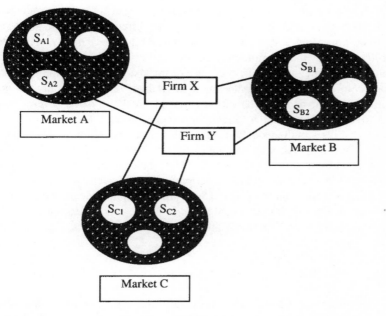

Fig. 1.

probability of whether or not a given firm will consider another firm as a source of knowledge. Specifically, the structural equivalence of firms, and resulting macroculture homogeneity present between them, increases the likelihood of a firm considering another as a source of knowledge.

AN EMPIRICAL EXEMPLAR

Our ideas regarding the factors that influence the knowledge transfer process among firms participating in multiple geographic markets are supported with an empirical illustration from the worldwide integrated circuit industry, a brief history of which follows. The integrated circuit (IC) industry developed as a result of innovation within the semiconductor industry, which in turn began with the invention of the transistor in 1947 by William Schockley, John Bardeen and Walter Brattain at Bell Labs. Similar to the vacuum tubes that preceded, the transistor allowed amplification of electrical signals but required less power, generated less heat, and was smaller. By 1952, difficulties in the manufacturing process had been overcome and active semiconductor production began.

The IC period of the semiconductor industry began with the introduction of two technological discontinuities: the integrated circuit and the planar process. The first introduced a completely new product to the industry. The second radically altered the manufacturing process of semiconductors. Until the development of the integrated circuit, use of transistors had been limited because of the requirement that separate components had to be physically connected on printed circuit boards. The introduction of the IC allowed several components to be combined on a single chip and increased the reliability of the products while simultaneously feeding the miniaturization process. The IC was an innovation that was commercially unviable until Fairchild's introduction of the planar process (Braun & MacDonald, 1982). After a very brief period of ferment, the industry adopted silicon over germanium as the semiconducting material of choice. The resulting technological regime consisted of the use of silicon as material, the planar as the manufacturing process, the IC as the product, and the integration of components and system as product concept.

Data Description:

The semiconductor industry, and specifically the subset of firms that produce integrated circuits (ICs), is an especially good candidate in which to test our argument given the higher reliance on using patents to protect intellectual property than seen in many other industries (Winter, 1987). Data for this example are drawn from the *Electronics Buyers Guide*, a source of industry information used in a number of previous studies of the semiconductor industry (Brittain, 1994; Brittain & Freeman, 1980; Hannan & Freeman, 1989). *The Electronics Buyers Guide* provides a very complete and reliable source of data for the worldwide population of merchant IC manufacturers. Brittain (1994) checked the coverage of U.S. firms relative to directories of manufacturers for the New England states, California, Arizona, and Texas (states that accounted for most of the U.S.-based firms), and found that the *Electronic Buyers Guide* included coverage for 95.9% of the firms listed in these other sources. The data were also cross-validated with another similar but more narrowly focused publication (*IC Master*). We also checked the data source for any coverage bias against non-U.S. producers by cross-referencing it with the *European Electronics Suppliers Guide* and the *Japan Company Handbook*. We found no evidence that non-U.S. firms are underrepresented in the *Electronics Buyers Guide*.

These data sources allow us to construct the total worldwide population of IC manufacturers, which consists of 254 unique organizations between 1978 and 1994. The second step in constructing our sample involves the elimination of firms from the population that do not patent their products or technologies, and therefore could not be "at risk" of either borrowing knowledge or having their knowledge borrowed through the patenting chain. This resulted in a sample of 141 unique firms used in our analysis, all of which participated in the patenting process to some degree within the time frame of the study. With respect to the construction of the yearly spells across the time frame, a firm was allowed to be at risk once they were granted their first patent. The firm remained at risk from that year forward because the firm's patent(s) provide a source of knowledge that could be borrowed and built on by another firm. Our unit of analysis was the $firm_i - firm_j - year$, where the first is the firm granted a patent and therefore able to cite others and the second is the firm whose patents are at risk of being cited. Our analysis is based on 11,738 $firm_i - firm_j - yearly$ observations.

Patent Citations as Proxies of Knowledge Transfer

To test our argument that a higher degree of multimarket contact, and hence structural equivalence, between firms is associated with a higher probability of knowledge transfer between those firms, we used a sub-sample of the IC industry consisting of firms that have patented their innovations in the U.S. Our data extend across a sixteen-year time period, from 1978 (the earliest we could obtain reliable data coverage for the firm patents in our sample) to 1994 (the point when the population seed data source, Electronics Buyers Guide, was acquired by a publisher that disrupted continuity in firm coverage). Previous work by Podolny, Stuart and Hannon (1996), and others (Almeida, 1996; Stuart & Podolny, 1996), supports the use of patents as proxies of knowledge in the semiconductor industry because of several characteristics of U.S. patenting in general and the semiconductor industry in particular. The U.S. is the primary technological marketplace in the world today, with extensive portions of that technology recorded by the U.S. patent system (Albert, Avery, Narin & McAllister, 1991). Additionally, all major innovations in the semiconductor industry have been patented in the U.S. (Wilson, Ashton & Egan, 1980).

As Cohen and Levinthal (1990) point out, firm knowledge is generated from combinations of new knowledge or extrapolations of existing knowledge. Patents document both the creation of new knowledge and the trail of preexisting knowledge from which new knowledge is derived (Griliches, 1990). Patent citations, similar to citations used to trace original ideas in academic research, trace the trail of knowledge as it is transferred between firms (Albert et al., 1991; Pavitt, 1985). These citations leave a clear trail back to the original knowledge, in effect, showing who borrows knowledge from whom (Narin, Carpenter & Woolf, 1984; Narin, Smith & Albert, 1993). Almeida (1996) also provides an extensive justification of the use of patents as proxies of knowledge in the semiconductor industry. As a reference, we have included a comprehensive justification for the use and limitations of patents as measures of knowledge transfer as an appendix to this chapter.

Geographic Market Overlap as Structural Equivalence

The integrated circuit industry has followed a globalization pattern similar to many others. What was once an industry characterized predominantly by one large market has changed over time to consist of forty-seven geographic markets located around the world. Information on each firm's participation in the markets located around the world was compiled from *The Electronics Buyers Guide* and *IC Master*. Because many firms also disclose the markets in which they participate in their 10-K or 20-F reports, spot validation of this information was possible. We used international geographic market presence to compute a continuous measure of structural equivalence using a method similar to that described in Stuart and Podolny (1996). For each firm, i, we determined the number of markets in common with another firm, j, using the equation:

$$Overlap_{ij} = \frac{\sum\limits_{m=1}^{M} i_m \times j_m}{\sum\limits_{m=1}^{M} i_m}, \forall i \neq j$$

Where i_m and j_m represent the presence of firms i and j in market, m, in a particular year. Our measure of geographic market overlap as a proxy of structural equivalence is both directional and asymmetric in the sense described by Chen (1996).

Controls

Because we are interested in testing the connection between structural equivalence and the probability of firms transferring knowledge between themselves, we need to control for other sources of heterogeneity that might provide alternative explanations for such a relationship. To that effect, we controlled for the age and size of the citing firm as a reflection of the experience and resources available to the firm. Whether these variables would be considered as either propensity or susceptibility effects might be subject to debate (Greve, 1998), but their inclusion in the model controls for the possibility that older and larger firms might be both more likely to absorb knowledge from other firms and more discerning about from whom it is absorbed. Because market size might also influence the dynamics that unfold regarding both the intent and opportunity to borrow knowledge from other firms, we also control for the worldwide consumption of ICs within each year of the study. Greve (1998) found that social similarity mattered in predicting the adoption of particular strategic positions, with organizations being more likely to mimic the actions of firms that were in markets of similar size. Along those lines, we controlled for the differences in size and age between the citing and cited firms, expecting the likelihood of knowledge transfer to decrease with increased social distance between the citing and cited firms. As a conclusive step in controlling for alternative explanations, we also included dummy variables in the analysis for each firm and year in the sample. Sorting through all of these potential firm and time effects better allows us to view our results as general effects within the industry rather than outcomes due to specific firms or time periods within our sample.

Methods and Results

We used binomial logistic regression to test the likelihood of a particular firm citing another firm's patents using PC-SAS software version 8.01, which

Table 1.   Logit Analysis Of A Firm's Probability of Citing Another
Firm's Patents
Model includes string of firm and year dummies (not shown).

Variable	Model coefficients (standard error)
Constant	2757.9
	(5035.6)
Multimarket contact	0.8783***
	(0.0823)
Log Size Of Citing Firm	0.2084**
	(0.0750)
Age Of Citing Firm	−0.7174
	(0.6558)
Difference In Size Between Two Firms	−0.1225***
(absolute value)	(0.0138)
Difference In Age Between Two Firms	−0.00774***
(absolute value)	(0.00171)
Total IC Market measured in dollars	0.0218
	(0.0394)
Likelihood Ratio X^2	2308.6829***
N	11,738

* $p < 0.05$, ** $p < 0.01$, *** $p < 0.001$

calculates the maximum likelihood estimate of the logistic regression equation in the following form: $\ln \dfrac{P_{ij}}{1 - P_{ij}} = a + BX_{ij}$, where P_{ij} is the probability that the ith firm will cite the patents of the jth firm, a is the intercept, and X_{ij} is the vector of covariates.

Table 1 illustrates the results of the analysis. Several of the variables used to control for alternative explanations of a firm's probability of borrowing knowledge from another are statistically significant, and therefore deserve comment. Firm size is positively related to the likelihood of a firm citing the patents of another, a result that seems logical given that we could expect larger firms to be able to patent more due to their relatively larger research budgets. In a broad sense, this result might also be interpreted somewhat differently. Firm size has long been associated with organizational inertia, and we might expect firms with higher degrees of inertia to be less likely to look outside for knowledge and more likely to build from within on their existing technologies. Our findings indicate that the relationship between size, inertia, and where firms look for knowledge might not be as clear as previously thought.

We also controlled for certain dimensions of proximity beyond the traditional lens of location and geography. Our findings indicate that proximity along the dimensions of size and age affect the likelihood of two firms borrowing and building on the knowledge of each other. More specifically, firms are more likely to borrow knowledge from other firms of the same or similar size and age than they are to do so from firms that are different from themselves. This relationship might be detrimental to larger, older firms that could build on the technologies and knowledge of the newer, smaller entrants within their industry to compensate for their inherent inertial tendencies. In short, our analysis confirms both Burt's (1987) and Greve's (1998) comments about social similarity playing a role in social emulation.

We also included a vector of firm and year dummies in the model to control for firm-to-firm and year-to-year variability. None of these firm and year dummies were statistically significant, and therefore are not reported in Table 1 to conserve space. This represents an especially strong control for the possibility that a single firm or year observation might be influencing the results. The presence of these dummies also absorbs any year-to-year variation in the data such as variability in the market or general economy.

Most importantly, our results indicate that a firm's tendency to borrow knowledge from another is positively related to their degree of international multi-market contact. In other words, firms are more likely to borrow knowledge from other firms that are viewed as structurally equivalent with respect to the multiple international markets that comprise the industry than from firms that are viewed as structurally dissimilar. This provides an important next step in understanding the dynamics involved in interfirm knowledge transfer, specifically when we consider recent studies on this topic and their findings. Almeida (1996) analyzed the transfer of knowledge between foreign subsidiaries and domestic firms in the U.S. semiconductor market, finding that this process was localized. Jaffe, Trajtenberg and Henderson (1993) also found that knowledge appears to be transferred more often among firms within the same geographic area. While these studies, and several others that focus on localization, provide a logical frame for the dynamics of knowledge transfer, their contribution diminishes as we step back and use a multimarket lens to model this phenomenon. As industries become increasingly global, and the firms that participate in these industries begin participating in the associated markets around the world with various types of structures and forms of commitment, it seems necessary to look beyond the localized effects that might occur between, say, two firm's subsidiaries located within a single common market. Our approach incorporates information about all the markets within an industry and the overlap that exists between the multiunit organizations that compete in these markets.

DISCUSSION

The implication of our argument and empirical results lies in the possibility that the industry-level outcomes of such a process of knowledge transfer, which unfolds as industries evolve, might be taken for granted to be optimal when in fact it is not. Understanding this implication and the forces behind it requires awareness of the dynamics of the knowledge transfer process and the larger social structure effects that can constrain it. Abrahamson and Fombrun (1994) argued that the stronger the barrier of a macroculture, the lower the rate of introduction of innovations invented by organizations outside the barrier. Given that innovations develop in settings involving flows and exchanges of knowledge between multiple organizations, the fact that multimarket competitors would tend to ignore potential sources of knowledge outside of their shared macroculture calls into question what sorts of knowledge might be overlooked? According to Schumpeter, small, young entrepreneurial firms are most likely to be the sources of innovation in our economy (Clemence, 1997; Schumpeter, 1934), yet it seems unlikely that these sorts of firms would be able or ready to compete with well-established multimarket competitors. Older, larger, better-established firms that can afford the costs associated with competing in multiple markets might overlook some of the sources of latest and greatest knowledge in their industries because their macrocultures tell them to ignore such organizations.

At the same time that these firms are overlooking potential sources of new knowledge on which to build their own innovations, their own disposition towards innovation can exhibit signs of inertia (Pouder & St John, 1996). This occurs because as firms continue their socialization into the macroculture binding them, imitation among them is likely. The shared beliefs and values of the managers of these firms lead to homogeneity on many dimensions, including their strategic profiles and technologies. Work in the area of institutionally informed strategy tells us that conformity to the norms of such a macroculture can be beneficial in early stages, facilitating legitimacy in the eyes of stakeholders and access to resources. But with time, the same institutional forces that once provided benefits can actually become a liability, contributing to strategic myopia and inflexibility (Oliver, 1991).

This combination of knowledge searching myopia and innovative inertia among multimarket competitors suggests that the knowledge transfer dynamics that unfold with industry evolution do not necessarily have to lead to optimal outcomes. This view fits well with the work of economists such as Arthur and David, each of which have addressed the possible "lock-in" that might occur in positive feedback or increasing-returns systems (Arthur, 1988, 1989; David,

1985). Increasing-returns mechanisms do more than just tilt competitive balances, they can cause economies and industries to become locked into inferior paths of development that are difficult to escape (Arthur, 1989). Rational outcomes are, of course, possible, but can be unknowingly diverted down sub-optimum paths. If path dependencies are possible, we cannot be certain that equilibrium situations are optimal. Indeed, any present situation might incorporate past inefficiencies. For example, if at some time in an industry's evolution two different but competing technologies appeared, and the competitive outcome was based on increasing returns, it's possible that the superior technology could fail while the inferior technology survives (Arthur, 1988). This was the case in the videocassette recording industry with the VHS and Betamax formats. Sony's Beta format was widely believed to be superior to VHS, but due to competitive factors and path dependencies, VHS survived and Beta failed. While this widely cited case suggests the survival of an inferior technology, in many cases we might never know if better technologies could exist today because of past "lock in by historical events" (Arthur, 1989). Efficiency is not necessarily the operative mechanism in the creation and transfer of knowledge.

This possibility has implications for the process of knowledge transfer in that the formation of industry groupings may be subject to path dependencies, suggesting that group composition may not be optimal. Knowledge flows within an industry may be constrained both by economic forces and historical accident. Firms within groups would be more likely to exchange knowledge with each other, while firms would be less likely to exchange knowledge with other firms across the group boundary due to reduced interaction with those firms. It would be incorrect to think of this group boundary as an impenetrable wall or barrier to entry as the strategic groups literature might view it. We prefer to view this boundary as similar to a small hill or berm encircling the group. Like a berm, the group boundary is not insurmountable provided the firm invests in mechanisms to facilitate capability to understand knowledge on the other side.

Our theory and empirical example suggest areas for further research in the other areas of multimarket knowledge transfer. For instance, will we find that the mechanisms of cooperation and rivalry operate in a generalizable way when we consider product or consumer multimarkets? Empirical questions of interest center on the magnitude of the macrocultural berm and the levels of multi-market overlap where rivalry and cooperation inflect.

In summary, this paper extends our understanding of multimarket phenomena by considering some of the factors that influence the transfer of knowledge between multimarket organizations and the spread of knowledge across industries comprised of multiple markets. Like many situations marked as path-dependent, our ability to view resulting outcomes as optimal or ideal is constrained. In fact, outcomes such as current views of "cutting-edge" technology and "leading" manufacturing processes might be far from the mark. It is the "what if question" embedded in increasing returns systems that forces us to question our assumptions regarding both organizational management and industrial policy decisions.

NOTES

1. In this context the term trading partners is intended to encompass all trading relationships in the production process from raw materials producer to final consumer.

2. Since knowledge can be transferred without additional production costs it will have some of the characteristics of public goods, the market for which is inefficient. Public goods are characterized by nondepletability and nonexcludability. Examples include public parks and national defense. The benefits provided by public goods are not diminished through consumption and it is costly to exclude free riders. The problem with public goods is that market inefficiencies prevent the producer from realizing the full economic benefit. This problem results in the underproduction of public goods due to costly methods of excluding freeriders.

REFERENCES

Abell, D. (1980). *Defining the Business*. New York: Prentice Hall.

Abrahamson, E., & Fombrun, C. J. (1994). Macrocultures: Determinants and Consequences. *Academy of Management Review, 19*(4), 728–755.

Albert, M. B., Avery, D., Narin, F., & McAllister, P. (1991). Direct validation of citation counts as indicators of industrially important patents. *Research policy, 20*, 251–259.

Almeida, P. (1996). Knowledge sourcing by foreign multinationals: Patent citation analysis in the U.S. semiconductor industry. *Strategic Management Journal, 17*(Winter), 155–165.

Appleyard, M. M. (1996). How does knowledge flow? Interfirm patterns in the semiconductor industry. *Strategic Management Journal, 17*(Winter), 137–154.

Arthur, W. B. (1988). *Self-reinforcing mechanisms in economics, The Economy as an Evolving Complex System*. Addison Wesley Publishing Company.

Arthur, W. B. (1989). Competing Technologies, Increasing Returns, And Lock In By Historical Events. *Economic Journal, 99*, 116–131.

Audretsch, D. B. (1998). Agglomeration and the location of innovative activity. *Oxford Review of Economic Activity, 14*(2), 18–29.

Axelrod, R. (1984). *The Evolution of Cooperation*. New York: Basic Books.

Barney, J. B. (1986). Strategic Factor Markets: Expectations, Luck, and Business Strategy. *Management Science, 32*(10), 1231–1241.

Barney, J. B. (1997). *Gaining and Sustaining Competitive Advantage*. Reading, Massachusetts: Addison Wesley.

Baum, J. A. C., & Korn, H. J. (1996). Competitive dynamics of interfirm rivalry. *Academy of Management Journal, 39*(2), 255–291.

Baum, J. A. C., & Korn, H. J. (1999). Dynamics of dyadic competitive interaction. *Strategic Management Journal, 20*, 251–278.

Bernheim, B. D., & Whinston, M. (1990). Multimarket contact and collusive behavior. *RAND Journal of Economics, 21*(1), 1–26.

Bierly, P., & Chakrabarti, A. (1996). Generic knowledge strategies in the U.S. pharmaceutical industry. *Strategic Management Journal, 17*(Winter), 123–135.

Braun, E., & MacDonald, S. (1982). *Revolution in Miniature* (2nd ed.). Cambridge, New York: University Press.

Brittain, J. W., & Freeman, J. H. (1980). Organizational proliferation and density dependent selection: Organizational evolution in the semiconductor industry. In: J. Kimberly & R. H. Miles (Eds), *The Organizational Life Cycle*. San Francisco, CA: Jossey-Bass.

Brittain, J. W. (1994). Density-independent selection and community evolution: Historical development of the semiconductor industry. In: J. A. C. Baum & J. V. Singh (Eds), *Evolutionary Approaches to the Dynamics of Organizing, Organizations, and Organizational Systems*, (pp. 355–378). New York: Oxford University Press.

Burt, R. S. (1987). Social contagion and innovation: Cohesion versus structural equivalence. *American Journal of Sociology, 92*, 1287–1335.

Carpenter, M., Cooper, M., & Narin, F. (1980). The linkage between basic research and patents. *Research Management, 13*(2), 13–19.

Carpenter, M., Narin, F., & Woolf, P. (1981). Citation rates to technologically important papers. *World Patent Information, 3*(4), 160–163.

Caves, R., & Porter, M. E. (1977). From entry barriers to mobility barriers. *Quarterly Journal of Economics, 91*, 241–261.

Chakrabarti. (1991). Competition in high technology: Analysis of patents of US, Japan, UK, France, West Germany, Canada. *IEEE, 38*(1).

Chen, M. J. (1996). Competitor analysis and interfirm rivalry: Toward a theoretical integration. *Academy of Management Review, 21*(1), 100–134.

Chposky, J., & Leonsis, T. (1988). *Blue Magic: The people power and politics behind the IBM personal computer*. New York: Facts On File Publications.

Clemence, R. V. (Ed.) (1997). *Joseph A. Schumpeter: Essays on entrepreneurs, innovation, business cycles, and the evolution of capitalism*. New Brunswick: Transaction Publishers.

Coale, K. (1991). *Redrawing the map; Will the IBM/Apple alliance shift the balance of power?* InfoWorld, 44. InfoWorld Media Group.

Cohen, W. M., & Levinthal, D. A. (1990). Absorptive capacity: A new perspective on learning and innovation. *Administrative Science Quarterly, 35*(1), 128–152.

David, P. (1985). Clio and the economics of QWERTY. *American Economic Review, 75*, 332–337.

Demarzo, R. C. (1993). Random Access; Fear of PC myopia foretold IBM's fate, *Computer Reseller News, 12*.

Dickson, M., & Kehoe, L. (1992). *The dinosaurs rise again: IBM is no longer a symbol of US industry, which is becoming more competitive*, Financial Times, 12. London.

DiMaggio, P. L., & Powell, W. W. (1983). The iron cage revisited: Institutional isomorphism and collective rationality in organizational fields. *American Sociological Review, 48*, 147–160.

Ekelund, R. B., & Tollison, R. D. (1994). *Economics*. New York, NY: Harper Collins College Publishers.

Elzinga, K., & Hogarty, T. (1978). The problem of geographic market definition revisited: The case of coal. *Antitrust Bulletin, 23*, 1–18.

Fitzgerald, M., & Klett, S. P. J. (1994). Radical shift for IBM PCs? *Computerworld, 28*(9), 1,14.

Friedman, J. W. (1983). *Oligopoly Theory*. Cambridge: Cambridge University Press.

Gibbons, R. (1992). *Game Theory for Applied Economists*. Princeton, NJ: Princeton University Press.

Gimeno, J., & Woo, C. Y. (1996). Hypercompetition in a multimarket environment: The role of strategic similarity and multimarket contact in competitive de-escalation. *Organization Science, 7*(3), 322–341.

Glismann, H. H., & Horn, E. J. (1988). Comparative invention performance of major industrial countries: patterns and explanations. *Management Science, 34*(10), 1169–1187.

Granovetter, M. (1985). Economic action and social structure: The problem of embeddedness. *American Journal of Sociology, 91*, 481–510.

Grant, R. M. (1996). Toward a knowledge -based theory of the firm. *Strategic Management Journal, 17*(Winter), 109–122.

Greve, H. R. (1996). Patterns of competition: The diffusion of a market position in radio broadcasting. *Administrative Science Quarterly, 41*(1), 29–60.

Greve, H. R. (1998). Managerial cognition and the mimetic adoption of market positions: What you see is what you do. *Strategic Management Journal, 19*(10), 967–988.

Griliches, Z. (1984). Patents R&D and Productivity. In: Z. Griliches (Ed.), *Patents R&D & Productivity*: University of Chicago Press.

Griliches, Z. (1989). *Patents: Recent trends and puzzles*, Brookings Papers: Microeconomics 1989, 291–330.

Griliches, Z. (1990). Patent statistics as economic indicators. *Journal of Economic Literature, 28*, 1661–1707.

Hall, B., Griliches, Z., & Hausman, J. (1983). *Patents and R&D: Searching for a lag structure*. Paper presented at the Conference on Quantitative Studies of Research and Development in Industry, L'Institut National de Statistique et des Etudes Economique, Paris.

Hamel, G. (1991). Competition for Competence and Inter-Partner Learning Within International Strategic Alliances. *Strategic Management Journal, 12*(Summer), 83–103.

Hannon, M. T., & Freeman, J. (1977). The population ecology of organizations. *American Journal of Sociology, 82*(5), 929–964.

Hannon, M. T., & Freeman, J. H. (1989). *Organizational Ecology*. Cambridge, MA: Harvard University Press.

Hawley, A. (1950). *Human Ecology: A Theory Of Community Structure*. New York, NY: The Ronald Press Company.

Haynes, P. (1994). The computer industry, The third age. *Economist, 332*(7881), SS3–SS5.

Jaffe, A. B., Trajtenberg, M., & Henderson, R. (1993). Geographic localization of knowledge spillovers as evidenced by patent citations. *The Quarterly Journal of Economics, 108*(3), 577–598.

Kirkpatrick, D. (1996). With new PCs and a new attitude, IBM is back. *Fortune, 134*(9), 28–29.

Kochen, W. L. (1994). Securing a secret trust. *Security Management, 38*(9), 142–147.

Langlois, R. N. (1992). External economies and economic progress: The case of the microcomputer industry. *Business History Review, 66*(1), 1–50.

Lorrain, F., & White, H. (1971). Structural equivalence of individuals in social networks. *Journal of Mathematical Sociology, 1*, 49–80.

Manasian, D. (1993). The computer industry: Personal best. *Economist, 326*(7800), SS5–SS6.

Mas-Colell, A., Whinston, M. D., & Green, J. R. (1995). *Microeconomic Theory*. New York, NY: Oxford University Press.

Mogee, M. E. (1991). Using patent data for technology analysis and planning. *Research Technology Management, Jul-Aug 1991*, 43–49.

Mowery, D. C., Oxley, J. E., & Silverman, B. S. (1996). Strategic alliances and interfirm knowledge transfer. *Strategic Management Journal, 17*(Winter), 77–91.

Narin, F., Carpenter, M. P., & Woolf, P. (1984). Technological performance assessments based on patents and patent citations. *IEEE Transactions on Engineering Management, EM–31*(4), 172–183.

Narin, F., & Noma. (1987). Patents as indicators of corporate technological strength. *Research policy*, *16*, 143–155.

Narin, F., Smith, V. M. J., & Albert, M. B. (1993). What patents tell you about your competition. *Chemtech, Feb 1993*, 52–59.

Oliver, C. (1991). Strategic Responses to Institutional Processes. *Academy of Management Review*, *16*(1), 145–179.

Pakes, A., & Griliches, Z. (1984). Patents and R&D at the firm level: A first look. In: Z. Griliches (Ed.), *Patents R&D and Productivity*: University of Chicago Press.

Pakes, A., & Schankerman, M. (1984). The rate of obsolescence of knowledge, research gestation lags and the private rate of return to research resources. In: Z. Griliches (Ed.), *Patents, R&D and Productivity*. University of Chicago Press.

Parker, R. (1990). Back to basics; IBM, Apple zero in on the low-end market, *InfoWorld*, 42.

Patel, P., & Pavitt, K. (1994). The continuing, widespread (and neglected) importance of improvements in mechanical technologies. *Research Policy*, *23*(5), 533–545.

Pavitt, K. (1985). Patent statistics as indicators of innovative activities: Possibilities and problems. *Scientometrics*, *7*, 77–99.

Phillips, O. R., & Mason, C. F. (1992). Mutual forbearance in experimental conglomerate markets. *RAND Journal of Economics*, *23*(3), 395–414.

Podolny, J. M., & Stuart, T. E. (1995). A role based ecology of technological change. *American Journal of Sociology*, *100*(5), 1224–1260.

Podolny, J. M., Stuart, T. E., & Hannan, M. T. (1996). Networks, knowledge, and niches: Competition in the worldwide semiconductor industry, 1984–1991. *American Journal of Sociology*, *102*(3), 659–689.

Porter, M. E. (1980). *Competitive Strategy: Techniques for Analyzing Industries and Competitors*. New York: Free Press.

Porter, M. E. (1985). *Competitive Advantage: Creating and Sustaining Superior Performance*. New York: Free Press.

Pouder, R., & St John, C. H. (1996). Hot spots and blind spots: Geographical clusters of firms and innovation. *Academy of Management Review*, *21*(4), 1192–1225.

Reger, R. K., & Huff, A. S. (1993). Strategic groups: A cognitive perspective. Strategic Management Journal, *14*(2), 103–123.

Rufford, N. (1999). Cloak and Dagger Ltd. Management Today, Feb 1999, 64–66.

Scherer, F. (1982a). Demand pull and technological invention: Schmookler revisited. *Journal of Industrial Economics*, *30*(1), 225–238.

Scherer, F. (1982b). *Inter-industry technology flows in the United States*. Research Policy, 11, 227 et suiv.

Scherer, F. (1983). The propensity to patent. *International Journal of Industrial Organization*, *1*(1), 107–128.

Scherer, F. M., & Ross, D. (1990). *Industrial Market Structure and Economic Performance* (3rd ed.). Boston: Houghton Mifflin Co.

Schumpeter, J. A. (1934). *The Theory of Economic Development*. Cambridge, MA: Harvard University Press.

Scott, J. T. (2001). Designing Multimarket-Contact Hypothesis Tests: Patent Citations and Multimarket Contact in the Product and Innovation Markets of the Chemicals Industry, In: J. A. C. Baum & H. R. Greve (Eds), *Multiunit Organization and Multimarket Strategy: Advances in Strategic Management*, Vol. 18 (pp. 175–203). Oxford UK: JAI Press.

Steiner, G. A., & Steiner, J. F. (2000). *Business, Government and Society: A Managerial Perspective* (9th ed.). Boston, MA: Irwin McGraw Hill.

Stigler, G., & Sherwin, R. (1985). The extent of the market. *Journal of Law and Economics*, 28, 555–585.

Stuart, T. E., & Podolny, J. M. (1996). Local search and the evolution of technological capabilities. *Strategic Management Journal*, *17* (Evolutionary Perspectives on Strategy Supplement), 21–38.

Tirole, J. (1988). *The Theory of Industrial Organization*. Cambridge, MA: The MIT Press.

Tushman, M. J., & Rosenkopf, L. (1992). Organizational determinants of technological change: Toward a sociology of technological evolution. In: L. L. Cummings & N. M. Staw (Eds), *Research in Organizational Behavior*, Vol. 14, (pp. 311–347). Greenwich, CT: JAI Press.

Van Wegberg, M., & Van Witteloostuijn, A. (2001). Strategic management in the new economy: Information technologies and multicontact competition, In: J. A. C. Baum & H. R. Greve (Eds), *Multiunit Organization and Multimarket Strategy: Advances in Strategic Management*, Vol. 18 (pp. 265–306). Oxford UK: JAI Press.

Walters, S. J. K. (1993). *Enterprise, Government and the Public*. New York, NY: McGraw-Hill Inc.

Wernerfelt, B. (1984). A Resource-Based View of the Firm. *Strategic Management Journal*, 5, 171–180.

Wilson, R. K., Ashton, P. K., & Egan, P. P. (1980). *Innovation, competition, and government policy in the semiconductor industry*. Toronto: Lexington Books.

Winter, S. G. (1987). Knowledge and competence as strategic assets. In: D. Teece (Ed.), *The Competitive Challenge* (pp. 159–184). Cambridge, MA: Ballinger.

Zachmann, PC Week, p. 19, Dec 19, (1988). IBM is pulling the PC back to mainframe legacy, *PC Week*, Vol. 5, 9.

APPENDIX

Patents as an Operationalization of Knowledge

It seems sensible to further justify our use of patents as a valid operationalization of knowledge and patent citations as a valid reflection of knowledge transfer. Specifically, what are patents and patent citations? There are certainly a lot of them. They contain enormous amounts of high quality, standardized information and are easily accessed. But what value do they hold for organizational researchers? This section attempts to provide critical justification for the use of patents as measures of knowledge. In it we ask several questions: Theoretically, what do patents represent? How have they been used in the past? What limits their usefulness?

Patents are approved applications for the property rights to a unique invention or process with commercial application. Inventors apply for patents as soon as they have developed a new invention or process. The patent is approved by the United States Patent and Trademark Office, USPTO, if the invention or process is determined to be acceptable. Each patent application lists the inventors, specifically describes the invention or process, and lists the prior patents on which the application is based. These citations to previous patents provide continuity to previous research and establish an "idea audit trail" similar to the citations listed in scholarly publications.

Since patents incorporate previously existing information about unique inventions and processes, there is strong face validity for the belief that patents can be used to represent the unique knowledge present in a particular discipline. There is also strong face validity for the idea that patent citations can be used to represent the transfer of unique knowledge. Undoubtedly there is some correlation between patents and constructs like knowledge, technology, innovation and performance. We further expect correlation between patent citations and constructs such as information flows, technology transfer, knowledge transfer and network relationships. The question remains as to whether the correlations are strong enough to support patents and patent citation as operationalizations of these constructs. While essentially an empirical question, we can do much on the theoretical side to support and refute these ideas.

First let's compare scholarly research to patents. Within all the sciences there is a strong tradition of publication. Scholarly publication fulfills three important functions. First, publications describe major advances within a field and transmit those ideas to all researchers. Second, publications list the contributors so that credit can be given to the originators and so researchers working on similar ideas can identify each other and come together. Third, publication citations trace precursor ideas back to progenitor ideas. Patents are similar to scholarly publications in those same three ways. First, patents convey new knowledge and information about technical advances with commercial applications in the same way that pure and applied research is conveyed by scholarly publication. Second, patents list those firms and inventors that were instrumental in the development of the new ideas. Finally, patents cite the body of previous research and previous patents that contributed to the new ideas. Structurally we can conclude that there are strong similarities between patents and scholarly research. If scholarly research can be said to contain and transmit scholarly knowledge, there is support for the notion that patents do the same with innovative knowledge contained by firms. Now lets look at the theoretical nature of knowledge from the resource-based perspective.

The resource based view of the firm, RBV, suggests that firms may gain a strategic competitive advantage based on firm specific resources that convey heterogeneous performance capability (Barney, 1997; Wernerfelt, 1984). In order to provide sustainable competitive advantage these resources must be: valuable, rare, non-substitutable and costly to imitate (Barney, 1986). Examples of these resources include: unique organizational processes, trademarks, brand names, customer loyalty, firm specific human capital, managerial talent, firm capacity to conduct innovative R&D, etc. The RBV perspective filled a niche in the strategic management literature for analyzing the internal environment of business. From this vantage point, the RBV perspective has been very beneficial. However, the RBV perspective is sometimes difficult to operationalize. For this reason some researchers have turned to patents and patent citations to operationalize various constructs of a firm's core competencies.

The use of patents to operationalize RBV constructs like tacit knowledge of unique firm processes or innovativeness of firm R&D seems logical. It is obvious that in order to generate patents the firm must have sufficient knowledge of the components of the underlying technology. It must also be able to harness the firm's R&D capability to that knowledge to be able to create the innovation described by the patent. Patents encapsulate the output of intangible firm processes and human specific knowledge that organizational members might not be able to articulate themselves. The rationalization for the use of patents is that few other operationalizations capture the intangible nature of firm specific knowledge. Because of these factors, patenting has high levels of face validity as an operationalization of inventions and inventive processes.

Despite the logical appeal of patents as a valid operationalization for both knowledge and innovative processes, they have been criticized on a number of fronts. Critics point out that it is difficult to know precisely what constructs patents actually operationalize. The fact that some researchers use patents to measure knowledge seems inconsistent when other researchers use patents to reflect innovativeness or inventiveness. It may be that patents can be used for several similar constructs with equal efficacy. This is an area where specific empirical investigation is needed.

Critics also point out that patents lack precision. While patents obviously capture some portions of knowledge and innovativeness, they fail to capture other portions of those constructs. Additionally, to the extent that the patenting process is affected by bureaucratic influences at the USPTO, patents may capture portions of other constructs to various degrees. Yet despite these shortcomings, patents are probably one of the best measures of knowledge that RBV, KBV and innovation researchers possess. Another problem with the use of patents is the fact that different disciplines patent to varying extents. Patents confer strong property rights in only a few industries: pharmaceuticals, plastics, chemicals and semiconductors (Winter, 1987). Other industries tend not to use patents because the legal system and market dynamics do not protect knowledge assets uniformly. These other industries have found strategies that protect knowledge assets better than patents: such as speed to market/first mover advantage, relationships with customers, secrecy, and developing economies of scale.

Therefore the ability of patents to appropriately capture the desired constructs is limited by the industry being studied.

The growth of the internet and the resulting availability of on-line patent data to researchers has served as a catalyst for its use in scholarly research. While the previous use of patents in organizational research doesn't constitute a validation of patents, it is useful to know what paths researchers have taken before. Specifically, what has been done previously in the way of using patent data?

Previous research into patents and patent citations has followed three major paths (Pavitt, 1985). There is one tradition of examining patents and patent citations using bibliometric methods to map the transmittal of ideas from patent to patent (Carpenter, Cooper & Narin, 1980; Carpenter, Narin & Woolf, 1981; Narin et al., 1984). A second path in an economic tradition follows the use of patent statistics to explore the causal relationships between patenting and organizational outcomes (Griliches, 1984; Hall, Griliches & Hausman, 1983; Pakes & Griliches, 1984; Pakes & Schankerman, 1984). The third research tradition focused on patenting is the use of patenting statistics to compare different organizations, industries and nations for use in competitor analysis (Scherer, 1982a, b, 1983). In his review of patents as an output of the innovative process, Pavitt (1985) showed that for the most part patents are valid measures over the whole range of innovative activities. Pavitt further points out the difficulty of collecting information on the inputs to the innovative process, suggesting that measures like patents and patent citations are needed.

Carpenter (Carpenter et al., 1980; Narin et al., 1993) argued that the number of patent citations to scientific papers shows a strong linkage between scientific knowledge and patenting. Mowery and colleagues (Mowery, Oxley & Silverman, 1996) argued that patent citation patterns could be used to assess the overlap in two firm's technological portfolios. The extent to which two firms cite a common body of patents suggests an overlap in the technological knowledge on which that technology is based. If patent portfolios are an indicator of aggregate innovation within a firm, the compiled list of patent citations from the portfolio should correspond to aggregate firm knowledge (Patel & Pavitt, 1994). Appleyard (1996) suggests that knowledge flows can be examined by patents in the semiconductor industry. These flows highlight various characteristics of information flows. Almeida (1996) suggests that patent citations can be used to track knowledge flows in the semiconductor industry. Patents and patent citations have also been used as proxies for firm performance and learning (Bierly & Chakrabarti, 1996), firm performance (Chakrabarti, 1991), technological strength (Narin & Noma, 1987), and niche participation and ties within a technological network (Podolny & Stuart, 1995).

These strengths notwithstanding, there are several empirical problems with using patents. Pavitt (1985) points out that the level of unexplained variance in most patenting studies is high, highlighting their imprecise nature. Griliches and colleagues (Griliches, 1984; Hall et al., 1983) failed to find the predicted relationship between patents and lagged R&D expenditures. While many reasons might have contributed to their inability to support such a relationship, the fact that they did not find a connection emphasizes the difficulty of using patent data in empirical research. Glismann and Horn (1988), Narin et al. (1993) point out that patents have been used as meaningful indicators in many types of economic analyses despite minor inaccuracies in patent class assignment and some double counting across industries. Griliches (1989) points out that the USPTO is an inefficient governmental bureaucracy that goes through a budgetary cycle and is subject to forces that distort the true nature of patents as measures.

There is no definitive answer to the question implied above: "Are patents effective measures of firm knowledge and are patent citations an effective measure of the transfer of that knowledge?" In a study in which she admits to minor problems with patent data in general, Mogee (1991) enthusiastically supports using patents as measures of technology and knowledge. The weight of opinion by many organizational researchers is that patents are valid measures of knowledge, innovativeness and technology in the social sciences and that patent citations are valid measures of knowledge transfer.

DESIGNING MULTIMARKET-CONTACT HYPOTHESIS TESTS: PATENT CITATIONS AND MULTIMARKET CONTACT IN THE PRODUCT AND INNOVATION MARKETS OF THE CHEMICALS INDUSTRY

John T. Scott

ABSTRACT

This paper discusses the design of hypothesis tests about multimarket contact and uses a sample of chemicals firms to illustrate researchers' choices and to provide new evidence about the effects of multimarket contact in product and innovation markets. Multimarket contact has a large, stable and statistically significant association with a firm's citations of the patents of another firm. The effect is present even when controls are added for each paired firm's pertinent characteristics (including the effects of its product and innovation markets) that would be expected to affect citations or reflect the effects of the research underlying the citations. New probability measures of multimarket contact are introduced and discussed, and their performance is compared with simple count measures.

Multiunit Organization and Multimarket Strategy, Volume 18, pages 175–202
Copyright © 2001 by Elsevier Science Ltd.
ISBN: 0-7623-0721-8

I. PURPOSE

The purpose of this paper is to reflect on some of the issues that face researchers designing hypothesis tests about multimarket contact and to illustrate the discussion with evidence about the association of multimarket contact with a dependent variable that has not been studied previously in the multimarket-contact literature. Although links to the growing literature are noted, the paper does not attempt to review that literature. Instead, new evidence about the effect of multimarket contact in product and innovation markets is presented with an emphasis on discussing the methodological choices available for the hypothesis tests. Section II addresses the reasons for interest in multimarket contact's effects. Section III discusses the selection of a sample. Section IV discusses the behavior, and hence the dependent variable, studied. Section V addresses the endogeneity issue. Section VI introduces the controls for explanatory variables other than multimarket contact. Section VII introduces and discusses the measures of multimarket contact. Section VIII presents the estimation of the effects of multimarket contact. Section IX concludes by emphasizing the challenges and the choices faced by the researcher designing tests of hypotheses about multimarket contact.

II. WHY STUDY MULTIMARKET CONTACT?

Perhaps the most fundamental distinguishing characteristic of the field of economics known as industrial organization is a focus on the strategic interaction of firms. For example, Scherer (1970, p. 9) begins his classic exploration of industrial organization by adopting "the term 'rivalry' to characterize much of the activity businessmen commonly call 'competition.'" And he observes that "there can be pure competition without rivalry. For instance, two Iowans growing corn on adjacent farms are pure competitors, but not rivals in the sense implied here." Although until recently its impact has typically been downplayed, multimarket contact is perhaps one of the most important structural characteristics that might affect such rivalry or what could alternatively be called strategic interaction.

Beginning with Edwards (1955), economists *have* developed conceptual and theoretical stories about how multimarket contact could affect the behavior and performance of market participants. However, the theories have been considered less compelling than the theories linking the presence of sellers within a single market to strategic interactions affecting market performance. An exception is Scott (1991) where I contend that for the typically diversified sellers of actual industries, multimarket contact may be a *sine qua non* of market power – the ability to control price in a given market as contrasted with simply taking price parametrically as textbook competitors would.

Although U.S. Supreme Court cases have established precedents for antitrust enforcement that blocks competition-reducing conglomerate mergers, multimarket contact is not among the Court's reasons for supporting such enforcement (Scott, 1993, pp. 19–21). Further, the merger guidelines of the U.S. Department of Justice and the Federal Trade Commission emphasize horizontal mergers, and actions against conglomerate mergers are even less likely than existing Supreme Court precedents would suggest (Scott, 1993, p. 21, pp. 194–195).

Does multimarket contact – often increased by conglomerate activity – affect the behavior of firms? In markets where behavior is captured reasonably well by the competitive model, firms take market price and the technologies available as given – as parameters of their environment that cannot be manipulated – and then do the best that they can for themselves while essentially ignoring their rivals. Competition is paradoxically non-rivalrous, entailing no strategic interaction among the competitors; competition is parametric. In markets where sellers are concentrated, rivalry – strategic interaction – is expected. A concentrated market is one where a few leading firms control a large proportion of output; seller concentration is said to be high in such a case. The question is whether multimarket contact adds anything to the story. The importance of multimarket contact is controversial. Presumably that is the reason the concept is not typically used in antitrust, while the conventional measures of seller concentration within markets are used regularly.

In my opinion (Scott, 1993, pp. 65–66), the theory suggests that the anti-competitive consequences of a horizontal merger would be less when the industry's oligopolists are diversified yet have little multimarket contact. The anti-competitive consequences would be greater if the merger increased concentration for an oligopoly where the sellers do meet significantly in other markets. Regarding conglomerate mergers, theory implies that concern about their price-raising effects should be greater if they increase the multimarket contact of concentrated sellers in particular markets.

The evidence supports the importance of multimarket contact. The evidence in my earlier work (Scott, 1982, 1988, 1989, 1991 and 1993) is just a part of what has become an increasing body of evidence. The literature has grown quite rapidly, with several different focuses. Much of the work examines the decrease in rivalry associated with multimarket contact for firms. The work includes both theoretical conjectures (Edwards, 1955; Adams, 1974; Feinberg, 1984; Bernheim & Whinston, 1990; Scott, 1993, Chap. 2; Van Wegberg, Van Witteloostuijn & Abbing, 1994; Phillips & Mason, 1996; and

Spagnolo 1999) and theoretical conjectures combined with detailed empirical work.

Many authors have interpreted Bernheim and Whinston (B&W) as showing that multimarket contact cannot affect firm behavior unless the markets in which the firms meet are asymmetric. For the B&W result, firms maximize profits or expected profits. Spagnolo (1999) allows for more general behavior and finds quite general effects for multimarket contact facilitating cooperative behavior if firms' objective functions are concave. If instead of maximizing profits or expected profits the firms' decision-makers are risk averse, objective functions are concave in profits following the von Neuman-Morgenstern approach. Spagnolo also adduces other types of actual decision making for which the objective functions are concave. Thus, to the B&W asymmetry reasons for behavioral effects of multimarket contact, we have the more general result that the contact will affect behavior when the firm's objective function is concave. To the list of reasons for effects of multimarket contact, I believe we should also add the greater contemporaneous game-playing experience of the firms that have multimarket contact.

I believe that even given the strict confines of the B&W model where firms maximize profits, the literature has erred when it has interpreted the B&W irrelevance proof as a proof that multimarket contact can have no effect on behavior in symmetric markets. As discussed in Scott (1993, pp. 22–31), the B&W irrelevance proof shows only that multimarket contact does not affect the set of Nash equilibria. For realistic multiperiod games there are innumerable equilibria and my point is that multimarket contact can affect the choice of a desirable Nash equilibrium from among the many equilibria that exist. Meeting in multiple markets increases the players' contemporaneous experience with each other and such experience could help players learn to choose an equilibrium that is better from their private perspectives. My point about multimarket contact and increased contemporaneous experience helping firms solve the equilibrium selection problem applies even in the strict B&W framework. It applies as well in the more general framework considered by Spagnolo.

Some of the literature has therefore made a compound mistake in its interpretation of the B&W irrelevance result. First, what the result shows is not entirely what the literature is claiming for it. Bernheim and Whinston do demonstrate the relevance of multimarket contact given asymmetry, but they do not prove its irrelevance given symmetry. Second, because of the erroneous interpretation, the literature is ignoring what may in fact be the real reason for the burgeoning empirical findings of an effect of multimarket contact on rivalry. Certainly real markets are asymmetric, but the reason for the effect of multimarket contact on behavior may be the greater familiarity of the players in a game with each other. That greater familiarity and contemporaneous experience playing the oligopoly game may increase their ability to chose desirable equilibria – a cause and effect that is present even for counterfactual symmetric markets and is distinct from the interesting B&W links from multimarket contact to behavior that emerge in asymmetric markets.

Some of the empirical work (Scott, 1982, 1988, 1989, 1991, 1993; Feinberg, 1985; Hughes & Oughton, 1993; and Vonortas, 2000) has examined firms meeting in many different manufacturing industries. Other papers have explored the intra-industry multimarket contact across geographic markets for firms operating in airlines (Evans & Kessides, 1994; Baum & Korn, 1996; Gimeno & Woo, 1996, 1999; Singal, 1996; Baum & Korn, 1999; Gimeno, 1999), cement manufacturing (Jans & Rosenbaum, 1997), banking (Heggestad & Rhoades, 1978; Mester, 1987; Pilloff, 1999; Greve, 1999), cellular telephones (Parker & Roller, 1997), and hospital services (Boeker, Goodstein, Stephan & Murmann, 1997). Additionally, experimental findings (Feinberg & Sherman, 1988; Phillips & Mason, 1992) have augmented both the theory and the empirical literatures. Further, the applications to public policy have gone beyond the focus on enforcement of U.S. antitrust law to include, among other things, a concern with the competitive effects of European integration (van Wegberg, Van Witteloostuijn & Abbing, 1994).

In addition to the studies of multimarket contact and rivalry, there are studies of organizational learning and efficiency advantages of multiunit and multimarket contact (Ingram & Baum, 1997a, b; Usher, 1999; Greve, 1999). There are studies considering the implications of multimarket contact for both improving efficiency and reducing rivalry (Scott, 1982, 1993; Gimeno & Woo, 1999; Greve, 2000). Attention has been directed to the evolution of multimarket contact whether by chance or other mechanisms such as when contact emerges as a consequence of firms pursuing strategic objectives (Scott, 1989, 1993; Korn & Baum, 1999; Greve, 2000).

Despite the burgeoning literature about the theory and evidence of the effects of multimarket contact, its importance is still quite controversial. In this paper, I shall introduce new evidence. I examine a well-defined type of behavior that has not been studied previously in the literature about multimarket contact. I control for all the product and innovation market characteristics by controlling for each firm's location in the product and innovation markets, and I control for other relevant firm characteristics as well. Then, given those controls, does multimarket contact matter? Once I have controlled for the effects of being in the various markets and other firm characteristics, multimarket contact should have no effect itself unless in fact being in the particular *collection* of markets where the contact occurs – in and of itself – affects behavior.

Of course, an open question is whether it is the contact between firms that affects their behavior or instead it is the presence in the particular *collection* of markets that would change the behavior of each firm even absent the contact and even with controls for the effects associated with each of the markets individually. Thus, the method that I use here will establish that even holding constant the effects of product and innovation markets (fixed effects for product markets and constant percentage effects for the innovation markets), there is an effect on firm behavior associated with multimarket contact. That effect of multimarket contact may reflect the contact itself or it may reflect the effect of the unique *collection* of markets where the contact occurs.

III. THE SAMPLE

Research about multimarket contact has studied whole companies in some papers and lines of business in others; some research has studied the multimarket contact for paired companies while other papers focus on measures of multimarket contact characterizing entire industries. The present sample is comprised of 42 of the 43 companies whose licensing behavior in chemicals-related technologies is studied in Link and Scott (1999). Because the present paper studies the multimarket contact of the companies in the several chemicals-related industries, the one of the 43 firms that did not have a significant share of its operations in at least one of those chemicals industries was dropped from the sample. The original 43 companies were those companies that had U.S. patents *and* were identified from searches of a number of electronic sources of information as companies having licensing agreements for chemicals technology that were reported in the news media from 1993 through 1997. Keyword searches for "licensing" and "chemicals" found the reported cases of licensing agreements for chemicals technology, and the electronic sources included ProQuest's (subsequently Bell & Howell Information and Learning) ABI/Inform, Information Access Company's Business Index and H. W. Wilson Company's Business Periodicals Index.

Link and Scott (1999) use the sample of 43 firms with U.S. patents and with licensing agreements reported during 1993 through 1997 to study the licensing of technology. In this paper, I shall use the 42 of those firms with substantial operations in chemicals industries to study the effect of multimarket contact on firms' citation behavior.

IV. THE BEHAVIOR AND THE DEPENDENT VARIABLE AFFECTED BY MULTIMARKET CONTACT

Previous studies (many discussed in Section II above) of the effects of multi-market contact on behavior or performance have examined many of the variables

– such as prices, price-cost margins, profits, entry and exit, and the variability of market shares – in the literature of industrial organization. Including the closely related studies of purposive diversification and resulting multimarket contact, the literature has also examined links from such diversification to R&D intensity, composition of patent portfolios, research joint ventures, mergers and acquisitions, and total factor productivity. Scott and Pascoe (1987) examine the productivity effects of R&D spillovers among the sets of markets where large diversified firms meet. Scott (1988, 1993), Van Wegberg, van Witteloostuijn and Abbing (1994) and Vonortas (2000) consider efficiency and rivalry-reducing implications of multimarket contact and multiproject contact associated with cooperative research ventures. Research linking multimarket contact or purposive diversification more generally to measures of profits, R&D intensity, systems orientation of patent portfolios, research joint ventures, mergers and acquisitions, and total factor productivity is provided in Scott (1993).

Here I introduce to the multimarket contact literature a new variable capturing behavior that is influenced by both product and innovation markets. The variable is the number of citations by firm i of the patents of firm j. Cassidy and Loree (this volume) also introduce the relation between patent citations and multimarket contact; they study contacts in geographic markets, and here I examine the contacts in product and innovation markets.

The Dependent Variable.

$Cite_{ij}$ is defined as the number of firm i's citations (for patents granted during 1990–1996) of firm j's patents (issued during 1975–1996).

The characteristics of each firm's product and innovation markets would determine both strategic motivations and simple non-strategic efficiency motives for the citations. The strategic motivations of cross-citations, for example, could include the desire to commit to a patent-sharing licensing agreement to avoid competition with substitute patent-protected products. The simple, parametric efficiency motivations in a competitive, non-rivalrous setting, for example, would include wholly non-strategic citations of prior art on which new technology was based. The non-strategic citations would not have the motive of shaping the rivalry between the citing and the cited firm. I do not attempt here to specify or to separate all such possibilities. Instead, by controlling for the product market and innovation market locations of both firm i and firm j, the empirical model will control for the associated strategic and non-strategic motivations for citations, whatever those motivations may be and whatever the product or innovation characteristics underlying those motivations may be. I then add to the specification measures of the multimarket contact of the pair of firms in their product and innovation markets and ask whether, other things being the same, multimarket contact matters for behavior.

In great contrast with previously studied variables such as profits or prices, for the dependent variable Cite$_{ij}$ here, the behavioral effect for multimarket contact is uncontroversial and certainly expected. Since the behavioral effect here is uncontroversial, I can use the experiment to focus on the methodological issues about measuring multimarket contact without any distractions about why the behavioral effect occurs. Clearly we expect the multimarket contact of two firms will increase their expected cross-citations holding constant the expected citations associated with particular market locations for the citing and cited firms. Most fundamentally, multimarket contact for the dependent variable *Cite$_{ij}$* reflects parsimoniously the interaction effects for product and innovation markets across the citing and the cited firms. Those effects in turn reflect what the innovation literature has termed the importance of investment in absorptive capacity – namely, a firm must do R&D in a particular technology area to be able to benefit from the spillovers of R&D insights or innovative outputs generated by the R&D of other firms (Martin, 2000). As Kealey and Al-Ubaydli (2000, p. 9) observe, "because science moves so fast, and because it takes personal expertise at the cutting edge to discriminate usefully between different research papers, patents and products, only *active* scientists have the judgement and tacit knowledge to capture others' science efficiently."

Thus, with multimarket contact comes interorganizational learning. In their study of hotel chains, Ingram and Baum (this volume) show that interorganizational relations are shaped by interorganizational learning. Their results and ideas about hotels are applicable to the interorganizational learning that occurs in the present paper through knowledge transfers reflected in patent citations and the subsequent licensing agreements and even mergers between the organizations that have borrowed technology from each other. Strategic research partnerships can increase the efficiency of interorganizational learning (Scott, 2000).

V.   ENDOGENEITY

In most studies of the behavior of firms in markets, there is an endogeneity issue that can render behavioral effects mere statistical associations whose driving force is yet to be determined. The present study is no exception. The goal for the evidence is to isolate the effect of multimarket contact in product and innovation markets on the citation behavior of the firms in those markets. Yet clearly over time patterns of citations in patents evolve and subsequent to the citations firms enter new markets. Hence, multimarket contact can emerge as a consequence of the patented research of firms, and any association between multimarket contact and citations can reflect not only the effect of the contact on citation behavior, but the effect of earlier research reflected in the patent citations on subsequent multimarket contact.

One way to face the issue is to model simultaneously (1) the time series of evolving patents and their citations and the evolution of firms' entry decisions and resulting multimarket contact with (2) the behavioral effect of multimarket contact on patent citations as firms meeting in multiple markets create a portfolio of substitutable products for which licenses are exchanged. Developing the data for such a comprehensive approach is beyond the scope of the present paper that has as its primary purpose pointing up and discussing the methodological issues, including introducing new measures of multimarket contact and discussing and illustrating them. Yet steps can be taken in the design of the statistical test for an association between multimarket contact and citation behavior to make more likely the observation of a behavioral effect of contact on citations rather than the observation of contact that resulted from the research underlying observed citations.

To that end, the present paper examines the broad product markets, within the broad chemicals industry, and the large chemicals firms that have occupied those product markets for decades and established patent portfolios while maintaining broadly stable product profiles. The multimarket contact in the broad product and innovation markets is measured and then recent citation behavior is analyzed as a function of the broad characterization of a firm's operations in product and innovation markets and its multimarket contact with other firms. Thus, the present paper does not consider a detailed time series documenting the evolution of citations and finely disaggregated market entries. Instead, the firms are described in cross-section by their positioning in broad product and innovation markets and by their recent citation behavior.

Despite the research design just described, the association of the firms' citation behavior with their multimarket contact, other things held constant, will potentially mingle the behavioral effect of multimarket contact on citations with the effect of past research on multimarket contact. To isolate the effect of multimarket contact on behavior, the research design uses broad markets and *recent* citation behavior. Further, the link from past citations and associated research to multimarket contact *and* the link from current market positions to recent citations are both controlled in the statistical association of citations with the included product market effects and innovation market effects. Ideally, no relation will remain between citations and multimarket contact unless there is a behavioral link from contact to citations.

VI. CONTROLLING FOR EXPLANATORY VARIABLES OTHER THAN MULTIMARKET CONTACT

The model then is that the number of recent citations by firm i of the patents of firm j is a function of characteristics of firm i and its product and innovation markets, characteristics of firm j and its product and innovation markets, and multimarket contact of firms i and j in their product and innovation markets. The characteristics of each firm include its number of patents and the closeness to science of its patent portfolio, its diversification, the product markets in which it operates, and the innovation markets in which it operates. The location of the firm in the various product and innovation markets is controlled with fixed product market effects and constant percentage innovation market effects. Ideally, the set of those controls for a firm picks up the effects on behavior of being in particular product and innovation markets.

Of course the underlying things about those markets that cause the effects are not observed. While for many purposes that would present a problem, for the purposes of asking whether multimarket contact matters, other things held constant, we need only control for the effects associated with a particular location in the product and innovation markets. The technique allows for a conservative test of the importance of multimarket contact on behavior because effects of multimarket contact that are common to all firms in a given product or innovation market are controlled by the locational variables alone. From my previous research (Scott, 1993), I know that there are great differences among an industry's firms in the extent to which they purposively diversify. Further, for those firms in an industry that do purposively diversify, there are a variety of diversification patterns. Thus, for any pair of firms in a market, the extent of multimarket contact will in general be different from the multimarket contact for other pairs of firms in the market.

The explanatory variables for the analysis here, apart from the multimarket contact variables to be introduced subsequently, are as follows.

The Firm-specific Controls

Numpat is the number of patents for the firm and therefore provides an appropriate measure of the scale of the firm's operations for purposes of studying its citations of other firms' patents. Other things being the same, more patents would be expected to imply more citations. With *Cite* covering the firm's citations in its patents granted during 1990–1996, *Numpat* is measured as the number of regular utility U.S. patents granted to the firm, 1990–1996, and was provided in a special tabulation by CHI Research.

Scilink is a measure of the closeness of the firm's patent portfolio to science – perhaps indicating more fundamental discoveries that would be more likely to have connections to the patents of other firms and more likely to generate cross-citations. The variable is what CHI Research calls the science linkage for a firm. It is CHI Research's TECH-LINE indicator (CHI Research, 1996) of how close a company's patents are to the scientific research base. It is defined to be the average number of "other references cited" on the front pages of the firm's U.S. patents (granted during the years 1990–1996 for the present sample). The "other references" are references to the scientific literature, such as journal papers and scientific meetings. References to books, reports, and other non-scientific literature sources are excluded. The variable was provided by CHI Research in a special tabulation.

Div is a measure of the diversification of the firm's sales across the six chemicals industry product areas defined below. The variable is defined to be the number of the six areas in which the firm has sales. *Divpat* is a measure of the diversification of the firm's patent activity across the 30 patent groups defined below. The variable is defined to be the number of the 30 patent groups in which the firm has at least 1% of its patents. Just as the number of patents provides an appropriate scaling variable, the diversification of the firm controls for another dimension of the firm's size that is important in the context of this study. The diversification variables will be used to distinguish diversification across product and innovation markets from multimarket contact in those markets, and its use in the controls will allow us to establish that multimarket contact affects behavior in a way that is distinct from the effect of diversification per se.

The Product Market Controls

The following 0–1 qualitative variables take the value 1 if the firm has sales in the category and take the value 0 otherwise. The product markets for the firms in the sample were ascertained from the various corporate directories available in Lexis-Nexis and from the web pages for the firms.

Dgen = 1 for operations in general chemicals or intermediate or specialty chemicals not classified elsewhere, and 0 otherwise.
Dpet = 1 for operations in petroleum and petrochemicals, and 0 otherwise.
Dpha = 1 for operations in pharmaceuticals, 0 otherwise.
Dplas = 1 for operations in plastics, 0 otherwise.
Dfib = 1 for operations in fibers, 0 otherwise.
Dagr = 1 for operations in agricultural chemicals, 0 otherwise.

The Innovation Market Controls

CHI Research, Inc. provided for each firm a special tabulation of the distribution of its patents across 30 product categories. There are then 30 patent location variables that show the percentage of the firm's patents in each of the 30 product groups into which CHI Research classified the patents of each firm. The resulting profile locates the firm in its innovation markets. The variables are defined for each firm as the CHI Research product group patent percentage denoted as $Pgpp_x$ for x = 1 to 30. The 30 groups combine the larger number of SIC product groups listed in CHI Research (1996).[1]

VII. MEASURES OF MULTIMARKET CONTACT

As detailed by Gimeno and Jeong (this volume), many different ways of measuring multimarket contact have been introduced in the literature. In the present paper, I use some novel measures to allow discussion of the nuances of alternative measures of multimarket contact. The alternative measures that I examine all tell broadly the same story for the present sample of chemicals firms and their multimarket contact across the six chemicals product markets and the 30 product groups into which their patents are distributed. Here the measures all have a large, stable, and statistically significant effect on strategic behavior. Yet the alternative multimarket contact measures can perform differently in some samples as the analysis of Gimeno and Jeong (this volume) shows.

Multimarket contact in product and innovation markets is measured in this paper in essentially two ways. First, a simple count g of the number of meetings across markets is used. Second, the probability *prob* of more meetings against the null hypothesis of random diversification is used.

Instead of the probability of more meetings, one could in principle use the probability of meeting more than or equal to the actual number of meetings. My choice here is just a practical matter of choosing the measure that distinguishes contact well given the parameters of the sample. For samples where the number of markets for each firm (and hence the number of potential meetings for a pair of firms) is large, I have used (Scott, 1982, 1989, 1991, 1993) the probability of more than or equal the number of actual meetings. Here, for diversification within the broad chemicals industry, the sampled firms are diversified into a relative handful of industries. With the limited number of potential meetings, I use the probability of a greater number of meetings than actually observed to distinguish clearly the probability of many meetings. For example, if each occupies 10 of a great many industries and the firms meet in

7, the probability of meeting in 7 or more is well-distinguished from a smaller number of meetings. For a pair where each occupies just 2 of a few industries and they meet in 1, the probability of meeting in more than 1 distinguishes the high meeting cases better than the probability of meeting in 1 or more would.

Another difference between this paper's probability measure of multimarket contact and the measures used earlier is that here I use the formal measure of the statistical significance of the contact, and that measures contact inversely. In the earlier papers, instead of using the inverse measure of contact (the probability of as much or more contact or, in the present paper, the probability of more contact), I measured contact directly as the probability of less contact (the analogy here would be the probability of less than or equal contact). Thus in the present paper, a positive effect of multimarket contact on behavior will show a negative sign on the coefficient of the probabilistic multimarket contact variable.

Let n denote the number of categories into which the firms could diversify their activities. For each pair of firms, s is the number of categories in which one firm has activity, while $t \leq s$ is the number of categories in which the other firm has activity. Let g denote the number of categories in which the two firms meet, and let $C_{x, y}$ denote the combination of x things taken y at a time where $C_{x, y} = x!/(y! (x - y)!)$ with $x!$ denoting x factorial, the product of the integer x with all the positive integers smaller than x. Then, the probability measure for a pair of firms is given by the formula:

$$prob = 1 - \sum_{f=0}^{g} p(f) = 1 - \sum_{f=0}^{g} \frac{C_{t,f} C_{n-t, s-f}}{C_{n, s}}$$

The formula gives the probability *prob* that the firms would meet more than they actually do if their diversification were random. $C_{n, t}$ has been canceled from the numerator and the denominator of the combinatorial expression for $p(f)$. Then, given a particular set of t activities for one firm, $C_{t, f}$ denotes the number of different combinations of f activities in which the two firms could meet. Conditional on the two firms meeting in a particular f activities, $C_{n-t, s-f}$ is the number of possibilities for s minus f categories that do not coincide with the t activities of the other firm. $C_{n, s}$ is the total number of ways the firm with s activities can be configured. Thus, $p(f)$ gives the proportion of all possible cases taken by those cases where the two firms meet in f categories. The summation of $p(f)$ from $f = 0$ to t equals 1.

The probability *prob* measures multimarket contact inversely, and also is a formal measure of the significance of the meetings across the several markets in which the firms could operate. For example, if one of a pair of the chemicals firms operates in four of the six chemicals product markets and the other operates in three of the markets, the probability that they meet more than twice in the six markets is 0.2. The probability that they meet more than three times is of course zero.

The probability measure provides a formal way to scale the number of observed meetings to reflect the fact that some meeting would occur simply by chance. Firms with more lines of business would by chance meet more than would firms with fewer lines of business, and yet as a proportion of the firms' activities, the smaller number of meetings may be more significant and have more influence on behavior. There is, however, a deeper reason why one might use the probability measure. If multimarket contact reflects the purposive pursuit of efficiencies or of market power by the diversifying firms, then when firms face similar opportunities for realizing efficiencies or market power through diversification, we would expect to find them meeting more than would happen by chance. The probability measure of multimarket contact for a set of diversified firms identifies the presence of such purposive diversifying behavior.

That distinction for the probability measure – the ability to distinguish purposive diversifying behavior leading to multimarket contact – was a key in the Federal Trade Commission Line of Business data in Scott (1982). The statistically significant relation between multimarket contact and profits occurred for significant multimarket contact as measured by the probability measure of contact, but not for the simple count measure although the sign of the effect was the same. Certainly it is conceivable that purely random contacts that do not reflect purposive pursuit of either efficiency or market power will not have noticeable effects on behavior, or that counts not scaled by the multimarket extent of firms' operations would not be associated with behavior. Yet that need not always be the case. As Hughes and Oughton (1993, note 19, p. 223) observe, even contact that occurs by chance may become the basis for tacit agreements. That of course does not imply that the probability based measures should not be used, but rather that with those measures the researcher can ask whether the behavioral effects of multimarket contact differ depending on whether the contact is the result of chance or instead the result of purposive behavior. Although Hughes and Oughton (1993, note 19, p. 223) conjecture that firms are unlikely to diversify for the purpose of creating multimarket contact, I believe that research along the lines of Scott (1989), Korn and Baum (1999), and Greve (2000) will establish the existence and importance of such behavior. Further, whether multimarket contact is the goal or not, it will result from the purposive pursuit of efficiencies or market power when firms face similar opportunities.

The potential differences in the performance of the simple count and the probability measures of multimarket contact suggest that comparing performance of different measures in different circumstances may yield insights about the behavior being studied. However, in the present sample and for the present type of behavior studied, the simple count measure and the probability measure are both significantly related to the dependent variable.

In this paper I would like to examine the extent of multimarket contact among all of the possible pairs of chemicals firms – do a particular two firms meet not at all, or once, or twice, and so forth across the several chemicals markets. Thus, I examine all of the pairs of firms, including those for which multimarket contact would be impossible because one or both of the firms are focused on a single market.

In the hypothetical example above, the two firms operated in multiple markets – one in four and the other in three of the product markets. Consider in contrast a pair of firms for which each firm operates in just one of the six markets; the probability that they would meet more than once is of course zero. If in fact these two hypothetical pairs met twice and once respectively, the probabilistic measure of multimarket contact shows that meeting once is in a sense more contact than meeting twice. The probabilistic, inverse measure of multimarket contact is 0.2 for the pair that meets twice, but the measure is 0.0 for the pair that meets once.

Thus, using only the probabilistic measure and the full sample of pairs, some pairs that meet once would have a greater measure of the extent of contact than pairs meeting more than once. Conceivably the importance of meeting and congruence of the pair's operations is measured, rather than multimarket contact per se. Scott (1982) treated this problem directly. There I began with pairs of firms in a particular market, and then used the distribution of their possible meetings across other markets, and I eliminated the cases where meetings in other markets were impossible because at least one of the firms operated in just the single market. In the earlier work, then, I used what could be called pure measures of multimarket contact alone, while here the measures are general measures of the congruence of the firms' activities across the markets into which they can diversify.

Here I want to use all of the pairs of firms, including those focused firms that either never meet others at all or meet others only once. I shall keep all of the observations, but present the statistics two ways – once using the absolute number of meetings, and then again using the probability measure of the significance of the number of meetings. The absolute measure of multimarket contact increases monotonically with the number of meetings, measuring the meetings directly. The probabilistic measure instead measures the significance of the meetings. Indeed, as we have seen in the example, for the small parameter space of the product markets, even a single meeting can be more significant than multiple meetings. Because fewer actual meetings can be associated with more significant meetings, the probabilistic measure for the full sample captures the importance of congruent operations in general, including the significance of the multiple meetings but also the significance of zero meetings or one meeting. In the present sample, both the absolute count of the number of meetings as well as probability measure that assesses the significance of the meetings tell the same story about the effect on behavior of the extent of meetings across multiple markets. Thus, examining the two sets of statistics together below shows that the extent of multimarket contact has a significant effect on behavior.

The distributions for the two cases discussed above are shown in Table 1, where $n = 6$ is the number of markets where the pair of firms can meet, s is the number of product markets for one firm, t is the number for the other, and $s \geq t$.

For the empirical work, the multimarket contact measures for the product markets are:

$Gprod_{ij}$ = the number of meetings between firm i and firm j in the six product markets.

prob ($>Gprod_{ij}$) = the probability of more product market meetings between firm i and firm j against the null hypothesis of random diversification.

For the multimarket contact measures in innovation markets, we know the complete distribution of each firm's patents across the 30 product groups and therefore have the number of patent categories into which its patents fall. For the empirical work, the multimarket contact measures for innovation markets are:

$Gpat_{ij}$ = the number of meetings between firm i and firm j in the 30 patent categories.

$Prob(>Gpat_{ij})$ = the probability of more patent category (hence innovation market) meetings between firm i and firm j against the null hypothesis of random

Table 1. Two Distributions for the Probability, $p(f)$, of Meeting when $n = 6$.

f	$p(f;\ s = 4,\ t = 3)$	$p(f;\ s = 1,\ t = 1)$
0	0.0	0.8<u>3</u>
1	0.2	0.1<u>6</u>
2	0.6	0.0
3	0.2	0.0
4	0.0	0.0
5	0.0	0.0
6	0.0	0.0

diversification. Although the sample space for the innovation market meetings is large enough to use the probability of more than or equal the number of meetings, for consistency with the definition of the probability measure for product market meetings, the probability of more meetings is used again here.

In computing the innovation market measures, I did not want to consider negligible proportions of a firm's patent portfolio. Thus, the proportion of the firm's patents in each of the 30 categories was rounded to the nearest percentage point, and the tiny percentages that rounded to zero were not counted.

Note that just as with the new probabilistic measure of multimarket contact in product markets, in principle the measure here is (unlike the measures of pure multimarket contact alone used in earlier work) a measure of the extent of congruence of the pair's patent profiles. For these new measures that examine the entire sample of firms, theoretically, high probabilistic contact can reflect a significant amount of meeting in a single category as well as a large amount of multimarket contact. For samples where the use of the complete-sample probability measures would measure congruence but not give a good ordering of multimarket congruence because of a predominance of meetings among undiversified firms, the researcher could simply examine the diversified pairs in each market and use the distribution of meetings in other markets as in Scott (1982). Here, however, the firms are well diversified across product and innovation markets, and the full-sample measures give general measures of congruence of activity across *multiple* markets.

The product market approach and the innovation market approach used here share the common foundation of the conscious choice to depart from my 1982 methodology and examine all firms, not just diversified ones. The new measures here are the same – one for product market meetings and the other for innovation market meetings. There is an interesting alternative measure when the complete percentage distribution of activity is available as for the innovation markets. Instead of counting the number of meetings in the markets and computing the probability of more meetings, one could count the number of times the 100 percentage points for each firm meet across the 30 patent groups and compute the probability of more such meetings. Such an alternative raises several interesting methodological issues about congruence versus multimarket contact per se and about the asymmetry of meetings when firms have very different proportions of their activities in the markets. I shall leave the alternative measure and a discussion of its properties for a future paper.

There is quite a bit of flexibility for developing appropriate probability measures, and often what is appropriate for one context is not appropriate for another. For example, at some point, all absolutely large numbers of contacts would appear significant and not be well distinguished by the probability measures. A researcher could encounter a sample where the probability measure essentially divides firms into those with high contact and those with low contact as pointed up by Singal (1996, p. 563), although that of course will not necessarily occur. When it does, and if the *a priori* hypothesis is one that must sort purposive from random behavior, then of course the dichotomous outcome in the data is the truth at hand.

For another example, simply because some papers have designed appropriate probability tests using just two or three firms in an industry, clearly it is not the case that a shortcoming of the probability measure is that it uses just two or three firms in an industry (Singal, 1996, p. 564). Scott (1991) and indeed the present paper use probability measures to consider all possible pairs of firms. Furthermore, not all contacts need be considered equivalent despite the number of firms (Singal, 1996, p. 564). In the initial paper using the probability measure of contact (Scott, 1982), the effect of multimarket contact was conditioned on the number and size distribution of the sellers in the market (seller concentration). Thus, in addition to the possibility of modeling the probability of a contact as a function of the number of firms, given the theoretical advantages of considering "dyadic competitive interaction" (Baum & Korn, 1999), an obvious way to control for the number of firms is by controlling for seller concentration and its interaction with multimarket contact for pairs of firms as in Scott (1982). Alternatively, one can examine dyadic interaction and control for the number of firms, among other things, with market effects as is done in the present paper.

My point is not to claim that probability measures are the only sensible ones; clearly they are not. Indeed, the present paper provides an example where the count and the probability measures tell broadly the same story. My point, instead, is that the probability measures are very flexible and can be designed to help identify purposive from random behavior when the effects of purposive behavior are important and might otherwise be difficult to distinguish.

VIII.   ESTIMATION

The dependent variable $Cite_{ij}$, the number of recent citations by one firm of another firm's patents, is modeled using the negative binomial model.[2] Statistical tests show that the negative binomial model, a count model that is a generalization of the Poisson count model, is appropriate. The likelihood ratio test for alpha, the over-dispersion parameter in the negative binomial model, equal to zero rejects the simpler Poisson model (which corresponds to alpha equal to zero) in all specifications.[3] The chi-squared value for that likelihood ratio test is extraordinarily high, and the probability of observing our sample if alpha equals zero is virtually zero. The negative binomial model is therefore appropriate; however, the basic findings about the significant effect of multi-market contact for both product and innovation markets and for both simple count measures and the probability measures are robust to other estimating procedures including ordinary regression.

Table 2 shows the negative binomial model's results for the model estimated with all 1722 pairs of firms – the permutations of the 42 firms. For the dependent variable studied here and given the present sample, whether measured with a count measure or a probability measure, multimarket contact is always associated with more citations.

The expected number of firm i's citations of firm j's patents is $e^{\beta_0 + \beta_1 x_1 + \cdots + \beta_k x_k}$. Holding constant all the explanatory variables except one, say x_i, the expected number of citations given a change of Δx_i in the one variable, relative to the expected number of citations without that change is:

$$\frac{e^{\beta_0 + \beta_1 x_1 + \cdots + \beta_i (x_i + \Delta x_i) + \cdots + \beta_k x_k}}{e^{\beta_0 + \beta_1 x_1 + \cdots + \beta_i x_i + \cdots + \beta_k x_k}} = e^{\beta_i \Delta x_i}$$

which for a unit change in x_i equals e^{β_i} which is called the incidence rate ratio or IRR. The incidence rate ratios (IRRs) for the probabilistic multimarket contact variables show the expected number of citations if the probability of more contact equals one relative to the expected number when the probability of greater contact equals zero. They show, then, the predicted citations with perfectly or completely insignificant contact relative to citations with perfectly or completely significant multimarket contact, other things being the same.

Using specification (2) in Table 2, Table 3 shows the incidence rate ratios for the probability measures of multimarket contact along with their standard errors. For product market contact, other things being the same the citations with insignificant contact are predicted to be 0.217 or 21.7% of the citations with significant contact. For innovation market contacts, other things being the same, the citations with insignificant contact are predicted to be 0.107 or 10.7% of the citations given significant contact. Both of these IRRs are estimated well, and Table 3 shows their 95% confidence intervals. Using specification (2), the average of the model's predicted expected number of citations for each of the 1722 observations is 32.1 with standard deviation of 75.8. For comparison, in the sample the average of the actual number of citations for each of the 1722 observations is 30.0 with standard deviation of 90.8.

Although in the present model the ordinary count measures and the probability measures both show that multimarket contact and more citations go together, as discussed in Section VII, there are nonetheless differences in the measures that

Table 2. Negative Binomial Model of Cite$_{ij}$ for 1722 pairs (42 firms).

Variable	coefficient (standard error)[a]	
	(1)	(2)
Numpat$_i$	0.000652	0.000589
	(0.000137)**	(0.000150)**
Numpat$_j$	−0.000114	−0.000130
	(0.000196)	(0.000205)
Scilink$_i$	0.451	0.610
	(0.120)**	(0.134)**
Scilink$_j$	0.774	0.898
	(0.184)**	(0.192)**
Div$_i$	0.460	0.588
	(0.474)	(0.523)
Div$_j$	2.52	2.62
	(0.566)**	(0.609)**
Divpat$_i$	0.722	0.935
	(0.0989)**	(0.102)**
Divpat$_j$	0.212	0.447
	(0.0672)*	(0.0708)**
Gprod$_{ij}$	0.627	
	(0.0651)**	
prob(>Gprod$_{ij}$)		−1.53
		(0.179)**
Gpat$_{ij}$	0.294	
	(0.0259)**	
prob(>Gpat$_{ij}$)		−2.24
		(0.367)**
constant	−12.3	−15.6
	(1.15)**	(1.22)**
Product Market Controls[b]	yes	yes
Innovation Market Controls[c]	yes	yes
Number of observations	1722	1722
chi-squared (degrees of freedom)[d]	2315.9** (78)	2170.9** (78)
Pseudo R-squared	0.2210	0.2072
Log likelihood	−4080.8	−4153.3
Alpha, over-dispersion Parameter (std error)	1.150 (0.0597)**	1.368 (0.0678)**
Likelihood ratio test of alpha = 0 Chi-squared (1)[e]	20138.1**	28633.9**

***Table 2*.** Continued

---

[a] Significance levels: ** = 0.001, * = 0.01
[b] Ten of the twelve industry variables (six for firm i and six for firm j) showing the production locations of the firms are included. The variables $Dgen_i$ and $Dgen_j$ are absorbed in the intercept; thus, the constant term reflects the impact of having both firms in general chemicals.
[c] $Pgpp_{ix}$ and $Pgpp_{jx}$ for $x = 1$ to 30, except that $Pgpp_{ichemicals}$ and $Pgpp_{jchemicals}$ were excluded and left in the intercept. Thus, there are included in this specification 58 control variables for patent locations, 29 of the 30 product group patent percentage variables for firm i and the same 29 variables for firm j. The percentages in the 30 categories add to 100%, and the variable dropped for firm i and the variable dropped for firm j and left in the intercept are the variables showing the percentage of firm i's or firm j's patents in the CHI Research product group for chemicals. Not surprisingly, that is the product group with the largest percentage of patents on average for the firms in the sample. Thus, the constant term reflects the effect of having both firms in general chemicals and with 100% of their patents in chemicals with the effects of the included $Pgpp$ variables to be added in to reach the effect for the exact patent distribution for firm i or the firm j.
[d] The chi-squared statistic is for the test of the coefficient vector (against the null hypothesis of the coefficients all being zero) for just the explanatory variables in the negative binomial model and equals minus two times the difference between the log likelihood in the negative binomial model with a constant only and in the model fitting coefficients for all of the explanatory variables.
[e] The chi-squared statistic here is for the test of just the over-dispersion parameter of the negative binomial model. The statistic is minus two times the difference between the log likelihood for the comparison Poisson model and for the negative binomial model fitting all parameters. The negative binomial maximum-likelihood estimation was performed using Stata (StataCorp., 1999, Vol. 2, pp. 423–431). The negative binomial regression example provided there also has a huge chi-squared value for the test of alpha = 0, and as here it is many times larger than the chi-squared for the model's coefficient vector for the explanatory variables. Evidently, not only are cases of over-dispersion common; the significance of the parameter measuring and controlling for over-dispersion can be extraordinarily high.

---

might prove important for different research projects and samples. Here I discuss some of the differences in the context of the present paper's experiment.

First, the probability measures may have a less uniform distribution than the count measures. Once a large count of contacts occurs, the significance is high for pairs with typical amounts of diversification. In such cases, the probability measure may be close to zero whether the number of meetings is large or larger still. The important point is that the researcher needs to understand that the count and probability measures capture different aspects of multimarket contact. The count measure captures multimarket contact absolutely. The probability measure captures the significance of such contact against the null hypothesis of random behavior. In some experiments, the researcher would want to distinguish purposive behavior from nonpurposive or random behavior, and the probability

Table 3. Incidence Rate Ratios for Probability Measures of Multimarket Contact.*

Variable	IRR	Standard error	z	Prob>|z|	95% confidence interval
Prob(>Gprod)	0.2168	0.03874	-8.555	0.000	0.1527 to 0.3077
Prob(>Gpat)	0.1067	0.03919	-6.090	0.000	0.05190 to 0.2192

*These statistics use specification 2 in Table 2. The z statistic is for the underlying coefficient shown in Table 2. The IRR shows the estimated coefficient transformed to an incidence rate ratio as explained in the text. The standard error and the confidence interval shown here are appropriately transformed as well.

measure allows that, but it does downplay the differences in multimarket contact once that contact is significant. In the present paper's experiment, those differences are associated with behavior as shown by the fact that the effect on the likelihood is somewhat greater for the simple count measures in specification (1) of Table 2 than for the probability measures used in specification (2).

Second, both the probability measure and the count measure pick up a large, significant, positive (recall that the probability measures multimarket contact inversely) effect of multimarket contact on citations that is independent of a firm's diversification per se. In some experiments an important distinction is that the count measure of multimarket contact captures diversification to some extent along with multimarket contact, because greater absolute contact can only come with greater diversification across the product markets. The probability measure does not pick up any of the diversification per se – after all it was designed to avoid confusion between effects of multimarket contact and diversification counts that may reflect random behavior. In the present experiment, both product (for just the cited firm) and innovation market diversification (for both firms in the pair) per se as well as both the count and the probability measures of multimarket contact are significant. The patents of diversified firms are cited more frequently, other things being the same, especially those diversified in their product markets. Firms diversified in their innovation markets cite the patents of others more frequently, other things being the same.

Multimarket contact, in all of the forms considered and for both product and innovation markets, is highly significant and has a large, stable, positive effect on citations. Those results are quite robust. They remain when the diversification variables are dropped from the specifications; they remain when the controls for product and innovation market locations are dropped from the specifications; and they remain across a variety of estimating models. The negative binomial model appears to summarize the data well and it seems appropriate, but other estimating techniques show the same story for multimarket contact in the product and innovation markets and for both the count and the probability measures of contact.

The scale effect for the number of patents of the citing firm is positive and significant as expected, while that effect is positive and significant for the cited firm only when the patent diversification variables are dropped from the specification. The effects of the science linkage variables are positive and significant as expected.

The importance of the measures of multimarket contact in the sample of 1722 pairs reflects the effects of the extent of their multimarket contact across the sets of six chemicals product categories and of 30 patent groups. The result remains whether the sample excludes focused firms or not. The behavior of pairs of firms changes with the extent of their contact across multiple markets, other things being the same.

To show the range of the values of the variables for the 1722 pairs studied, Table 4 provides descriptive statistics for the variables used in the negative binomial model.

Table 4. Descriptive Statistics for the 1722 pairs for the full sample of 42 firms[a].

Variable	n	mean	standard deviation
All observations			
$Cite_{ij}$	1722	30.0	90.8
Numpat	1722	842.5	1148.7
Scilink	1722	0.99	1.10
Div	1722	1.81	1.20
Divpat	1722	11.2	6.08
$Gprod_{ij}$	1722	0.59	0.72
$prob(>Gprod_{ij})$	1722	0.19	0.21
$Gpat_{ij}$	1722	5.80	4.24
$prob(>Gpat_{ij})$	1722	0.057	0.128

[a] Because each firm appears once as the citing firm and once as the cited firm in combination with every other firm, in the models reported the complete set of 1722 observations for a variable's firm i values ($Numpat_i$ for example) includes the same values as the complete set of 1722 observations for a variable's firm j values ($Numpat_j$ for example) although of course their ordering is different. Thus for the summary statistics the variable (Numpat, for example) appears once and unsubscripted.

IX. CONCLUSION

This paper compares count and probability measures of the extent of the contact of a pair of firms across product and innovation markets. A difference with my previous work on multimarket contact is that the measures here examine the full sample, not just the diversified firms. The extent of multimarket contact for all possible pairs of firms is measured – for each pair of firms, contact can be in zero, one, two, or more markets.

For the product markets, I use alternatively:

- a count of the number of product markets where contact for the pair occurs, and
- the inverse probability measure of the contact that shows the significance of the contact – that is, the probability of more contact against the null hypothesis of random diversification.

For the innovation markets, I use alternatively:

- the count of the number of innovation markets where contact for the pair occurs, and
- the inverse probability measure of the contact – that is, the probability of more contact against the null hypothesis of random allocation of patent activity.

The results show that multimarket contact in both product and innovation markets is associated with a substantial, statistically significant effect on behavior, other things being the same.

Despite efforts to design the test to capture effects of multimarket contact on citation behavior, clearly the research results underlying the sequence of citations over time can affect the evolution of multimarket contact. The hypothesis test here was designed to capture the broad, stable product and innovation market positions of large chemicals firms and then isolate the effects of the patterns of their multimarket contact on their recent citation behavior. An alternative design would trace the evolution of citations through time and the subsequent changes in multimarket contact. Estimating the evolutionary link from citations to subsequent multimarket contact simultaneously with the behavioral effects of multimarket contact on citations is beyond the scope of the present essay which had the goal of adducing methodological issues while presenting evidence for an effect of multimarket contact that is not itself controversial.

The effect of multimarket contact on citations, given controls for the product and innovation market effects in citations, is expected because the R&D of other firms is most useful to a firm when it is actively involved in the same product and innovation markets as the firms whose R&D it borrows. To the extent that the research design explained in Section V addresses endogeneity successfully, the evidence does show a behavioral effect of multimarket contact on patent citations. Certainly there is evidence of a strong statistical association between contact and citations, even given controls for the other effects in citations. Congruence of two firms' operations across the product and innovation markets of each is extraordinarily important for their ability to absorb each other's research and development ideas.

ACKNOWLEDGMENTS

I am indebted to Joel A. C. Baum, William L. Baldwin and Henrich R. Greve for many helpful comments on the earlier version of the paper.

NOTES

1. The 30 groups are: (1) Agriculture, (2) Oil & Gas, Mining, (3) Power Generation & Distribution, (4) Food & Tobacco, (5) Textiles & Apparel, (6) Wood & Paper, (7) Chemicals, (8) Pharmaceuticals, (9) Biotechnology, (10) Medical Equipment, (11) Medical Electronics, (12) Plastics, Polymers & Rubber, (13) Glass, Clay & Cement, (14) Primary Metals, (15) Fabricated Metals, (16) Industrial Machinery & Tools, (17) Industrial Process Equipment, (18) Office Equipment & Cameras, (19) Heating, Ventilation, Refrigeration, (20) Miscellaneous Machinery, (21) Computers & Peripherals, (22) Telecommunications, (23) Semiconductors & Electronics, (24) Measurement & Control Equipment, (25) Electrical Appliances & Components, (26) Motor Vehicles & Parts, (27) Aerospace & Parts, (28) Other Transport, (29) Miscellaneous Manufacturing, (30) Other.
2. The negative binomial model is estimated using Stata (StataCorp., 1999, Vol. 2. pp. 423-431).
3. See StataCorp. (1999, Vol. 2, p. 425).

REFERENCES

Adams, W. J. (1974). Market Structure and Corporate Power: The Horizontal Dominance Hypothesis Reconsidered. *Columbia Law Review*, *74*, 1276–1297.

Baum, J. A. C., & Korn, H. J. (1996). Competitive Dynamics of Interfirm Rivalry. *Academy of Management Journal*, *39*, 255–291.

Baum, J. A. C., & Korn, H. J. (1999). Dynamics of Dyadic Competitive Interaction. *Strategic Management Journal*, *20*, 251–278.

Boeker, W., Goodstein, J., Stephan, J., & Murmann, J. P. (1997). Competition in a Multimarket Environment: The Case of Market Exit. *Organization Science*, *8*, 126–142,

Bernheim, B. D., & Whinston, M. D. (1990). Multimarket Contact and Collusive Behavior. *Rand Journal of Economics*, *21* (Spring), 1–26.

Cassidy, C., & Loree, D. (2001). Dynamics of Knowledge Transfer Among Multimarket Competitors. In: J. A. C. Baum & H. R. Greve (Eds), *Multiunit Organization and Multimarket Strategy*: *Advances in Strategic Management*, Vol. 18 (pp. 141–174). Oxford U.K.: JAI Press, 2001.

CHI Research, Inc. (1996). *TECH-LINE-CD: Indicators of Technological Excellence Manual*, revised 1996, and special tabulations by CHI Research.

Edwards, C. D. (1955). Conglomerate Bigness as a Source of Power. In: *The National Bureau of Economic Research conference report, Business Concentration and Price Policy* (pp. 331–339). Princeton: Princeton University Press.

Evans, W. N., & Kessides, I. N. (1994). Living by the Golden Rule: Multimarket Contact in the U.S. Airline Industry. *Quarterly Journal of Economics, 109*, 341–366.

Feinberg, R. M. (1984). Mutual Forbearance as an Extension of Oligopoly Theory. *Journal of Economics and Business, 36*, 243–249.

Feinberg, R. M. (1985). 'Sales at Risk': A Test of the Mutual Forbearance Theory of Conglomerate Behavior. *Journal of Business, 58*, 225–241.

Feinberg, R. M. & Sherman, R. (1988). Mutual Forbearance Under Experimental Conditions. *Southern Economic Journal, 54*, 985–993.

Gimeno, J. (1999). Reciprocal Threats in Multimarket Rivalry: Staking out 'Spheres of Influence' in the U.S. Airline Industry. *Strategic Management Journal, 20*, 101–128.

Gimeno, J., & Jeong, E. (2001). Multimarket Contact: Meaning and Measurement at Multiple Levels of Analysis. In: J. A. C. Baum and H. R. Greve (Eds), *Multiunit Organization and Multimarket Strategy: Advances in Strategic Management*, Vol. 18 (pp. 357–408). Oxford U.K.: JAI Press, 2001.

Gimeno, J., & Woo, C. Y. (1996). Hypercompetition in a Multimarket Environment: The Role of Strategic Similarity and Multimarket Contact in Competitive De-escalation. *Organization Science, 7*, 322–341.

Gimeno, J., & Woo, C. Y. (1999). Multimarket Contact, Economies of Scope, and Firm Performance. *Academy of Management Journal, 43*, 239–259.

Greve, H. R. (1999). Branch Systems and Nonlocal Learning in Populations. In: A. Miner & P. Anderson (Eds), *Population-Level Learning and Industry Change: Advances in Strategic Management* (pp. 57–80), Vol. 16. Stamford, Conn.: JAI Press.

Greve, H. R. (2000). Market Niche Entry Decisions: Competition, Learning, and Strategy in Tokyo Banking, 1894–1936. *Academy of Management Journal, 43*, 816–836.

Heggestad, A. A., & Rhoades, S. A. (1978). Multi-Market Interdependence and Local Market Competition in Banking. *Review of Economics and Statistics, 60*, 523–532.

Hughes, K., & Oughton, C. (1993). Diversification, Multi-market Contact and Profitability. *Economica, 60*, 203–224.

Ingram, P., & Baum, J. A. C. (1997a). Chain Affiliation and the Failure of Manhattan Hotels, 1898–1980. *Administrative Science Quarterly, 42*, 68–102.

Ingram, P., & Baum, J. A. C. (1997b). Opportunity and Constraint: Organizations' Learning from the Operating and Competitive Experience of Industries. *Strategic Management Journal, 18*, 75–98.

Ingram, P., & Baum, J. A. C. (2001). Interorganizational Learning and the Dynamics of Chain Relationships. In: J. A. C. Baum & H. R. Greve (Eds), *Multiunit Organization and Multimarket Strategy: Advances in Strategic Management*, Vol. 18 (pp. 109–139). Oxford U.K.: JAI Press).

Jans, I., & Rosenbaum, D. I. (1997). Multimarket Contact and Pricing: Evidence from the U.S. Cement Industry. *International Journal of Industrial Organization, 15*, 391–412.

Kealey, T., & Al-Ubaydli, O. (2000). *Science as an Invisible College Good: Remodelling Endogenous Growth Theory, manuscript.* University of Cambridge, Department of Clinical Biochemistry, Cambridge, U.K., August.

Korn, H. J., & Baum, J. A. C. (1999). Chance, Imitative, and Strategic Antecedents to Multimarket Contact. *Academy of Management Journal, 42,* 171–193.

Link, A. N., & Scott, J. T. (1999). *Development of an Industrial Database on Licensing Patterns, Final Report submitted to the National Science Foundation, Division of Science Resources Studies, Research and Development Statistics Program,* SGER Project 9615976, July.

Martin, S. (2000). *Spillovers, Appropriability, and R&D,* manuscript. University of Amsterdam, The Netherlands, July.

Mester, L. J. (1987). Multiple Market Contact between Savings and Loans. *Journal of Money, Credit and Banking, 19,* 538–549.

Parker, P. M., & Roller, L. H. (1997). Collusive Conduct in Duopolies: Multimarket Contact and Cross-ownership in the Mobile Telephone Industry. *Rand Journal of Economics, 28,* 304–322.

Phillips, O. R., & Mason, C. F. (1992). Mutual Forbearance in Experimental Conglomerate Markets, *Rand Journal of Economics, 23,* 395–414.

Phillips, O. R., & Mason, C. F. (1996). Market Regulation and Multimarket Rivalry. *Rand Journal of Economics, 27,* 596–617.

Pilloff, S. J. (1999). Multimarket Contact in Banking. *Review of Industrial Organization, 14,* 163–182.

Scherer, F. M. (1970). *Industrial Market Structure and Economic Performance.* Chicago: Rand McNally.

Scott, J. T. (1982). Multimarket Contact and Economic Performance. *Review of Economics and Statistics, 64* (August), 368–375.

Scott, J. T. (1988). Diversification versus Co-operation in R&D Investment. *Managerial and Decision Economics, 9,* 173–186.

Scott, J. T. (1989). Purposive Diversification as a Motive for Merger. *International Journal of Industrial Organization, 7,* (March), 35–47.

Scott, J. T. (1991). Multimarket Contact among Diversified Oligopolists. *International Journal of Industrial Organization, 9* (June), 225–238.

Scott, J. T. (1993). *Purposive Diversification and Economic Performance.* Cambridge, England: Cambridge University Press.

Scott, J. T. (2000). *Strategic Research Partnerships: What Have We Learned?* Presented at the Workshop on Strategic Research Partnerships sponsored by the National Science Foundation and convened at SRI International, Washington, D. C., October 13, and forthcoming in a special report about strategic research partnerships to be published by the National Science Foundation.

Scott, J. T., & Pascoe, G. (1987). Purposive Diversification of R&D in Manufacturing. *The Journal of Industrial Economics, 36* (December), 193–205.

Singal, V. (1996). Airline Mergers and Multimarket Contact. *Managerial and Decision Economics, 17,* 559–574.

Spagnolo, G. (1999). On Interdependent Supergames: Multimarket Contact, Concavity and Collusion. *Journal of Economic Theory, 89* (November).

StataCorp (1999). *Stata Statistical Software: Release 6* with *Stata Reference Manual: Release 6.* College Station, Texas: Stata Press.

Usher, J. M. (1999). Specialists, Generalists, and Polymorphs: Spatial Advantages of Multiunit Organization in a Single Industry. *Academy of Management Review, 24,* 143–150.

Van Wegberg, M., Van Witteloostuijn, A., & Abbing, M. R. (1994). Multimarket and Multiproject
    Collusion: Why European Integration May Reduce Intra-Community Competition. *De
    Economist, 142* , 253–285.
Vonortas, N. S. (2000). Multimarket Contact and Inter-firm Cooperation in R&D. *Journal of
    Evolutionary Economics, 10*, 243–271.

Part Three:
MARKET BEHAVIOR

COLLUSION IN HORIZONTALLY CONNECTED MARKETS: MULTIMARKET PRODUCERS AS CONDUITS FOR LEARNING

Owen R. Phillips and Charles F. Mason

ABSTRACT

Two duopoly market structures are experimentally constructed. Payoff tables describe basic conditions in an X market and a Y market. In one market structure two rivals choose X quantities and a different set of rivals choose Y quantities. These markets develop equilibria independently. A second market structure creates a multiproduct producer that chooses both an X and Y output. Separate X and Y duopolists are rivals to the multiproduct producer. The multiproduct/multimarket rival creates a horizontal connection for the X and Y markets. Subjects choose outputs from payoff tables for at least thirty five periods. Compared to the independent duopolies, the horizontal connection raises outputs in the X market and lowers outputs in the Y market. These impacts are statistically significant. We find Granger causality for output choices moving from X to Y and from Y to X in the connected markets; however learning that moves through the horizontal connection is less influential than learning within the market. Further testing shows that competitive learning travels better than cooperative learning through the multimarket firm.

Multiunit Organization and Multimarket Strategy, Volume 18, pages 205–227.
ISBN: 0-7623-0721-8

I. INTRODUCTION

We begin with a very fundamental idea that "connected markets" have one or more firms that operate in multiple markets. These multiunit, multimarket (MUMM) enterprises establish a linkage whereby behavior in one market can impact behavior in another market. A well-known example of possible cross-market influence is mutual forbearance. Firms that confront each other in multiple markets use cooperative behavior in one market to induce cooperation in other markets. Such effects could be tied to learning, in that firms come to understand the cooperative tendencies of their rivals in one area of competition and transfer this learning to other markets. Alternatively, the behavioral connection has been modeled in a game theoretic framework with linked incentive constraints (Bernheim & Whinston, 1990). The costs and benefits of cooperation in one market are not independent of rivalry with the same firm in another market. Cooperative strategies between the firms are pooled to cover the multi-market rivalry, and this leads to joint output and pricing decisions.

In this paper we study connected markets without multimarket rivalry, recognizing there is a difference between multimarket contact and multimarket competition (Stephen & Boeker, this volume), and there can be contact without competition. Our focus is on a MUMM firm that is a rival to independent producers in two other markets. These two markets, we shall say, are *horizontally connected*, through the MUMM firm. Specifically there is one firm that produces X and Y products for different markets; this firm faces one rival in the X market and a second, distinct rival in the Y market. In this setting, there is no reason to expect the pooling of incentive constraints in the two markets. We believe the potential influence of one market upon behavior in the other will come from learning. We propose some very simple lines of study. Given the horizontal connection, does the interaction of rivals in the X market impact the interaction of rivals in the Y market and/or vice versa? Does the interaction, if it exists, lead to more or less cooperation in markets? Can cooperation be transferred from one market to the other through the multimarket conduit? Does intensely competitive behavior in one market filter into another market? Addressing these questions compares behavior in a connected market structure to behavior in markets without the multimarket link.

This study would be a difficult undertaking if data in naturally occurring markets were relied upon; instead, we analyze data from laboratory markets. Subjects are presented with payoff tables that show them how much they earn for every row choice they might make, given the column choice of a rival. The intersection of a row and column choice is profit for the period. These choices correspond to production outputs in the market. For each $q_i + q_j = Q$ set of quantities, underlying demand and cost conditions determine profit to the seller. These experimental markets are real; subjects are paid in cash what they earn from the payoff tables.

Using experimental methods we create horizontally connected markets and compare outcomes to markets with the same basic conditions, but without the connection. Figure 1 provides a sketch of the two market structures. In both cases rivalry is a duopoly. In panel (1a) the multimarket agent produces both the X and Y product. In the laboratory, this person has two payoff tables and makes an X and Y row choice each production period of the game. There is another X agent making a quantity choice and a different Y agent making a quantity choice, so the multimarket producer faces two distinct rivals in two distinct markets. We compare what happens in this environment to the market structures illustrated in panel (1b), where there is an X and Y duopoly market without a linkage through the multiproduct seller.[1] Such controlled experimental environments will allow us to better understand the influence of multimarket contacts. In this context we investigate how learning in the market and the perceptions of a rival player in one game can affect learning and perceptions in another game. Learning can be carried into the other market through the multimarket contact.

These two particular market structures keep demand and costs the same; further the number of firms in the markets is unchanged. Nevertheless these market structures can have different influences on the cooperative nature of rivals. The simple independent duopoly structure puts a silo around interaction

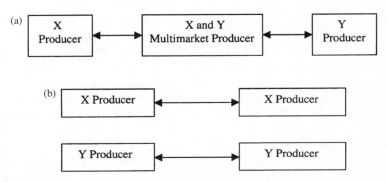

Fig. 1. Connected and Unconnected Duopoly Markets: (a) Horizontally Connected Duopoly Markets; (b) Horizontally Unconnected Duopoly Markets.

and learning that goes on between two rivals. The duopoly relationship is self-contained. Commitments to a price, signaling to cooperate, punishment strategies, and generally reputation are learned through the interaction of the two firms (Saloner, 1994; Ingram & Baum, 1997). This learning is not transferred to a population of organizations, nor is other learning from the population of firms transferred into the X and Y duopolies. The linked market structure, on the other hand, creates an environment through which duopoly learning in either of the two markets can be transferred to the other through the multiproduct producer. It is in this sense we label the multimarket rival a conduit across markets in the population.

There are limits to learning. Just as rationality is bounded in decision making, the capability of managers to understand and put their experiences in perspective is bounded (Levinthal & March, 1993). The history of interaction between agents is a filter through which current actions by one agent are seen by the other. In the horizontally connected design the multiproduct seller generates two histories. This agent must undertake simultaneous learning, and this creates a "noisy environment" that makes learning difficult (Levinthal & March, 1993, p. 97). The histories in the connected market structure can get tangled and this can lead to very different outputs and prices than those observed in the "siloed" duopolies. From field studies, e.g. Greve (1999), Korn and Baum (1999), and Baum and Ingram (1998), the added contact through multimarket interaction is not necessarily beneficial to the linked enterprises.

II. THEORETICAL CONSIDERATIONS

Behavior in a duopoly market is widely modeled with a trigger strategy in a repeated game (Tirole, 1988, Chap. 6; Green & Porter, 1984; Friedman, 1983). Such a strategy is comprised of two parts: cooperative-looking choices that players select so long as there are no defections by either player from these choices, and a "punishment phase," consisting of a punishment choice and a period over which these choices are made, in the event of defection. Consider a two-person infinitely repeated game with payoffs identical to a quantity choosing, duopoly market. Two players simultaneously make choices q_{1t} and q_{2t} in each period $t = 1, 2, \ldots$; subjects make a row choice from a payoff table before the column choice of a rival is known. In any period t, player i's payoffs are $\pi_i(q_{it}, q_{jt})$, for $i, j = 1, 2$. The weight placed upon next period's payoffs in a market, i.e. the discount factor, is δ for both player. It is generally argued (Rasmusen, 1989; Kreps, 1990) that δ captures much more than the simple time structure of payoffs. The discount factor can capture the probability of the game ending as the players know it. Importantly it can reflect the beliefs players have over the cooperative tendencies of their rival; it need not be the same across markets. When learning takes place within a market and across markets, δ may change.

For simplicity of exposition, we restrict the model to stationary, symmetric equilbria of the repeated game; these are combinations of strategies that are the same for each player at each point in time. It can be argued that such strategies are easily identified by agents and more likely to represent "self-evident patterns of play," and therefore are most likely to be selected from the set of subgame perfect equilibria (Kreps, 1990). Subgame perfection exists if play at any point in the game is consistent with Nash equilibrium behavior for the remainder of the game.

Perhaps the best-known example of a trigger strategy is the "grim reaper strategy." Under this strategy, the cooperative quantity, q^c, is selected so long as both players have chosen this quantity in all previous periods. The punishment quantity is the one-shot Cournot/Nash equilibrium choice, q^n, and the punishment phase lasts forever. If either player defects in some period τ, both choose q^n in all future periods $t = \tau + 1$, $\tau + 2$, and so on. Let $q^d(q^c)$ be the optimal one-period defection to the cooperative choice. Then, we may write symmetric cooperative payoffs as $\pi^c \equiv \pi(q^c, q^c)$ and defection profits as $\pi^d \equiv \pi(q^d(q^c), q^c)$. It is evident that both payoffs are uniquely determined by q^c, and so henceforth we shall write them only as functions of q^c. It is assumed that π^c is a concave function of q^c. Finally, we write the one-shot Cournot/Nash equilibrium payoffs as π^n. For the choice q^c to be supported as part of a subgame perfect equilibrium path, these payoffs must satisfy the incentive constraint:

$$\pi^d(q^c) + \delta\pi^n/(1-\delta) \leq \pi^c(q^c)/(1-\delta). \tag{1}$$

The interpretation of this constraint is that rivals in a market can realize the cooperative payoff perennially if no one defects. Following any defection, however, play reverts to an infinite sequence of one-shot Cournot/Nash equilibrium choices. Thus, each player must compare the present discounted value of continued cooperation, the right side of (1), against the present discounted value of defection, the left side of (1), which includes the one-shot gain from defection and the discounted flow of one-shot Cournot/Nash profits.

It is well-known that there are many values of q^c that satisfy this constraint, but we shall consider the most profitable of these. This choice yields strategies that payoff dominate all alternative (stationary symmetric) subgame perfect equilibria. Let us write this value as q^*; it solves the constrained optimization problem

$$\text{Max } \pi^c$$
$$q^c \quad \text{s.t. } (1-\delta)\pi^d(q^c) + \delta\pi^n \leq \pi^c(q^c).$$

The unconstrained optimum choice q^m will have at the margin $\pi^{c\prime}(q^m) = 0$. Since π^c is concave, $\pi^{c\prime}(q^c) < 0$ for $q^c > q^m$. If complete collusion is not feasible then $q^c > q^m$ in the relevant range, and so it follows that q^* is the smallest value of q^c that satisfies the incentive constraint. At this choice the incentive constraint is just binding and:

$$\pi^c(q^*) - (1-\delta)\pi^d(q^*) - \delta\pi^n = 0. \tag{2}$$

It is against this backdrop that Bernheim and Whinston (1990) have analytically demonstrated that multimarket rivalry in a conglomerate setting can lead to more cooperative-looking choices in some markets but less cooperative-looking choices in others. In the case of duopolists meeting in two markets, contact will decrease quantities in one market and raise them in the other. The pooled incentive constraint from multimarket rivalry allows firms to increase profits by breaking the incentive constraint in one market and relaxing the constraint in the other market. Where the constraint is broken, outputs decrease; where there is compensating slack, outputs increase. The appropriate market in which to break the constraint is the market in which it is relatively more profitable to collude. Phillips and Mason (1992, 1996) discuss this in more detail and provide support for this kind of mutual forbearance in experimental markets for multimarket duopolies.

The multiproduct seller in Fig. 1 faces two incentive constraints that cannot be pooled. It must reach distinct equilibrium in each of the X and Y markets. In one or both markets it is likely that one or more agents at some point in the game will be inclined to move choices toward more cooperative and higher profit levels. These tendencies reflect different degrees of "rationality" between agents (Kreps, 1990). In such an event, it is not unreasonable to envision the multiproduct seller attempting to convey the possibilities of larger joint profits to the other seller. This behavior transfers learning across markets. Learning alters the incentive constraints by changing δ (the weight put on future returns), and this will change the quantities at which the constraint becomes binding. To the extent that such learning moves from one market to another, our interest is in determining the direction and the extent to which learning occurs. Do cooperative or noncooperative changes in behavior in market X lead to similar changes in Y, or do changes in Y predate changes in X? In our econometric analysis below we investigate this issue, by testing the hypothesis that lagged choices in the X market are useful in explaining current behavior in the Y market (and conversely).

III. EXPERIMENTAL DESIGN AND DATA

Subjects in our experimental design make choices from a payoff table for an indefinite number of periods. The row choice made by one subject becomes the column value of a counterpart. The intersection of the row and column in the payoff table shows earnings for the period. The payoff table represents the normal form of a stage game (Friedman, 1983). The use of payoff tables in experiments has a history that predates their description of oligopoly markets. Rapoport, Guyer and Gordon (1976) and Colman (1982), for instance, provide extensive surveys of literally hundreds of experiments that use payoff tables to generally learn more about rivalry and bargaining behavior. Surveys of how researchers have used payoff tables to study non-cooperative behavior are provided by Davis and Holt (1993, Chapter 2), Friedman and Sunder (1994, Chapter 9), Kagel and Roth (1995), and Plott (1989).

Subjects for each of the three experimental market structures were recruited from upper level undergraduate economic classes. They reported to a reserved classroom with a personal computer at each seat. At the beginning of a session, instructions were read aloud as subjects followed along on their own copy. Questions were taken and one practice period was held with sample payoff tables different from those used in the experiment. In the practice period, a monitor randomly chose a column value while subjects, at the same time, chose a row value from one or two sample payoff tables. Payoffs from the intersection of a row and the monitor's column were recorded on a record sheet by every subject. Each person was checked during the practice period to insure that everyone understood payoff tables and that they were correctly recording their choices and earnings. Earnings were measured in a fictitious currency called tokens. At the end of the experiment, tokens were exchanged for cash at the rate of $1.00 = 1000$ tokens.

In each market period subjects were instructed to type their row choices into their personal computer. These computers were linked together and networked by the University's VAX cluster. Subjects were anonymously paired for the duration of the experiment, and paired individuals were not in proximity to each other. Once everyone had made their choices, the computer screen reported back to each subject his or her choices, earnings, and balance. Subjects kept track of this information and they always could check the computer's calculations from the payoff tables provided to them. Subjects also were informed of the rival's choice and earnings. Finally, all participants knew that the experiment would last at least 35 periods, and at the end of each period thereafter, the computer would randomly generate a number between 0 and 100, and that the experiment would end in the first period the random number did not exceed

20.[2] Sessions generally ended between periods 35 and 40, and took about 1½ hours. Earnings averaged about $25 per subject.

Each of the three markets represented in Fig. 1 are experimentally designed as two-person repeated games, where the payoff table are derived from linear demand and cost conditions. In the X market each agent faced fixed costs of 1300/19, and no variable costs. The inverse demand function was $P_x = 150/19 - 5(q_i + q_j)/76$. Every entry in the X payoff table for the primary treatment, therefore, came from the payoff or profit function:

$$\pi_{ix} = [150/19 - 5(q_{ix} + q_{jx})/76] \, q_{ix} - 1300/19.$$

In the payoff table seen by the subjects, quantity choices were rescaled to values between 1 and 22, where a choice of 1 corresponded to an output of 28, and so on. A reduced-in-size copy of the payoff table is attached at the end of this paper. Subjects were never told they were picking outputs, just that they were choosing values from a payoff table where the intersection of their row choice and the other player's column choice determined earnings for the period. With the renumbering of output choices, the Cournot/Nash choice in the X payoff table was 13, and the symmetric joint profit maximizing choice was 3.

The Y market had fixed costs of 63.426 for each seller, no marginal costs, and inverse demand $P_y = [1800 - 15(q_{iy} + q_{jy})]/289$. Again choices were rescaled, with subjects choosing values between 1 and 27. Here a choice of 1 corresponded to an output of 25, a choice of 2 corresponded to an output of 26, and so on. The non-cooperative Cournot/Nash equilibrium in the Y market was (16,16). Perfect, symmetric collusion was at (6,6). A copy of this payoff table also is attached at the end of this paper.

Two experimental sessions where subjects participated in just the Y market were conducted for a total of 14 markets (8 markets in one session and 6 markets in the other). Two sessions of 7 markets each, were conducted for all subjects choosing an X value. The horizontally connected market sessions required one subject, choosing an X and Y value, grouped with two other subjects choosing either an X or Y value but not both. Three connected experimental sessions were conducted with a total of 14 groups. Two sessions had fifteen subjects (a total of 10 groups) and one had twelve subjects (4 groups). In these connected groups, therefore, there were 14 X-connected markets and 14 Y-connected markets.

Figure 2 shows the average *market* choice of subject pairs in the X independent and X connected markets. The dashed line is the average market output or paired choices of players in the independent X market. The solid line is the average paired choices of players in the horizontally connected X market. After period five, Fig. 2 shows that connected market choices are consistently greater

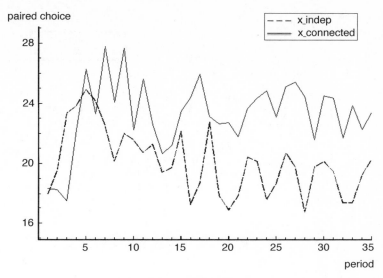

Fig. 2. X Market Choices.

than choices in the independent market. As the sessions progress the spread between the trends appears to widen and become stable. The horizontally connected X markets are relatively more competitive than the independent X duopoly markets.

Figure 3 compares the average market choice of subject pairs in the Y independent and Y connected markets. Once again, the connected market is the solid line. The pattern of paired choices is less definite than that in Fig. 2, but the connected Y market choices are lower than the independent market outputs until period 18. Between periods 19 and 25 choices appear about the same, and then after period 25 the connected Y market choices are again lower than the independent Y choices. The data generally show less Y competitiveness in the connected markets. Taking Figs 2 and 3 together, the horizontal connection seems to cause greater X outputs and lower Y outputs, and the X output increase seems to be substantial.

IV. ECONOMETRIC ANALYSIS OF THE DATA

The structural econometric model we estimate in order to test for differences in the X and Y markets, across the independent and connected structures, is

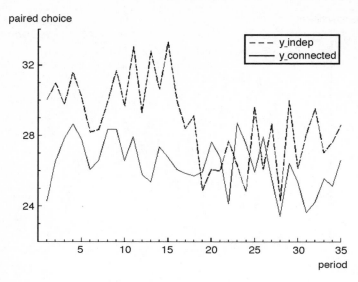

Fig. 3.   Y Market Choices.

drawn from our earlier work (Mason, Phillips & Nowell, 1992; Mason & Phillips, 2000a, b; Phillips & Mason, 1992, 1996). We assume that each subject's choice is dependent on his or her prediction of a rival's period t action, and that the game's history is a key determinant of a subject's prediction of a rival's choice. Subjects operating in only one market of a connected structure know only about outputs in that market, and therefore would only care about the outputs in this market, while subjects operating in both markets would presumably try to predict the upcoming market choice of rivals in each market. Since we use the aggregated output in each market as the focus of our empirical investigation we allow current market output in each market to be influenced by past choices in both markets. In particular, we allow for effects from the two preceding periods to influence current behavior.[3] We therefore posit the following relations for paired outputs:

$$X_{it} = \beta_n^X + \mu_n^{XY}Y_{it-1} + \mu_n^{XX}X_{it-1} + \theta_n^{XY}Y_{it-2} + \theta_n^{XX}X_{it-2} + \varepsilon_{it}^X \qquad (3)$$

$$Y_{it} = \beta_n^Y + \mu_n^{YY}Y_{it-1} + \mu_n^{YX}X_{it-1} + \theta_n^{YY}Y_{it-2} + \theta_n^{YX}X_{it-2} + \varepsilon_{it}^Y \qquad (4)$$

where X_{is} (respectively, Y_{is}) represents the X (respectively, Y) market output chosen by subject pair i for period s = t, t−1 or t−2; n = 1 if pair i is in group

1 (independent), and $n = 2$ if pair i is in group 2 (connected). The parameters μ_n^{jh} measure the impact of a small change in period $t-1$ output in market h upon period t output in market j, for j, h $\in$ {X,Y}, n = 1 or 2. Similarly, the parameters θ_n^{jh} measure the impact of a small change in period $t-2$ output in market h upon period t output in market j, for j, h $\in$ {X,Y}, n = 1 or 2. Notice that the various parameters are assumed to be the same for all subject pairs in a given design. Finally, we assume the disturbance term ε_{it}^k is white noise for k = X, Y (i.e. it has mean zero, is homoscedastic within a market, and is serially uncorrelated).[4]

These relations are expected to hold without qualification for subjects in the connected design. However, there is no reason to expect subjects in the X market of the independent experiments to be influenced by Y market subject behavior, or conversely. Correspondingly, we impose the parameter restrictions $\mu_1^{YX} = \mu_1^{XY} = \theta_1^{YX} = \theta_1^{XY} = 0$ when estimating this system for the independent markets.

The first test has to do with the ultimate equilibrium values for the two markets. Let us call these values X_1^e and Y_1^e for the independent design and X_2^e and Y_2^e for the connected design. In constructing estimates of these values, we take the perspective that subject choices converge toward the true equilibrium over the course of the experimental session. Starting from equations (3) and (4), estimates of the ultimate equilibrium values can be derived in terms of the parameters in the system above by substituting X_n^e for X_{is} and Y_n^e for Y_{is}, s = t, t-1, t-2, assuming $\varepsilon_{it}^X = \varepsilon_{it}^Y = 0$ (Fomby, Hill & Johnson, 1988). Solving the resultant matrix equations for X_1^e and Y_1^e, we obtain

$$X_n^e = [(1 - \mu_n^{YY} - \theta_n^{YY})\beta_n^X + (\mu_n^{XY} + \theta_n^{XY})\beta_n^Y]/D; \tag{5}$$

$$Y_n^e = [(\mu_n^{YX} + \theta_n^{YX})\beta_n^X + (1 - \mu_n^{XX} - \theta_n^{XX})\beta_n^Y]/D; \tag{6}$$

where $D = (1 - \mu_n^{YY} - \theta_n^{YY})(1 - \mu_n^{XX} - \theta_n^{XX}) - (\mu_n^{XY} + \theta_n^{XY})(\mu_n^{YX} + \theta_n^{YX})$, and n indexes the group as 1 or 2. We note that the formulae for X_n^e and Y_n^e are continuous functions of the βs, μs, and θs so long as $D \neq 0$. It follows from Slutsky's theorem[5] that X_n^e and Y_n^e can be consistently estimated by inserting consistent estimates of the βs, μs, and θs into equations (5) and (6).

To obtain estimates of the various parameters, and then test hypotheses regarding the equilibrium levels of outputs, we pooled the paired choices for each period from the three experimental sessions. With 14 paired choices in the connected market design, this gave us 462 data points for the estimation procedure. Likewise, we have 14 pairs in each of the independent X and Y markets, which yields 462 observations for each of the separate markets. In

Table 1. Regression Results For Paired Choices.

Parameter	Independent Design point estimate	Connected Design point estimate
β_n^X	5.537*	5.411*
	(0.3007)	(1.204)
μ_n^{XY}	–	0.0862*
		(0.0406)
μ_n^{XX}	0.5535*	0.4196*
	(0.0167)	(0.0461)
θ_n^{XY}	–	0.0528
		(0.0411)
θ_n^{XX}	0.18873*	0.2003
	(0.0168)	(0.0461)
X_n^e	20.778	24.004
	(0.5040)	(0.3074)
β_n^y	12.413*	5.3456*
	(0.4488)	(1.2834)
μ_n^{YY}	0.3771*	0.3131*
	(0.0152)	(0.0433)
μ_n^{YX}	–	0.0573
		(0.0491)
θ_n^{YY}	0.17552*	0.3710*
	(0.0153)	(0.0438)
θ_n^{YX}	–	0.0717
		(0.0491)
Y_n^e	27.746	26.724
	(0.3167)	(0.3699)

* significant at better than 1% level.
chi-squared test stat for Y Granger causes X: 10.835 (p-value = 0.004).
chi-squared test stat for X Granger causes Y: 6.822 (p-value = 0.033).
chi-squared test stat for H_0: $X_1^e = X_2^e$ and $Y_1^e = Y_2^e$: 18.424 (p-value = 0.0001).
t-stats on differences between connected & ind. steady state estimates are 9.257 (X);–2.099 (Y).
number of observations: 462 (independent X), 462 (independent Y), 462 (connected).

each case, we estimated the system of equations defined by (5) and (6) for all subject pairs in a given design, using ordinary least squares. The resultant parameter estimates are given in Table 1.

Estimated equilibrium market outputs are numerically and statistically larger in the connected design than in the independent design for the X market. By contrast, estimated equilibrium market outputs are numerically and statistically smaller in the connected design than in the independent design for the Y market. To test the joint hypothesis that both equilibrium outputs are unaffected by the horizontal connection, i.e. H_0: $X_1^e = X_2^e$ and $Y_1^e = Y_2^e$, we use a likelihood ratio test. The resultant test statistic is distributed as a chi-squared variate with 2 degrees of freedom under the null hypothesis (Fomby, Hill & Johnson, 1988). In this application the value of the test statistic is 18.424, which is significant at better than the 1% level. Thus, we reject the null hypothesis, and conclude that subject behavior in the connected and independent designs is statistically different.

In light of the observation that steady-state outputs are different in the connected design, we are led to inquire into the cause. Specifically, we wish to investigate the possibility that actions in one market drive those in the other. Formally, variable A is said to "Granger cause" variable B if past values of A are valuable in explaining B (Jacobs, Leamer & Ward, 1979). In the context of our connected design, choices in X Granger cause choices in Y if past values of X are useful in explaining current values of Y, i.e. if one can reject the joint hypothesis that $\mu^{YX} = 0$ and $\theta^{YX} = 0$. Similarly, choices in Y Granger cause choices in X if one can reject the joint hypothesis that $\mu^{XY} = 0$ and $\theta^{XY} = 0$. We test these two hypotheses using a likelihood ratio test. Under the null hypothesis, the test statistic has a chi-squared distribution with two degrees of freedom. We obtain a test statistic of 10.835 for the hypothesis that Y choices do not Granger cause X choices, and a test statistic of 6.822 for the hypothesis that X choices do not Granger cause Y choices. Each of these statistics is significant at the 5% level; the first also is significant at the 1% level (the critical values at the 5% level and 1% level are 5.99 and 9.21 respectively). We note that none of the four key parameter estimates is very large. Thus, while there is evidence that Y choices Granger cause X choices, and that X choices Granger cause Y choices, these two effects are small in comparison to the own-effect (lagged choices in k upon current choices in k, k = X or Y). We conclude that while there is a transfer of learning across markets – in that past values of one market impact current values of the other – this impact is not as strong as the history of behavior between rivals in the same market.

Despite the secondary importance of Granger causality, it would appear that behavior in each market *is* impacted by the presence of the other market in the connected design. Interestingly, the impact is reminiscent of the effect that multimarket rivalry has upon the behavior of the two firms meeting in X and Y duopoly markets (Phillips & Mason, 1992), where there is both contact and rivalry between two MUMM firms. In experiments using the identical payoff tables, the independent market outcomes compared to those in the multimarket structure showed that behavior was relatively less cooperative in the X multimarket duopolies and more cooperative in the Y multimarket duopolies. When the X and Y markets are horizontally connected, behavior also becomes less cooperative in the X market, but more cooperative in the Y market. It would appear that the impact of multimarket contact on relative outputs need not require all firms to participate in all markets. Contact with competition and contact without competition have similar impacts on the X and Y market equilibria.

Evidence that there is Granger causality between markets, leads us to further investigate whether the transfer of learning is related to the level of cooperation in the two markets. We delineate three sets of market player groups in the connected design, three players to a group. A market group may be "cooperative," "combative," or fall into a classification we call "neither." Our interest is in comparing any differences in learning between the cooperative and combative groups. We ranked each of the 14 connected groups in terms of its degree of cooperation in each of the two markets. The set of "cooperative" groups is defined by those with outputs in the final ten periods prior to the random termination that were smaller than the average outputs across all groups in each market. Combative groups tend to have average outputs at least as large as the Cournot/Nash level, with output in one market that is significantly larger than Cournot/Nash. Table 2 provides detail on how we identified the cooperative and combative market groups of three subjects. Based on average choices in

Table 2. Relative Levels of Cooperation for Connected Market Groups.
Based on Periods 26–35 Average Choices.

Market Group	Average X Market Choice	X Rank	Average Y Market Choice	Y Rank	Sum of X, Y Ranks
1	20.8	4	14.6	3	7
2	14.2	3	24.9	7	10
3	7.5	2	18.8	4	6
4	6.0	1	12.0	1	2
5	25.8	7	37.6	14	21
6	27.6	10	12.0	1	11
7	26.3	9	20.4	5	14
8	30.1	11	30.4	9	20
9	24.6	6	30.0	8	14
10	36.0	14	31.2	10	24
11	23.2	5	22.8	6	11
12	30.5	12	36.6	13	25
13	32.5	13	32.5	12	25
14	26.2	8	31.3	11	19

"Cooperative": X Rank ≤ 7 and Y Rank ≤ 7. Market Groups 1,2,3,4,11.
  "Combative": X Rank ≥ 10 and Y Rank ≥ 10. Market Groups 5,8,10,12,13.
  "Neither": Market Groups 6,7,9,14.
Note: Cournot X paired choice is 26 and Cournot Y paired choice is 32.

the X and Y markets, market groups were ranked from most to least coopera-tive and the ranks were added. Cooperative groups choose quantities below the average quantities in *both* markets. Combative groups chose well above the average quantities in *both* markets.

With this scheme, there are five cooperative groups and five combative groups. Restricting our attention to the first 35 observations, as above, and taking into account the presence of two lags in the regression specification, we have 33 usable observations per group. There are therefore 165 observations for each cohort. We re-ran equations 3 and 4 using these two subsets of the database; results are given in Table 3. Based on these estimates, we again test the null hypotheses of no Granger causality against the alternative (a) that X causes Y and (b) that Y causes X. Associated test statistics are given at the bottom of Table 3, with p-values in square brackets. We see that there is substan-tial evidence that X Granger causes Y in the combative groups, but little evidence of any other causality (though the hypothesis that Y causes X in the cooperative groups is somewhat close to significant, with a p-value of 15%). Our conclusion is that the "learning" that takes place, at least for these extreme cohorts, is largely confined to learning that is of a competitive, rather than a cooperative, nature. That is, in groups that ultimately are combative, move-ments towards larger X outputs appear to precede movements towards larger Y outputs. Put differently, a breakdown in cooperation within the X market tends to drive players towards significant reductions in cooperation across the board. Conversely, and somewhat surprisingly, there is little indication that enhanced cooperation in the Y market engenders greater cooperation in X.

V. CONCLUSION

In the horizontally connected markets, behavior in one market is influencing behavior in the other. The multimarket producer is a conduit for learning between the duopolies. The impact of the conduit producer is to raise produc-tion and lower prices in the X market and to lower production and raise price in the Y market. Both effects are statistically significant. However the magni-tudes of these intermarket influences are about *one-fifth* of the measured own-market influences. The dominant learning arena is the rival's own market.

Our earlier experimental work has studied the impact of mutual forbearance in conglomerated markets (Phillips & Mason, 1992). The market structure in this work created two multiproduct producers both meeting in the X and Y market. Referring to Fig. 1 it would be the case of the two single product producers of X and Y in (1a) merging, or in panel (1b) the four firms combing into two firms, each producing the X and Y products. Remarkably this 1992

Table 3.   Comparison of Cooperative and Combative Groups.

Parameter	Cooperative groups point estimate	Combative groups point estimate
β_n^X	10.727*	25.527*
	(2.187)	(3.931)
μ_n^{XY}	0.1410*	−0.0212
	(0.0780)	(0.0707)
μ_n^{XX}	0.3620*	0.1783*
	(0.0864)	(0.0788)
θ_n^{XY}	−0.0316	0.0394
	(.0877)	(0.0696)
θ_n^{XX}	−0.0797	−0.1122
	(0.0798)	(0.0808)
X_n^e	18.132	27.968
	(1.742)	(3.361)
β_n^y	15.909*	23.836*
	(2.423)	(4.188)
μ_n^{YY}	0.1869*	0.0403
	(0.0864)	(0.0753)
μ_n^{YX}	0.0994	0.2324*
	(0.0957)	(0.0840)
θ_n^{YY}	0.0815	0.1845*
	(0.0884)	(0.0742)
θ_n^{YX}	−0.0464	−0.1828*
	(0.0971)	(0.0861)
Y_n^e	23.061	32.539
	(2.221)	(3.948)
test stat for Y Granger causes X:	3.798	0.3957
	[0.150]	[0.092]
test stat for X Granger causes Y:	1.101	10.465
	[0.577]	[0.001]

Notes: asymptotic standard errors in parentheses below point estimates; probability of true null hypothesis (no causality) is in square brackets below Granger causality test statistics.
* significant at better than 1% level.
number of observations: 165 (cooperative groups), 165 (combative groups).

study shows the same effect of the multimarket conglomerate contact, as compared to behavior in the independent doupoly markets, that we now observe in the horizontally connected market structure. The impact on X and Y production is virtually identical when moving from the independent silo duopolies to a multimarket environment with competition and one that does not have competition between the two X and Y markets.

The multiproduct producer in the connected market structure is acting as if it has pooled the incentive constraints described in the trigger model, and as if it faced an identical conglomerated rival. This is supported by the significant measure of Granger causality in the X and Y markets, and that an increase in X outputs causes an increase in Y outputs and vice versa. This causality creates a market environment that reflects the underpinnings of mutual forbearance and the pooled incentive constraints. Namely that defection from agreement, if it occurs, will take place in both markets, and punishment, if it occurs, will take place in both markets. Simple learning rules in the market environment may promote this kind of mirrored behavior. As discussed earlier, learning is bounded and in complicated environments controlled by experience. Agents facilitate their learning from experience by simplifying. Complex developments through a series of price changes that signal cooperation or punishment may be difficult for the multiproduct producer to associate and interpret when the actions come from independent sources. Learning is less noisy when the same two agents meet in different markets and implicit understanding is one market transfers to other markets. It is possible that the multiproduct producer in the horizontally connected design, in order to interpret the actions of different rivals, treats the rivals as having a single common strategy. The multimarket producer therefore uses the same rule by which to adjust to the actions of either rival. In turn, this strategy may force the X and Y market rivals to adjust quantities in different directions. The strategy of the multimarket agent may break "the constraint" in the Y market and create slack in the X market.

There is a second related argument along this line that is less strategic. The multimarket conduit operating in multiple markets with multiple rivals may reach the limit of learning. If this limit is reached, simple rules of thumb might be developed that help the firm transfer learning between markets. The conduit firm may take an "averaging approach" to cooperation across markets, not trusting itself to too much cooperation in one market and moving toward further cooperation in the relatively competitive market. Such a learning rule would create a similar contrast to the single market learning silos used as the control environment. There may of course be other simplifying rules used by agents, and even more complicated conduit market relationships could change learning further by forcing different algorithms on agents attempting to understand behavior and respond to the actions of rivals. In more natural decision environments complicated relationships can exist within and across organizations that make it difficult to learn and develop business strategies. The decision-making culture, itself, evolves as a result of the learning that takes place from the contact (Stephan & Boeker, this volume).

Our estimates show that the multimarket conduit causes outputs in the X market to rise 15.5% and outputs in the Y market to fall by 3.7%. These changes are significant. The experimental markets constructed in this paper offer a first look at how integration by *one* firm into another market affects the outputs and prices of previously independent market structures. It appears from our Granger causality tests that "combative" learning transfers well through the multimarket conduit, while "cooperative" learning does not. This is consistent with the relatively large rise in X market choices; and by comparison the overall small decreases in Y market choices. The combative choices in the X market precede larger choices in the Y market for market groups that are generally uncooperative. Market groups that cooperate do not exhibit a significant transfer of learning. It appears cooperation is learned within the confines of the single market structure, while competitive behavior spreads with relative ease through a population of firms. To establish robustness further study needs to be done in markets that have different basic cost and demand conditions than our particular X and Y markets. But these particular markets show that with the horizontal connection, there on balance is more competitive behavior than if the markets were independently structured.

As mentioned early in the paper there are other types of multimarket conduits. For instance we have described a possible vertical conduit, for which there are additional cost relations between the enterprise. At the horizontal level the multimarket firm may have extensions into numerous markets, rather than two as we have studied. The multimarket firm could be a hub through which learning can be transferred from several markets to another. The structure would be similar to the Japanese *Keiretsu* system of cooperate links. Through added experience, the hub may become a more efficient coordinator of learning, or because of the increased learning noise, the hub could have less of an impact than the two-market MUMM created in our experiments. There are a variety of intermarket connections that deserve study. According to van Wegberg and van Witteloostuijn (this volume) we have constructed in this paper a simple type of indirect contact. They describe a number of similar, but more complicated relationships, that can develop through business consultants, shareholders, upstream suppliers, downstream distributors, and boards of directors. All of these potential points of contact represent information conduits, and connect markets. A firm may have a portfolio of connections without rivalry, and this portfolio is a learning vehicle by which firms can form competitive strategies. The experimental methods that we have described offer a viable means by which to identify and understand the fundamental outcomes generated through such connections.

Payment Table X.

Value Selected by the Other Participant.

	0	1	2	3	4	5	6	7	8	9	10	11	12	13	14	15	16	17	18	19	20	21	22
1	984	495	476	458	439	421	403	384	366	347	329	311	292	274	255	237	218	200	182	163	145	126	108
2	990	518	499	480	461	441	422	403	384	365	346	327	308	289	270	251	232	213	193	174	155	136	117
3	994	539	520	500	480	461	441	421	401	382	362	342	322	303	283	263	243	224	204	184	164	145	125
4	998	560	539	519	499	478	458	438	417	397	376	356	336	315	295	274	254	234	213	193	172	152	132
5	999	579	558	537	516	495	474	453	432	411	389	368	347	326	305	284	263	242	221	200	179	158	137
6	1000	597	575	553	532	510	488	466	445	423	401	380	358	336	314	293	271	249	228	206	184	163	141
7	999	613	591	568	546	524	501	479	457	434	412	389	367	345	322	300	278	255	233	211	188	166	143
8	998	628	605	582	559	536	513	490	467	444	421	398	375	352	329	306	283	260	237	214	191	168	145
9	994	642	618	595	571	547	524	500	476	453	429	405	382	358	334	311	287	263	239	216	192	168	145
10	990	655	630	606	582	557	533	509	484	460	436	411	387	363	338	314	289	265	241	216	192	168	143
11	984	666	641	616	591	566	541	516	491	466	441	416	391	366	341	316	291	266	241	214	191	166	141
12	976	676	650	624	599	573	547	522	496	470	445	419	393	368	342	316	291	265	239	211	188	163	137
13	968	684	658	632	605	579	553	526	500	474	447	421	395	369	342	316	289	263	237	206	184	158	132
14	958	691	664	638	611	584	557	530	503	476	449	422	395	368	341	314	287	260	233	200	179	152	125
15	947	697	670	642	614	587	559	532	504	476	449	421	393	366	338	311	283	255	228	193	172	145	117
16	934	702	674	645	617	589	561	532	504	476	447	419	391	636	334	306	278	249	221	193	164	136	108
17	920	705	676	647	618	589	561	532	503	474	445	416	387	358	329	300	271	242	213	184	155	126	97
18	906	707	678	648	618	589	559	530	500	470	441	411	382	352	322	293	263	234	204	174	145	115	86
19	889	708	678	647	617	587	557	526	496	466	436	405	375	345	314	284	254	224	193	163	133	103	72
20	872	707	676	645	614	584	553	522	491	460	429	398	367	336	305	274	243	213	182	151	120	89	58
21	852	705	674	642	611	579	547	516	484	453	421	389	358	326	295	263	232	200	168	137	105	74	42
22	832	702	670	638	605	573	541	509	476	444	412	380	347	315	283	251	218	186	154	122	89	57	25

Payment Table Y.

Value Selected by the Other Participant.

	0	1	2	3	4	5	6	7	8	9	10	11	12	13	14	15	16	17	18	19	20	21	22	23	24	25	26	27
1	537	274	261	248	235	222	209	196	183	170	157	144	131	118	105	92	79	66	53	40	28	15	2	-11	-24	-37	-50	-63
2	548	297	283	270	256	243	229	216	202	189	175	162	148	135	121	108	94	81	67	54	40	27	13	0	-13	-27	-40	-54
3	558	319	305	291	277	263	249	235	221	207	193	179	165	151	135	122	108	94	80	66	52	38	24	10	-4	-18	-32	-46
4	566	339	325	310	296	281	267	252	238	223	209	194	180	165	151	136	121	107	92	78	63	49	34	20	5	-9	-24	-38
5	575	359	344	329	314	299	284	269	254	239	224	209	194	179	163	148	133	118	103	88	73	58	43	28	13	-2	-17	-32
6	582	378	362	347	331	316	300	284	269	253	238	222	207	191	175	160	144	129	113	98	82	66	51	35	20	4	-11	-27
7	587	396	379	636	347	331	315	299	283	267	251	235	219	202	186	170	154	138	122	106	90	74	58	42	25	9	-7	-23
8	592	412	396	379	362	346	329	312	296	279	263	246	229	213	196	180	163	146	130	113	97	80	63	47	30	13	-3	-20
9	595	428	411	393	376	359	342	325	308	291	274	256	239	222	205	188	171	154	137	119	102	85	68	51	34	17	-1	-18
10	598	442	425	407	389	372	354	336	319	301	283	266	248	230	213	195	178	160	142	125	107	89	72	54	36	19	1	-17
11	599	456	438	419	401	383	365	347	329	310	292	274	256	238	220	201	183	165	147	129	111	92	74	56	38	20	2	-17
12	600	468	449	431	412	393	375	356	337	319	300	281	263	244	225	207	188	169	151	132	113	94	76	57	38	20	-1	-18
13	599	480	460	441	422	403	384	364	345	326	307	288	268	249	230	211	192	172	153	134	115	96	76	57	38	19	-1	-20
14	598	490	470	451	431	411	391	371	352	332	312	293	273	253	234	214	194	174	155	135	115	94	76	57	38	19	-3	-23
15	595	499	479	459	439	418	398	378	358	337	317	297	277	256	236	216	196	175	155	135	115	94	74	54	34	13	-7	-27
16	592	508	487	466	445	425	404	383	362	342	321	300	279	258	238	216	196	175	154	133	111	90	68	46	25	4	-17	-32
17	587	515	494	472	451	430	408	387	366	345	323	302	281	260	238	217	196	174	153	132	111	89	68	47	25	4	-17	-38
18	582	521	499	478	456	434	412	390	369	347	325	303	281	260	238	216	194	172	151	129	107	85	63	42	20	-2	-24	-46
19	575	526	504	482	459	437	415	393	370	348	325	303	281	260	238	216	194	172	151	129	107	85	63	42	20	-2	-24	-54
20	566	530	508	485	462	439	416	393	371	348	325	302	279	256	234	211	188	165	142	119	97	74	51	28	5	-18	-40	-63
21	558	534	510	487	463	440	417	393	370	347	323	300	277	254	230	207	183	160	137	113	90	66	43	20	-4	-27	-50	-74
22	548	536	512	488	464	440	416	392	369	345	321	297	273	249	225	201	178	154	130	106	82	58	34	10	-13	-37	-61	-85
23	537	537	512	488	463	439	415	390	366	342	317	293	268	244	220	195	171	146	122	98	73	49	24	0	-24	-49	-73	-98
24	526	537	512	487	462	437	412	387	362	337	312	288	263	238	213	188	163	138	113	88	63	38	13	-11	-36	-61	-86	-111
25	512	536	510	485	459	434	408	383	358	332	307	281	256	230	205	180	154	129	103	78	52	27	2	-24	-49	-75	-100	-126
26	498	534	508	482	456	430	404	378	352	326	300	274	248	222	196	170	144	118	92	66	40	15	-11	-37	-63	-89	-115	-141
27	483	530	504	478	451	425	398	372	345	319	292	266	239	216	186	160	133	107	80	54	28	1	-25	-52	-78	-105	-131	-158

NOTES

1. We recognize that there can be more complicated horizontal links. For example there may exist other multiproduct seller configurations that create additional links. For a product Z it is possible to envision:

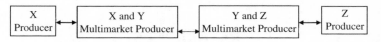

There is also a vertical link that we do not address in this study. Imagine an upstream supplier of an input used in different markets.

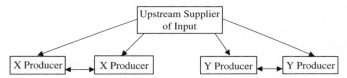

The X and Y markets are connected through the common supplier of the input.

2. The unknown endpoint creates a game that is like a discounted infinite game, because the game has no identified last period. See Rasmusen (1989), chapter 4. These experimental games are not stationary. However, the class of subgame perfect equilibria that satisfy the incentive constrains for a stationary game also satisfy the incentive constraints in each period of non-stationary games such as these.

3. While our past studies identified the second order autoregressive model as providing the best explanatory power, there are good reasons to expect *ex ante* that more than one lag ought to matter. These include subjects' attempts at signaling collusive desires (Shapiro, 1980) and learning about the rival's rationality (Kalai & Lehrer (1993), Mason & Phillips (2000)). Cason and Friedman (1995) model subject behavior with a partial adjustment model, and also find past actions have a significant influence upon current behavior. One can then regard the second order lagged model as providing a parsimonious description of the evolutionary process.

4. Because our regression model includes lagged dependent variables, the traditional Durbin-Watson statistic cannot be used to test for the presences of serial correlation (Fomby, Hill & Johnson (1988)). One can, however, use Durbin's h-statistic. Under the null hypotheses that the disturbance term in our regression model is not serially correlated, Durbin's H-statistic is asymptotically distributed as a standard Normal random variable, and so one may infer significance of the test statistic by applying a t-test. In all the regressions reported below in Table 3, the h-statistic is small. Thus, we cannot reject the hypotheses that the ε_{it}^{k} are serially uncorrelated.

5. Slutsky's theorem states that a continuos function $f(\theta)$ of a vector of parameters, θ, can be consistently estimated by evaluating the function at a vector of a consistent estimates of the parameters: see Fomby, Hill and Johnson (1998, p. 58) for further discussion. The variance of $f(\theta)$ can then be consistently estimated by the quadratic form where $g(\theta) = \partial f(\theta)/\partial \theta$ and $V(\theta)$ is the associated maximum likelihood estimator of the covariance matrix for θ (Fomby, Hill & Johnson, Corollary 4.2.2).

ACKNOWLEDGMENT

This work has been supported by the College of Business, University of Wyoming. The findings and conclusions expressed in this paper are those of the authors and do not reflect the views of the funding agency. The authors have made equal contributions to the manuscript.

REFERENCES

Baum, J. A. C., & Ingram, P. (1998). Survival-Enhancing Learning in the Manhattan Hotel Industry, 1898–1980. *Management Science*, *44*(7), July, 996–1016.

Bernheim, B. D., & Whinston, M. (1990). Multi-market Contact and Collusive Behavior. *Rand Journal of Economics*, *21*(1), Spring, 1–26.

Cason, T., & Friedman, D. (1995). Learning in Markets with Random Supply and Demand, Working Papers, University of California, Santa Cruz.

Colman, A. (1982). *Game Theory and Experimental Games*. New York: Pergamon Press.

Davis, D., & Holt, C. (1993). *Experimental Economics*. Princeton, New Jersey: Princeton University Press.

Fomby, T. R., Hill, R. C., & Johnson, S. (1988). *Advanced Econometric Methods*. New York: Springer-Verlag.

Friedman, D., & Sunder, S. (1994). *Experimental Methods: A Primer for Economists*. New York: Cambridge Press.

Friedman, J. *Oligopoly Theory*. (1993). New York: Cambridge Press.

Green, E., & Porter, R. (1984). Non-cooperative Collusion Under Imperfect Price Information. *Econometrica*, *52*(1), 87–100.

Greve, H. R. (1999). Branch Systems and Nonlocal Learning in Populations. In: A. Miner & P. Anderson (Eds), *Advances in Strategic Management*, *16*, (pp. 57–80). Stamford, CT: JAI Press.

Ingram, P., & Baum, J. A. C. (1997). Opportunity and Constraint: Organizations' Learning From the Operating and Competitive Experience of Industries. *Strategic Management Journal*, *18*, 75–98 (Special Summer Issue).

Jacobs, R., Leamer, E., & Ward, M. P. (1979). Difficulties with Testing for Causation. *Economic Inquiry*, *17*(8), July, 401–413.

Kagel, J. H., & Roth, A. E. (1995). *The Handbook of Experimental Economics*, Princeton, New Jersey: Princeton University Press.

Kalai, E., & Lehrer, E. (1993). Rational Learning Leads to Nash Equilibrium (A New Extended Version). *Econometrica*, *61*(5), 1019–1045.

Korn, H. J., & Baum, J. A. C. (1999). Chance, Imitative, and Strategic Antecedents to Multimarket Contact. *Academy of Management Journal*, *42*(2), 171–193.

Kreps, D. M. (1990). *Game Theory and Economics Modelling*. New York: Oxford University Press.

Levinthal, D., & March, J. (1993). The Myopia of Learning. *Strategic Management Journal*, *14*, 95–112.

Mason, C., Phillips, O., & Nowell, C. (1992). Duopoly Behavior in Asymmetric Markets: An Experimental Evaluation. *Review of Economics and Statistics*, *74*(4), 662–670.

Mason, C., & Phillips, O. (2000a). An Experimental Analysis of the Effects of Vertical Integration. *International Journal of Industrial Organization*, March, *18*(3), 471–496.

Mason, C., & Phillips, O. (2000b). Dynamic Learning in a Two-Person Experimental Game. *Journal of Economics Dynamics and Control, forthcoming.*

Phillips, O., & Mason, C. (1996). Market Regulation and Multimarket Rivalry. *Rand Journal of Economics,* Autumn, *27*(3), 596–617.

Phillips, O., & Mason, C. (1992). An Experimental Investigation of Mutual Forbearance in Conglomerate Markets. *Rand Journal of Economics, 23*(3), Autumn, 395–414.

Plott, C. (1989). An Updated Review of Industrial Organization: Applications of Experimental Methods. In: R. Schmalensee & R. Willig (Eds), *Handbook of Industrial Organization,* Vol. II. Amsterdam: Elsevier Science Publishers, B.V.

Rapoport, A., Guyer, M., & Gordon, D. (1976). *The 2×2 Game.* Ann Arbor: University of Michigan Press.

Rasmusen, E. (1989). *Games and Information: An Introduction to Game Theory.* Cambridge MA: Basil Blackwell.

Saloner, G. (1994). Game Theory and Strategic Management: Contributions, Applications, and Limitations. In: R. P. Rumelt, D. E. Shendel & D. J. Teece (Eds), *Fundamental Issues in Strategy* (pp. 155–194). Boston, MA: Harvard Business School Press.

Shapiro, L. (1980). Decentralized Dynamics in Duopoly with Pareto Optimal Outcomes. *Bell Journal of Economics, 11*(2), Autumn, 730–744.

Stephan, J., & Boeker, W. (2001). Getting to Multimarket Competition: How Multimarket Conact Affects Firms' Market Entry Decisions. In: J. A. C. Baum & H. R. Greve (Eds), *Multimarket Organization and Multimarket Strategy: Advantages in Strategic Management,* Vol. 18. Oxford U.K.: JAI Press.

Tirole, J. (1988). *The Theory of Industrial Organization,* Cambridge, MA: MIT Press.

van Wegberg, M., & van Witteloostuijn, A. (2001). Strategic Management in the New Economy: Modern Information Technologies and Multichannel Contact Strategies. In: J. A. C. Baum & H. R. Greve (Eds), *Multiunit Organization and Multimarket Strategy: Advances in Strategic Management,* Vol. 18a. Oxford U.K.: JAI Press.

GETTING TO MULTIMARKET COMPETITION: HOW MULTIMARKET CONTACT AFFECTS FIRMS' MARKET ENTRY DECISIONS

John Stephan and Warren Boeker

ABSTRACT

Studies of multimarket contact typically hypothesize (and find) that the relationship of contact levels between firms and the likelihood of aggressive competitive behaviors is linear and negative. This includes the likelihood of entry moves by multimarket rivals. However, a linear negative relationship between market entry and multimarket contact, which implies that deterrence exists at lower levels of contact, makes it unlikely that firms' will enter into each others' markets in order to create that deterrent.

We address this theoretical issue by distinguishing between multimarket contact and multimarket competition. Lower levels of multimarket contact provide models for a focal firm that both guide and legitimize its strategic moves. As multimarket contact levels increase, multimarket competition eventually ensues as multimarket rivals recognize their mutual interdependence and further entry into shared markets is deterred. We develop the logic for this non-linear relationship by incorporating theory from the strategic, institutional, and decision-making literatures that has direct

Multiunit Organization and Multimarket Strategy, Volume 18, pages 229–261.
Copyright © 2001 by Elsevier Science Ltd.
All rights of reproduction in any form reserved.
ISBN: 0-7623-0721-8

implications for the way in which contact between firms across multiple markets is likely to affect managerial cognitions and firm actions.

    Since firms must enter into the markets of their (multimarket) competitors to build multimarket structures which yield competitive benefits, we conclude by developing several propositions about how such entry might best be achieved to avoid retaliatory responses by multimarket competitors.

INTRODUCTION

Early work on multimarket competition sought to find empirical support for the theoretical idea that when firms meet each other in several different markets, they exhibit a 'forbearance effect.' It was hypothesized that firms meeting the same rivals across multiple markets would refrain from aggressively attacking each other due to the greater potential retaliatory costs they faced (Karnani & Wernerfelt, 1985). That is, firms would forbear from escalating competitive rivalry in the markets they shared with their multimarket rivals. Although there were some conflicting results (Baum & Korn, 1999; Phillips & Mason, 1992), multimarket studies tended to support the contention that markets with greater numbers of multimarket competitors exhibited lower levels of rivalry. Primary supporting evidence included performance levels that were found to be higher in these markets than in those with fewer multimarket competitors (e.g. Heggestad & Rhodes, 1978; Gimeno & Woo, 1996). These findings are consistent with the general idea that a firm's performance is enhanced to the extent that it can avoid competition with its rivals (e.g. Roberts, 1999). Like the structure-conduct-performance paradigm in I/O economics, these studies inferred that the intensity of rivalry had to be lower in markets where multimarket contact levels were high in order for the performance differences they observed to occur. It was rarely the case that competitive behaviors were explicitly examined.

    Later work began to investigate how varying levels of multimarket contact affected the likelihood firms would exhibit specific competitive behaviors. For example, the likelihood of exit from a market was found to be lower when a firm had higher levels of multimarket contact with market incumbents (Baum & Korn, 1996; Boeker, Goodstein, Stephan & Murmann, 1997). Conversely, Baum and Korn (1996) found that the likelihood of a firm's entry into a target market declined with increasing levels of multimarket contact with firms already in the target market. Similar results were obtained by Boeker and his colleagues (Boeker, Goodstein, Stephan & Murmann, 1993).

    In the case of entry, these results were interpreted to mean that firms were more likely to refrain from aggressively encroaching on their rivals' turf when they could expect a more costly (to themselves) response (Chen, 1996). The logic stressed that the potential costly response implicit in multimarket contact posed an effective deterrent to overly aggressive competitive behavior. The resulting situation has been construed to produce 'spheres of influence' (Gimeno, 1999) – where firms accept subordination to their rivals in one or more jointly contested markets in exchange for similar consideration by these rivals in other jointly contested markets.

More recent work has sought to present more refined analyses of multimarket effects. Previously, multimarket contact had been depicted as having a monotonic effect on a firm's competitive intensity in the markets it shares with its multimarket rivals (Baum & Korn, 1996; Boeker et al., 1997). Departing from this empirical base, Baum and Korn (1999) hypothesized, and found, a non-linear influence of the level of multimarket contact on a firm's likelihood of entry into and exit from markets shared with its multimarket competitors. For both entry and exit, an inverted-U shaped relationship was found between levels of multimarket contact and the strategic behaviors of market entry and exit. This development is of considerable interest as it points the way toward a more detailed description of when and how multimarket linkages matter. A similar result, obtained by Haveman and Nonnemaker (2000) in their study of entry behavior among savings and loan institutions, provides additional evidence that multimarket relationships are more complex than earlier models assumed. While these results expand our view of the nature of multimarket competition effects, the treatments did not fully address the changing forces at work over different levels of multimarket competition.

To date, multimarket theory (and most research) has concentrated on the forbearance effects that contact between firms across multiple markets produces (e.g. Baum & Korn, 1996). The theory does not, however, offer any insight into determining the point at which forbearance effects begin to operate. That is, how much multimarket contact is necessary for a firm to establish a credible deterrent? In addition, the possible effects, if any, of multimarket contact *before* this point is reached have remained unexamined from a theoretical standpoint. Finally, if one considers market entry as the specific competitive action involved, there are additional strategic reasons for firms to avoid additional entry into the markets of their multimarket rivals.

In light of recent work and these remaining theoretical questions, we describe the changing forces at work as multimarket contact levels between firms change. In order to understand the role of interfirm relationships within a competitive environment more fully, it is essential to understand exactly how multimarket influence operates at all levels of contact – and what influences those levels to change. This will result in more fine-grained multimarket theories and a better understanding of how multimarket structures affect firm actions. This refinement will expand the theory beyond a concern with just the forbearance effect, while at the same time recognizing its importance and the fact that it is not immediately forthcoming at all levels of multimarket contact.

More generally, our approach will provide a more comprehensive depiction of competitive interaction between firms within and across markets. It will also aid in identifying the factors that managers pay attention to regarding their rivals as they guide their organizations through competitive waters. Understanding more fully how multimarket relationships operate will consequently permit a better grasp of the linkage between competitive environments and managerial cognitions and actions. It also provides a mechanism for identifying tactics managers might employ within competitive environments to avoid aggressive competition with their rivals (beyond those associated with forbearance effects) in order to achieve organizational objectives.

To address these issues, we contend that a distinction needs to be made between multimarket *contact* and multimarket *competition*. We recognize that in order to establish a deterrent effect through multimarket contact, firms must, at some point, enter into the markets of their rivals. Thus, over some range, multimarket *contact* levels by themselves, do not deter entry, but in fact might encourage it. For example, multimarket contact is likely to aid in managerial sense-making (Porac, Thomas, Wilson, Paton & Kanfer, 1995; Schwenk, 1984) and offer action alternatives which are likely to have greater legitimacy in the eyes of the firm's constituencies (Deephouse, 1999). Eventually, though, the deterrent effect arising from multimarket contact begins to operate and multimarket *competition* ensues. At this point, the motivations influencing managerial decisions change to reflect a greater concern over potential competitive consequences. We expect, however, that this point will not be the same across every set of markets in which multimarket competitors compete.

We begin by describing the evolving nature of multimarket relationships, focusing on its impact on market entry. We discuss the various motivations operating at lower levels of multimarket contact, where, *ceteris paribus*, managers are encouraged to increase their levels of multimarket contact with existing multimarket rivals. Following this, we turn to motivational changes that occur when multimarket contact levels between firms reach the threshold level at which deterrence begins to become effective.

Given that entry into the markets of a firm's multimarket rivals is a requirement for establishing a deterrent and producing multimarket equilibriums (Karnani & Wernerfelt, 1985), we then develop several propositions regarding how market entry might be accomplished by multimarket rivals so that aggressive retaliation is minimized. That is, entering certain markets or entering a market in a particular way is less likely to result in an outbreak of escalating competition among incumbent multimarket rivals. These kinds of entry moves would permit the new entrant to increase its level of multimarket contact with rivals in the new market without igniting competitive responses.

Finally, we conclude with some observations related to the balance that successful firms need to strike between legitimacy – which is created when a firm resembles its competitors – and superior competitive positioning which comes from effectively differentiating itself from them (Deephouse, 1999). Non-linear depictions of multimarket relationships must be careful to separate those effects that are directly due to the (potential) competitive responses of multimarket rivals and those that are associated with managers' attempts to position their firm in an advantageous competitive position.

THE CASE FOR NON-LINEAR MULTIMARKET EFFECTS

Multimarket structures have, for the most part, been depicted as having linear or monotonic negative effects on competitive intensity across shared markets (Baum and Korn's (1999) study represents a notable recent exception). Multimarket theory has been built on the idea that contact across multiple markets between firms creates a significant deterrent to aggressive competition between these firms and thus reduces rivalry across all of the markets they share (Edwards, 1955; Karnani & Wernerfelt, 1985). The strength of the deterrent lies in the fact that the repertoire of competitive responses available to a firm increases with the extent of multimarket contact it has with its rivals (Karnani & Wernerfelt, 1985). Single point competitors, who meet their rivals only in one market, are limited to competitive responses in the particular market where aggressive actions toward its position takes place. Multimarket rivals, however, can respond in a different market that is shared with the multimarket aggressor – a market where the damage inflicted upon the aggressor is likely to be higher than in the market where the aggression initially took place and where the responder's own costs are lower. Response can also occur across several shared markets, potentially raising the overall cost of the aggressor's initial move to an unacceptably high level. Because the consequences of these responses increase the (potential) costs associated with an initial aggressive action, multimarket structures that give rise to such responses deter aggression and reduce rivalry across the markets that multimarket competitors share.

This reduction in rivalry has been shown to enhance firm performance, including enabling the firms involved to charge higher prices (Feinberg, 1985;

Gimeno & Woo, 1996) and stabilizing their market shares (Heggestad & Rhoades, 1978). Similarly, Hughes and Oughton (1993) found that industry rates of return were higher the greater the level of multimarket contact in the industry. These outcomes provide a solid rationale to explain the results of several studies that find that firms are less likely to exit from markets in which they meet more of their multimarket rivals than from those where they meet fewer (Barnett, 1993; Baum & Korn, 1996; Boeker et al., 1997). Thus, the potential performance benefits that derive from multimarket relationships provide a strong incentive for firms and their managers to create multimarket structures proactively and maintain them once they are established.

This situation raises an interesting theoretical paradox. In order for firms to improve performance by establishing deterrence through (higher) levels of multimarket contact with rivals, they must enter markets where their rivals in other markets already compete. But the deterrent effect underlying multimarket theory argues that this aggressive entry behavior is just the sort that would be avoided by firms competing in a multimarket environment. Indeed, prior work on multimarket competition has stressed that firms must increase their multi-market ties with competitors in order to establish a credible deterrent to future aggressive behavior. Gimeno and Woo unequivocally state that mutual forbearance, the reluctance of firms to aggressively attack their rivals in exchange for similar restraint on their rivals' part, demands that "firms need to increase their multimarket overlap" (Gimeno & Woo, 1996; p. 338). So, if multimarket contact is construed as having a monotonic, negative impact on competitive intensity, for firms to increase their multimarket contact implies that either they do so despite the deterrent effect present in multimarket relationships (indicating that they are willing to bear the costs of retaliation, an outcome that multimarket theory disputes) or that the deterrent, over some range of multimarket contact levels, has yet to become effective.

The inconsistency of this situation is reinforced by that fact that it is not unusual for firms to have reasonably high levels of multimarket contact between them. For example, Gimeno (1999) calculated the average level of multimarket contact between his sample of firm pairs at nearly 400 markets. Another study found average levels of multimarket contact ranged from 33 to 345 markets, depending on the level of resource sharing across markets (Gimeno & Woo, 1999), while a third put it at an average of 72% of the markets served by firms in their sample (Boeker et al., 1997).

One can only conclude from the above that the relationship between multi-market contact and market entry is unlikely to be a purely negative one. In order to establish a credible deterrent and position itself within a multimarket structure, firms have to enter markets where their (potential) multimarket rivals currently compete. This implies that some range of multi-market contact might encourage market entry by multimarket rivals. More specifically, the incentives to establish additional multimarket ties are strongest and the costs least when existing levels of multimarket contact are relatively low.

MULTIMARKET CONTACT VERSUS MULTIMARKET COMPETITION

Multimarket Contact

We propose that to resolve the issue it is necessary to consider the multimarket phenomena more broadly and to make a distinction between the types of influence that differing levels of multimarket contact have on firm behavior. Whether multimarket contact serves to forestall competitive behavior that would increase multimarket contact or encourages a firm to build additional multimarket ties can be traced to different motivations that operate as the level of multimarket contact between firms changes. Over some range of lower levels of multimarket contact, firms are motivated to increase their number of multimarket ties with their rivals to eventually establish a credible deterrent (Gimeno & Woo, 1996). More importantly, lower levels of multimarket contact operate in additional ways to influence firm behavior even though it has yet to provide the benefits ascribed to it by multimarket theory. We discuss these influences below. Table 1 summarizes these factors and their effects on multimarket contact.

Creating Deterrence
The most compelling reason for a firm to increase levels of multimarket contact with it rivals is, of course, to reach the point where a credible deterrent to future aggression will be achieved. If, as much of the multimarket literature has shown, multimarket structures are less competitive and capable of yielding higher, more stable performance, firms are likely to actively pursue these arrangements (Greve, 2000). Without a presence in a number of its rivals' markets, it is impossible for a firm to threaten responses across multiple markets or in markets where the damage will be more severe to the aggressor. Baum and Korn (1999) lean heavily on the desire to create a deterrent to support their findings regarding the entry decisions of the multimarket firms in their sample. Some firms will move into particular markets first, but for multimarket structures to take shape, others must follow. Additional entry would cease when the increment to a firm's deterrent capability from establishing an additional tie is outweighed by the costs of creating the additional tie.

Table 1. Incentives for Increasing Multimarket Contact.

Factor	Key Issues & Processes	Effect on Multimarket Contact
Creating Deterrence	Create environment of mutually perceived interdependence between firms. Improve interpretation of signaling effects between firms.	Increases contact until deterrent established and cost of additional contact outweighs incremental increase in deterrence
Modeling Behavior	Bounded rationality; Heuristic decision making and cognitive simplification. Similarity Assessment: basis for selection of 'similar' firms to model behavior on (greater cognitive availability of multimarket rivals as models) Phase in CEO's tenure: Is CEO ready to establish enduring theme?	Increases contact until demands for establishing unique firm position and CEO's own reputation outweigh benefits of 'following the leader.'
Competitive Intelligence	Experienced-based actions - entry moves more likely in known (rather than in relatively more unknown) environments Enhancing depth of existing competitive information preferred over expanding its breadth. Extent of need for additional information is affected by heterogeneity of top management team in terms of prior experience with other rivals across different markets.	Increases contact until marginal benefit of additional information exceeds potential cost of obtaining it via additional contact
Legitimacy	Resource dependence; Impression management & political coalition building by CEO. Nature and power of key constituencies; Nature and degree of political opposition to strategic changes.	Increases contact until demands for differentiating firm from its rivals outweigh demands for and benefits of legitimation

Modeling Opportunities

Second, as strategic decisions, market entry presents a firm and its managers with high levels of uncertainty, complexity and ambiguity (Mintzberg, Raisinghani & Theoret, 1976) . Success in a new market is never assured, even when competitive advantages can be leveraged from existing operations. When faced with a highly uncertain decision situation, managers have been shown to employ a variety of heuristic decision-making tactics to simplify the problem and reduce the level of uncertainty they face (Schwenk, 1984; Porac, Thomas, Wilson, Paton & Kanfer, 1995). It has been noted by several observers that under these circumstances, firms and their managers will model their actions after those of other, similar organizations (DiMaggio & Powell, 1983; Vernon, Wells & Rangan, 1996). Other work has specifically noted that it is not at all unusual for firms to 'follow the leader' and mimic the entry decisions of their rivals (Haunschild & Miner, 1997; Haveman, 1993; Knickerbocker, 1973; Tsurumi, 1976).

In such situations, the extent of multimarket contact should figure prominently as a proxy for similarity. Greve (2000) states that firms use attributes of other firms that are easily observable to decide which firms to model their entry behaviors on. Similarly, Porac and Thomas (1990) note that managers use an organization's most salient features when assessing its similarity to their own firm. Chen (1996) observed that multimarket contact is the characteristic most visible to other firms and should consequently be a large consideration in strategic decision-making. van Wegberg and van Witteloostuijn (this volume) note that contact across multiple markets is likely to be a key determinant of which rivals a focal firm seeks to emulate. Thus, in the context of uncertain market entry decisions, then, managers of a focal firm would seek to emulate rivals that have similar market coverage to themselves. In addition, the fact that these rivals already have a presence in other markets presents prospective growth paths for similar firms to follow. That is, a firm with multimarket rivals will mimic those rivals who compete in other markets that their firm has yet to enter. Firms of this type would be ones with low to moderate levels of multimarket contact with the focal firm. Emulating firms with lower levels of multimarket contact takes advantage of a readily available growth model while it also moves the entering firm closer to the point at which it will have a credible deterrent in place.

Competitive Intelligence

A second characteristic of (lower levels) of multimarket contact that encourages additional entry into the markets of a firm's existing competitors is that such entry takes advantage of the most comprehensive information managers have available (Boeker et al., 1997). This increases the chances for a successful outcome. MacMillan (1982) points out that accurate competitive intelligence is indispensable for reinforcing a firm's strategic position. Such information provides the basis on which the moves, countermoves and changes in product-market positions by competitors are assessed and anticipated. Since this information is best obtained through direct observation (Smith, Grimm & Gannon, 1992), firms will possess better information about their existing competitors than about those they have yet to meet. Entering a market populated by competitors a firm is already familiar with lets it draw on its experience of its competitors' past behavior to assess their likely response to its actions (Smith et al., 1992; van Wegberg & van Witteloostuijn, this volume). Consequently, its conjectures about their future responses are likely to be more accurate (Caves & Porter, 1977). This will allow the firm to develop plans that are less likely to invoke a response, devise counter-responses should an initial response occur and be more successful in identifying unique positions in the market (Porac et al., 1995). These capabilities make it more likely that the entry move will be successful compared with entering a market where the firm would meet all new competitors. The latter situation would put a firm in a poor position to judge the likely responses of these new rivals and reduce the effectiveness of any contingency plans that were developed. Prospects for success in these situations would be much more uncertain.

The information gained from observation of the actions and responses of a firm's rivals in new settings also enhances the firm's competitive intelligence about its rivals. Conditions in the new market are unlikely to exactly mirror those in the markets already shared with multimarket rivals. Thus, managers can refine their mental images of their competitors by observing their rivals' behavior under a wider variety of circumstances. This fine-grained knowledge helps managers better anticipate future actions in more varied situations (Ingram & Baum, 1997) including other markets it shares with its rivals. This knowledge is indispensable for maintaining the reduced competition characteristic of multimarket environments. It not only permits more accurate interpretations of rivals' motives but also reduces the likelihood of incorrect, potentially costly misunderstanding.

Kim (this volume) notes that information asymmetry has come to be a dominant characteristic of firms' relationships. Multimarket firms, by virtue of their ability to send multiple signals to their competitors, are arguably in a better position to expect that these signals are more accurately interpreted. Baum and Korn (1999) build on the work of Boeker et al, (1997) as they described the motivating role of relying on and adding to competitive information regarding multimarket rivals as a key determinant of market entry in a multimarket context when existing contact levels were low. Their results were consistent with this reasoning.

Legitimacy

Finally, entry into markets already populated by similar firms is likely to be seen as more legitimate by critical stakeholders of the firm. Managers are often faced with a difficult tradeoff between differentiating their firm from its rivals to establish a competitive advantage and remaining similar enough so that the marketplace accepts it as a legitimate competitor (Deephouse, 1999; Porac, Thomas & Baden-Fuller, 1989). To the extent that managers can point to similar decisions reached by their competitors, they can increase the chances that important stakeholders will perceive that these decisions were indeed appropriate (Haunschild, 1993; Haveman, 1993). Increased legitimacy will encourage key stakeholders to provide necessary resources much more readily (Hybels, 1995; Pfeffer & Salancik, 1978; Stone & Brush, 1996). This minimizes some of the difficulties involved in entering new markets and would consequently make mangers tend to favor such actions.

In summary, when levels of multimarket contact between firms are low, multimarket contact does not yet function as a deterrent. Instead, it provides a set of positive motivations to increase the level of such contact. Additional contact moves a firm closer to the point when it will possess a credible deterrent against future aggression, builds on existing competitive information about a firm's rivals at the same time that it offers the opportunity for refining this information base. It also provides a model on which a firm can base its decisions, providing a source of legitimacy which can enhance its prospects in the eyes of key constituencies.

Multimarket Competition

When a firm's multimarket contacts reach higher levels, the motivation to enter additional markets that its competitors are already in is likely to decline, reducing the likelihood of further entry into such markets. Three key factors contribute to this reduction. Following from traditional multimarket theory, higher levels of market overlap eventually provide firms with a credible deterrent against further aggressive behavior by their multimarket rivals. Second, managers themselves will eventually refrain from engaging in more 'follow the leader' behavior. Excessive mimicry will limit their firm's ability to establish a competitive advantage (Deephouse, 1999; Porac, Thomas & Baden-Fuller, 1989). Resembling rivals too closely can also jeopardize managers' ability to enhance their professional and personal reputations (Hambrick & Fukutomi, 1991). Table 2 summarizes how multimarket competition affects future firm actions as a result of these factors.

Deterrence and Mutual Forbearance

When contact between firms across multiple markets reaches a high enough level, managers begin to recognize the mutual interdependence between their firms and the competitive stakes associated with further incursions into each others' markets (Edwards, 1955; Karnani & Wernerfelt, 1985). The deterrent effect stemming from multimarket contact begins to kick in and firms begin to refrain from aggressively attacking each other's positions across their shared markets. Possessing a credible deterrent against aggression enables multimarket competitors to divide up their shared markets into so-called 'spheres of influence' where particular firms are granted primacy in certain markets while granting similar status to their multimarket rivals in other markets (McGrath, Chen & MacMillan, 1998). Realizing the potentially escalating cost of encroachment on their multimarket rivals' turf, mutual forbearance behavior begins to dominate firm activity and competitors refrain from aggressive behavior toward each other. Mutual forbearance will limit additional entry into markets shared by a firm's multimarket rivals.

The deterrent power of this established network of multimarket ties is supported by the improved competitive intelligence the network provides. Competitive information available to multimarket rivals furnishes a sufficient amount of reliable intelligence to aid in maintaining the established spheres of influence. When firms' interconnectedness reaches a high enough level, they are better able to engage in the types of tacit collusion and normative agreements that yield less competitive environments (DiMaggio & Powell, 1983; Oliver, 1991). High levels of multi-market contact increase the likelihood that signaling and competitive information is accurately interpreted by market participants (Heil & Robertson, 1991; Srinivasan, 1991; van Wegberg & van Witteloostuijn, this volume). Consequently, the incidence of misinterpretation of a rival's intent leading to competitive escalation will decline. With a greater ability to predict competitors' behaviors from extensive experience across different settings, a given multimarket rival with high levels of contact will be more aware of the greater response potential of its rivals, should it engage in additional aggressive actions such as market entry (Chen, 1996). This awareness is likely to cause them to think twice about undertaking such a risky, and potentially costly, course of action. Rather than attack each other and endure performance declines, firms within fully elaborated multimarket structures adopt a 'live and let live' policy toward their rivals (Edwards, 1955).

Table 2. The Effects of Multimarket Competition on Market Entry.

Factor	Key Issues & Processes	Effect on Multimarket Contact
Deterrence and Mutual Forbearance	Cost-benefit analysis: Increased response options of multimarket rivals (cross party, response across multiple markets) raises costs of aggression for multimarket competitors. Mutual interdependence now highly salient to multimarket rivals.	Incidence of aggressive behavior by multimarket rivals declines across shared markets. Firms mutually forbear from future aggression and establish spheres of influence.
Strategic Balance	Competitive positioning: to generate top performance, firm needs to establish unique competitive position, different from its rivals (depends on assessment of extent of strategic similarity to multimarket rivals) Bounded Rationality and Heuristic decision making: Extent of perceived benefit from additional information about multimarket rivals is reduced and exceeded by costs of potential responses generated by aggressive behavior.	Firms seek to avoid complete isomorphism with competitors (and poor competitive positioning). Future entry moves more likely into other markets where multimarket competitors are not present.
Management Reputation	CEO now seeks to establish own enduring theme. Resource dependence; Political coalitions in place to support enduring theme. Impression management focuses on establishing independence from the past.	Development of shared markets (multimarket structure) now complete. Reputation-building actions more likely to focus on different/newer markets and unique actions.

Strategic Balance

Porac and his colleagues (Porac et al., 1989) observed that managers are continually searching for the proper balance between competitive distinctiveness and legitimacy. Trying to find the appropriate position on this 'competitive cusp' requires that at some point, firms reject the legitimacy that mimicking the moves of a rival provides in favor of locating the firm in a unique competitive position capable of securing a competitive advantage for itself (Deephouse, 1999). Managers of firms engaged in multimarket relationships will realize, at some point, that using their rivals' moves to justify their own will only produce an excessive isomorphism between their firm and its rivals. It will become increasingly hard for the marketplace to distinguish between these firms. Consequently, continuing to 'follow the leader' will decrease the likelihood that a firm will develop its own competitive advantage. While imitation by rivals is a key threat to a firm's existing competitive advantage, it rarely confers advantage on the imitator (Barney, 1991). The result is often competitive parity, which gives customers the choice between the original and its imitators to obtain similar value. The net result is diminished performance for competitively similar firms.

Management Reputation

One of the key responsibilities of top management is to develop the competitive advantages that will distinguish its firm from its rivals (Peteraf, 1993). This is especially true of CEOs. If a CEO is able achieve a sustainable competitive advantage by positioning his or her firm in a unique competitive position, he or she leaves a lasting impression on the firm while at the same time enhancing his or her own reputation. Hambrick and Fukutomi (1991) have described how the actions of typical CEOs evolve over their tenure in the job. During the experimentation phase of the CEO's tenure, mimicking the moves of rivals can serve as a mechanism for CEOs to learn what their organization is capable of doing well and what it is not. Imitation can also help enhance the CEO's reputation as an individual capable of initiating and managing organizational change, which can build support among key resource providers that he or she can draw upon at a later time (Stone & Brush, 1996).

Eventually, though, most CEOs seek an enduring theme or paradigm for their organization, with which they ultimately become identified (Hambrick & Fukutomi, 1991). Competitive interaction remains an important consideration, but attention now turns to distinguishing the firm from its rivals, rather than assuring its legitimacy through them. To continue to imitate others in the market would result in the firm being seen by its stakeholders as an 'also-ran' in the market and compromise the possibility of the CEO establishing a reputation as a dynamic and visionary leader.

The selection of an enduring paradigm is likely to coincide with CEOs feeling less of a need for additional legitimation of their actions. Prior successful imitative moves would have secured the cooperation of critical resource providers and stakeholders through the legitimacy the moves created. As a result, CEOs will be more confident of acceptance and support, which enables them to lay out a new direction for their firms. In addition, they are likely to anticipate little political resistance which could not be overcome (Hambrick & Fukutomi, 1991; Pfeffer, 1992). These pressures and motivations are consequently likely to reduce the incidence of 'follow the leader' types of behavior. It is important to note that a reduction in the incidence of imitation strategies will make firms more heterogeneous which normally *increases* the level of competition between them (Caves & Porter, 1977; Cool & Schendel, 1988; Khandwalla, 1981). However, the forbearance effect of multimarket competition should limit this occurrence.

The mutual forbearance logic, the eventual decline in the added value of additional competitive intelligence obtained from establishing more points of contact, and the eventual performance and personal limitations inherent in imitation strategies all support the idea that the influence of multimarket contact on market entry changes when multimarket ties reach higher levels. Consistent with classic multimarket theory, firms with moderate to high levels of multimarket ties to their rivals become increasingly less likely to enter markets that their multimarket competitors are already in. This reluctance is characteristic of the muted competition that results from high levels of multimarket contact between firms. It is important to note that the above discussion makes clear that the motivations at work are not limited to mutual forbearance.

Taken together, the distinction between multimarket contact and multimarket competition depicts the relationship between the extent to which a firm competes in the same markets as its competitors and its propensity to enter into additional markets that these competitors are already in as an inverted-U. This is consistent with the empirical results obtained by Baum and Korn (1999) and Haveman and Nonnemaker (2000).

IMPLICATIONS FOR MARKET ENTRY IN A MULTIMARKET CONTEXT

The foregoing discussion raises a number of interesting questions and issues regarding a firm's market entry behavior in pursuit of the benefits that come with being positioned within multimarket structures. In particular, to build an effective deterrent, firms must enter the markets of their (current and future) multimarket competitors. The success of such moves depends, in part, on their ability to avoid attracting the attention of these competitors and evoking an aggressive response.

Although multimarket competitors are very likely to respond to an aggressive move by their multimarket rivals (Chen, 1996), they must be aware of the move in order to respond, as well as possess the motivation to do so (Chen & Miller, 1994; Miller & Chen, 1994). To achieve the benefits of an elaborated multimarket structure, then, firms need to enter into the markets of their multimarket competitors, but in ways that are less visible or make it difficult for their competitors to respond (MacMillan, McCaffrey & Van Wijk, 1985; Smith, Grimm, Chen & Gannon, 1989).

Whether a particular entry move elicits a response from competitors rests on two fundamental aspects of the entry decision: the particular market chosen and the method of entry. Both choice of market and method of entry have several key characteristics that are more or less likely to provoke a response to the entry by multimarket rivals. In the following, we discuss a number of ways in which additional ties to multimarket competitors can be established that will increase multimarket contact (up to the threshold level) and thus create a credible deterrent to future aggressive action while also reducing the likelihood of immediate response. The extant studies of market entry in a multimarket context have used a broad definition of market entry and did not distinguish between the types of markets nor the way in which market entry was achieved (Baum & Korn, 1996, 1999; Boeker et al., 1993). These areas represent important avenues for future research.

In a multimarket context, the choice of which markets to enter, of course, is dependent on the markets in which one's multimarket competitors are already in. That is, if a firm is seeking to increase multimarket contact levels with its rivals, its set of possible markets to enter is limited to those already entered by its multimarket competitors. As a result, a firm's decisions to enter into these markets are likely to be instances of 'follow the leader' behavior, since by definition, they would be following their rivals into the market. They would be able to use the fact of their rivals' prior entry as a key point in legitimizing the move. Additionally, since improving competitive intelligence is a key benefit of increasing multimarket contact, firms are likely to choose markets that are less similar to the ones it currently meets its multimarket competitors in. By following rivals into less similar markets, the firm has a better opportunity for observing a wider range of behavior than it would if it concentrated in similar markets, which are likely to have similar environmental opportunities and threats and elicit similar behaviors from market incumbents.

It should be kept in mind that the propositions presented below are not meant to imply that multimarket concerns are of paramount importance or interest to managers planning their firm's strategic future. However, studies have demonstrated that, *ceteris paribus*, when firms compete with similar rivals across a common set of markets, multimarket concerns do, in fact, play a significant role in their decision calculus. Boeker et al. (1997) found multimarket contact to be in the middle of their set of variables in terms of its impact on market exit in a multimarket context. Similarly, Baum and Korn (1996) find strong effects for their multimarket measures on both market exit and market entry. It is within this context that we discuss the role that multimarket contact plays regarding market entry. Multimarket concerns may not be *the most important factor* in firm entry decisions, but prior research indicates that multimarket concerns do factor into the decision. Gimeno and Woo (1994) explicitly encourage managers to include multimarket concerns in their strategic decision-making.

Market Choice

Gimeno and Woo (1999) presented some initial theorizing about which markets multimarket competitors are more likely to enter. In their paper, they hypothesized that firms would be more likely to share multimarket ties with other firms in markets that offer resource-sharing opportunities. They also noted that the efficiency gains associated with economies of scope that such markets offered to multimarket competitors would result in greater forbearance in these markets. Their findings supported their expectations. In addition to the benefits resulting from resource-sharing across markets, there are competitive concerns that multimarket rivals are likely to consider as they decide how to increase their level of contact with their multimarket rivals. We develop several propositions related to these concerns below.

Peripheral Markets

One of the key characteristics of competitive actions that has been shown to evoke quicker responses from competitors is the visibility of the attack (Chen & Miller, 1994; MacMillan et al., 1985). If a competitor is aware that a move is directed at a firm's most important markets, a response is very likely to be undertaken (Chen & Miller, 1994). MacMillan (1982) supports this logic by identifying inertial barriers to response that are negatively related to a particular market's priority to a firm. That is, the more a market is considered a low priority for the firm, the less likely the firm will be to defend the market against threats associated with additional market entries. This suggests that to increase the level of multimarket contact with its rivals, a focal firm would be well advised to direct its attention to markets where its current multimarket rivals have only a minor presence. Such markets are ones where the rival receives relatively little of its total revenues and/or profits, or ones where it employs fewer of its core competencies. These markets are likely to be defended with less vigor should a competitor establish new operations in them.

The advantage to a multimarket competitor of establishing additional points of contact in peripheral markets relates to its ability to escalate the costs of entry to unacceptably high levels. Having a presence in multiple markets from which to respond to an aggressors' action in one market, raises the potential overall costs of the action dramatically and reduces the likelihood of its initial occurrence. Thus, establishing positions in markets peripheral to one's competitors increases the breadth with which a response can be launched.

Another advantage of targeting peripheral markets is that these are the markets that are likely to be relatively more dissimilar to the core markets of a firm's multimarket competitors. As noted, they may be ones where fewer core competencies are employed. The dissimilarities of peripheral markets are likely to increase the kinds of situations in which a firm can view the behaviors of its rivals, which can enhance the scope of competitive intelligence dramatically. Recent work supporting the idea that the degree to which firms occupy market space with greater variety enhances their learning opportunities (regarding efficiency and effectiveness, for example (Greve, 2000, 1999; Usher, 1999)) suggests that this effect may also favorably impact learning about the competition. Observing rivals under a wider variety of conditions would improve competitive intelligence more than increasing the number of observations available under more similar situations.

> *Proposition 1*: Multimarket rivals with low levels of multimarket contact will be more likely to increase multimarket contact with their rivals through entry into their multimarket rivals' peripheral markets.

Footholds

Multimarket theory leans heavily on the idea that even a token presence in the markets of one's competitors may be sufficient to deter aggressive action (Karnani & Wernerfelt, 1985; Gimeno, 1999). Karnani and Wernerfelt (1985) described this situation as one of a 'mutual foothold equilibrium.' Gimeno (1999) illustrates the capacity such footholds have for forestalling competitive behavior within competitively asymmetric firm dyads. His results demonstrate that the intensity of competitive behavior between a particular market leader and a challenger is lessened if these roles are reversed in another shared market. That is, with so-call 'reciprocal multimarket contacts,' neither has an incentive to aggressively attack the other in either market because of the threat of retaliation in their more important market. By virtue of the deterrent power inherent in the costs associated with this type of 'cross-parry' response in the rival's more important market (Porter, 1980), a multimarket competitor has a strong incentive to establish such footholds.

Equally important, though, is the fact that such footholds may be established without evoking an immediate response from a market leader. Although the market is clearly important to the leader, a challenger coming into the market at the small scale characteristic of a foothold may be interpreted as posing a minimal threat to the entrenched interests of the dominant player, particularly if the new entrant can accurately signal its intention to occupy only a small portion of the market space. Results obtained by Chen, Smith and Grimm (1992) tend to support this contention. They found that competitive responses were lower and fewer in number if the initial move was relatively low in competitive impact. That is, response was less severe if the action did not directly challenge a large portion of the market of the attack's target. In addition, Chen et al. (1992) found that the smaller the attack intensity and the more strategic the move, the less likely were responses to be. A small entry into a competitor's market is unlikely to be interpreted as a massive assault, and the fact that it involves a clearly strategic, rather than tactical, objective should also work to reduce the likelihood of response (Smith et al., 1992). Entering at a small scale with appropriate signaling as to the limits of one's expansion plans might be enough to allay the fears of market leaders.

Small scale entry into the major markets of a firm's multimarket competitors will also impact competitive intelligence. Since the entering firm is not yet in this major market, its knowledge of the incumbents' behaviors in such markets is limited to second-hand vicarious observations (Bandura, 1977), which are unlikely to be as comprehensive or accurate as first-hand observations (Fazio & Zanna, 1981). In addition, without detailed knowledge of the specific context, second-hand observations are not likely to be correctly interpreted. Since such markets will be of critical importance to firms for whom they represent major sources of revenue, their behaviors in these markets are likely to be extremely reliable indicators of their likelihood to defend their market position, and their propensity to act aggressively. First-hand observation of the moves of a firm's rivals in markets of major importance to them will add immeasurably to the richness of its manager's mental images of these rivals and their assessments of their future actions.

> *Proposition 2*: Multimarket rivals with low levels of multimarket contact will be more likely to increase multimarket contact with their rivals through small foothold entries into their multimarket rivals' existing markets.

Quick following into new markets
One of the recognized limitations of past studies of market entry within a multi-market context is that the risk sets of possible markets to be entered were

relatively fixed and stable. That is, they did not adequately capture pioneering behavior into new, emerging markets by the firms in the samples used (Baum & Korn, 1996). However, such new markets might easily facilitate increasing levels of multimarket contact between firms.

Most research regarding entry into new markets has focused on whether or not a pioneering firm achieves significant and long-term first-mover advantages (e.g. Lambkin, 1988; Lieberman & Montgomery, 1988, 1998). The basis for these advantages includes the incidence of followers entering into the market quickly upon the heels of the pioneer (Lieberman & Montgomery, 1988). In new markets with low imitation barriers (MacMillan et al., 1985) and where first movers have not been able to successfully establish barriers to entry such as technological leadership, the preemption of critical resources or buyers' switching costs (Lieberman & Montgomery, 1988) might represent viable avenues for multimarket competitors to increase their levels of multimarket contact with their multimarket rivals with a lower likelihood of response from these rivals, should their rivals be among the first into the new market.

MacMillan (1982) makes clear that competitive response is less likely if the firms in the market under attack are distracted by internal problems or external opportunities. Entry into new markets presents challenges to pioneering firms on both of these fronts. Initially, first movers are often subject to a great amount of technological and market uncertainty in the new market (Lieberman, 1988). In this case, resolving this uncertainty (in its favor) is likely to require a great deal of the first mover's attention, distracting it from other events in its environment.

Internal problems can also plague first movers. From inertia generated through the accumulation of relatively inflexible fixed assets to internal political dynamics (Hannan & Freeman, 1984), the attention of first movers may be directed inward to such an extent that they overlook the entry moves of followers into the market. This situation is more likely to be the case if followers are quick to enter after the pioneer. Facing an unsettled situation in the new market, the pioneer may not be able to respond effectively to the competitive moves of its rivals, making response less likely (Chen & Miller, 1994).

The earlier a rival follows a pioneer into an emerging market, the less entrenched will be the first mover's position. Consequently, the pioneer is not likely to feel as threatened by additional entry moves of its rivals, even if it is aware of it. This would reduce its motivation to respond to the threat implicit in the entry move (Chen & Miller, 1994).

The situation may be similar even if the market is not in the early stages of its life cycle. The market will still be new to the recent entrants and these firms may not be adequately prepared to respond to additional new developments in the competitive environment. Multimarket competitors can take advantage of this temporary inability by establishing themselves in these new markets shortly after their rivals do. In so doing, they increase their multimarket contact with early movers, creating additional avenues for a multiple-market response at a later time.

These types of 'follow the leader' actions are likely to be the most effective at increasing multimarket contact while averting response from multimarket rivals. They are also likely to be very effective at building the reputations of top managers. Because the markets are completely, or comparatively new to the firms involved, entry can easily be construed as an innovative and risk-taking action, even if a firm is not the first into such markets. These types of behaviors help a CEO cement a reputation for being able to lead a firm through difficult, risky decisions and can help set the stage for more radical departures from the status-quo at a later time. In short, they can build the political support needed when the CEO eventually defines his or her enduring theme (Hambrick & Fukutomi, 1991).

> *Proposition 3*: Multimarket rivals with low levels of multimarket contact will be more likely to increase multimarket contact with their rivals through following their multimarket rivals' into emerging markets.

> *Proposition 4*: Multimarket rivals with low levels of multimarket contact will be more likely to increase multimarket contact with their rivals through quickly following their multimarket rivals into established markets in which none of them currently competes.

Method of Entry

Firms have several choices regarding the method of entry into a new market. They can invest in their own assets and build a presence from the ground up. Alternatively, they can merge with or acquire a firm already competing in the market they wish to enter. For example, Singal (1996) describes how airlines have increased their level of multimarket contact through mergers. Scott (1989) has noted that merger and/or acquisition to increase multimarket contact is unlikely to generate intense regulatory scrutiny when the new contacts are across very dissimilar markets. A third option for firms seeking to enter new markets is to contract with another firm for provision of goods and/or services in the desired market.

Contracting is unlikely to help a multimarket competitor secure either a better deterrent or improve its competitive intelligence. First, the contracted firm remains a separate legal entity, under the control of its own owners and managers. The nature of this market-based transaction makes it difficult for the multimarket competitor to secure its cooperation in any planned response it might need to undertake (Combs & Ketchen, 1999). Second, because the contracted firm remains separate, there is less of an incentive for it to share its market knowledge with the multimarket competitor. What knowledge it does share would be second-hand to the multimarket competitor. This exposes the information to various mis-communications, misinterpretations and distortions, rendering it less useful as reliable intelligence than first-hand knowledge.

Boeker et al. (1997) provide some supportive evidence for these claims in a multimarket environment. In their analysis, they divided their sample of firms into two subsamples depending on whether the firms provided the services they offered under contract or in-house. For the contracting subsample, their multi-market measure had no significant effect on their dependent variable, market exit (although the sign was in the appropriate direction). This result supports the notion that contracting for product or service provision is an ineffective way for firms to gain the benefits of multimarket contact with their rivals. From the above, we conclude that while multimarket competitors may choose to enter markets through a contracting route (the above arguments do not *preclude* entry via contracting), they would most likely do so without taking into account multi-market considerations.

The fact that contracting for product or service provision appears to be an ineffective way to secure multimarket advantages raises a very important point. It may be the case that market entry through contracting is a viable route to market entry when multimarket contact levels with rivals have passed the threshold where deterrence begins to operate. If contracting does not provide the benefits of multimarket competition, then moves by multimarket rivals into new markets using this method might not be seen as inherently threatening by multimarket firms already in these markets. An additional rationale supporting this contention is that the entry of the new firm via contracting does not alter the number of competitors in the market. The firm with which the multimarket entrant is contracting has received additional business, but no new firm has entered the market. Thus, a new entry through contracting will be less likely to evoke a retaliatory response.

Proposition 5a: At low to moderate levels of multimarket contact, levels of multimarket contact will be unrelated to the likelihood of multimarket competitors' entry into the markets of their multimarket competitors through contracting methods.

Proposition 5b: When firms have higher levels of multimarket contact with market incumbents, entry into the markets of multimarket competitors will be more likely through contracted means.

The choice then reduces to merger/acquisition or developing one's own market presence in-house. Focusing strictly on scale, an acquisition can quickly increase the level of multimarket contact the acquirer has with its multimarket rivals as it can create new and (possibly) large positions in several markets at once for the acquiring firm. For example, Kimberly-Clark's planned acquisition of Scott Paper would have been a major move into several of Proctor & Gamble's product markets in both Europe and North America (Brierly, 1996). This advantage seems to favor acquisition as a more attractive approach to building multimarket ties than a slower method of internal development. This notion is supported by Singal's (1996) observation that acquisition is a popular choice for airlines seeking to enter new routes. The question remains as to whether acquisition or in-house development would be more likely to generate competitive responses from multimarket rivals.

The likelihood of response rests on the assessment by multimarket rivals of the strategic nature of the acquisition versus the threat to their most important markets. Prior research indicates that responses are less likely the more strategic the attack (Chen et al., 1992). However, other work suggests that when an acquisition involves the entry of a competitor into a market important to a focal firm, response likelihood or frequency is predicted to rise (Chen & Miller, 1994; MacMillan et al., 1985). Clearly, the expenditure of funds for an acquisition or merger represents a significant investment in assets and psychological commitment on the part of top management that are not easily reversed. The investment is clearly strategic in nature. However, if the acquisition involves only peripheral markets of multimarket competitors, it is reasonable to conclude that the likelihood of response would be low. By joining both strategic action and a less-important peripheral market, it is likely that multimarket competitors choosing to enter such markets in this way, contrasted with de novo entry (i.e. starting from the ground up using their own assets), will face a greatly reduced likelihood of response by their multimarket competitors.

It may be the case that the acquisition of a multi-business firm would bring the acquirer into major markets of one or more multimarket competitors. This kind of action has been hypothesized to result in swift retaliation (Chen, 1996). To avoid a competitive response, the firm can elect to spin off this part of the acquisition, clearly signaling its intention to do so. Such a requirement can be avoided and a retaliatory response precluded if the acquisition provides the acquirer entry into its rivals' markets at only relatively modest scales. Firms seeking to increase their multimarket contact, but avoid competitive response, would strive to make sure that if an acquisition brings it into markets of primary importance to its competitors, that it creates only a foothold presence in these markets.

Proposition 6a: Multimarket rivals with low levels of multimarket contact will be more likely to increase multimarket contact with their rivals in peripheral markets through acquisitions than through de novo entry.

Proposition 6b: When acquisitions by firms include entry into more central markets of the firm's multimarket competitors, the entry is more likely to be a foothold presence than on a large scale.

IMPLICATIONS, EXTENSIONS AND CONCLUSION

This paper began by pointing up an inconsistency in the multimarket literature regarding market entry. Most prior work depicted the relationship between multimarket competition and competitive firm behaviors as a monotonic, often linear, negative relationship. This depiction, however, is inconsistent with the fact that entry into the markets of a firm's multimarket competitors is an essential precursor to the establishment of more fully elaborated multimarket structures. We offered a theoretical explanation for how, at lower levels of multimarket contact, such contact actually encourages market entry by offering firms models on which to fashion their strategic moves, enables firms to utilize their best, most comprehensive competitive intelligence and eventually affords them the benefits of a less competitive environment when levels of multimarket contact reach the point were multimarket competition ensues and mutual forbearance occurs. We followed these conceptual arguments with several propositions that described how, if multimarket competitors are to enter into the markets of their multimarket rivals, they might do so with a higher likelihood of not incurring a competitive response from these rivals.

Generalizability of Non-Linear Multimarket Effects
Our analysis of firm behavior within a multimarket context raises a number of additional interesting questions that can help to further the development of multimarket theory and direct empirical investigations into the effects of multi-market contact and competition. While our argument for the necessity of a non-linear relationship between levels of multimarket contact and market entry seems to us quite compelling, it should not be automatically generalized to other types of firm behaviors in a multimarket setting without the appropriate theoretical development.

In one case, Baum and Korn (1999) hypothesize and find a non-linear effect for market exit and levels of multimarket contact between pairs of multimarket competitors. Their inverted-U shaped relationship shows that the likelihood of market exit by firms with some small amount of multimarket contact with their rivals increases with multimarket contact levels up to some point, and then declines. If the focus is on individual firm behaviors (i.e. the likelihood for **a** firm to exit from **a particular market** based on the multimarket characteristics of that market among other things), such a result implies that just when a firm is attempting to increase its multimarket contact with its rivals (through additional entry), it is exiting from the very markets that enable it to do so.

This implication highlights several issues. An inverted-U shaped relationship may be an appropriate depiction of the effect of multimarket contact (generally) on market exit if aggregate rates (from a market overall) are considered. For example, if the sum of all entry and exit decisions for a particular firm within a specified time period yielded a net increase in multimarket contact then the effect of this contact on exit decisions may be of an inverted-U form. However, this requires taking both entry and exit decisions into account simultaneously, rather than looking at exit decisions alone. At the very least, this concern raises the importance of considering the full range of firm behaviors when testing for effects related to a specific action of interest. It makes clear that researchers may have to control for other firm behaviors while investigating the effects of multimarket contact on the behavior(s) of interest.

Taking both entry and exit decisions into account simultaneously seems to represent an particularly revealing way to assess the impact of multimarket ties on these two key firm behaviors. Many researchers have noted that multimarket studies need to address the fact that, by definition, in a multimarket context entry and exit decisions cannot be considered independent events (Barnett, 1993; Boeker et al., 1997). Consequently, an argument can be made that it is essential that both decisions be included in any model that tests for the impact of multimarket ties on either one. As noted, an alternative would be for models to incorporate the net effect of a firm's entry and exit decisions during a time period in order to assess how multimarket contact levels change over time and the effect that these changing levels have on other firm behaviors. Baum and Korn (1999) do just this in a supplemental analysis in their study. Their findings show that at low to moderate levels of multimarket contact (between dyads of firms), entry behavior by firms dominates their exit behavior, enabling them to increase levels of multimarket contact with their rivals.

Of particular interest is their speculation that a multimarket competitor may use exit as the means to signal subordination. This possibility raises a host of interesting questions regarding the characteristics such a move would need to have to communicate subordination in a credible way. For example, would exits have to be from markets in which the firm has had a long term (but, perhaps, relatively minor) presence in in order to convincingly demonstrate its commitment to subordination (Chen et al., 1992)? Conversely, exit from a more recently entered market might be more effective at signaling a firm's intention of ceding superiority in a market to a particular multimarket rival. The bang-bang nature of the combination of entry followed by a relatively quick exit in a shared market might be more visible to rivals (Chen & Miller, 1994). If so, by better attracting the attention of the firm's multimarket competitors, the moves would more effectively signal the firm's intention to acknowledge spheres of influence.

Alternatively, chance might play a key role in building and maintaining multimarket relationships (Korn & Baum, 1999). If so, multimarket environments could represent an ideal context for exploring the boundedly rational behavior of managers (and, of course, for subsequently developing prescriptive strategies that address its deficiencies). Phillips and Mason (this volume) note that managers of firms operating in multiple markets may be overly disposed to see connections between actions in different markets that may not be related. If chance does play a role in establishing multimarket contact, it is not hard to imagine that a multimarket presence could lead managers to draw inappropriate conclusions from their experiences across these markets (Levinthal & March, 1993). As Korn and Baum (1999) describe, a vicious circle may result whereby firms imitate their multimarket rivals and learn based on a limited sampling of their own experiences which in turn reinforces the subsequent impact that multimarket competitors have on strategic decision making. Take for example an imitative acquisition by a firm, focused on gaining entry into a particular market. Coincidentally, the acquisition brings with it a dramatic increase in the level of multimarket contact between the focal firm and its rivals because the target competes in a number of other markets. This could then make management extremely attentive to multimarket issues, which then increases the influence of multimarket concerns regarding subsequent firm actions. The process was set in motion by chance, but due to the use of simplifying heuristics, multimarket concerns become increasingly important.

Although chance can provide an explanation for changes in multimarket contact, the perspective still seems inadequate to explain fully how over some range entries will consistently outpace exits (so that multimarket contact levels increase). The fact that entries must exceed exits seems to point to at least some non-chance-related factors at work. In any event, multimarket phenomena present researchers with a fascinating challenge to tease out the effects that are directly linked to managers' assessments of multimarket environments and those that merely appear to mimic these concerns. As Phillips and Mason (this volume) demonstrate in their provocative paper, firms that compete in multiple markets are liable to coordinate their actions across these markets even when they do not meet any similar multimarket competitors. More thorough theoretical developments regarding the influences multimarket contact has on specific firm behaviors is necessary for theory to move beyond some of the incomplete and inconsistent findings that have been generated about multimarket effects.

Other competitive behavior may be provocatively explored by hypothesizing an inverted-U shaped relationship as well. Several studies have examined the pricing behavior of airlines within multimarket environments. Results have repeatedly shown that fares are higher on routes that are flown by carriers with extensive multimarket ties (Evans & Kessides, 1994; Gimeno & Woo, 1996; Singal, 1996). That is, the relationship between aggressive pricing behavior and multimarket ties is negative. This suggests that the periodic price wars that plague the airlines industry seem to affect such markets less strongly than markets with fewer multimarket competitors in them (or markets with multimarket rivals with lower levels of multimarket contact between them).

An inverted-U shaped relationship between aggressive pricing actions and multimarket contact might capture both the fact that price wars do occur while also remaining consistent with the multimarket studies of airline pricing behavior. An inverted-U implies that when routes are dominated by airlines that compete in relatively few other routes (i.e. multimarket ties are in the low range and multimarket contact is operating), these airlines are increasingly likely to respond to their rivals' price reductions as their levels of contact increase. Eventually this relationship reverses and once multimarket competition ensues, increasing levels of contact would make response to such competitive actions less likely (while also reducing the incidence of the initial aggressive actions).

The negative relationship found in earlier studies may indicate a relatively low threshold for multimarket competition. The incentive to refrain from excessive price rivalry may start at relatively low levels of multimarket contact between carriers. In the studies to date, the forbearance effect of multimarket competition may have been so strong as to overwhelm the propensity to engage in price wars at lower multimarket contact levels – yielding the negative relationship that has been reported. Clearly, this becomes an empirical question. Even casual observation of the real-world behavior of air carriers demonstrates convincingly that price competition between them does occur, with sometimes significant consequences. This is an intriguing issue and deserving of investigation.

The Onset of Multimarket Competition
This paper also has relevance for the competitive implications of the tradeoff managers must make between the legitimacy gained from imitating their rivals and the competitive advantage that comes from staking out unique space in the markets in which their firms compete (Deephouse, 1999; Porac et al., 1989). We stated earlier that we did not feel that the point at which multimarket contact

becomes multimarket competition was likely to be identical across all sets of markets or all sets of multimarket competitors. The above discussion of multi-market competition in the context of airlines pricing behavior suggests a relatively low threshold for multimarket competition. Conversely, Boeker and his colleagues (1993) estimate that in their sample of hospitals, multimarket competition does not begin until firms share, on average, 75% of their markets with multimarket competitors. This suggests that the extent to which individual markets or industries exhibit institutional effects is likely to influence this point dramatically (Glynn & Abzug, 1998). In addition to hospitals, banks and educational institutions are perhaps the most well-known examples of such industries. Banks have been the setting for a number of prior multimarket studies (Heggestad & Rhoades, 1978; Ma & Jemison, 1994; Rhoades & Heggestad, 1985), but none have looked for possible non-linearities in the relationship of multimarket contact to firm behaviors or performance outcomes.

A number of other factors can be suggested that might influence where multi-market contact becomes multimarket competition. Phillips and Mason (1996) argue that demand and cost conditions prevailing in the shared markets will determine when and if cooperation (i.e, multimarket competition and mutual forbearance) across these markets occurs. Another factor is the degree of product innovation present with an industry or across a collection of firms. For example, firms in pharmaceutical industry have been described by several authors as strong exemplars of pioneering organizations (Henderson & Cockburn, 1994; Hill & Hansen, 1991). These firms typically devote much attention to producing new chemical compounds to treat conditions that had previously not been addressed. To the extent that an industry is driven by the development of these kinds of new markets, the firms within them might exhibit a high degree of multimarket contact (due to 'follow the leader' type behavior into markets in which entrenched positions have yet to be established).

Firms producing commodity-like products may also exhibit higher levels of multimarket contact with their rivals before forbearance occurs, but for different reasons. Since price competition is the primary competitive lever available to such firms, they may persist in such behaviors over a wider range of multimarket levels. This possibility suggests that the more limited the number of strategic actions a group of firms can take, the more multimarket contact is necessary before forbearance begins to occur. The above examples highlight the fact that a more detailed explication of where the 'competitive cusp' (Porac et al., 1989) might be located in different sets of markets and firms remains an important issue for development of the full implications of the non-linearities associated with multimarket competition. As the last example hints, there may also be some factors that may be generalizable across different industries and markets (or groups of firms) to determine where the competitive cusp is located.

Interaction Effects

Finally, our propositions highlight primarily direct effects regarding the impact of multimarket contact and market entry. Several of the factors could easily be examined in an interaction context. That is, multimarket competitors seeking to increase their multimarket contact with their rivals can do so through foothold entries and entry by acquisition. The arguments for each that were presented above suggest that establishing a foothold through acquisition may be the most effective way to accomplish this to avoid competitive responses. There seem to be additional factors that make the joint use of acquisition and foothold entry more likely to be successful. While most acquisitions experience significant integration difficulties (Buono & Bowditch, 1989; Chatterjee, Lubatkin, Schweiger & Weber, 1992), the small scale of a foothold acquisition might permit easier integration as the acquiring firm will be clearly the controlling force in the combined firm. Consequently, fewer problems may emerge as the new entity builds the internal coordinated decision structures across its markets that are ultimately necessary for the firm to pursue multimarket strategies (Gimeno & Woo, 1994). Other interaction effects between form of entry and market characteristics can also be profitably investigated.

This paper offers a sound theoretical basis for refining multimarket theory along non-linear lines. It represents a first step toward a more thorough understanding of the impact of multimarket contact on firm behaviors as the level of multimarket contact a firm has with its rivals changes. It also offers some important avenues for further investigating this impact in the area of market entry. It begins to consider some of the more intriguing aspects of extending theorizing about the possible non-linear effects of multimarket contact to other competitive behaviors. As is frequently the case with emerging areas of research, we have only begun to perceive the tip of the iceberg.

REFERENCES

Bandura, A. (1977). *Social Learning Theory*. Englewood Cliffs, NJ: Prentice-Hall.

Barnett, W. P. (1993). Strategic Deterrence Among Multipoint Competition. *Industrial and Corporate Change, 2*, 249–278.

Barney, J. (1991). Firm Resources and Sustained Competitive Advantage. *Journal of Management, 17*, 99–120.

Baum, J. A. C., & Korn, H. J. (1996). Competitive Dynamics of Interfirm Rivalry. *Academy of Management Journal, 39*, 255–291.

Baum, J. A. C., & Korn, H. J. (1999). Dynamics of Dyadic Competition. *Strategic Management Journal, 20*, 251–278.

Boeker, W. J. G., Stephan, J., & Murmann, J. P. (1993). The Dynamics of Market Entry: The Role of Multipoint Competition. Paper presented at Academy of Management Annual Meeting, Atlanta GA.

Boeker, W. J. G., Stephan, J., & Murmann, J. P. (1997). Competition in a Multimarket Environment: The Case of Market Exit. *Organization Science, 8*, 126–142.

Brierly, S. (1996). Andrex Dog Has Its Day. *Marketing Week, 19*(29), 46–47. October 11.

Buono, A. F., & Bowditch, J. L. (1989). T*he Human Side of Mergers and Acquisitions* . San Francisco: Jossey Bass.

Caves, R. E., & Porter, M. E. (1977). From Entry Barriers to Mobility Barriers: Conjectural Decisions and Contrived Deterrence to New Competition. *Quarterly Journal of Economics, 91*, 241–261.

Chatterjee, S., Lubatkin, M. H., Schweiger, D. M., & Weber, Y. (1992). Cultural Differences and Shareholder Value in Related Mergers: Linking Equity and Human Capital. *Strategic Management Journal, 7*, 119–139.

Chen, M. J. (1996). Competitor Analysis and Inter-Firm Rivalry: Toward a Theoretical Integration. *Academy of Management Review, 21*, 100–134.

Chen, M. J., & Miller, D. (1994). Competitive Attack, Retaliation and Performance: An Expectancy-Valence Framework. *Strategic Management Journal, 15*, 85–102.

Chen, M. J., Smith, K. G., & Grimm, C. M. (1992). Action Characteristics as Predictors of Competitive Responses. *Management Science, 38*, 439–454.

Combs, J. G., & Ketchen Jr., D. J. (1999). Explaining Interfirm Cooperation and performance: Toward a Reconciliation of Predictions from the Resource-based View and Organizational Economics. *Strategic Management Journal, 20*, 867–888.

Cool, L., & Schendel, D. (1988). Performance Differences Among Strategic Group Members. *Strategic Management Journal, 9*, 207–223.

Deephouse, D. L. (1999). To Be Different or the Same? It's a Question (and Theory) of Strategic Balance. *Strategic Management Journal, 20*, 147–166.

DiMaggio, P. J., & Powell, W. W. (1983). The Iron Cage Revisited: Institutional Isomorphism and Collective Rationality in Organizational Fields. *American Sociological Review, 48*(April), 148–160.

Edwards, C. (1955). Conglomerate Bigness as a Source of Power. The NBER Report: Business Concentration and Price Policy. Princeton University Press. 331–359.

Evans, W. N., & Kessides, I. N. (1994). Living by the 'Golden Rule:' Multimarket contact in the U.S. Airline Industry. *Quarterly Journal of Economics, 109*, 341–366.

Fazio, R. H., & Zanna, M. P. (1981). Direct experience and attitude-behavior consistency. In: L. Berkowitz (Ed.), *Advances in Experimental Social Psychology, 14*. NY: Academic Press.

Feinberg, R. M. (1985). Sales at Risk: A Test of the Mutual Forbearance Theory of Conglomerate Behavior. *Journal of Business, 58*, 225–241.

Gimeno, J. (1999). Reciprocal Threats in Multimarket Rivalry: Staking Out 'Spheres of Influence' in the U.S. Airline Industry. *Strategic Management Journal, 20*, 101–128.

Gimeno, J., & Woo, C. Y. (1994). Multipoint Competition, Market Rivalry and Firm Performance: A Test of the Complete Mediation Hypothesis. *Academy of Management Best Papers Proceedings*, 1994. 32–36.

Gimeno, J., & Woo, C. Y. (1996). Hypercompetition in a Multimarket Environment: The Role of Strategic Similarity and Multimarket Contact in Competitive De-Escalation. *Organization Science, 7*, 322–341.

Gimeno, J., & Woo, C. Y. (1999). Multipoint Competition, Economies of Scope, and Firm Performance. *Academy of Management Journal, 43,* 239–259.

Glynn, M. A., & Abzug, R. (1998). Isomorphism and Competitive Differentiation in the Organizational Name Game. In: J. A. C. Baum (Ed.), *Disciplinary Roots of Strategic Management: Advances in Strategic Management,* Vol. 15 (pp. 105–128). Stamford, CT: JAI Press.

Greve, H. R. (1999). Branch Systems and Nonlocal Learning in Populations. In: A. Miner & P. Anderson (Eds), *Population-Level Learning and Industry Change: Advances in Strategic Management,* Vol. 16 (pp. 57–80). Stamford, CT: JAI Press.

Greve, H. R. (2000). Market Niche Entry Decisions: Competition, Learning and Strategy in Tokyo Banking, 1984–1936. *Academy of Management Journal, 43,* 816–836.

Hambrick, D. C., & Fukutomi, G. D. S. (1991). The Seasons of a CEO's Tenure. *Academy of Management Review, 16,* 719–742.

Hannan, M., & Freeman, J. (1984). Structural Inertia and organizational change. *American Sociological Review, 49,* 149–184.

Haunschild, P. R. (1993). Interorganizational Imitation: The Impact of Interlocks on Corporate Acquisition Activity. *Administrative Science Quarterly, 38,* 564–592.

Haunschild, P. R., & Miner, A. S. (1997). Modes of Interorganizational Imitation: The Effects of Outcome Salience and Uncertainty. *Administrative Science Quarterly, 42,* 472–500.

Haveman, H. A. (1993). Follow the leader: Mimetic Isomorphism and Entry into New Markets. *Administrative Science Quarterly, 38,* 593–627.

Haveman, H. A., & Nonnemaker, L. (2000). Competition in multiple geographic markets: The impact on growth and market entry. *Administrative Science Quarterly, 45,* 232–267.

Heggestad, A. A., & Rhoades, S. A. (1978). Multi-market interdependence and local market competition in banking. *Review of Economics and Statistics, 60,* 523–532.

Heil, O., & Robertson, T. S. (1991). Toward a Theory of Competitive Market Signaling: A Research Agenda. *Strategic Management Journal, 12,* 403–418.

Hemmasi, M., Graf, L. A., & Kellogg, C. E. (1990). Industry Structure, Competitive Rivalry and Firm Profitability. *Journal of Behavioral Economics, 19*(4), 431–448.

Henderson, R., & Cockburn, I. (1994). Measuring Competence? Exploring Firm Effects in Pharmaceutical Research. *Strategic Management Journal, 15,* 63–84.

Hill, C. W. L., & Hansen, G. S. (1991). A Longitudinal Study of the Cause and Consequences of Change. *Strategic Management Journal, 12,* 187–199.

Hughes, K., & Oughton, C. (1993). Diversification, Multi-market Contact and Profitability. *Economica, 60,* 203–224.

Hybels, R. C. (1995). On Legitimacy, Legitimation, and Organizations: A Critical Review and Integrative Theoretical Model. *Academy of Management Best Papers Proceedings,* 241–250.

Ingram, P., & Baum, J. A. C. (1997). Opportunity and Constraint: Organizations' Learning from the Operating and Competitive Experience of Industries. *Strategic Management Journal, 18* (Summer Special Issue), 75–98.

Khandwalla, P. N. (1981). Properties of Competing Organizations. In: P. C. Nystrom & W. H. Starbuck (Eds), *Handbook of Organizational Design* (pp. 411–432). NY: Oxford University Press.

Karnani, A., & Wernerfelt, B. (1985). Multipoint Competition. *Strategic Management Journal, 6,* 87–96.

Kim, S. (2001). Markets and Multiunit Firms from an American Historical Perspective. In: J. A. C. Baum & H. R. Greve (Eds), *Multiunit Organization and Multimarket Strategy; Advances in Strategic Management, 18* (pp. 307–328). Oxford, UK: JAI Press.

Knickerbocker, F. T. (1973). *Oligopolistic Reaction and Multinational Enterprise*. Harvard University.

Korn, H. J., & Baum, J. A. C. (1999). Chance, imitative, and strategic antecedent to multimarket contact. *Academy of Management Journal, 42*, 171–193.

Lambkin, M. (1988). Order of Entry and Performance in New Markets. *Strategic Management Journal, 9*, 127–140.

Levinthal, D. A., & March, J. G. (1993). The Myopia of Learning. *Strategic Management Journal, 14*, 95–112.

Lieberman, M. B., & Montgomery, D. B. (1988). First-Mover Advantages. *Strategic Management Journal, 9*, 41–58.

Lieberman, M. B., & Montgomery, D. B. (1998). First-Mover (Dis)advantages: Retrospective and Link with the Resource-based View. *Strategic Management Journal, 19*, 1111–1125.

Ma, H., & Jemison, D. B. (1994). Effects of Spheres of Influence and Differentials in Firm Resources and Capabilities on the Intensity of Rivalry in Multi-Market Competition. Paper presented to Business Policy and Strategy Division, Academy of Management Annual Meeting, Dallas, TX.

MacMillan, I. C. (1982). Seizing Competitive Advantage. *Journal of Business Strategy, 2*(4), 43–57.

MacMillan, I. C., McCaffrey, M. L., & Van Wijk, G. (1985). Competitors' Responses to Easily Imitated New Products – Exploring Commercial Banking Product Introductions. *Strategic Management Journal, 6*, 75–86.

McGrath, R. G., Chen, M., & MacMillan, I. C. (1998). Multimarket maneuvering in uncertain spheres of influence: Resource diversion strategies. *Academy of Management Review, 23*, 724–740.

Miller, D., & Chen, M. J. (1994). Sources and Consequences of Competitive Inertia: A Study of the U.S. Airline Industry. *Administrative Science Quarterly, 39*, 1–23.

Mintzberg, H., Raisinghani, D., & Theoret, A. (1976). The Structure of 'Unstructured' Decision Processes. *Administrative Science Quarterly, 21*, 246–275.

Oliver, C. (1991). Strategic Responses to Institutional Processes. *Academy of Management Review, 16*(1), 145–179.

Peteraf, M. A. (1993). The Cornerstones of Competitive Advantage: A Resource-Based View. *Strategic Management Journal, 14*, 179–191.

Pfeffer, J. (1992). *Managing with Power: Politics and Influence in Organizations*. Boston, MA: Harvard Business School Press.

Pfeffer, J., & Salancik, G. R. (1978). *The External Control of Organizations*. NY: Harper and Row.

Phillips, O. R., & Mason, C. F. (1992). Mutual Forbearance in Experimental Conglomerate Markets. *RAND Journal of Economics, 23*, 395–414.

Phillips, O. R., & Mason, C. F. (1996). Market Regulation and Multimarket Rivalry. *RAND Journal of Economics, 27*, 596–617.

Phillips, O. R., & Mason, C. F. (2001). Collusion in Horizontally Connected Markets: Multimarket Producers as Conduits for Learning. In: J. A. C. Baum & H. R. Greve (Eds), *Multiunit Organization and Multimarket Strategy; Advances in Strategic Management, 18* (pp. 207–229). Oxford, UK: JAI Press.

Porac, J. F., & Thomas, H. (1990). Taxonomic mental models in competitor definition. *Academy of Management Review, 15*, 224–240.

Porac, J. F., Thomas, H., & Baden-Fuller, C. (1989). Competitive Groups as Cognitive Communities: The Case of Scottish Knitwear. *Journal of Management Studies, 26*, 397–416.

Porac, J. F, Thomas, H., Wilson, F., Paton, D., & Kanfer, A. (1995). Rivalry and the industry model of Scottish knitwear producers. *Administrative Science Quarterly, 40*, 203–227.

Porter, M. (1980). *Competitive Strategy*. New York, Free Press.

Rhoades, S. A., & Heggestad, A. A. (1985). Multimarket Interdependence and Performance in Banking: Two Tests. *Antitrust Bulletin, 30,* 975–995.

Roberts, P. W. (1999). Product Innovation, Product-market Competition and Persistent Profitability in the U.S. Pharmaceutical Industry. *Strategic Management Journal, 20,* 655–670.

Schwenk, C. R. (1984). Cognitive Simplification Processes in Strategic Decision Making. *Strategic Management Journal, 5,* 11–18.

Scott, J. T. (1989). Purposive Diversification as a Motive for Merger. *International Journal of Industrial Organization, 7,* 35–47.

Singal, V. (1996). Airline Mergers and Multimarket Contact. *Managerial and Decision Economics, 17,* 559–574.

Smith, K. G., Grimm, C. M., Chen M. J., & Gannon, M. J. (1989). Predictors of Response Time to Competitive Strategic Actions: Preliminary Theory and Evidence. *Journal of Business Research, 18,* 245–258.

Smith, K. G, Grimm, C. M., & Gannon, M. J. (1992). *Dynamics of Competitive Strategy.* Newbury Park, CA: Sage.

Srinivasan, K. (1991). Multiple Market Entry, Cost Signaling and Entry Deterrence. *Management Science, 37,* 1539–1555.

Stone, M. M., & Brush, C. G. (1996). Planning in Ambiguous Contexts: The Dilemma of Meeting Needs for Commitment and Demands for Legitimacy. *Strategic Management Journal, 17,* 633–652.

Tsurumi, Y. (1976). *The Japanese are Coming: A Multinational Interaction of Firms and Politics.* Cambridge, MA, Ballinger Publishing Company.

Usher, J. M. (1999). Specialists, Generalists and Polymorphs: Spatial Advantages of Multiunit Organization in a Single Industry. *Academy of Management Review, 24,* 143–150.

van Wegberg, M., & van Witteloostuijn A. (2001). Strategic Management in the New Economy: Modern Information Technologies and Multichannel Contact Strategies, In: J. A. C. Baum & H. R. Greve (Eds), *Multiunit Organization and Multimarket Strategy; Advances in Strategic Management, 18* (pp. 265–306). Oxford, UK: JAI Press.

Vernon, R., Wells, L. T., & Rangan, S. (1996). *The Manager in the International Economy.* Upper Saddle River, NJ: Prentice-Hall.

STRATEGIC MANAGEMENT IN THE NEW ECONOMY: MODERN INFORMATION TECHNOLOGIES AND MULTICHANNEL CONTACT STRATEGIES

Marc van Wegberg and Arjen van Witteloostuijn

ABSTRACT

The so-called information revolution has loosened many tongues in the academic, business and policy worlds. The communis opinio is that the diffusion of modern information technologies in the global village is about to radically change the rules of the competitive game in many, if not all, industries. What the new rules may be, nobody really knows for sure. The New Economy, being characterized by the penetration of information technologies and the dominance of network arrangements, is born. Firms face the daunting task of developing a response to this new environment. How they respond depends in part on what they learn from their contact portfolio. Which contacts they have, and what information they get out of these contacts, shapes their response to the New Economy. A case in point is the Internet. Apart from stimulating the emergence of new value-adding products and efficiency-enhancing processes, an argument is that the Internet will shake up the century-old market institution by introducing

Multiunit Organization and Multimarket Strategy, Volume 18, pages 263–304.

information transparancies and network economies. This chapter's objective is fivefold. First, we summarize the current state of the art in the multimarket competition literature. Second, we develop a multichannel contact framework that builds upon the established multimarket contact theory. Third, we briefly evaluate the New Economy debate. Fourth, we analyze what the emergence of this New Economy may imply for issues of competitive rivalry and strategic management in the context of multichannel contact management. Fifth, we illustrate part of the argument by briefly discussing the case of Java software.

INTRODUCTION

Industry competition and corporate performance do not only depend on objective features of a market, such as cost functions and demand curves, but they also reflect the subjective interpretations of relationships between companies – their communication, interaction and learning behavior. The theory of multimarket contact is an example of a framework that reflects this insight. If firms have overlapping multimarket scope, the fact that they meet each other in multiple markets as competitors (multimarket contact) helps them to recognize their interdependence. Moreover, multimarket contact facilitates the exchange of the strategic intent to behave friendly, or to exchange threats to retaliate upon aggressive behavior across the board. Multimarket contact theory's counter-intuitive hypothesis is that, as a result of this recognition of interdependence and transmission of reputation, overlapping market scope may well weaken the intensity of competition by promoting (tacit) collusion. Additionally, multimarket contact can also transmit information to a focal firm from her contacts that stimulates the former's learning behavior, particularly in the area of innovative technologies. In this chapter, we build upon this multi**market** contact argument to develop a multi**channel** contact framework that may be well-suited to analyze the strategic consequences of the emergence of the New Economy.

A well-established argument is that firms choose their behavior on the basis of information they obtain from their contacts, with whatever party and of whatever nature, with their environment. A case in point here is the well-studied boundary-spanning function that helps to manage a firm's resource dependencies [see e.g. a textbook such as Daft's (1998)]. In this context, multimarket contact is only one channel out of many. We focus especially on contact through inter-firm alliances and Internet commerce, next to multimarket contact. These and other contact channels (or networks) are information conduits through which firms learn about new developments and possible strategies. The Internet is an example of a new development, closely related to the emergence of the so-called New Economy, that challenges a modern firm's strategic adaptability. This raises the general question as to how the Internet technology impacts upon corporate interaction and performance, as well as the specific question as to how this will affect the importance of multimarket and multichannel contact. The chapter is organized as follows. We begin with an abbreviated survey of the multimarket contact literature, summarizing the theory's core in five propositions. We then extend this multi**market** contact theory to a multi**channel** contact approach to business strategy, which is illustrated by developing three additional propositions. Firms have a portfolio of contacts, which includes multimarket contacts next to contacts through a variety of alternative channels. By way of intermezzo, a brief introduction into the New Economy debate is included. Subsequently, we apply the multichannel contact framework to the Internet case, particularly by elaborating upon the strategic responses to new Internet opportunities, such as *e*-commerce, by formulating eight hypotheses. As a first step, we continue by describing an illustrative case study of the diffusion of the Java Internet programming language among computing firms. The chapter is concluded with an evaluating appraisal.[1]

MULTIMARKET CONTACT THEORY

Collusion from Multimarket Contact

Multimarket contact analysis, with roots in the industrial organization (IO) and strategic management (SM) literatures, argues that firms reduce competition by (tacitly) coordinating behavior with companies whom they meet in various markets (van Witteloostuijn & van Wegberg, 1992). Multimarket contact refers to the number of markets where, say, two firms 'meet', that is, where they compete with each other. It indicates the extent to which two (or whatever number) diversified companies have an overlapping multimarket scope, in terms of locations and/or products. On the basis of game-theoretic analyses, IO economists have proven that overlapping multimarket scope facilitates the transmission of (tacit) collusion from one market to several others (Feinberg, 1984; Bernheim & Whinston, 1990; van Wegberg & van Witteloostuijn, 1992; van Witteloostuijn, 1993). The central argument is that the benefit of cheating in market 1 is dominated, under specific conditions, by the cost of the collapse of the collusive equilibrium in markets 2 to n. After all, if firm A cheats upon firm B in market 1, then firm B can exploit their full multimarket overlap, including markets 2 to n, in her retaliation strategy. This multimarket retaliation threat may facilitate the sustainability of spheres-of-influence, reciprocal-hostage and market-sharing equilibria. This line of reasoning produces multimarket contact theory's central (tacit) collusion prediction, which is captured by Proposition 1.

> *Proposition 1* (Collusion from multimarket contact): The higher multi-market contact between two (or more) firms, the less intense their rivalry will be, leading to, for example, higher prices and higher profit margins, or less entry by either of both rivals in the other firm's markets.[2]

Baum and Korn (1999) identify three, closely related, types of argument to support the counterintuitive prediction as to the anticompetitive effect of multimarket contact. Briefly, multimarket contact: (a) offers experiments that facilitate learning (learning vehicle), (b) acts as a reputation-transmission mechanism (reputation device) and (c) produces instruments for enforcing (tacit) collusion (retaliation power). Via these three routes multimarket contact tends to blunt the intensity of competition (Proposition 1's multimarket contact collusion hypothesis) by operating as an information conduit that facilitates learning behavior, communicates reputation and carries a retaliation threat. The result is that multimarket firms may downplay competition by, for example, differentiating their products, moving towards different market segments or raising price levels. To set the scene, we start with a summary of the central information conduit argument, with an emphasis on the learning angle. Subsequently, we briefly discuss both subtle underlying mechanisms of multimarket contact (reputation and retaliation) in turn.

Multimarket Contact as Learning Vehicle

As noted, multimarket contact serves as a conduit for communicating strategic intentions to another firm. This is the crucial information effect. By engaging in some action in one market, a firm may signal her intentions to her rivals. This is the key argument underlying Proposition 1's 'static' prediction of multimarket collusion. In a dynamic interpretation, the firm may probe a market in order to learn about the incumbent firms as to how they react to her move. Subsequently, she can use that information in other markets where she interacts with these companies. Competition is, in this story, a learning process where firms finetune their interaction with one another by playing a subtle information-transmitting multimarket game (cf. Cassidy & Loree, this volume). In particular, they try to establish an equilibrium that may take the form of either, on the one hand, competing for profitable positions in an industry or, on the other hand, maintaining a collusive order so as to avoid cut-throat competition across the board. Smith and Wilson's (1995) study, for example, indicates that there is indeed a potential for competitive learning.[3] They investigate the effects of multimarket contact on how an incumbent firm reacts to entry into her market. If the entrant and incumbent have multimarket contact, the incumbent firm may retaliate by entry into or price cutting in the entrant's markets. Unexpectedly, they find that in approximately 57% of all entry moves studied, the incumbent firms did not respond at all. If they do respond, they may not respond aggressively, but may rather *raise* price upon entry. A typical multimarket strategy – the counterattack in the entrant's market – is only the third most frequently observed response in their sample. This suggests that entrants may face a high degree of uncertainty about how the incumbent firm may react to their initial move. This finding supports the idea that firms may use entry as a probing device so as to learn about the incumbent firms' competitive strategies.[4] Moreover, by raising rather than reducing price the incumbent may signal her willingness to collude across markets, which relates to the issue of reputation building (see below).

Much learning amounts to imitation (Nelson & Winter, 1982; DiMaggio & Powell, 1983). Firms are likely, in choosing their strategic moves such as investing in their scope, to emulate the behavior of firms they have much contact with. Greve (1998) found evidence for this in an interesting study of how U.S. radio stations adopt new radio formats. Greve's (1998) approach focuses on learning and imitation, and suggests a new direction for multimarket contact research that focuses on the broader issue of multimarket contact as an information conduit that facilitates all kinds of learning. If we recognize multimarket contact's nature as an information conduit, we can envision firms operating in multiple markets as a multimarket information network. Each firm is a node in the network. Each dyad of two firms meeting in one market represents a link in the network. The higher the multimarket contact between two firms, the more linked they are, and the more central is their place in the network. That is, a firm with many concentrated multimarket contact links, on the one hand, takes up a central place in the network. A firm whose activities are scattered across multiple markets, on the other hand, tends to have low levels of multimarket contact with her rivals, and is thus a peripheral player. The same holds true for a firm who is active in few markets only. A central firm is likely to have a larger impact upon the nature of an industry's competitive equilibrium than a peripheral player. Network analysis can reveal the structure of the network, and the place of firms within this structure (Gulati, 1995; Madhavan, Koka & Prescott, 1998). Measuring multimarket contact in terms of a multimarket contact network structure implies a step toward exploring *how* multimarket contact may affect industry competition and corporate performance. The structure of the multimarket contact network may reveal information flows throughout the industry. In a static context, a more closely knit network can be hypothesized to be associated with high price and profit levels in the industry. A tightly-knit multimarket contact network increases the pressure toward mimetic adoption (Greve, 1998). This argument suggests a 'dynamic' learning addendum to Proposition's 1 'static' multimarket collusion prediction, as reflected in Proposition 2.

Proposition 2 (Learning from multimarket contact): (a) Firms are likely to learn from the behavior (e.g. entry, exit and pricing moves, as well as advertising and R&D strategies) of firms with whom they have a high level of multimarket contact. (b) An industry equilibrium is particularly affected by the behavior of firms who occupy a central place in the multimarket contact network. (c) A tightly-knit multimarket contact framework is associated with high price and profit levels.

Multimarket Contact as Reputation Device

An important multimarket contact mechanism pertains to influencing the rivals' expectation about the nature of future interaction (Hughes & Oughton, 1993). Game theory has taught us that the sustainability of a (tacitly) collusive arrangement critically depends upon the expectation of firms that they will continue to interact in the future (see e.g. the textbook exposition in Bierman & Fernandez, 1993). Colluding firms limit output to raise prices (in a so-called Cournot context), or avoid price-cutting strategies (in a Bertrand setting). The individually rational action is to free ride: let others reduce their output or keep their price at a high level, and increase one's own output level to benefit from the high price or obtain large sales after a one-sided price cut. To sustain a collusive equilibrium, firms threaten each other that if a rival cheats, others will punish the cheater in the future. Cheating destroys a reputation, to which other firms react by reverting from collusive behavior to competitive strategies. This threat is credible if firms will indeed continue to interact in the future. On the one hand, anything that increases the expectation of continued future interactions, therefore, tends to stabilize the collusive arrangement. Meeting each other in multiple markets has precisely this effect. If firms meet in multiple markets, there is a greater chance that they will continue to interact in the future. In this case, multimarket contact (in markets with a higher survival potential) may protect the collusive *status quo* in a case where otherwise the collusive equilibrium would break down. On the other hand, anything that undermines the expectation of future interaction destroys a collusive settlement. In a declining market, for example, a selection of the established firms may be expected to exit from the market. The exit candidates tend to cheat, as they have nothing to lose from punishments in the future. This end-game effect is likely to eliminate the collusive arrangement.

So, reputation is a relational asset with foresight that is produced by transmitting information: the reputation of firm X is what other firms think about X's future features, behavior or performance, which clearly is the outcome of a learning process. Thus, multimarket contact as a reputation device relates to multimarket contact as an information conduit. By communicating credible signals across markets, a firm may develop a reputation of aggressive multimarket punishment (so as to threaten any potential cheater) and peaceful multimarket cooperation (so as to protect the profit from collusion). That is, one kind of experiment that firms enact upon each other in developing their reputation is to see how each individual rival reacts to market opportunities. For example, by responding in a tit-for-tat manner to competitive moves across multiple markets, a firm may provide the right signals to set in motion a process of softening competition, which may produce (tacit) multimarket collusion. Then, the short-run cost of the reputation-building aggressiveness today is outweighed by the long-run benefit of the resulting reputation of aggressiveness tomorrow. Proposition 3 summarizes this reputation argument.

Proposition 3 (Multimarket contact as reputation device): A firm's reputation of aggressive multimarket punishment and peaceful multimarket cooperation facilitates the sustainability of a (tacitly) collusive arrangement across a set of markets.

Multimarket Contact as Retaliation Power

Theories of multimarket competition that apply game theory or conjectural variation modeling have explored an aspect of multimarket contact that is inextricably bound up with the reputation device side of the coin: the threat of multimarket retaliation. Building upon the path-breaking work of Bain (1956), many IO economists have finetuned the game theory of the incumbent's (threat of) retaliation strategy to a newcomer's (threat of) entry move (Gilbert, 1989). A key issue in this stream of literature is the game-theoretic analysis of credibility. That is, the incumbent's threat to retaliate upon a newcomer's entry move is credible if, and only if, the incumbent's execution of the *ex ante* retaliation threat signal is the *ex post* profit-maximizing strategy. Then the retaliation announcement is a credible threat that may well keep the newcomer from entering the incumbent's market in the first place. The impressive stock of incumbent – entrant game models that have occurred in this tradition reveal the credibility-enhancing devices that can be exploited by an incumbent firm to develop a successful retaliation threat strategy, suggesting the potency of such strategies as irreversible sunk cost investment (by e.g. installing overcapacity) and aggressive response reputation building (by e.g. launching price wars). In particular, this literature is very informative as to the underlying conditions that may transform an empty threat into a credible announcement, with examples being low discount (interest) and high growth (demand) rates (cf. Proposition 3). In the 1980s, the single-market setting of this branch of IO theory has been extended to the multimarket context. Basically, this extension: (a) enlarges the set of credible threat strategies (i.e. another-market retaliation move) and (b) adds another credibility-enhancing condition (i.e. the number and size of contact markets). This is reflected in Proposition 3.

So, IO's multimarket competition theory focuses on analyzing threat – reciprocal threat equilibria in multimarket settings.[5] Basically, depending upon the game's conditions, three different types of 'pure' (ignoring the many betwixt-and-between cases, such as the reciprocal-hostages arrangement) equilibria may emerge: (i) spheres-of-influence, (ii) market-sharing or (iii) head-on rivalry outcomes. The third equilibrium is the benchmark case in which a competition-avoiding multimarket arrangement fails to materialize: in each of the contact markets, that is, the multimarket firms are involved in aggressive fights for market share. The first and second equilibria are particularly interesting when multimarket contact operates as the condition that facilitates the emergence of a collusive arrangement that would have collapsed in a single-market setting. The strength of this multimarket contact effect derives from the ability to punish a rival's non-collusive behavior in market 1 in the other markets 2 to n as well (cf. Proposition 1). This relates to the power to retaliate. That is, the threat of other-market retaliation operates as a disciplinary device in the focal market. As Bernheim and Whinston (1990) have argued, firms may collude on a market-by-market basis, implying that the multimarket dimension as such is immaterial. The 'real' multimarket contact effect comes in only when there is an asymmetry in the abilities of firms to sustain the collusive equilibria in different markets. That is, firms export their ability to collude in market A to a market B and vice versa, whilst, taken in isolation, they would not be able to sustain collusion in neither market A nor market B. The multimarket contact notion thus measures the number of markets in which multimarket firms have the instruments at hand to punish each other for cheating in whatever market in their portfolio of activities. This multimarket retaliation transfer argument, which sets apart multimarket collusion from its single-market (or market-by-market) counterpart, is summarized in Proposition 4.

Proposition 4: (Multimarket contact as retaliation power): The multimarket contact effect by transferring retaliation power from one market to the other may materialize if the ability of the multimarket firms to sustain a collusive arrangement in different markets, is characterized by asymmetry.

A Multimarket Contact Framework

Without doubt, the multimarket contact literature has explored in great depth and *ditto* detail a striking effect that multimarket contact may have on a firm's behavior – i.e. the ability to sustain collusive arrangements across markets that would collapse in a single-market setting. This is an insightful result that is very helpful in deepening our understanding of the (non-)competitive dynamics in industries that are characterized by a plethora of multimarket contacts. On top of the key insights summarized in the four propositions introduced above, much multimarket contact modeling has revealed the collusion-enhancing and impeding conditions that may interact with the central multimarket contact effect. This additional set of results is summarized in a fifth proposition, which lists a number (but not all) of such contingencies.

Proposition 5 (Multimarket collusion contingencies): The multimarket contact effect interacts positively with the expectation of continued interaction, discount rate level, firm-level survival chances, behavioral transparancy, market growth rate, industry concentration, managerial continuity, firm size, ownership stability and strategic homogeneity.

The arguments underlying Proposition 5 are embedded in game-theoretic reasoning of the kind we discussed above. A representative example of an advanced game-theoretic analysis is Bernheim and Whinston (1990). According to this game-theoretic interpretation of multimarket contact, conditions that enhance an aggressive punishment or peaceful cooperative reputation will support the sustainability of (tacit) collusion.[6] Equivalently, any condition that increases the chance that two firms have a reciprocal profit at stake in the future will enhance the sustainability of a collusive arrangement. On both accounts, game-theoretic modeling has revealed that the multimarket contact effect (cf. Proposition 1) interacts positively with conditions such as the survival chances of the individual firms, height of exit barriers, level of the discount (interest) rate, behavioral transparancy, market growth rate, industry's concentration level and homogeneity of corporate strategies. Reversely, changes in ownership or management of a firm may disrupt her original reputation, thus threatening any collusion built on this reputation. Similarly, acquisitions or mergers may initially have this pro-competitive effect.

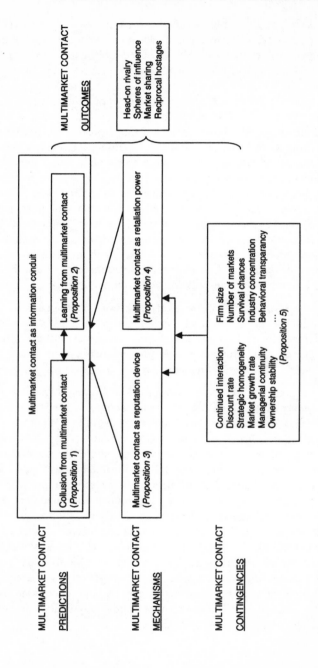

Fig. 1. Multimarket Contact Framework.

By way of summary, Fig. 1 offers an overview of the multimarket contact framework, distinguishing multimarket contact predictions, mechanisms, contingencies and outcomes, and linking the theory's key elements to the five propositions.

The multimarket contact literature is associated with two important **predictions**: Proposition 1, multimarket contact may facilitate the sustainability of across-market (tacit) collusion, and Proposition 2, multimarket contact facilitates across-market learning. The effect of multimarket contact is best understood by recognizing multimarket contact's nature as information conduit. Particularly two **mechanisms** underlie the collusive effect of multimarket contact: (a) a multimarket firm may develop an across-market reputation of aggressive multimarket punishment and peaceful multimarket collusion (multimarket contact as reputation device: Proposition 3); and (b) a multimarket firm may transfer her retaliation power from one market to the other (multimarket contact as retaliation power: Proposition 4). From game-theoretic analyses, a list of multimarket collusion-enhancing and impeding **contingencies** is derived that impact upon multimarket contact's effectiveness as information conduit, reputation device and retaliation power (Proposition 5). Together, the five key propositions of this multimarket contact framework produce a theory that explains why, when and how different multimarket contact **outcomes** will occur.

A MULTICHANNEL CONTACT FRAMEWORK

From Multimarket to Multichannel Contact

Starting from multi**market** contact theory, an extended and enriched multi-**channel** contact framework can be developed that may increase the explanatory power of the argument by adding another insight to the existing multimarket competition apparatus: a firm can exploit other contact channels besides multi-market encounters. That is, firms do not only experience inter-rivalry interaction in the product market, but they also interact in resource markets, as well as in (anti or pro-competitive) strategic alliances, cross-shareholdings and interlocking directorates. These additional contact channels, too, may offer powerful instruments to reward or punish each other in the context of a multichannel contact game. As such, this insight is anything but new. For example, antitrust authorities are aware that inter-firm alliances may have an anti-competitive effect. Such alliances may be permitted, however, if they are expected to support useful activities such as (joint) research and development that, by the end of the day, benefit society at large. In this context, van Wegberg, van Witteloostuijn and Roscam Abbing (1994) and van Wegberg and van Witteloostuijn (1995) make the point that inter-firm R&D alliances might offer additional punishment instruments, next to and on top of traditional product market interdependencies, that support tacit collusion in product markets. Extending this line of reasoning produces the argument that firms may have a portfolio of different contact channels that they can use as instruments in supporting collusive arrangements (an adapted Proposition 1) and learning opportunities (a revised Proposition 2).

The case of the information conduit argument is illustrative. As an information conduit, multimarket contact complements many other forms of contact. As is well known from the organization sciences literature in such areas as network analysis and organizational learning, firms exchange information with rivals in various ways. They cooperate in all kinds of inter-firm alliances, such as R&D joint ventures and closely-monitored outsourcing contracts. They may also communicate indirectly, by sharing consultants, suppliers, shareholders, banks and/or directors (the so-called interlocking directorates). Contact plays a dual role for learning. It provides access to rich information that needs an elaborate context (such as gestures, persuasion or example) to be transmitted and interpreted sensibly. And it exposes an organization to environmental pressure by rivals or partners. Thus contact may be especially important because of bounded rationality.

Multimarket contact is part of a portfolio of different contact channels. For example, contact in inter-firm alliance networks may substitute for multimarket contact, and thus blur the latter's effect on performance (van Wegberg & van Witteloostuijn, 1995). Boundedly rational players may postpone (radical) decisions until they are directly confronted with the need to act through their contact portfolio. Adam Smith (1970: 232), who else!, already conjectured that firms seek contact with each other, through a wide variety of routes, in a conspiracy against the public interest. Firms want to establish reciprocal contact when price signals fail to offer information timely or adequately enough to coordinate behavior, provided that society allows them to collude in this way. Whether or not firms design their scope with a view to creating multimarket contact (as Scott, 1989, suggests that they do), may thus depend on the alternative contact routes available to them.

The above bits and pieces point the way to a full-fledged framework of multichannel contact. Developing such a framework is too ambitious an undertaking in this chapter, though. Rather, we can offer a first step by summarizing the intuition behind four stepping stones for a multichannel contact framework by briefly discussing: (1) channel sources, (2) channel features, (3) channel purposes, and (4) channel externalities. Together, these four stepping stones offer input for multichannel contact management. This preliminary multichannel contact framework is summarized in Fig. 2.

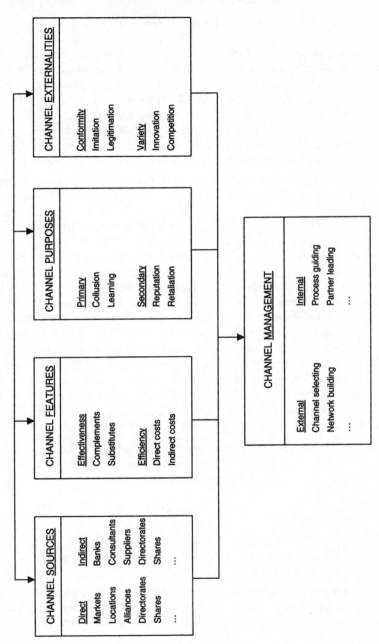

Fig. 2. Multichannel Contact Framework.

Channel Sources

A firm has a portfolio of contacts, within and across different channels. She has contacts with other firms by means of e.g. their shared markets, alliances, inputs, contracts, locations, shares and/or directorates. For example, firm A may meet firm B in similar product domains (markets), R&D joint ventures (alliances), shared relationships with consultancy agencies (inputs), outsourcing contracts with suppliers (contracts), production plants in the same countries (locations), portfolios of cross-holdings (shares) and reciprocal board memberships (directorates). The contact through such channel sources may be either *direct* or *indirect* in nature.

(1a) A *direct* contact arises whenever focal firm A and her rival B operate face-to-face in the context of this channel source. For example, they compete for market share in the same market, they cooperate within a joint technology alliance, they operate selling units in the same regions, they buy cross-ownership stocks and their CEOs are on each other's boards. Such direct contacts offer ample opportunities to sustain a collusive arrangement by effectively communicating reputation and retaliation signals, as well as to facilitate across-firm learning.

(1b) An *indirect* contact emerges whenever focal firm A meets her rival B through a shared channel source with party C. For instance, firm A and rival B may ask for advice from the same consultancy firm C, they may cooperate with the same partner C in different technology alliances, their CEOs may sit on different boards with the same colleague C and they may buy a key intermediate product from the same supplier C. Such indirect contacts can be exploited to transmit information from firm A to rival B (and vice versa) *via* channel C, which, again, helps to facilitate cartel-like conduct and across-firm learning.

By operating a portfolio of channel sources, associated with both direct and indirect contacts, firm A and rival B may manipulate their reciprocal information transfer to their (mutual) competitive advantage.

Channel Features

In the context of a multichannel contact framework, managing a multichannel portfolio of contacts may benefit from carefully distinguishing four different within-channel and across-channel features.

(2a) Different contact channels can be *complements*. For instance, different contacts may give access to different kinds of information or may strengthen the threat of multichannel retaliation. Additionally, a firm with many different contacts, within and across channels, is likely to obtain valuable information, competitive reputation or retaliation power, which makes her an attractive contact target for others. Through this virtuous cycle, a well-connected firm develops a new network or a valuable position in an established network.

(2b) Different contact channels can be *substitutes*. A firm may exploit alternative contact routes to achieve equivalent (i.e. competition-reducing or learning-enhancing) benefits. For example, a retaliation threat may be communicated effectively (credibly) by either: (a) a foothold strategy in a rival's home market, or (b) signaling the willingness to destroy a successful R&D joint venture. Deploying both contact channels simultaneously may well be an overinvestment in the capability to retaliate, implying a cost-benefit disbalance.

(2c) Different contact channels are associated with different *direct costs*. The development of a contact channel requires an investment in and over time. A firm must put money and time in e.g. drafting outsourcing contracts or creating R&D joint ventures. Additionally, maintainance of a contact channel does not come for free. Without the direct cost of monitoring an outsourcing contract or running an R&D joint venture the contact channel is very likely to break down.

(2d) Different contact channels are associated with different *indirect costs*. The indirect cost concept pertains to the benefit of foregone alternatives. On the one hand, if a firm decides to allocate scarce resources to maintaining e.g. a foreign foothold or a cross-holding participation, then this contact channel strategy limits her discretion to invest elsewhere. On the other hand, the option to appropriate firm-level technological knowledge may be history when valuable information is given away through the R&D joint venture contact channel.

The effectiveness (1a and 1b: contact channels' complementarity or substitutability) and efficiency (1c and 1d: contact channels' direct and indirect costs) of a contact channel are likely to depend on the features of the parties involved and the kind of information being transmitted. For instance, inter-firm R&D alliances will be relatively efficient transmitters of technological information, whilst multimarket contact may be an efficient vehicle for competitive learning.[7]

Channel Purposes

From the perspective of a value-maximizing firm, maintaining a portfolio of multichannel contacts must serve a number of purposes. After all, developing and sustaining such a portfolio is anything but consuming a free lunch. In line with Propositions 1 to 4, the careful management of a multichannel contact portfolio may produce four related benefits.

(3a) The key objective that is central to much original work in the multimarket contact tradition pertains to the establishment and maintainance of a *collusive arrangement* that would collapse in the context of single-market competition. This is reflected in Proposition 1 above, but now in a multi-channel rather than multimarket setting.

(3b) A multichannel contact portfolio can be exploited to obtain information that enhances learning. Then, the multichannel contact portfolio operates as a *learning vehicle*. This is the dynamic extension of the well-established static mutual forbearance argument. This is the multichannel version of Proposition 2.

(3c) By establishing and manipulating a multichannel contact portfolio a firm may develop a tailor-made reputation of aggressiveness and peacefulness. So, a multichannel contact portfolio can be a *reputation device*. This is Proposition 3 in a multichannel context.

(3d) A multichannel contact portfolio can be a source of *retaliation power*. Having multiple contacts makes a firm flexible, and helps her to retaliate against a firm that threatens her competitive position. This helps swift recognition of and reaction to competitive actions. This is the multichannel adaptation of Proposition 4.

The *secondary* purposes of reputation and retaliation signaling are instrumental in reaching the *primary* objectives of across-firm learning and collusive conduct. That is, the effectiveness of a multichannel portfolio is dependent upon the firm's reputation and retaliation profiles. For example, firm A's objective, in her confrontation with her rival B, of collusive conduct in market I is not only enhanced by developing a reputation of aggressive retaliation in the markets I and II in which both firms compete for market share (the multimarket collusion Proposition 1), but also by a credible threat of undermining the firm A–firm B technology alliance III.

Channel Externalities

Multimarket contact theory has shown that multimarket contact has significant effects on competitive behavior by enhancing collusive conduct. Above, we have extended this argument in a multichannel contact setting by exploring the key argument that this collusive effect derives from the information conduit nature of whatever contact. In such a multichannel contact portfolio context, the value added of the portfolio externalities of a firm's contact set cannot be ignored. To this aim, we may envision the firm as the focal node in a *network* of multichannel contacts that is associated with a number of network *externalities*. The value of a position in such a contact network consists of access to a wide variety of information, reputation and retaliation channels. The more contacts a firm has, the more adequate she can respond to threats and opportunities in her environment. By and large, four different network externalities can be distinguished.

(4a) Contact transmits information that can speed up the diffusion of an innovation (Greve, 1998). The multichannel contact network creates a group a firms (players) with shared information. This is likely to be relevant especially when information is tacit and the market is non-transparent. The multichannel network provides ample opportunities to imitate the best practices that a firm observes in her multichannel contact portfolio. For example, firm A may learn from her alliance partner firm B how to increase the efficiency of her production processes, which she then transfers to firm C through the board membership of her CEO and to firm D as a result of the experience of the consultancy firm that firms A, C and D share. This is the network's *imitation* effect.

(4b) Contact may help to enhance the legitimacy of new ways of conduct. For example, contact may legitimize change by enabling a manager or employee of firm A to justify the introduction of new organization structures by referring to an innovative, and well-performing, contact B as an example to be followed. Generally, the legitimacy of new conduct is highly dependent upon what is happening in the firm's environment at large. For instance, the legitimacy of a new product is enhanced if high-status firms launch the new product, too, or if high-status banks are willing to finance the new venture. All this refers to the network's *legitimation* effect. Legitimation may also create contact. In their chapter in this book, Stephan and Boeker explore the aspect of legitimacy in great depth. They argue that at **low** levels of multimarket contact, a firm will enter a market of her rival because the rival's presence in that market legitimizes the firm's managers to enter that market, too.

(4c) As explained above, a multichannel contact portfolio can fuel learning. That is, by obtaining information from a wide variety of sources, through the exploitation of a diverse portfolio of contact channels, a firm may enhance her creativity. For instance, focal firm A may learn from her partner B in their technology alliance C how to combine the new process technology, as developed within the alliance, with the information technology expertise of her consultancy firm D to produce a leapfrogging efficiency gain. This way of combining different pieces of information into something new relates to the network's *innovation* effect.

(4d) The multichannel network may offer firm A information that she can use to obtain a competitive advantage. Clearly, information influences decision making. Knowing a firm's information sources makes her somewhat predictable. However, the more varied a firm's information sources (contacts) are, the less predictable she becomes to her individual contact partners. In a competitive environment, this very diversity and unpredictability can be a source of competitive advantage. This is the network's *competition* effect.

The multichannel contact forces of imitation and legitimation induce within-network conformity (or homogeneity), whereas the multichannel forces of innovation and competition enhance within-network variety (or heterogeneity). This homogeneity–heterogeneity forces are well-known from the literatures on, for example, institutional theory (e.g. DiMaggio & Powell, 1983) and organizational ecology (e.g. Hannan & Freeman, 1977) that focus on the explanation of (the lack of) organizational variety. Our argument here is that the understanding of organizational homogeneity and heterogeneity may benefit from systematically taking notice of the above multichannel contact externality effects that are so inextricably bound up with the portfolio's network nature.

Channel Management

Together, the above four features of a multichannel contact portfolio suggest a framework that can help a firm to manage her network. As said, Fig. 2 summarizes this multichannel contact management framework. From an external environment perspective, multichannel portfolio management involves the selection of contact channels, as well as the development of the portfolio's network features. In this context, the above story offers a list of channel sources, channel features, channel purposes and channel externalities that must be taken on board whilst deciding on the selection and development of the network. From an internal perspective, multichannel contact management requires carefully guiding and leading the (wide) variety of different contacts. This offers many challenges to the way the firm organizes multichannel contact management internally. On the one hand, information overload or a bureaucratic structure may make the firm insensitive to information, and thus to the information advantage of contact. On the other hand, well-functioning internal communication structures reinforce the firm's absorptive capacity of new information. The better the internal communication and learning (absorption) skills are, the higher the usefulness of external contacts. Improvements of internal communication – as brought about, for example, by using an Intranet infrastructure – increase the exchange of information internally, which helps a firm to make sense of her contacts. The internal organization of multichannel contact management, although very important, is only a side issue in the context of the current chapter. For now, we restrict the argument to an illustration of how Fig. 2's multichannel contact framework can be used to derive new insights. To this aim, we focus on developing three illustrative propositions in the context of a technology shock.

The emerging multichannel contact management approach to business and corporate strategies will, we believe, be able to explain how firms react to important shocks that affect their entire industry. The emergence of the Internet is a key example of such a shock: many managers and gurus liken it to a revolution (see below). Firms are extremely uncertain as to how to best react to the Internet revolution. If they are followers rather than pioneers, they may use their established multichannel network of contacts to find out how others cope with the Internet technology. This raises questions such as "When do you follow a leader?" (timing of the adoption of an Internet strategy: this relates to the network's imitation effect) and 'Whose lead do you follow?" (if first movers develop different Internet strategies: this is associated with the network's legit-imation effect). Some Internet providers offer free access to Internet, whereas others still charge a fee: which example must be followed? If a firm receives conflicting signals, she needs to decide which example to imitate. We argue that firms attach different weights to different contacts, depending on how relevant contacts are to a particular signal and decision.

A revolutionary technology shock forces firms to search for the unknown. In such a condition of fundamental uncertainty, a firm cannot restrict her contact scanning strategy to the traditional inner circle of multimarket contacts. The reason for this is, at least, twofold. First, in times of technological revolution, much of relevance to the focal firm may be happening in many different corners of the economy. In Schumpeterian terminology, innovative behavior is inextri-cably bound up with finding new combinations, of old and/or new elements. Such new combinations may well emerge in contacts with new partners. Higher contact heterogeneity increases the changes of tracing new interesting ideas or practices. Hence, in an era of high innovativeness and much technological uncertainty, a contact portfolio's learning effectiveness can be increased by promoting intra-portfolio's contact channel diversity. This can be reached by seeking contact with non-traditional partners outside the traditional inner circle, particularly by including contacts with innovators in different industries. Second, a revolutionary new technology is associated with much tacit knowledge that is not yet widely diffused throughout the economy. Such tacit knowledge is best appropriated through direct and intimate contact with those most likely to have developed innovative knowledge, thus facilitating the transmission of the unspoken. This is not easily done *via* traditional, arm's length multimarket contact. Rather, explicit cooperation – and thus intimate contact – in alliances or through cross-ownership is a much more effective learning vehicle in this context. This suggests Proposition 6 about the relative importance of different contact channels.

> *Proposition 6* (Relative importance of multichannel contacts): In the case of a technology shock (major innovation), firms attach a greater weight to multichannel contacts than to multimarket contacts since the former provide: (a) heterogeneous contacts, and (b) intimate (tacit) knowledge transmisson.

If a firm receives conflicting signals, which is very likely in an era of funda-mental technological uncertainty, she will also attach different weights to different contact partners, depending upon the characteristics of the contact firms involved. In line with the above argument, particular contacts are more promising than others in times of revolutionary technological change as new (tacit) knowledge transmitters. Here, at least three contact firm characteristics spring to mind. First, some contacts are more relevant than others by offering access to important technological knowledge. This is obvious. In the Internet age, an alliance with an Internet *e*-tailer makes more sense for a retailer than an additional contact with an old-fashioned wholesaler. Second, the desired increase of multichannel contact portfolio heterogeneity can be obtained by allying with dissimilar firms, in terms of their contact network or in-house resources, rather than by connecting even further with similar contacts. So, the retailer above can better join forces with an Internet firm than with yet another retailer. Third, technological benchmarking is a performance-related exercise, where firms attempt to learn-by-imitation from well-performing contacts. Hence, our retailer is particularly keen to develop a learning contact with a high-performing Internet partner (in terms of e.g. new product growth, business process innovativity or new market entry). This argument is summarized in Proposition 7.

> *Proposition 7* (Relative importance of new contacts): In the case of a tech-nology shock (major innovation), a firm is likely to attach more importance to information from a firm that she has new contacts with when: (a) the contacts with this firm are more relevant to obtaining (tacit) technological knowledge, (b) she is more dissimilar to that firm and/or (c) the contact firm is outperforming others on technology-relevant criteria.

So, in times of technological revolution, multichannel contacts are argued to be more important than their multimarket counterparts (Proposition 6), and new contacts are conjectured to be more important than their old equivalents (Proposition 7). However, technological turbulence comes with anything but multichannel contact network stability. That is, new developments occur frequently, rapidly and unexpectedly. This implies that a firm must re-assess her multichannel contact network on a quasi-continuous basis. In the face of rapidly shifting competitive conditions, the new contacts of yesterday may be outdated today, forcing the firm to establish even newer contacts tomorrow. Particularly in the early days of a technological revolution, before a new equilibrium is reached, the quickly changing competitive setting frequently disrupts a firm's multichannel contact portfolio. This produces Proposition 8.

> *Proposition 8* (The disruptive dynamics of new contacts): In the case of a technological shock (major innovation), the rapid shifts in competitive conditions and the associate dynamics of new contacts disrupt a firm's just-established multichannel contact portfolio time and again.

This set of three propositions, together with the multichannel versions of Propositions 1 to 5, suggest an approach that may help to explore how firms develop multichannel contact strategies for the Internet age. The bottom line is that we expect that in the early days after the introduction of a revolutionary break-through technology the multichannel learning argument (cf. Proposition 2) dominates over the multichannel collusion story (cf. Proposition 1) because: (i) technological uncertainty induces an omni-present need for learning, and (ii) the collusion-enhancing conditions are overshadowed by their collusion-impeding counterparts (cf. Proposition 5). Below, we return to this issue of the short *versus* the long run in a bit more detail. But first, in the next section, we set a preliminary step toward the analysis of multichannel contact management in the New Economy.

MULTICHANNEL CONTACT MANAGEMENT IN THE NEW ECONOMY

Three Different Revolutions

The impressive period of sustainable economic growth in the U.S. in the 1990s has induced an equally impressive stream of guru-type publications that announce the birth of the New Economy [see e.g. *Wired* (www.wired.com)]. To emphasize the revolutionary nature of what is happening, the advocates of the New Industrial Revolution promote the New Economy by introducing a lengthy list of language novelties. Apart from the habit to use capitals, this is reflected in inventing new acronyms (e.g. B2B), in putting a new *e* in front of well-established words (e.g. *e*-banking) and in revealing a preference for the new @ symbol (e.g. @lli@ncies). As we want to be taken seriously by those in New Economy circles, this chapter fits nicely in this New Tradition.

The key argument is that the modern information technologies (IT) radically alter the ways in which businesses are organized, products are developed and transactions are shaped. The chapter by Kim (this volume) supports this idea by a historical account of how new technologies affected the organization and strategies of U.S. businesses around the turn of the (nineteenth) century. Our chapter focuses on recent changes in information technology, notably the Internet and *e*-commerce. While Kim's chapter explores how information changed the market interaction between suppliers and buyers, we focus on the effect of the Internet on interactions among companies. Both chapters have one message in common. Advances in information technology change the structure of the economy toward greater interdependence among economic agents. In the context of the current chapter, we cannot discuss all the details that are so inextricably bound up with this revolution. Rather, we wish to underline what we think is essential. Basically, this involves three different revolutions (van Witteloostuijn, 2001). In a nutshell, our argument is summarized in Fig. 3.

First, the IT revolution that attracts most attention in the (business) press is related to the emergence of the many dotcom firms. This pertains to the rise (and fall?) of new industries, breeding new firms and offering new products, and their impact upon the behavior and design of old industries. The figure-heads of this micro revolution are associated with new organizational forms such as network and virtual organizations (e.g. Volberda, 1998), and new information products such as browsers and portals (e.g. Shapiro & Varian, 1999). On top of the birth of such new industries, the micro revolution is said to radically alter the way old industries are organized as modern IT offers ample opportunities to, so to say, re-animate the business process reengineering hype by introducing new efficiency-enhancing and IT-driven coordination, communication and design devices (e.g. Nouwens & Bouwman, 1995). Second, the meso IT revolution is argued to change the rules of the competitive game at the industry level. The key argument here is that advanced IT reduces the cost of economic transaction by providing virtual market places and electronic trading places in new and old industries. In such an on-line environment, demand can meet supply in an efficient and transparant way. The result is the entry of a large number of new 'cybermediaries' that facilitate this 'demand-meets-supply' process (e.g. Sarkar, Butler & Steinfield, 2000). Third, the IT-driving increase of firm-level efficiency and industry-level effectiveness are the forces,

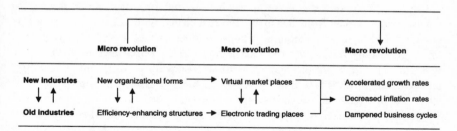

Fig. 3. The Three IT Revolutions of the New Economy.

according to New Macroeconomists, that underly accelerated growth rates, decreased inflation rates and dampened (or even disappearing) business cycles. Therefore, the New *E*-conomy has brought the macroeconomic paradise to Earth (e.g. Cohen, DeLong & Zysman, 2000). The reason for this is that IT is a break-through technology that produces an impressive productivity jump throughout the economy, so providing the fuel for sustainable macroeconomic prosperity (e.g. Gordon, 2000). Together, that is, the interacting micro and macro revolutions produce a really global macro revolution.

For the purposes of the current chapter, we can restrict the argument to the meso revolution at the industry level. Clearly, the New Economy proponents expect much from the (micro and) meso IT revolution: not only will *e*-organizing within and between firms increase cost efficiency and reduce transaction costs, but also *e*-trade will reduce prices as a result of the increased intensity of competition that comes with the transparent *e*-market places. By way of illustration, we develop an argument as to what the New Economy may imply for the sources and features of multichannel *e*-contacts in relation to (the multichannel versions of) Propositions 1 to 8. This exercise produces eight hypotheses that set an agenda for future empirical research, and that run opposite to the New Economy *communis opinio*. That is, after the revolutionary on-line dust has settled down, the Internet revolution may **decrease** rather than increase the force of competition as a consequence of multichannel *e*-contact collusion.

The Sources of Multichannel E-contacts

The New Economy is characterized by an impressive acceleration of the already impressive development of alliance networks. By way of example, Figure 4 provides an overview of a knowledge @lli@nce network in the Internet industry in the September 1998 – July 1999 period.

Clearly, the network formation in the Internet industry is not limited to dotcom firms. Apart from the many Internet firms, with such exotic names as Comone, G-Magic and Fatbrain, a large number of well-established high-tech firms are heavily linked into the Internet knowledge @lli@ance network. Here, revealing examples are the major electronic companies (from Philips to Sony) and telecom firms (from Bell babies to Nokia). And the Internet network is even extented into other than high-tech industries (such as banking: from ABN AMRO to Citibank). So, the acceleration of @lli@nce development is not restricted to the IT industries. Figure 5 lists a number of examples of @lli@ncies in 'old' and well-established industries, so connecting the Old Economy with the New Economy.

To give some examples from B2B, which stands for "business to business", and B2C, which is the *e*-acronym for "business to consumer":[8] the Deutsche Bank enters into B2B *e*-banking by teaming up with Internet provider AOL and software producer SAP; Kmart attempts to penetrate the B2C *e*-tail market by joining forces with the webmaster Yahoo!; an international @lli@ance of leading retailers (including Dutch Ahold, British Tesco and American Kmart) is set up to organize powerful *e*-procurement; et cetera.

Clearly, the IT revolution has further increased the contact intensity in many industries through the impressive @lli@nce network development movement. From the preliminary evidence in Figs. 4 and 5, we suggest Hypothesis 1.

Hypothesis 1 (Increasing importance of @lli@nce contacts): The IT revolution induces the accelerated growth of @lli@nces network formation, within and across new and old industries.

Additionally, and related to the above, IT has initiated the birth of new contact channels. That is, the electronic world of the Internet is occupied by new organizational forms that organize different channels of inter-firm contact. Here, the key example is the cybermediary (e.g. Sarkar, Butler & Steinfield, 2000). Firms now meet in such electronic environments as *e*-auctions, *e*-malls and *e*-platforms, on top of and in addition to their traditional non-electronic contacts. These *e*-contact devices increase the number of different contact channels. Of course, the motives for innovative *e*-contact development and @lliance network formation may be anything from sharing *e*-customer bases and combining complementary *e*-capabilities to *e*-product development and chain *e*-management. However, in line with Proposition 1 and the preliminary evidence in Figs 4 and 5, we suggest an important additional effect of the increasing incidence of @lli@nces and other *e*-contacts. This is Hypothesis 2.

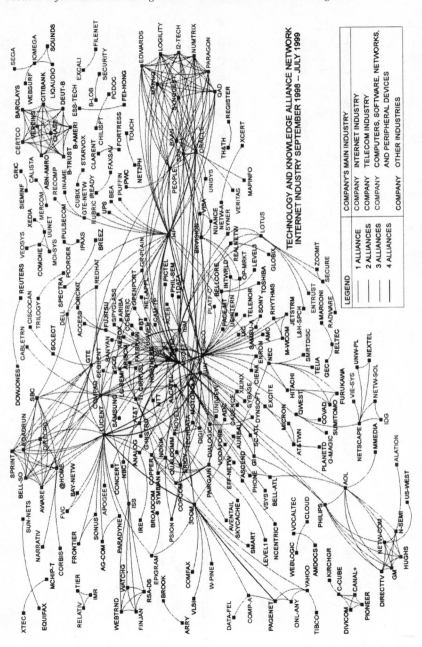

Fig. 4. An @lli@nce Network in the Internet Industry (September 1998–July 1999).

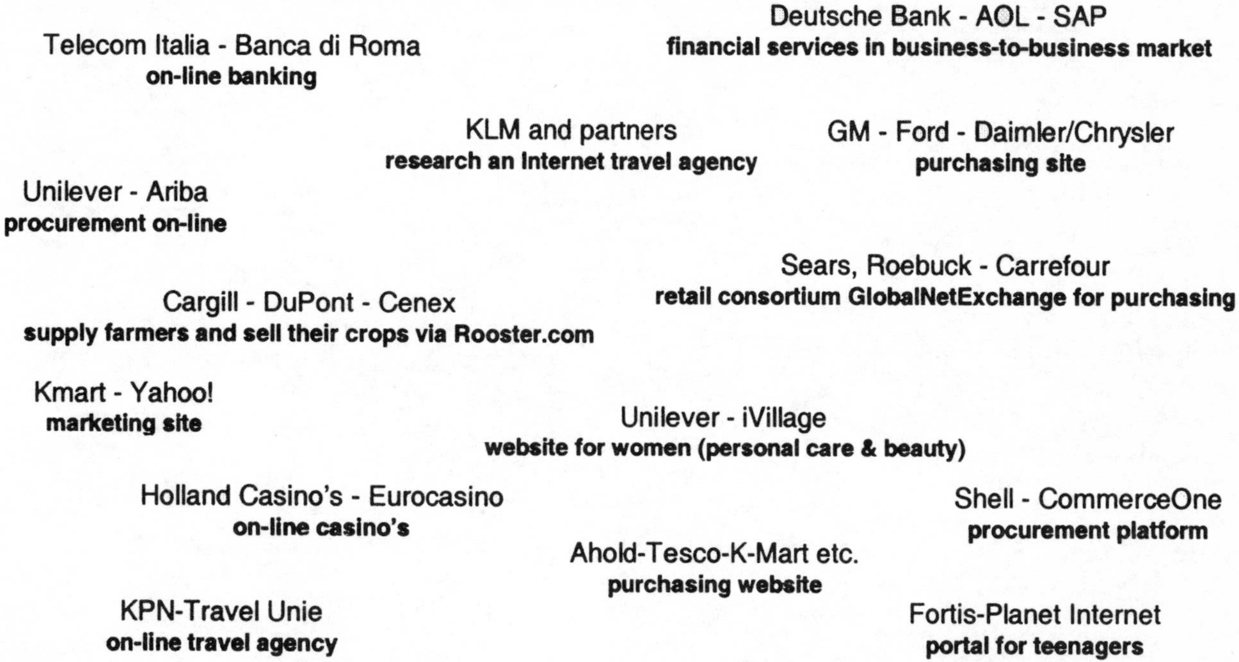

Telecom Italia - Banca di Roma
on-line banking

Deutsche Bank - AOL - SAP
financial services in business-to-business market

Unilever - Ariba
procurement on-line

KLM and partners
research an Internet travel agency

GM - Ford - Daimler/Chrysler
purchasing site

Cargill - DuPont - Cenex
supply farmers and sell their crops via Rooster.com

Sears, Roebuck - Carrefour
retail consortium GlobalNetExchange for purchasing

Kmart - Yahoo!
marketing site

Unilever - iVillage
website for women (personal care & beauty)

Holland Casino's - Eurocasino
on-line casino's

Shell - CommerceOne
procurement platform

Ahold-Tesco-K-Mart etc.
purchasing website

KPN-Travel Unie
on-line travel agency

Fortis-Planet Internet
portal for teenagers

Fig. 5. Examples of @lli@nces Connecting the 'Old' with the New Economy.

Hypothesis 2 (Increasing collusion through *e*-contacts): The extension of the number of multichannel contacts and the expansion of the range of different contact channel opportunities, including @lli@ncies and cyber-mediaries, increase the incidence and sustainability of collusive conduct.

The argument underlying Hypothesis 2 is standard multimarket or multichannel contact theory, relying on the reputation device (the multichannel version of Proposition 3) and retaliation power (the multichannel variant of Proposition 4) stories, that is likely to be applicable to what might happen in the New Economy's long run (see below). This argument is supported by the firm asymmetry suggested by Figure 4, which according to Proposition 4 enhances the opportunities for sustainable multimarket collusion.

The Features of Multichannel E-contacts

Apart from the increase in the number of contacts and the expansion of the range of different channels, the emergence of a 'virtual' business world, next to and on top of the good-old physical one, may well change competitive conditions and channel features. Table 1 offers a list of six examples of changing competitive conditions and ditto channel features. Thinking through the consequences of this set of six examples implies the application of Proposition 5 to the New Economy case.

On the one hand, the growth of the New Economy stimulates a restructuring within and across industries. First, the merger between AOL and TimeWarner symbolizes the current M&A wave that affects many – if not all – parts of the economy, which increases industry concentration. From game theory, we know that the sustainability of a collusive (multimarket) arrangement correlates positively with industry concentration (e.g. Bernheim & Whinston, 1990). Second, many old firms diversify into new electronic markets, as is revealed by the examples in Figs. 4 and 5. Much empirical multimarket contact studies have produced evidence that diversification is positively associated with collusion (e.g. Scott, 1989). Third, by its very nature, the virtual world is global as national

Table 1. New Channel Features in the New Economy.

Changing competitive conditions	Changing channel features
E-concentration	*E*-speed
E-diversification	*E*-transparancy
E-globalization	*E*-uncertainty

boundaries are meaningless in cyberspace. So, separate national markets integrate in the global Internet world such that the number of cross-border contacts increases substantially, which facilitates the emergence of multicontact collusion (e.g. van Witteloostuijn & van Wegberg, 1991). This reasoning produces Hypothesis 3.

> *Hypothesis 3* (Collusion-enhancing *e*-competitive features): The *e*-concentration, *e*-diversification and *e*-globalization movement that is so inextricably associated with the New Economy increase the incidence and sustainability of collusive conduct.

On the other hand, the virtual world changes the nature of contact. *E*-contact channels may be associated with features that are rather different from those linked to 'traditional' contact sources. Here, three examples are particularly revealing. First, high speed is a key characteristic of the Internet world. To make contacts and to execute transactions is easily and quickly done in Internet space, compared to the old-fashioned non-electronic world. Moreover, the transparancy of the electronic meeting places is much larger, on average, than the transparancy of the non-virtual world. Together, the increased *e*-speed and *e*-transparancy facilitate the immediate detection and punishment of a collusion-breaking cheater. Pre-modern and modern IO has produced the robust result that the opportunity to quickly and effectively detect and punish a cheater is very helpful in sustaining any cartel-like arrangement (Tirole, 1988). On top of this, the New Economy is – for the time being, at least – associated with an abundance of uncertainty as everybody starts to 'interact' with everyone (cf. Figs 4 & 5) without a clue about how long all this will take, which is typical for interaction in an era of technological revolution. Since uncertainty about the duration of interaction is equivalent to the infinite horizon condition, which is a key facilitator of cooperation in an iterative game setting (Rasmusen, 1990), *e*-uncertainty helps to sustain collusive conduct. This argument is summarized in Hypothesis 4.

> *Hypothesis 4* (Collusion-enhancing *e*-features): The *e*-speed, *e*-transparancy and *e*-uncertainty-enhancing features of the new *e*-contact channels increase the incidence and sustainability of collusive conduct.

Of course, Hypotheses 1, 2, 3 and 4 fail to tell the full story. In this context, Proposition 5's list of multimarket (or multicontact, for that matter) collusion contingencies suggests that the old multicontact collusive arrangements may well break down, as hinted at above, in the new economic short or medium run. After all, in many new industries or markets – as is clear from, for example, the endless list of NASDAQ stories about dotcom failures – firm-level survival chances may well be low, market growth tends to be associated with negative profitability, managerial continuity is quite rare, ownership stability is often absent and strategic homogeneity is the exception rather than the rule. In response, three arguments can be put forward. First, the above story is unlikely to be valid in old industries – to the contrary – in which well-established firms add *e*-contacts to their existing multichannel contact portfolio. Second, Hypotheses 3 and 4 reflect *ceteris paribus* predictions that, together with the above counterforces, suggest a subtle balancing act that may tip either way, depending upon the strength of the opposing forces in specific settings. Third, the collusion-disruptive forces may well be the temporary labor pains of the early stages in an industry's life cycle. Following this line of argument, Hypotheses 3 and 4 particularly relate to the New Economy's long-run equilibrium state.

Learning Through Internet and E-commerce

So far, the argument is basically restricted to the New Economy application of the static version of multichannel contact theory. The next question is what the emergence of the New Economy does to multichannel contact strategies in a **dynamic** context – i.e. multichannel contact learning – which relates to Proposition 2, as well as Propositions 6 to 8. In the New Economy, this dynamic perspective is crucial. After all, the Internet has, and will have, profound effects on technological developments, market structures and business processes. This calls for strategic (re)actions, both from new and from old companies, which involves much *e*-learning. As a result, the New Economy increases the demand for information so as to facilitate such learning processes. Here, firms can draw on their contact network for information about new events, interpretations and expectations. This is the imitation, innovation and legitimation effect of multi-channel contact, which is particularly important in the uncertain times of technological revolution.

There are many conjectures as to the effect of the New Economy on markets, processes and technologies. A number of key 'traditional' constraints in the market lose their relevance (Shapiro & Varian, 1999). Information products can be distributed without capacity constraints. Transactions can be conducted independent of locations, across traditional country and industry boundaries. Internet-based information transfer is timely, detailed and easy-to-access. Web browsers are considered to be an effective and user-friendly interface for intermediating between information users and information sources. As a result, information costs fall, especially the costs of distributing and decoding infor-mation (i.e. the costs of gaining access to information). Once diffusion of the Internet network exceeds a certain threshold, these falling information costs may be expected to stimulate economic growth (see Dudley, 1999, for a general model). If transaction costs fall, this will stimulate the further division of labor. Internet produces new patterns of cooperation between people in different countries and time zones. With increased possibilities for cooperation, they can specialize, which raises the division of labor. With various constraints on economic transactions and labour divisions relaxed, new opportunities arise. To explore these opportunities, companies experiment with new business models and competitive strategies. This *e*-experimenting is a vehicle for *e*-learning, which may well benefit from exploiting multichannel (*e*-)contact portfolios. So, the multichannel (*e*-)contact version of Proposition 2 is likely to gain even more relevance in the New Economy.

A fundamental change, such as the Internet surely is, calls for players to develop new 'theories of the world'. This refers to an important cognitive aspect of corporate culture: culture as beliefs, as an understanding of how the economy works, and culture as beliefs about where your company stands relative to rivals. A company is a learning environment that offers a conceptual framework which guides and coordinates decision making by her employees and managers (Loasby, 1994). Basic innovations, such as the Internet, throw these corporate cultures into crisis. The solution to this is an intensified search for new theories – in other words: learning. Hence, contacts are more important now than ever. In order to get access to new ideas, firms should not limit contacts to their traditional rivals (multimarket contact) or partners (network contacts). This suggests that basic innovations weaken the link between multimarket contacts and competitive moves. As a corollary of Proposition 6, this suggests Hypothesis 5.

> *Hypothesis 5* (Decreasing importance of multimarket contact): In the New Economy, the importance of multimarket contact decreases in favor of multichannel contact.

So, new contacts are a major source of new information in the New Economy. However, what kind of information are companies and their managers looking for? Obviously, data about stable equilibrium states are not a key issue in the New Economy. Rather, firms and their managers need to understand new and dynamic processes. They are interested in expectations and understandings of new kinds of relationships between economic players, including the behavior of new *e*-players. Meaningful, profound changes must be distinguished from opportunistic experiments and uninformed herd behavior. Slow movers may be paralyzed, or may be preparing thoughtful actions. Many mega-mergers, deep-cutting divestitures and major reorganizations are attempts to cope with the new uncertainty. These change processes contain learning behavior that is constrained by bounded rationality and political behavior. Information is impacted by proselytizing behavior and advocacy practices. Information is a source of change power. Information channels play different roles in this regard. Communication tends to provide information in a two-way exchange setting. Contact may therefore increase predictability. In a time-honoured way, the next step may be collusion, where communication serves to stabilize environments.

One aspect that companies need to reassess in this New Economy, is their optimal scope. The firm's productive resources, scope economies and competitive patterns determine her scope. The Internet leads to new forms of multimarket scope, revealing examples being the emerging combinations of telecom and datacom or new and old media firms. Basically, organizations face a choice between, on the one hand, being a pure Internet firm or pure 'physical' (so-called brick-and-mortar) firm and, on the other hand, becoming a combined Internet-physical (so-called click-and-mortar) organization. For efficiency reasons, John Hagel III and Marc Singer (1999) argue in favor of unbundling established companies into separate firms for customer relationship management, product innovation and infrastructure management. In the case of airlines, for example, this would suggest a merger of brands (like, say, Air Italia, British Airways and KLM), while simultaneously outsourcing many operations (as already occurs in the case of ground handling and airplane maintenance).

These outsourcing strategies may create many new forms of contact. For example, the new unbundled firms may share the same bank and the same supplier. Additionally, the new alliances formation might influence the extent of a firm's multimarket scope. In a networked environment, the firms' opportunities increase to learn from each other and to exchange signals. A case in point is, again, the airline industry. In this industry, many formal networks operate side by side. If Air France would meet KLM in one market and Northwest in another, is this a multimarket contact?[9] If we look at the level of alliance networks (where KLM and Northwest are partners), an affirmative answer is appropriate; if we look at individual firms, the answer must be negative. In the former case, if the networks are strong, alliance networks are complementary to multimarket contact. If the latter case holds, which occurs when the information-transmitting and coordinating power of the network is weak, firms may merge instead so as to increase their multimarket contact.[10] In the New Economy, networks are gaining importance, and so do network contacts (next to and on top their firm-level counterparts). Overall, the above argument suggests Hypothesis 6, which provides further detail to Hypothesis 5.

Hypothesis 6 (New contact sources): In the New Economy, increasing vertical unbundling and network formation are associated with the emergence of many new sources of contact.

The emergence of new contact sources is one thing, but using those new contacts effectively is quite another matter. In re-assessing their scope in the New Economy, firms may imitate the behavior of firms with whom they have a high amount of technology-relevant contact, with firms who are dissimilar to her and/or with firms who are technologically successful (cf. Proposition 7). However, bad friends may have the wrong influence. Firms may hesitate in learning from newcomers when they have a well-established high multichannel (or multimarket, for that matter) contact with firms who have a stable pattern of decision making about scope, entry, exit and/or pricing. So, by the end of the day, those firms who attach greater weight to developing new contacts may outperform their counterparts who stick to their old contact network partners. This produces Hypothesis 7, which is a corollary of Proposition 7.

> *Hypothesis 7* (New *versus* old contacts): In the New Economy, those firms who develop a new multichannel contact portfolio and who attach more weight to their new contacts, are likely to outperform their counterparts who hang on to their 'old' and well-established multichannel contact network.

To argue that, in the New Economy, new contacts emerge (Hypothesis 6) that leapfrog old contacts in importance (Hypothesis 7) might suggest a move toward a new stable equilibrium. However, nothing can be more beside the mark. In the turbulent and uncertain early days of the Internet revolution, the apparent *status quo* is a moving target. In this context, in line with Proposition 8, we can add a number of effects of *e*-commerce on the dynamics of market behavior in the New Economy. Clearly, the New Economy is inextricably bound up with shifting competitive conditions. And related to this, the New Economy produces newness in all corners of the business world. Below is a revealing, but incomplete, list of examples.

- New players are entering. Companies re-arrange their product portfolio, foreign companies enter through virtual portals, and newly created *e*-companies penetrate cyberspace.
- New transaction systems are introduced. New cybermediaries help to reduce the cost of *e*-transactions, new on-line auctions facilitate market efficiency, and electronic payment services reduce the customers' barrier to engage in B2C purchasing.
- New value chains are designed. Manufacturers may cut out traditional distribution intermediaries, suppliers may focus on interaction with customers, and firms may outsource production while using fewer subcontractors.

- New multimarket scope strategies arise. As argued above, many firms re-assess their multimarket scope, merging horizontally, unbundling vertically and allying diagonally.
- New information channels are installed. Electronic feedback from customers deepen and enrich a company's information, enabling her to design quick and tailor-made responses to customer-specific events and features.
- New business models are invented. The introduction of Internet and Intranet offers opportunities to re-design business processes, both within and across organizations, so as to improve efficiency and effectiveness.
- New product strategies are implemented. Information products, with their unique combination of features (such as low marginal production costs, high switching costs, powerful lock-in effects and significant network externalities), ask for different strategies in terms of e.g. product versioning, price discrimination, property rights and complementary bundling.
- New competitive rules of the game are developing. As a result of any (combination) of the above new ways doing business, industries may well be confronted with new competitive games, either by moving from collusion to competition or *vice versa*.

The bottom line is that the above and many other new developments imply that the dynamics of competition in the New Economy are impressive. Partly, this is the result of the very nature of the Internet technology. That is, the electronic speed and transparancy of information travel reduce the ability to keep sources of competitive advantage secret for very long. It induces firms to protect their sources of competitive advantage (intellectual property rights) by patents and copyrights. If that fails, conditions of hypercompetition occur (Gimeno & Woo, 1996). In the New Economy, as a result, competitive advantages tend to have a short life cycle (which defines hypercompetition) as information travels fast, is easy to replicate and distribute, and difficult to protect. In the context of the multichannel contact perspective, this story points to the necessity to frequently re-assess any multichannel contact portfolio. After all, what might be a central and promising new contact today may well be relegated to the periphery of competitive irrelevance tomorrow. This suggests Hypothesis 8 as the New Economy complement to Proposition 8.[11]

> *Hypothesis 8* (disruption of multichannel contact portfolios): In the New Economy, the rapid development and diffusion of new ways of doing *e*-business, together with the associated competitive *e*-dynamics, disrupt a firm's just-established multichannel contact portfolio time and again.

Multichannel Contact Management in the New Economy

The above argument offers a first step toward the analysis of multichannel contact management in the New Economy – and nothing more. After all, multi-channel contact management must deal with a number of key issue at the **portfolio** level, too. Here, Fig. 2 offers a stepping stone for a tentative reflection. Below, by way of wrap-up, we reflect briefly on the five different elements of our multichannel contact framework.

1. **Channel sources**. The immediate implication of the New Economy is the emergence of additional *e*-channel sources, apart from the accelerated @lli@nce network formation (Figs. 4 & 5). For instance, the many *e*-trading websites offer a direct contact channel that operates next to or instead of the traditional market places. Moreover, cybermediaries, which help firms to smooth their transaction conduct in an electronic world of information overload, are clear examples of additional indirect *e*-contact channel sources.
2. **Channel features**. Next to and on top of the *e*-speed, *e*-transparancy and *e*-uncertainty features of Internet contact (Table 1), with their likely effect of enhancing (the sustainability of) multichannel collusion, the new *e*-channels may either complement or replace current non-Internet channel sources, so stimulating a re-assessment of the effectiveness of a multichannel contact portfolio. In the context of this re-assessment exercise, the relative direct and indirect cost of developing and maintaining *e*-contact channels must be taken on board. For instance, the management of an @lli@nce network may absorb so much energy and time that the firm can dispose of an inefficient cross-shareholding portfolio, because the @lli@nce network is an effective substitute for the cross-shareholding contact channel.
3. **Channel purposes**. The issue of the *e*-channel purposes is reflected in Hypotheses 1 to 8 above. Clearly, the primary objectives of collusive *e*-conduct and across-firm *e*-learning operate side by side the secondary aims of developing and sustaining *e*-reputation device and *e*-retaliation power, the latter twin being instrumental in reaching the former couple. Here, the argument produces *e*-versions of Propositions 1 to 4.
4. **Channel externalities**. A key question is whether the new Internet tech-nolgy will prove to be either a conformity-stimulating or variety-producing shock. On the one hand, the Internet, and the many associated contact networks, may facilitate across-firm imitation, so enhancing the new technology's conformity-enhancing legitimation. On the other hand, the world of *e*-contact may offer ample opportunities to develop innovative *e*-novelties, thus producing competitive variety.

5. **Channel management**. The New Economy's Internet break-through technology is inextricably bound up with many uncertainties, which offers an exciting challenge to multimarket contact channel management. From an external environment perspective, many – if not all – firms face the need to re-asses their channel selection and network building strategies, taking on board the new threats and opportunities in the *e*-world. From an internal organization angle, many firms are just starting to explore such issues as electronic process guiding and *ditto* partner leading.

Fair enough, the above reflection is only a first step toward an in-depth exploration of multichannel contact management in the New Economy, being associated – for the time being – with asking interesting questions rather than providing definitive answers. As a second step, the next section introduces a tentative empirical investigation of the case of the diffusion of Java software so as to put empirical flesh on the theoretical bones of a selection of the issues that are associated with the multichannel contact framework.

A Case: the Diffusion of Java

Java is a programming language that has become popular for Internet applications. Sun developed Java in the early 1990s, initially as a tool for interactive television applications. In 1994, Sun relaunched Java for the world wide web. Its diffusion has been very fast, and it is widely used now as something close to a *de facto* standard for Internet programming. Computer makers are among the companies who needed to adopt Java for their software and *e*-commerce applications. For the short Java case below we used data from the Dutch IT journal *Automatisering Gids* (their latest CD-rom data set covers the period from August 1994 to September 1999). We determined the timing of the computer makers' adoption of Java by looking at the alliances they engaged in that explicitly refer to Java, as well as to product announcements that relate to Java. The results that we report here are very preliminary. The only message we would like to bring home in this section is how (part of) the multichannel contact perspective can be applied to a real-world case that is related to the New Economy of IT and Internet. A rigorous empirical study will have to be a second step, as is the application of the full multichannel contact framework. That is, the analysis below is, basically, restricted to the **incidence** of multimarket and multichannel contact, ignoring the consequences of such contact. Taking the latter on board requires additional data collection as to the conduct and performance of the firms operating in the Java network.

Table 2. Twelve Firms Announcing @lli@nces with a Java Basis.

Company	Country	Date
International Business Machines (IBM)	U.S.	December 15 1995
Apple	U.S.	March 22 1996
Hewlett-Packard	U.S.	May 10 1996
Digital Equipment Corporation (DEC)	U.S.	May 24 1996
Mitsubishi	Japan	May 24 1996
Motorola	U.S.	May 24 1996
Olivetti	Italy	May 24 1996
Toshiba	Japan	June 7 1996
Compaq	U.S.	August 26 1996
NEC	Japan	May 31 1997
Siemens	Germany	August 15 1997
Fujitsu	Japan	October 10 1997

As a stepping stone for our analysis, Tables 1 and 2 provide relevant Java-related information. It is clear from both tables that IBM was the first adopter of Java, after the inventor Sun. It is widely believed that IBM has currently more programmers working on Java, in her San Francisco project, than Sun herself. We may then raise the question what has determined the sequence of the subsequent adopters. To see that, we looked at all reported cooperative moves (in the data source mentioned above) by the companies listed in Tables 2 and 3. The result is provided in Table 4 (cf. Hypothesis 1).[12]

Comparing this Table 4 to Tables 2 and 3 makes clear that, roughly, the computer companies who cooperate frequently with IBM (Apple, HP and DEC), were the ones who rapidly followed IBM's adoption of Java. Some companies who had few cooperative links with IBM also were relatively late to adopt Java – notably NEC, Siemens and Fujitsu. There are some anomalies, though, as

Table 3. Companies That Sell Products Using the Java Standard.

Company	Year	Purpose
IBM	1996	Minicomputers and higher OS
Mitsubishi	1996	(Set-top box for) TV with Internet access
Hewlett-Packard	1998	Mobile phone / PDA Internet access

Table 4. Number of IBM-Based Cooperative and Standard-Setting Events.

Company	Number
Apple	23
Hewlett-Packard	29
Digital Equipment Corporation (DEC)	17
Mitsubishi	3
Motorola	6
Olivetti	1
Toshiba	3
Compaq	10
NEC	5
Siemens	4
Fujitsu	4

Mitsubishi, Motorola and Olivetti were fast followers without having that many cooperative links with IBM. For a fuller picture, we therefore need additonal information about multimarket and multichannel contact events.

To collect more information about multimarket contact, we used the Worldscope CD-rom which contains information about firms and their industries. For IBM, this source lists the following markets (four-digit SIC codes): 3570, 357, 3571, 3575, 7372 and 7378. All firms selected are computer firms, and are thus active in the SIC-code 3571 industry (which refers to "electronic computers"). Table 5 reveals the resulting multimarket contacts within our sample of computer makers.

In absolute terms, Compaq has the greatest multimarket contact overlap with IBM (in five industries), closely followed by Apple, Digital and Olivetti (three markets each). In relative terms, Compaq's lead is even larger (contact in five of her six markets). Sun has contacts with all companies listed in the single industry she is recorded to be active in (with the SIC code 3571). Thus, she does not have multimarket contact with these companies (at the four-digit SIC level).

Comparing the alliance contacts in Tables 2 and 4 to the multimarket contacts in Table 5 suggests that the alliance data much better explain what is happening in the business world of Java software than the multimarket contact data – i.e. why Apple and Hewlett-Packard were swift to follow IBM in adopting Java, compared with Compaq. On the one hand, Apple and Hewlett-Packard had a higher alliance contact incidence with IBM than Compaq. On the other hand, they did have less multimarket contacts with the central Java-player IBM. This is consistent with Propositions 6 and 7: since Java is a technological

Table 5. Industry Overlap in IT Businesses.

Company	357	3570	3571	SIC code 3575	7372	7378	Other codes
Apple			x	x	x		3572, 3577
Hewlett-Packard			x			x	3577, 3841, 5049
Digital (DEC)			x	x	x		3572, 3577, 7373, 7379
Mitsubishi							36, 363, 3651, 3554, 3570
Motorola							366, 367, 3650
Olivetti	x		x			x	3695, 5045, 7373, 7374
Toshiba				x			3612, 3674, 3651, 3663
Compaq	x	x	x		x	x	3575
NEC	x						366, 3674
Siemens			x				3661, 3823, 4911, 3743, 3670, 3845, 3641
Fujitsu			x				3572, 3577, 3669, 3674
Sun			x				

phenomenon that plays an important role in the Internet revolution, alliance contacts are more relevant to firms, particularly those with the leading Java-applying pioneer IBM, than are multimarket contacts. Additionally, our preliminary findings suggest that multi-alliance and multimarket contacts are probably viewed as substitutes rather than complements (cf. Fig. 2). Multimarket contact may have an effect, of course, specifically when alliance contacts are very limited. For example, Olivetti was relatively quickly involved in Java (see Table 2), but she has only one alliance with IBM and only one with Sun (see Table 4). But she does meet IBM in three different markets. Fujitsu's relatively late adoption of Java (in late 1997) is consistent with both her low alliance contact (four alliances) and her low multimarket contact (one market out of her five industries) incidence with IBM.

APPRAISAL

Multimarket contact theory envisions competition as a subtle multi-level play, where multiple players coordinate their moves over different playing fields. For one, this kind of competition does have high informational requirements. We suggest in this chapter that the theory of multimarket contact needs to be re-assessed, with greater emphasis than before on the informational and expectational conditions of contact, reputation building and coordinated decision making. Additionally, and related to the above, forms of contact other than through market competition may also communicate strategic intent. Networks may coordinate pricing in novel ways by creating new forms of contact and overlapping scope. Alliances and shared suppliers, such as consultants and financiers, may also act as conduits of information. This suggests a multi**channel** rather than multi**market** contact perspective. In this context, we know little about the relative importance of various contact channels for the learning that goes on in firms. Contact is important in situations where firms need more information than they can get from analyzing the raw data that can be derived from observing a market (business intelligence). Here, by way of illustration, we have discussed the cases of the New Economy, which – in all likelihood – increases the relevance of a multichannel contact perspective, and the business world of the Java programming language. Hopefully, our chapter may contribute to developing such a multichannel contact approach of corporate and business strategy.

NOTES

1. To avoid disappointment, we would like to remark that this chapter is an explorative, and hopefully thought-provoking, essay. That is, the aim is to offer stepping stones for future reseach by: (i) developing a multichannel contact framework, and (ii) applying the argument to the New Economy case. So, as yet, we neither propose a mathematical model nor offer an econometric test.

2. For the sake of parsimony, Proposition 1 ignores nonlinearities. On this, Stephan and Boeker (this volume) offer interesting insights.

3. Phillips and Mason (this volume) present an interesting experimental study that focuses on competitive learning through a player who horizontally connects two separate (duopoly) markets.

4. An important aspect of this learning perspective on multimarket contact is that firms must be free to experiment in individual markets. In this context, arbitrage trade, economies of scope or scale, network economies or other basic conditions may place constraints on a firm's behavior in an individual market, which would reduce the freedom for firms to experiment in that market. But if such restrictions are not binding, then higher multimarket contact is associated with more opportunities to learn from each other as to how the competitive game can be played. This, in turn, increases the chance that the firms involved are able to establish an equilibrium in which they avoid disruptive competition. The effect of such competitive learning behavior are higher prices and higher profits. These high prices and high profits need not reflect the presence of (tacit) collusion, though. They may instead point to the absence of aggressive price cutting as a result of firms jockeying for position. This interpretation, then, challenges the view that the positive impact of multimarket contact on prices and profits reflects tacit collusion *per se*.

5. As an important side effect, IO's multimarket game theory repairs another shortcoming of much IO: in a multimarket setting, the threat of potential entry is no longer an anonymous *deus ex machina*, as is the case in the majority of entry threat games (Gilbert, 1989), but rather takes the shape of a potential entrant with a face. This offers

promising opportunities in the context of the welfare-theoretic analysis of competition by providing a multimarket interpretation of perfect contestability (van Witteloostuijn, 1992).

6. So, much of IO's multimarket collusion modeling is a natural extension of industrial economics' well-established single-market cartel theory that has produced a list of cartel-enhancing and cartel-disrupting conditions. Scherer and Ross (1990) offer an insightful textbook treatment of this subbranch of IO.

7. Arm-length forms of contact are likely to be less efficient information conduits than internal information conduits, though. This may be one factor why a firm might prefer a merger to an alliance. This is an issue that lies beyond the scope of the current chapter.

8. Perhaps New Economy prophets follow pop musicians (e.g. U2), when they play around with letter and number symbols.

9. Phillips and Mason (this volume) offer an in-depth treatment of this issue of indirect multimarket contact.

10. This relates to the entry mode issue (cf. Stephan & Boeker, this volume).

11. For the sake of brevity, the argument does not distinguish new from old firms. This is not to say that this distinction is irrelevant. For example, new forms of collusion can very well appear in new industries. New Internet companies need to build up reputations. Since their position in output markets is still very new, they may derive reputation from their inputs rather than from their outputs, such as well-known top managers, employees, investors or owners. This implies a bias of their multichannel contact network formation to developing and maintaining input links.

12. Note that these cooperative moves occur partly after the firm concerned adopted Java. This is one of the weaknesses that must be improved upon in the context of a rigorous empirical study.

ACKNOWLEDGMENTS

We gratefully appreciate the comments of Joel Baum and Henrich Greve. We thank Geert Duijsters (Eindhoven University) for providing Figs 4 and 5. Of course, the usual disclaimer applies.

REFERENCES

Bain, J. S. (1956). *Barriers to New Competition*. Cambridge MA: Harvard University Press.

Baum, J. A. C., & Korn, H. J. (1996). Competitive Dynamics of Interfirm Rivalry. *Academy of Management Journal, 39*, 255–291.

Baum, J. A. C., & Korn, H. J. (1999). Dynamics of Dyadic Competitive Interaction. *Strategic Management Journal, 20*, 251–278.

Bernheim, B. D., & Whinston, M. D. (1990). Multimarket Contact and Collusive Behavior. *RAND Journal of Economics, 21*, 1–26.

Bierman, H. S., & Fernandez, L. (1993). *Game Theory with Economic Applications*. Reading MA: Addison Wesley.

Cassidy, Chr., & Loree, D. (2001). Dynamics of Knowledge Transfer among Multimarket Competitors. In: J. A. C. Baum & H. R. Greve (Eds), *Multiunit Organization and*

Multimarket Strategy: Advances in Strategic Management, 18 (pp. 141–174). Oxford, UK: JAI Press.

Cohen, S. S., DeLong, J. B., & Zysman, J. (2000). Tools for Thought: What is New and Important About the 'E-conomy'?, BRIE Working Paper No. 138, Berkeley: University of California at Berkeley, http://econ161.berkeley.edu

Daft, R. L. (1998). *Organization Theory and Design.* Cincinnati: South-Western College Publishing.

DiMaggio, P. J., & Powell, W. W. (1983). The Iron Cage Revisited: Institutional Isomorphism and Collective Rationality in Organizational Fields. *American Sociological Review, 48,* 147–160.

Dudley, L. (1999). Communications and Economic Growth. *European Economic Review, 43,* 595–619.

Feinberg, R. M. (1984). Mutual Forbearance as an Extension of Oligopoly Theory. *Journal of Economics and Business, 36,* 243–249.

Gilbert, R. J. (1989). Mobility Barriers and the Value of Incumbency. In: R. Schmalensee & R. D. Willig (Eds), *Handbook of Industrial Organization.* Amsterdam: North-Holland.

Gimeno, J., & Woo, C. Y. (1996). Hypercompetition in a Multimarket Environment: The Role of Strategic Similarity and Multi-market Contact on Competitive De-escalation. *Organization Science, 7,* 322–341.

Gordon, R. J. (2000). Does the 'New Economy' Measure up to the Great Inventions of the Past? *Journal of Economic Perspectives, 14,* 49–74.

Greve, H. R. (1998). Managerial Cognition and the Mimetic Adoption of Market Positions: What You See is What You Do. *Strategic Management Journal, 19,* 967–988.

Gulati, R. (1995). Social Structure and Alliance Formation Patterns: A Longitudinal Analysis. *Administrative Science Quarterly, 40,* 619–652.

Hagel III, J., & Singer, M. (1999). Unbundling the Corporation: What Business Are You In? Chances Are, It's Not What You Think. *Harvard Business Review,* March–April, 133–141.

Hannan, M. T., & Freeman, J. (1977). The Population Ecology of Organizations. *American Journal of Sociology, 82,* 926–964.

Hughes, K. S., & Oughton, C. (1993). Diversification, Multi-market Contact and Profitability. *Economica, 60,* 203–224.

Kim, S. (2001). Markets and Multiunit Firms from an American Historical Perspective. In: J. A. C. Baum & H. R. Greve (Eds), *Multiunit Organization and Multimarket Strategy: Advances in Strategic Management, 18* (pp. 307–328). Oxford, UK: JAI Press.

Loasby, B. J. (1994). Organisational Capabilities and Interfirm Relations. *Metroeconomica, 45,* 248–265.

Madhavan, R., Koka, B. R., & Prescott, J. E. (1998). Networks in Transition: How Industry Events (Re)shape Interfirm Relationships. *Strategic Management Journal, 19,* 439–459.

Nelson, R. R., & Winter, S. G. (1982). *An Evolutionary Theory of Economic Change.* Cambridge MA: Harvard University Press.

Nouwens, J., & Bouwman, H. (1995). Living Apart Together in Electronic Commerce: The Use of Information and Communication Technology to Create Network Organizations. *Journal of Computer-Mediated Communication, 1.* (http://www.ascusc.org/jcmc/vol1/issue3/nouwens.html)

Phillips, O. R., & Mason, C. F. (2001). Collusion in Horizontally Connected Markets: Multimarket Producers as Conduits for Learning. In: J. A. C. Baum & H. R. Greve (Eds), *Multiunit Organization and Multimarket Strategy: Advances in Strategic Management, 18* (pp. 207–229). Oxford, UK: JAI Press

Rasmusen, E. (1990). *Games and Information: An Introduction into Game Theory.* Oxford: Basil Blackwell.

Sarkar, M. B., Butler, B., & Steinfield, C. (2000). Intermediaries and Cybermediaries: A Continuing
    Role for Mediating Players in the Electronic Marketplace. *Journal of Computer-Mediated
    Communication, 6.* (http://www.ascusc.org/jcmc/vol6/issue3/sarkar.html)
Scherer, F. M., & Ross, D. (1990). *Industrial Market Structure and Economic Performance.* Boston
    MA: Houghton Mifflin.
Scott, J. T. (1989). Purposive Diversification as a Motive for Merger. *International Journal of
    Industrial Organization, 7,* 35–47.
Shapiro, C., & Varian, H. R. (1999). *Information Rules: A Strategic Guide to the Network Economy.*
    Boston MA: Harvard Business School Press.
Smith, A. (1970). *The Wealth of Nations.* Harmondsworth: Penguin.
Smith, F. L., & Wilson, R. L. (1995). The Predictive Validity of the Karnani and Wernerfelt Model
    of Multipoint Competition. *Strategic Management Journal, 16,* 143–160.
Stephan, J., & Boeker, W. (2001). The Changing Effects of Multipoint Contact: Refining the
    Relationship between Multimarket Contact and Firm Behavior. In: J. A. C. Baum &
    H. R. Greve (Eds), *Multiunit Organization and Multimarket Strategy: Advances in Strategic
    Management, 18* (pp. 231–263). Oxford, UK: JAI Press.
Tirole, J. (1988). *The Theory of Industrial Organization.* Cambridge MA: MIT Press.
Volberda, H. (1998). *Building the Flexible Firm: How to Remain Competitive.* Oxford: Oxford
    University Press.
Wegberg, M. van, & Witteloostuijn, A. van (1992). Credible Entry Threats into Contestable Markets:
    a Symmetric Multimarket Model of Contestability. *Economica, 59,* 437–452.
Wegberg, M. van, & Witteloostuijn, A. van (1995). Multicontact Collusion in Product Markets and
    Joint R&D Ventures: The Case of the Information Technology Industry in an Integrating
    Europe. In: J. Hagedoorn (Ed.), *Technical Change and the World Economy: Convergence
    and Divergence in Technology Strategies.* Aldershot: Edward Elgar Publishing Limited.
Wegberg, M. van, & Witteloostuijn, A. van, & Roscam Abbing, M. (1994) Multimarket and
    Multiproject Collusion: Why European Integration May Reduce Intra-Community
    Competition. *De Economist, 142,* 253–285.
Witteloostuijn, A. van (2001). The 'Old' versus the 'New' Economy Debate: How Well-Established
    Laws Rule New Paradoxes, Research Memorandum, Groningen: University of Groningen.
Witteloostuijn, A. van (1992). Theories of Competition and Market Performance: Multimarket
    Competition and the Source of Potential Entry. *De Economist, 140,* 109–139.
Witteloostuijn, A. van (1993). Multimarket Competition and Business Strategy. *Review of Industrial
    Organization, 8,* 83–99.
Witteloostuijn, A. van, & Wegberg, M. van (1991) Multimarket Competition and European
    Integration. In: Rugman, A. M., & Verbeke, A. (Eds), *Research in Global Strategic
    Management: Global Competition and the European Community.* London: JAI Press.
Witteloostuijn, A. van, & Wegberg, M. van (1992). Multimarket Competition: Theory and Evidence.
    Journal of Economic Behavior and Organization, 18, 273–282.

MARKETS AND MULTIUNIT FIRMS FROM AN AMERICAN HISTORICAL PERSPECTIVE

Sukkoo Kim

ABSTRACT

The expansion of markets and industrialization greatly increased the benefits of specialization in the U.S. economy. However, since the benefits of specialization can only be realized through trade, specialization significantly increases the volume of market transactions in the economy. The analysis presented in this paper suggests that a better understanding of the historical changes in the nature of market transactions costs, especially those related to information, is likely to provide considerable insights on the rise of the modern business enterprise and a richer understanding of the industrial organization of the U.S. economy.

I. INTRODUCTION

The revolutions in transportation and communications technologies have increased the extent of the U.S. domestic markets over the last two centuries. Moreover, the expansion of markets is associated with major changes in the course of American economic history. The introduction of canals in the late eighteenth and the early nineteenth centuries is credited with increasing the

Multiunit Organization and Multimarket Strategy, Volume 18, pages 305–326.

levels of inventive activity and triggering industrialization (Sokoloff, 1988). The extension of markets and industrialization is associated with the growth of Smithian division of labor of all kinds. Households became less self-sufficient and became specialized consumer-laborers; firms that specialized in the production of various goods emerged in great numbers. The division of labor within firms led to a re-organization of production and increased levels of productivity (Sokoloff, 1984a, b). Finally, as regional domestic markets became increasingly integrated between the late nineteenth and the early twentieth centuries, geographic specialization in economic activities increased (Kim, 1995, 1998).

While gains from specialization and trade are likely to be enormous, these gains do not come freely. Specialization increases productivity, but it also leads to greater costs in making transactions (Wallis & North, 1986). Indeed, it is precisely because specialization introduces new costs that specialization will not occur until these additional costs are brought below the benefits of specialization. What kinds of costs does specialization produce? Every trade must overcome two types of costs: transportation and information. Since gains to specialization are realized through trade between agents, specialization increases the volume of goods and people that are transported. Specialization also reduces the information set of the agents. Compared to a more self-sufficient economy, buyers lose information on supply and firms lose information on demand. In addition, specialization exacerbates the problems of asymmetric information. When the quality of products is not easily verifiable upon casual observation, firms will know the quality of the products whereas the buyers will not.

This paper argues that the rise and growth of multiunit firms between the late nineteenth and the twentieth centuries are explained by changes in the nature of transaction costs associated with specialization. In the late nineteenth century, due to advances in science and technology, products became more sophisticated and consumers became less and less able to use their senses to identify the quality of the products they consumed. When consumers know less about the quality of products than producers, the conditions are ripe for the classic "lemons" problem where the presence of low quality products drives higher quality products out of the market (Akerlof, 1970). Multiunit firms arose in this environment because they were better able to solve the problem of asymmetric information than the traditional single-unit firms. One important solution to the "lemons" problem is for firms to use advertising and brand-names as a commitment device not to cheat (Klein & Leffler, 1981; Carlton & Perloff, 1994). In this task, the multiunit firms had two significant advantages over single-unit firms: they were able to economize on advertising costs and the sheer size of multiunit firms became a commitment device which credibly signaled to buyers that the cost of reneging was significant.

This paper is organized as follows. Section II will examine the historical relationship between the U.S. domestic market and industrial organizations. Section III will explore the growth of multiunit firms in the twentieth century and Section IV will conclude with a summary.

II. THE EVOLUTION OF MARKETS AND INDUSTRIAL ORGANIZATIONS OVER AMERICAN HISTORY.

In colonial British North America, the markets for the products of agriculture and extractive industries were well integrated into the British imperial and world economies. International transportation costs fell significantly with advances in shipping and the various colonies specialized in the production of goods of their comparative advantages. The northern colonies specialized in sea, wood and grain products and the southern colonies specialized in tobacco, rice, indigo and other extractive industries (Shepherd & Walton, 1972; McCusker & Menard, 1985). In these well developed export markets, the merchants in port cities coordinated the supply of and demand for these products in the world market. On the other hand, the markets for manufactures were small and undeveloped. The population was thinly spread and overland transportation by wagons was prohibitively costly. Given the relatively small market for manufacturing, households manufactured many basic products such as food, clothing and farm implements. It was typical for households to grind their own flour and bake their own bread, make jellies, jams, honey, and maple syrup, brew their own beer, rum and whiskey, and knit various articles of clothing such as mittens and sweaters (Tryon, 1917; Walton & Rockoff, 1998).

In the late eighteenth and the early nineteenth centuries, the expansion of the U.S. domestic markets and industrialization caused a rapid decline in household production and a proliferation of specialized manufacturing firms in the American economy. In this period, the industrial structure was composed of single-unit firms who specialized in the production of manufacturing goods and wholesale merchants and retail store owners who distributed these goods. Since the manufacturing firms typically specialized in a narrow line of products, it was simply too costly for them to market their products directly to consumers. In this setting, the wholesale merchants, who bought and sold sufficient lines of products, were able to lower the costs of transactions more efficiently. The wholesale merchants were not only able to collect information on various manufacturers by locating in major cities but were also able to collect information on rural consumer demand through the use of sales agents who traveled to rural country stores (Jones, 1937; Porter & Livesay, 1971; Chandler, 1977). In this period, most consumers were able to judge the quality of most products upon visual inspection. However, for some goods, they relied on the local producers' and retail merchants' reputation for honesty.

In the late nineteenth century, with advances in science and technology, it became increasingly difficult for consumers to discern the quality of products which they consumed. As incomes rose, consumers purchased a growing number of products for which they lacked basic knowledge to discern quality. Moreover, even the manufacturing processes of the most basic of products such as food became so sophisticated that consumers no longer had enough knowledge to discern whether a product was healthy or poisonous. Ellen Richards, one of the figures of the home economics movement, wrote in *Food Materials and Their Adulteration* in 1885; "We buy everything, and have no idea of the processes by which articles are produced, and have no means of knowing beforehand what the quality may be. Relatively, we are in a state of barbarous innocence, as compared to our grandmothers, about the common articles of daily use (Strasser, 1989, p. 255)."

For many products, it became easier for firms to use the science of chemistry to adulterate or substitute ingredients without the knowledge of consumers. It was widely suspected that firms substituted cane for maple sugar, extended flour and ground coffee with sawdust and chalk fillers, and made blended whiskey from ethyl alcohol, water and coloring (Kallet & Schlink, 1933). In addition, new potentially dangerous preservatives were often used without the consumers' knowledge. Unlike the historic preservatives, such as salt, sugar, vinegar, and wood smoke, the new preservatives, such as borax, salicyclic acid and salicylates, sulfurous acids and sulfites, benzoic acids and benzoates, formaldehyde, were without taste or odor in the dosages used. Indeed, Harvey Wiley, the chief chemist of the Department of Agriculture, believed that the most deleterious substance in foods were those added to prevent decay (Young, 1989, p. 151).

The meat packing industry provides an excellent illustration of the emergence of the asymmetric information problem associated with an increasingly specialized economy. In the mid-nineteenth century, given the prohibitive costs of transporting meat prior to the invention of refrigerated cars, the industry was characterized by small, local slaughterhouses. In this setting, the local butchers served a small area and built reputations for the freshness of their meat. As the use of refrigerated cars lowered the costs of transportation in the late nineteenth century, geographic specialization of meat packing increased significantly. Meat packing became concentrated in the Midwest which had considerable comparative advantage in the production of beef (Yeager, 1981; Libecap, 1992). The geographic specialization of the meat packing industry exacerbated the asymmetric information concerning meat. The consumers no longer knew the identity of the butchers who supplied them with their meat. While it may be relatively easy to distinguish fresh versus rotten meat, it was more difficult to verify the claims of the local slaughterhouses that refrigerated meat was butchered under horrible conditions, and that it was diseased and was detrimental to the consumers' health.

Glucose sugar, a product quite different from beef, also came to the forefront of public debate concerning quality of food and drugs. In the late nineteenth century, a growing number of firms began producing glucose sugar manufactured from corn as a substitute for cane sugar. Pure glucose had about two-thirds the sweetening power of cane sugar, but it was much cheaper. Soon glucose was used in the making of confectionaries, jellies, canned fruit and meat, and bakery goods. However, numerous individuals, including the cane sugar producers, claimed that glucose sugar was unsafe. Since sulfuric acid and metals were used in the manufacturing process, it was claimed that syrup made from glucose was poisonous as it contained residues of tin, iron, calcium and magnesia. Thus, even though most glucose sugar was safe, it was impossible for consumers to know whether a product was made from glucose sugar and whether it was safe to consume.

"Because of the unfairly bad press glucose had received, argued Frank H. Madden, representing the Wholesale Grocers of Chicago, the public would cease to buy products containing that sweetener should a law be enacted requiring ingredient labeling. At least 98% of the 'thinking public,' Madden asserted, deemed glucose 'something vile and unfit for food.' He admitted that 95% of the jelly consumed in the nation was made from glucose and the skins and cores of apples, although labeled strawberry or raspberry or whatever other flavor the processor chose to call it. This cheap, wholesome food did not deserve disparaging by physicians and chemists, who were 'always discovering bugaboos,' many of which were merely products of their own imaginations (Young, 1989, p. 158)."

The introduction of another basic ingredient in cooking, margarine, raised the public's concern for the potential dangers of food. Patented by a French chemist Hippolyte Mège-Mouriés, margarine made from animal fat was so close in resemblance to butter that experts and chemists could tell the difference only after extensive tests. When the Chicago meatpackers began to produce margarine or "butterine" in significant quantities, the dairy interests fought back. The butter interests accused margarine, the "midnight assassin," for causing numerous deaths. Witnesses testified that margarine was made from the fat of dead horses, dead cows and dead dogs; others argued that diseases such as tuberculosis and trichinosis were transferable to consumers of margarine. In addition, the chemical process, or the use of acids and alkalis, which transformed fat into margarine was claimed to leave poisonous by-products (Young, 1989, pp. 70–94). Once again, even if most margarine was safe, consumers became wary of using it in every-day cooking.

If consumers had a difficult time detecting fraud, honest firms had an equally difficult time convincing their customers that their product was of high quality. In this period called the Progressive Era, the asymmetric information problem concerning food and drugs received the most public attention. Moreover, these concerns led to a greater involvement by the federal government with the passages of the Meat Inspection Act of 1891 and the Food and Drug Act of 1906 (Libecap, 1981; Young, 1989). However, the asymmetric information problem was much more general and involved products in many industries. In a wide range of goods from automobiles, tires, and gasolines and basic chemicals such as soaps and new emerging medicines, consumers lacked scientific knowledge to independently judge the quality of these products. In a growing number of industries, the traditional firms faced the "lemons" problem for which they had few answers. In this new technologically sophisticated environment, new firms emerged to solve the growing asymmetric information problem and forged a new industrial structure for the United States.

III. THE RISE AND GROWTH OF MULTIUNIT FIRMS IN THE TWENTIETH CENTURY

The modern multiunit firms arose in the late nineteenth and the twentieth centuries because they were better able to solve the asymmetric information problem which grew in importance over this period. Unlike most single-unit firms, the multiunit firms were able to use advertising and brand-names to credibly signal a certain level of quality of their products to their consumers. In addition, a variety of factors enabled the multiunit firms to use this strategy in this period. Advances in transportation and communications technologies and organizational innovations in advertising lowered the costs of marketing products directly to consumers. Furthermore, the federal government lowered the cost of developing brand names as it provided more secure property rights to a firm's trademarks and passed laws on product quality.

For a growing number of products in this period, the traditional industrial structure composed of single-unit firms in manufacturing, wholesale trade and retail trade was unable to solve the asymmetric information problem efficiently. When the population was dispersed in rural areas, the asymmetric information problem, if it existed at all, was solved largely through the reputation of local producers or retail store owners. For example, the retail store owners were able to develop a level of reputation through repeated, long-term customer relationships. However, as the population became increasingly more concentrated in urban areas, the traditional retail store owners were less able to develop a reputation for honesty. Unlike the traditional general store owner who knew the family histories of his customers, the urban retailers faced a growing number of anonymous shoppers. In this setting, the retailers found it increasingly difficult to find a credible mechanism for signaling honesty.

Klein and Leffler (1981) outlines conditions under which firms will honor their commitments to supply a high level of quality when product quality is difficult to measure. The model assumes that when a firm cheats, the consumers in the market will know that it cheated. In this setting, firms will choose not to cheat if they earn a stream of income from a price that is greater than the perfectly competitive price. However, competition will lead firms to make "sunk" non-salvageable firm-specific assets in brand-name that is equal to the rental value of premium quality assuring price. Thus, the model predicts that when asymmetric information is present, firms will make investments in brand name but will also receive higher prices.

Multiunit firms were able to solve the asymmetric information problem through the use of advertising and the development of brand names. In the presence of uncertain quality and the absence of a credible third party enforcer, the main private-contract enforcement mechanism relies on the value of repeat sales to a firm. One solution to signaling a firm's value of repeated sales is to invest in firm-specific and non-salvageable assets such as advertising and developing brand names. Since the value of repeat sales is limited for most single-unit firms, these firms have little incentive to advertise and develop brand names. On the other hand, for multiunit firms, the value of repeat purchase is potentially much greater. Thus, the economies of marketing for multiunit firms come not only from their ability to spread their costs over many plants or stores, but also from the fact that the cost of reneging on their product quality is significantly higher.

In the late nineteenth and early twentieth centuries, various laws passed by the federal government aided in enforcing the private solution to the asymmetric information problem. In the nineteenth century, there was much confusion concerning a firm's legal ownership of trademarks. Once a firm established a brand-name using a certain trademark, many firms imitated the established trademark (Strasser, 1989). In 1905, the Congress passed a trademark law which clarified the legal property rights of trademarks. The new act established that trademarks are legal property under the law and, unlike patents and copyrights, property rights on trademarks did not expire. The federal government also became an important third party enforcer with the passage of the Meat Inspection Act of 1891 and the Food and Drugs Act of 1906. If the advances in sciences and enabled firms to adulterate foods, it also became possible for scientists employed by the government and non-profit consumer watch-dog organizations to verify the claims made by producers (Young, 1989; Rao, 1998). Thus, for both firms and consumers, the federal government and consumer research organizations became important third party agents that could provide independent information on the quality and safety of products.

While the benefits of solving the asymmetric information problem were high, firms could not use the strategy of advertising and developing brand-names until the costs of marketing products fell sufficiently. For most of the nineteenth century, the task of marketing a product directly to consumers at the national level was simply daunting. Since the predominant media of communication was the local newspaper dailies and weeklies, a firm needed to collect information on the cost and benefits of advertising in each of these local newspapers. Given the lack of systematic data on the demographics and the size of readership of any given local newspaper, it was difficult to know what a firm should pay for a particular advertisement. In addition, it was not clear how a manufacturer would monitor whether the advertisements in all these local newspapers were placed honestly and correctly.

Just as the wholesale merchants emerged to coordinate the supply and demand of goods in an earlier era, advertising agencies arose to coordinate the supply and demand of advertisement space in geographically dispersed newspapers and periodicals (Hower, 1949; Pope, 1983). These agencies collected information on the benefits and costs of placing an advertisement for different types of products, bought space from these newspapers in bulk, and then re-sold these spaces in smaller blocks to advertisers. The growth of advertising agencies lowered the costs of marketing sufficiently for a growing number of manufacturers, but the real growth in national advertising by manufacturers did not occur until the rise of national mass-media magazines, radio and television.

In the early twentieth century, the retail multiunit firms, or chain stores, became the first important category of businesses to use the modern method of solving the asymmetric information problem (Lebhar, 1963). Although a growing number of manufacturing firms used advertising and brand-names to signal the quality of their products, it was still too costly for most producers to market their products directly to consumers. For retail chains, as population density increased with urbanization, the cost of marketing multiple stores in a given area fell dramatically. In addition, due to technological innovations such as the rotary steam press, the cost of printing local urban daily and weekly newspapers fell significantly. (See Wegberg & Witteloostuijn, this volume, for an analysis of the impact of new information technologies such as the internet and e-commerce on the structure of the economy.)

Table 1. Distribution of Chains Owning Private Brands, 1929–1930.

Stores per Chain	Chains	Stores	Chains w/ brands	Stores w/brands
2 to 5	886	2,901	14.2%	15.1%
6 to 10	323	2,412	21.4	21.4
11 to 25	224	3,529	37.5	37.4
26 to 50	99	3,481	44.4	46.2
51 to 100	57	4,236	57.9	58.5
101 to 500	53	11,679	77.4	81.5
501 to 1,000	8	4,831	75.0	79.1
1,001 and over	10	32,555	90.0	94.5
Total	1,660	65,624	24.8	76.9

Source: "Chain Store Advertising," *Chain Stores*, Federal Trade Commission, 1934.

The unique data on chain stores collected by the Federal Trade Commission (FTC) in the early 1930s provide unusually rich information on the costs and benefits of marketing products for multiunit retail firms. In May 1928, in order to investigate whether the chain stores violated anti-trust laws, the Senate approved an inquiry by the FTC that collected considerable information on the advantages and disadvantages of chain store distribution. The report took six years to complete and consists of 2,694 pages in four volumes. The FTC sample of firms consists of 1,727 retail chains in 26 lines of retail businesses. These retail chains operated 66,246 stores and sold more than $5 billion worth of merchandise and represented about one-half of all stores and sales operated by chains in 1928. In addition to collecting basic information on chain stores, the FTC conducted field studies and interviews (Kim, 1999b).

The FTC data on chain stores provide considerable evidence that these multi-unit retail firms arose to solve the asymmetric information problem by making firm-specific, sunk-cost investments in advertising and brand-names. The data indicate that retail chains like A&P developed their own private brand labels and advertised extensively to cultivate a reputation for their brands. Unlike the traditional retail stores who bought most of their goods from wholesalers and sold them to consumers in bulk, the retail chains increasingly purchased products directly from manufacturers and sold them as branded items. Moreover, there is considerable anecdotal evidence that many retail chains integrated backward into manufacturing only to preserve their brand identity by ensuring a consistent level of quality of their products.

The FTC data demonstrate that retail chains used private brands to signal quality to their consumers. The data shown in Table 1 indicate that chains with

Table 2. Private Brand Sales for Grocery Chain Stores.

	Chains	Stores	Sales ($1,000)	Brand Sales
1919*	26	1,467	$127,437	18.8%
1922*	57	2,133	192,631	21.3
1925*	95	3,986	377,333	27.7
1928*	187	14,751	1,270,128	20.4
1929*	255	19,754	1,815,567	28.3
1930*	274	21,450	1,859,311	27.9
1925	97	20,876	933,592	24.3%
1928	189	35,188	2,437,369	20.3
1929	257	40,748	3,140,821	24.3
1930	276	42,353	3,177,556	24.3

Source: "Chain Store Advertising," *Chain Stores*, Federal Trade Commission, 1934.
Note: *Excluding A&P and Kroger.

larger numbers of stores were more likely to use private brands. If a chain owned 2 to 5 stores, only 14% of these chains carried private brands and, if they owned 51–100 stores, 58% carried private brands. However, if the chain owned 1,001 stores or more, 90% of the chains used private brands. Table 2 shows the share of private brand sales for grocery chain stores. By 1930, private brand sales accounted for close to 30% of total sales and the figure was much higher for the very largest grocery chains.

The advertising data on chain stores suggest that the large multiunit retail firms spent significantly more on advertising than the smaller chain stores. Table 3 shows that, in 1929, if a chain owned 2 to 5 or 6 to 10 stores, it spent an average of $19,444 and $45,051 in advertising respectively. However, for the very large multiunit firms the advertising expenditure was significantly higher. If a chain owned 501 to 1,000 or over 1,000 stores, it spent $225,000 and $1,425,000 respectively. Thus, the value of firm-specific investments that would be lost by reneging on quality was significantly higher for the larger multiunit firms. In addition, there were significant economies in making this firm-specific investment for chain stores. For the smaller chains, advertising expenditures were about $6000 per store; for the very largest chains, they were less than $400.

The retail chains were acutely aware that private brands were devices that signaled a certain level of quality to consumers. An A& P executive noted: "Where the brand A&P is used, it is employed for the highest quality products

Table 3. Economies in Advertising for Multiunit Firms
in Retail Trade, 1928.

Stores Per Chain	Chains	Number of Stores	Advertising ($ mil.)	Advertising per chain	Advertising per store	Adv./Sales (percent)
2 to 5	792	2,595	$15.4	$19,444	$5,934	3.57%
6 to 10	293	2,17	13.2	45,051	6,058	3.74
11 to 25	205	3,248	6.7	32,683	2,063	2.58
26 to 50	97	3,404	5.1	52,577	1,498	1.88
51 to 100	55	4,052	3.9	70,909	962	1.63
101 to 500	48	10,600	8.1	168,750	764	1.15
501 to 1000	8	4,831	1.8	225,000	372	0.51
1,001 and over	8	29,030	11.4	1,425,000	393	0.67
Total	1,506	59,939	65.6	43,559	1,094	1.52

Source: "Chain Store Advertising," *Chain Stores*, Federal Trade Commission, 1934.

which are sold by this company under private label. The A&P brand never appears on a product having a quality lower than the highest quality we market ... At one time the top grade of all our private brands bore the A&P label. Now we have so-called family groups: A&P, Quaker Maid, Rajah, Encore, etc., any one of which labels may be on the highest quality of a given product; Rajah, in the case of salad dressing; Quaker Maid in the case of cocoa; Encore, in the case of spaghetti and macaroni; A&P, in the case of canned peas; Sunnyfield, in the case of flour. The other qualities of these products are under any one of a number of labels. The Iona brand is used for products of standard grade, and the Sultana brand for an intermediate grade, just under the standard set for highest quality. In some cases there is a second intermediate grade also. Thus, in canned peas, the A&P label designates a very fancy pea – the very best we can buy. Then there are Sultana, Reliable, and Iona peas, each a step further down in grade (*Chain Stores*, FTC, Vol. 3, 'Chain-Store Private Brands,' p. 50–51.)"

However, the retail chain stores faced significant challenges in controlling the quality level of their private brands. Many retail chains discovered that wholesale merchants were unreliable in providing products of consistent quality. The growing importance of the asymmetric information problem led to the rise of multiunit retail firms, but it also squeezed out the wholesalers in the distribution channel as retail chains contracted directly with manufacturers. The data in Table 4 indicate that many large retail chains purchased their private brand

Table 4. Proportion of Merchandise Purchased from Manufacturers by
Retail Chain Stores, 1928.

Stores Per Chain	(A) Dry Goods & Gen Mer.	(B) Grocery	(C) Drug, Tob., Hard., Music	(D) Meat, Variety, Dry Goods	(E) Apparel, Dept. Store, Furniture
2 to 5	29.4%	27.2%	39.5%	61.2%	83.8%
6 to 10	16.9	40.6	53.8	56.0	93.5
11 to 25	25.0	35.3	76.6	70.0	92.9
26 to 50	–	43.2	73.0	88.4	98.7
51 to 100	–	53.2	91.9	72.4	96.4
101 to 500	–	54.4	77.2	89.6	95.0
501 to 1000	–	38.9	95.2	90.0	–
1,001 and over	–	66.4	95.1	95.0	–

Source: "Sources of Chain-Store Merchandise," *Chain Stores*, Federal Trade Commission, 1934.

items directly from the manufacturers. In some instances, retail chains found that the only way to maintain consistent quality was to produce the goods themselves. While it was costly to integrate backward into manufacturing, it was necessary to maintain the reputation of the brand.

The FTC field interviews of many different types of chain store businesses provide wonderful anecdotal evidence that chain stores manufactured goods mainly due to their concerns on maintaining a consistent quality. A confectionary firm responded: "Our line is not adaptable to wholesale manufactures principally because it does not keep fresh long enough for that purpose. We use butter, fresh cream, and other highly perishable ingredients which make much finer goods but are not suitable for use with the wholesaler's methods of manufacture and distribution." A shoe store manager responded: "Our principal reason and advantage for manufacturing shoes for ourselves is that we are certain to continually keep the standard of construction that we desire. Too often manufacturers who have not the 100% interest of the retailer at heart will deviate even if only slightly from the standard if necessity compels them to." A drug store manager wrote: "We actually have better chemists and at higher salaries than most manufacturers employ, and we think our merchandise, either ice cream or shaving cream, is of standard that is not surpassed by anybody else. This is very important with things like milk of magnesia and other similar items and we know that our merchandise is very high grade. In other words, if your farm out private-brand stuff there is a certain tendency to cut corners and we insist on high quality, not because we are saints but because it is good business."

Finally, a testimony of an apparel chain manager suggests that consumers are uncertain whether a certain type of clothing is fashionable and that the retail chain store builds its reputation on up-to-date style: "Our company is engaged primarily in manufacturing, and the principal reason for our operating our chain of retail stores is to enable us to foresee the consumer demand for styles and colors and to regulate manufacturing accordingly. Through having these chain of retail stores, we are enabled to see from day to day the trend in styles and colors, and through doing this, have been able to effect large savings in our manufacturing operations by not piling up merchandise that is not readily salable; we also sell our merchandise to retailers throughout the country and the experience gained in our own retail shops which, incidentally, are located entirely in metropolitan district with one exception, has enabled us to tell our dealers from time to time the style and color trend (*Chain Stores*, FTC, Vol. 3, 'Chain-Store Private Brands.')"

The FTC data suggest that the retail chains were also able to establish a reputation for lower prices than the single-unit establishments. The FTC collected information on prices of identical products sold by chains and independent stores for groceries and drugs in four cities, Washington DC, Cincinnati, Memphis and Detroit. The data in Table 5 show that in groceries, the chain store prices were lower than that of independent stores by 6 to 10%; in drugs, the difference was even larger and ranged between 10 to 20% depending upon how one averaged the different products (see also Tedlow's (1996: 201) review of 11 additional studies). The theoretical literature on the use of advertising and brand-names to solve the asymmetric information problem on quality do not apply to those on prices. In fact, in the Klein and Leffler (1981) model, firms who commit to higher quality through advertising and branding are able to charge higher prices. Nevertheless, even if the theory is less well developed with respect to prices, the data suggests that multiunit firms are also able to build reputations for lower prices.

Despite the success of urban retail chains, manufacturing firms quickly adopted the multiunit form of organizing production and soon replaced retail chains in importance. Once the costs of marketing fell sufficiently, multiunit manufacturing firms discovered that they were generally more effective in solving the asymmetric information problem than the retail chains. Even though the retail chains were able to develop a certain level of reputation for their private brands through advertising, they faced enormous challenges in maintaining a consistent level of quality. Since manufacturers and wholesalers did not make the same firm specific investments in advertising and private brands, these firms did not have the same incentive for maintaining the proper level of quality as the retail chains. Consequently, there was always an incentive for

Table 5.   Prices of Chain and Independent Distributors.

Independents	Groceries		Drugs	
	Chains		Independents	Chains
Washington DC	$58.03	$54.08	$130.09	$117.49
Cincinnati	23.35	21.95	143.34	130.54
Memphis	38.11	35.96	119.17	106.02
Detroit	35.66	33.26	144.73	129.67
	Groceries		Drugs	
	Unweighted	Geometric Avg	Unweighted	Geometric Average
Washington DC	7.3%	6.4%	10.7%	22.7%
Cincinnati	6.4	8.8	9.8	20.4
Memphis	6.0	8.3	12.4	20.7
Detroit	7.2	10.5	11.6	17.5

Source: "Chain Store Advertising," Chain Stores, Federal Trade Commission, 1934.
Note: Prices cannot be compared across cities. The bundle of goods used to compare prices of chains and independents differ across cities. In groceries, the number of items used is as follows: DC, 274; Cincinnati, 120; Memphis, 193; Detroit, 183. In drugs, they are: DC, 226; Cincinnati, 268; Memphis, 212; Detroit, 256.

manufacturers and wholesalers to pass lower quality products onto the retail chains.

Unfortunately, there is little systematic information on the extent to which firms in manufacturing were organized as multiunit firms in the early twentieth century (see Thorp (1924); Thorp, Crowder et al. (1941)). Nevertheless, there is considerable indirect evidence on their growing importance. One compelling source of information comes from data on advertising expenditures. In the early twentieth century, advertising expenditures grew significantly. Between 1890 and 1929, advertising expenditures are estimated to have risen from $190 million to $2.987 billion, or as a percentage of gross national product, from 1.5% to 2.9% (Pope, 1983, p. 23). There is strong evidence that the growth of advertising expenditures over this period was driven by national advertising campaigns of manufacturers. For example, the largest advertisers in national magazines were manufacturers. Of the 58 firms who spent at least $100,000 for advertising in major national magazines in any one of the years between 1913 and 1915, the data show that 57 firms were in manufacturing. In addition, the largest advertisers were clustered in a few industries; fourteen in foods, thirteen in automobiles and tires, and nine in chemicals (see Pope (1983, 44–46)).

In the second half of the twentieth century, with the introduction of the *Enterprise Statistics* program, the U.S. census bureau began providing census level information on firms. Until this publication, most of the data published by the U.S. census bureau was based on establishments or plants. When the various census programs were established, most firms were single-unit establishments and it was natural for the census bureau to report data categorized at the plant level. However, when firms became multiunit and owned multiple establishments, the traditional census data no longer provided information on firms. In the second half of the twentieth century, when it finally became feasible to coordinate all the censuses to construct data at the firm level of aggregation, the census bureau began reporting this information in its publication called the *Enterprise Statistics* (see Kim (1999a, b) for more detailed information).

The *Enterprise Statistics* published between 1954 and 1987 provide the first systematic account of the extent to which economic activity in the United States is organized by multiunit firms. Although most establishments or plants continue to be organized as single-unit firms, the data in Table 6 indicate that multiunit firms accounted for over half of all employees in 1954. Surprisingly, the overall level of multiunit activity has remained relatively constant over the second half of the twentieth century. Between 1954 and 1987, the proportion of employment in multiunit activity remained consistently between 50–60%.

The *Enterprise Statistics* reports do not provide information on topics such as advertising and the use of national brands by multiunit firms, but they provide considerable indirect information which can be used to examine whether or not they arose to solve the asymmetric information problem. Since products in some industries are more likely to have an asymmetric information problem than in others, the benefits of using advertising and brand-names as devices to signal product quality are likely to differ across industries. Thus, the extent of multiunit activities in different industries may provide interesting clues to whether

Table 6. The Share of Employment in Multiunit Firms, 1954–1987.

	1954	1958	1963	1967	1972	1977	1982	1987
All	52.0%	53.8%	55.8%	55.4%	57.5%	58.6%	51.4%	55.5%
Minerals	57.2	56.7	51.9	58.1	67.3	64.6	55.5	55.5
Construction	–	–	–	17.0	21.5	24.6	23.7	16.9
Manufacturing	64.4	67.4	70.0	74.5	77.4	77.9	77.0	76.2
Public warehouse	24.7	34.6	30.0	–	–	–	–	–
Wholesale trade	26.8	29.8	29.3	32.4	35.1	39.8	39.4	43.1
Retail trade	38.7	40.2	43.0	44.4	49.9	51.6	53.3	58.8
Services	23.4	27.5	29.0	30.1	36.0	37.1	–	40.3

Source: *Enterprise Statistics*, 1954–1987.

the costs and benefits of marketing in different industries are likely to explain the industry variations in multiunit activity.

The data on multiunit activity by industries show that the extent of multi-unit activity differed significantly across the major sectors of the economy. Table 6 shows that, in 1954, multiunit activity was most important in manu-facturing and minerals and least important in services and wholesale trade. In that year, multiunit employment in manufacturing and minerals accounted for 64% and 57% of employment in these sectors. In services and wholesale trade, the respective figures were 23% and 27%. The figure for retail trade was in between at 39%. Except for the mineral industry which fluctuated over time, the importance of multiunit activity grew over the second half of the twentieth century. In manufacturing, the percentage of multiunit employment rose to 77% in 1977 but plateaued at that level thereafter. On the other hand, multiunit firms in retail trade, wholesale trade and services steadily grew in importance over this period so that in 1987, 59%, 43% and 40% of the employment in these respective sectors was organized under these firms.

The industry data on multiunit firms suggest an interesting hypothesis on the historical changes in the industrial structure of the U.S. economy. In the late nineteenth and the early twentieth centuries, as argued in the previous section, retail chains arose to solve the asymmetric information problem when costs of marketing fell in urban areas. In the first half of the twentieth century, with the introduction of new national media of communications such as the radio and the television, the costs of marketing fell sufficiently for manufacturing firms to use advertising, brand-names and multiunit organization as a mechanism for signaling product quality. In the second half of the twentieth century, as the population became increasingly more mobile, the benefits of establishing brand-names in services increased. Thus, the extent of multiunit activity in the various services increased steadily over the second half of the twentieth century.

The *Enterprise Statistics* data on industry specialization or diversification by multiunit firms are also likely to provide important information on whether the multiunit firm arose to solve the asymmetric information problem. Since these firms are more likely to develop a reputation for brands for a similar class of products, they are more likely to be organized as horizontal rather than as vertical firms. (See Phillips & Mason, this volume, and Stephan & Boeker, this volume, for alternative analyses of markets which are horizontally connected.) The data in Table 7 show that multiunit firms in most sectors were more special-ized than diversified. In 1954, over 75% of employment in manufacturing and over 90% in minerals, wholesale trade, retail trade, and services were in the same industry at the 3-digit industry level. Although the specialization ratio for most sectors declines over the twentieth century, the ratio remains above 90%

Table 7. The Share of Employment of Multiunit Firms in Same Industries, 1954–1987.

	1954	1958	1963	1967	1972	1977	1982	1987
All	84.7%	84.0%	80.2%	78.9%	77.1%	76.9%	79.8%	83.0%
Minerals	90.9	85.3	84.6	83.0	73.2	73.7	76.9	79.9
Construction	–	–	–	96.4	94.9	93.4	93.0	95.8
Manufacturing	77.3	75.8	70.2	65.4	60.8	60.2	58.0	63.8
Public warehouse	98.3	93.0	96.3	–	–	–	–	–
Wholesale trade	95.4	96.6	95.3	93.8	93.0	91.0	90.3	90.0
Retail trade	94.5	93.4	91.4	90.2	88.4	88.1	88.1	89.4
Services	98.3	97.4	95.8	96.2	94.0	93.6	–	93.9

Source: *Enterprise Statistics*, 1954–1987.

for the service sectors. In manufacturing, the specialization ratio declines to a low of 58% in 1982 before rising to 64% in 1987.

Even in the manufacturing sector, a more careful examination suggests that industry diversification was much lower if one defined products more broadly. In 1958, the *Enterprise Statistics* reports provide a detailed list of other industry activities by multiunit firms so that a relatively complete picture of diversification can be constructed at various levels of industry aggregation. If one defines industries at the 3-digit industry level, the data indicate that only 13 of 91 3-digit industries in manufacturing employed more than 30% of their employees in vertical or unrelated industries. However, if horizontal integration is measured by 2-digit rather than 3-digit categories for these 13 industries, the level of diversification falls sharply for many industries except for the integrated petroleum industry (Kim, 1999b).

Finally, the data on the number and size of establishments operated by multi-unit firms provide additional information on whether these firms arose to solve the asymmetric information problem. If multiunit firms arose to take advantage of economies of marketing rather than those of scale, then there should be little correlation between plant sizes and multiunit firms since there is no relationship between marketing and production technologies. Indeed, Kim (1999a, b) finds that horizontal multiunit firms grew in size predominantly by operating many more establishments rather than by operating plants of large sizes.

The analysis of the rise and growth of multiunit firms presented in this paper differs sharply with that of Alfred Chandler. Chandler in his works, the *Visible Hand* (1977) and *Scale and Scope* (1990), argued that the fundamental advantage of the modern multiunit firm is related to production technology rather than its ability to lower market transactions costs. For Chandler, the modern multiunit firm arose to take advantage of economies of speed and flow of throughput (or economies of scale) in production. Since it was necessary for firms to integrate forward into distribution to ensure sales of sufficient volume and vertically integrate backwards into raw materials to ensure a constant flow of inputs, the traditional single-unit firms did not have the organizational structure necessary for taking advantage of economies of scale and scope.

Chandler (1977) also provides a narrative history of the evolution of industrial organizations in the United States. In the eighteenth and the nineteenth centuries, when transportation costs were high, traditional single-unit firms produced and distributed goods in the economy. However, as transportation costs fell and markets expanded, modern multiunit firms arose to take advantage of economies of throughput. For Chandler, the multiunit firms arose first in the mass distribution sector because the decline in transportation and communications costs was all that was necessary to take advantage of speed of throughput. However, it required more time for multiunit firms to arise in the manufacturing sector since many basic inventions and innovations in production technology were necessary to achieve economies of scale. Finally, the revolution culminated with the integration of mass production and mass distribution as the modern industrial firms integrated forward into distribution and backward into raw materials.

In contrast, this paper suggests that the modern multiunit firm arose because it was better able to solve the asymmetric information problem concerning the quality and price of products. In the late nineteenth century, with advances in science and technology, consumers no longer possessed sufficient knowledge to judge the quality of the products which they routinely purchased. This paper argues that the multiunit firms arose in this period because they were able to use the strategy of making firm-specific, sunk-cost investments in advertising and branding to credibly earn the trust of consumers on the quality of their products. Since the value of advertising and brand-names is designed to signal the value of repeat sales that is lost if one reneged on quality, the large multiunit firms had significant advantages over the traditional single-unit firms.

However, the multiunit firms could not use the strategy of advertising and branding until the costs of marketing fell sufficiently. Since the costs of national marketing was simply too prohibitive in the late nineteenth and the early twentieth century, the multiunit firms first arose in retail trade. As the population became urbanized and as urban newspapers lowered the costs of advertising, retail firms re-organized as multiunit chains and developed private brands to signal product quality. Unfortunately, the urban retailers had a significant problem in maintaining the quality of their branded products since their suppliers did not make the same firm-specific investments in the brand.

The wholesalers and manufacturers who sold the products to retailers did not have the same incentive to maintain product quality as specified by a brand. Thus, when the costs of national marketing fell with the introduction of national mass magazines, radio and television, manufacturing firms quickly re-organized as multiunit firms. For many products, the multiunit manufacturing firms discovered that they were more effective in solving the asymmetric information problem than the retail chains.

IV. CONCLUSION

Ever since the publication of Adam Smith's *Wealth of Nations*, scholars have understood the potential benefits of specialization. Yet, given that these benefits can only be achieved through trade, economists, especially in international economics, have also known that specialization introduces new transaction costs, namely transportation costs. Indeed, this is precisely the reason why division of labor is limited by the extent of the market or why specialization is triggered by a decline in transportation costs in the standard models of trade. Surprisingly, the idea that specialization introduces transactions costs associated with loss in information has received much less attention. With specialization, consumers know their demands but not the supply conditions of production and firms know their costs but not the demand for their products. While market prices provide valuable information to both buyers and sellers, they are not provided without costs. The existence of the vast array of middlemen who coordinate and facilitate transactions, and the fact that cities arise in part to lower the costs of these transactions, are signs that costs of providing market prices are far from trivial (Wallis & North, 1986; Kim, 2000).

In the late nineteenth and the twentieth centuries, specialization greatly increased the information costs of a different type associated with asymmetric information. In an earlier era, most goods were produced using craft technology that used hand tools and simple machines and were often produced in local homes and small shops. Given the relative simplicity of the production process, consumers could easily discern the quality of the product either through visual inspection or through the reputation of the local producer or retail store owner. In the new era, as production technology became scientifically sophisticated and as goods were produced in factories far from consumers' residences, information became increasingly asymmetric. While firms knew the quality of their products, consumers were less able to use their four senses and knowledge to judge even the most basic of products such as food and household chemicals, let alone the endless variety of new durable consumer goods which emerged over time. In this environment, an increasing number of firms faced the "lemons" problem where lower quality goods tended to out-compete ones of higher quality.

In the early twentieth century, modern multiunit firms emerged in a number of industries because they were better able to solve the asymmetric information problem. While the traditional industrial structure composed of specialized single-unit producers, wholesale merchants, and retail store owners was able to efficiently produce and distribute goods when information was dispersed, it was unable to solve the problem of asymmetric information. In a variety of industries, as firms re-organized as multiunit firms to tackle the asymmetric information problem, a new industrial structure emerged. Since the value of repeat sales was significantly higher for multiunit rather than single-unit firms in many industries, the multiunit firms were able make large firm-specific, sunk cost investments in advertising and branding to credibly signal to buyers that the costs of reneging on quality were high. Thus, this paper suggests that a better understanding of the transaction costs associated with specialization, especially those associated with information costs, are likely to shed considerable insights on the rise of multiunit firms and the evolving structure of American industry.

ACKNOWLEDGMENTS

I am grateful to Doug North for the many encouraging and stimulating conversations which led to the ideas presented in this paper. I thank the two editors, Joel Baum and Henrich Greve, for providing many helpful suggestions and constructive editorial advice, and Andrew Godley for his incisive comments on my earlier papers.

REFERENCES

Akerlof, G. A. (1970). Market for 'Lemons': Quality Uncertainty and the Market Mechanism. *Quarterly Journal of Economics*, *84*, 488–500.
Carlton, D. W., & Perloff, J. M. (1994). *Modern Industrial Organization* (2nd ed). New York: NY: HarperCollins.
Chandler, A. (1977). *The Visible Hand*. Cambridge, MA: Belknap Press.
Chandler, A. (1990). *Scale and Scope*. Cambridge, MA: Belknap Press.
Federal Trade Commission. (1931–1934). *Chain Stores*. Volumes I–IV. Washington DC: GPO.
Hower, R. M. (1949). *The History of an Advertising Agency: N.W. Ayer & Son at Work 1869–1949*. Cambridge, MA: Harvard University Press.
Jones, F. M. (1937). *Middlemen in the Domestic Trade of the United States 1800–1850*. Urbana, IL: University of Illinois.
Kallet, A., & Schlink, F. (1933). *100,000,000 Guinea Pigs: Dangers in Foods, Drugs, and Cosmetics*. New York, NY: Grosset & Dunlap.

Kim, S. (1995). Expansion of Markets and the Geographic Distribution of Economic Activities: Trends in U.S. Regional Manufacturing Structure, 1860–1987. *Quarterly Journal of Economics, 110*(4), 881–908.

Kim, S. (1999a). The Rise of Multiunit Firms in U.S. Manufacturing. *Explorations in Economic History, 36*(4), 360–386.

Kim, S. (1999b). The Growth of Modern Business Enterprises in the Twentieth Century. *Research in Economic History, 19*, 75–110.

Kim, S. (2000). Urban Development in the United States, 1690–1990. *Southern Economic Journal, 66*(4), 855–880.

Klein, B., & Leffler, K. B. (1981). The Role of Market Forces in Assuring Contractual Performance. *Journal of Political Economy, 89*, 615–641.

Lebhar, G. M. (1963). *Chain Stores in America, 1859–1962.* Clinton, MA: Colonial Press Inc.

Libecap, G. D. (1992). The Rise of the Chicago Packers and the Origins of Meat Inspection and Antitrust. *Economic Inquiry, 30*, 242–262.

McCusker, J. J., & Menard, R. R. (1985). *The Economy of the British America, 1607–1789.* Chapel Hill, NC: University of North Carolina Press.

Nelson, P. (1970). Information and Consumer Behavior. *Journal of Political Economy, 78*, 311–329.

Phillips, O. R., & Mason, C. F. (2001). Collusion in Horizontally Connected Markets: Multimarket Producers as Conduits for Learning. In: J. A. C. Baum & H. R. Greve (Eds), *Multiunit Organization and Multimarket Strategy: Advances in Strategic Management, 18* (pp. 207–229). Oxford, UK: JAI Press.

Pope, D. (1983). *The Making of Modern Advertising.* New York, NY: Basic Books.

Porter, G., & Livesay, H. C. (1971). *Merchants and Manufacturers.* Chicago, IL: Ivan R. Dee, Inc.

Rao, H. (1998). Caveat Emptor: The Construction of Nonprofit Consumer Watchdog Organizations. *American Journal of Sociology, 103*, 912–961.

Schmalensee, R. (1978). A Model of Advertising and Product Quality. *Journal of Political Economy, 86*, 485–503.

Shepherd, J. F., & Walton, G. M. (1972). *Shipping, Maritime Trade, and the Economic Development of Colonial North America.* Cambridge, UK. Cambridge University Press.

Sokoloff, K. L. (1984a). Investment in Fixed and Working Capital during Early Industrialization: Evidence from U.S. Manufacturing Firms. *Journal of Economic History, 44*, 545–556.

Sokoloff, K. L. (1984b). Was the Transition from the Artisanal Shop to the Non-Mechanized Factory Associated with Gains in Efficiency? Evidence from the U.S. Manufacturing Censuses of 1820 and 1850. *Explorations in Economic History, 21*, 351–382.

Sokoloff, K. L. (1988). Inventive Activity in Early Industrial America: Evidence From Patent Records, 1790–1846. *Journal of Economic History, 48*, 813–849.

Stephan, J., & Boeker, W. (2001). Getting to Multimarket Competition: How Multimarket Contact Affects Firms' Market Entry Decisions. In: J. A. C. Baum & H. R. Greve (Eds), *Multiunit Organization and Multimarket Strategy: Advances in Strategic Management, 18* (pp. 231–263). Oxford, UK: JAI Press.

Strasser, S. (1989). *Satisfaction Guaranteed.* Washington, DC: Smithsonian Institutions Press.

Taylor, G. (1951). *The Transportation Revolution.* Cambridge, MA: Harvard University Press.

Tedlow, R. S. (1996). *New and Improved.* Cambridge, MA: Harvard Business School Press.

Thorp, W. (1924). *The Integration of Industrial Operation.* Washington, DC: GPO.

Thorp, W., & Crowder, W. et al. (1941). *The Structure of Industry.* Washington, DC: GPO.

Tryon, R. M. (1917). *Household Manufactures in the United States, 1640–1860.* New York, NY: Sentry Press.

U.S. Bureau of the Census, *Enterprise Statistics* (Washington, DC: G.P.O.), various years.

Wallis, J., & North, D. (1986). Measuring the Transaction Sector in the American Economy, 1870–1970. In: S. Engerman & R. Gallman (Eds), *Long-Term Factors in American Economic Growth*. Chicago: University of Chicago Press.

Walton, G. M., & Rockoff, H. (1998). *History of the American Economy* (8th ed.). New York: NY: Dryden Press.

Wegberg, M. van, & Witteloostuijn, Arjen van. (2001). Strategic Management in the New Economy: Information Technologies and Multicontact Competition. In: J. A. C. Baum & H. R. Greve (Eds), *Multiunit Organization and Multimarket Strategy: Advances in Strategic Management, 18* (pp. 265–306). Oxford, UK: JAI Press.

Yeager, M. (1981). *Competition and Regulation: The Development of Oligopoly in the Meat Packing Industry*. Greenwich, CT: JAI Press.

Young, J. H. (1989). *Pure Food: Securing the Federal Food and Drug Act of 1906*. Princeton, NJ: Princeton University Press.

Part Four:
OUTCOMES

RACING FOR MARKET SHARE: HYPERCOMPETITION AND THE PERFORMANCE OF MULTIUNIT-MULTIMARKET FIRMS

Stan Xiao Li and You-Ta Chuang

ABSTRACT

Research linking firms' hypercompetitive strategic actions and performance focuses on firm level performance, and assumes that the impact of each firm's strategic actions affects only a limited number of other firms. We advance a complementary perspective for multiunit-multimarket firms in which the action-performance linkage operates at the market-unit level (i.e. within a specific geographic product or service market), and strategic actions within a market-unit are assumed to affect all other firms participating in that market-unit. Supporting the perspective, our analysis of Canadian insurance firms shows that these firms' performance in a market-unit depends on the number and simplicity of their strategic actions in that market unit – both absolutely and vis-à-vis those of others competing in the market unit. Our study offers new insight into how multiunit-multimarket firms compete across a series of market-units – and how they can compete more effectively.

Multiunit Organization and Multimarket Strategy, Volume 18, pages 329–355.
2001 by Elsevier Science Ltd.
ISBN: 0-7623-0721-8

INTRODUCTION

Researchers in strategic management and industrial organization have increasingly come to view firms' strategic actions designed to create a series of short-term advantages by challenging the status quo of the market process as vital to their performance (D'Aveni, 1994; Jacobson, 1992; Miller & Chen, 1994). The theoretical foundation for this view, first set out over 60 years ago by Austrian economists, advances the idea that firms' strategic advantages will be eroded if they are too slow to respond and insufficiently aggressive in defending their positions and initiating attacks on their competitors (Kirzner, 1997; Schumpeter, 1934; Young, Smith & Grimm, 1996). Empirical research on the linkage between such 'hypercompetitive' rivalry and firm performance remains rare. Recently, however, Ferrier, Smith and Grimm (1999) demonstrated that industry leaders – firms with greatest market share – were more likely to experience market share erosion and dethronement from their lead position when their rivals adopted more aggressive, complex and swift attacks.

Although Ferrier et al.'s (1999) research offers compelling evidence of the impact of hypercompetitive strategic actions on firm performance, these insights have not yet been applied to hyercompetition among multiunit-multimarket (MUMM) firms. A MUMM firm is one that engages in business activities in more than one 'market unit' – a geographic product or service market (e.g. marine insurance sold in the Province of Ontario). MUMM firms within the same industry usually engage in multipoint competition, facing off against one another in a series of market-units. The complexity of a MUMM firm's strategic interactions is best reflected in the potential that its strategic actions in one market-unit have for triggering its rivals to retaliate in other market-units. This added complexity may result from a firm and its rivals viewing the importance of the same market-unit differently (McGrath, Chen & MacMillan, 1998), because, for example, they have carved out their respective strongholds in different market-units (Baum & Korn, 1999).

In this study, we examine the linkage between hypercompetitive strategic action and firm performance among MUMM firms. We articulate the linkage between MUMM firms' strategic actions and performance, and test four hypotheses relating the characteristics – number and simplicity – of MUMM firms' strategic actions in a market-unit to their performance in that market-unit. We consider the characteristics of firms' strategic actions in both absolute terms and relative to the strategic actions of other firms competing in the same market-unit. We employ hierarchical linear modeling (HLM) to analyze our data on 232 MUMM firms competing in the 193 market units comprising the Canadian property and casualty insurance industry from 1993 to 1998. The nature of this market and firms competing within it provides an excellent opportunity to examine the relationship between MUMM firms' hypercompetitive strategic actions and their market-unit performance.

HYPERCOMPETITIVE STRATEGIC ACTIONS AND FIRM PERFORMANCE

The relationship between a firm's strategic actions and its performance is central to the field of strategic management. Rooted in the structure-conduct-performance (SCP) paradigm (Bain, 1951), traditional theory in strategic management suggests that firms employ strategic actions to stake out superior and defensible positions from which they can fend off threats imposed by industry-level forces (Andrews, 1971; Caves & Porter, 1977; Porter, 1980). Such positions enable firms to earn abnormal rents by creating and sustaining imperfectly competitive markets (Teece, Pisano & Shuen, 1997). For some time now, however, this traditional view has been challenged on the grounds that it overlooks the competitive impact of innovative firms' efforts and achievements (Jacobson, 1992; Nelson & Winter, 1982; Schumpeter, 1934). Innovative firms undermine the sustainability of rivals' competitive advantages by overcoming barriers to entry, changing the rules and basis of competition, increasing the uncertainty and speed of change, and raising customer expectations – and demands. The more transitory nature of competitive advantages under such circumstances makes application of SWOT analysis (Andrews, 1971; Steiner, 1979), McKinsey's 7S's (Gluck, 1986), or generic strategies (Porter, 1980) of limited use for providing insight into the motivation for, or the consequences of, strategic actions. Indeed, in dynamic competitive environments, possibilities for specifying 'optimal configurations' for organizational strategies seem limited.

In contrast to traditional approaches, the hypercompetitive rivalry perspective embraces the idea that firms' competitive advantages will be short-lived as competitors' aggressive strategic actions frequently disrupt causal linkages between strategic conduct and firm performance (Jacobson, 1992; Kirzner, 1997; Schumpeter, 1934). The dynamic, disequilibrium nature of hypercompetitive industries forces firms competing within them to launch strategic actions continuously as they pursue a stream of temporary competitive advantages. From this perspective, firms must endeavor, through their strategic actions, to continuously generate new competitive advantages and destroy, render obsolete, or neutralize their rivals' advantages (D'Aveni, 1994). These incessant strategic actions aim to keep competitors off balance, restructure the basis of industry competition, and provide new albeit fleeting advantages that improve firm performance.

Despite their differences, SCP and hypercompetition perspectives agree that a key determinant of firms' success or failure is their purposeful strategic actions. The SCP framework assumes that firms take purposeful actions to achieve a sustainable, advantageous position given industry conditions. In contrast, the hypercompetition perspective views firms' continuous strategic actions as resulting in superior performance when they produce a series of transitory advantages.

Hypercompetitive Strategic Actions and MUMM Firm Performance

Relating MUMM firms' hypercompetitive strategic actions to their performance poses two conceptual issues: level of analysis incongruence and range of strategic actions' impact (see Gimeno & Jeong for an in-depth discussion of the theoretical and empirical implications of level incongruence for MUMM research). For MUMM firms, the level at which strategic interaction unfolds is not necessarily the firm. Strategic actions and reactions are often undertaken in one or a few market-units, rather than at the level of the entire firm. One implication of this contrast in levels is that MUMM firms' strategic actions, while systematically related to market-unit performance, may be only weakly related to overall firm performance. Another is that impact of strategic actions on MUMM firms' performance depends crucially on the market-units in which the actions occur. Below we briefly consider each issue.

Level of Analysis Incongruence
MUMM firms are reluctant to launch across-the-board strategic actions because they are costly and, if unsuccessful, can threaten the viability of the entire corporate entity. Airlines, for example, offer discounts on selected routes, rather than across-the-board, having learned the hard way that such actions can damage corporate performance severely, particularly for a market leader. MUMM firms' strategic actions are thus typically focused at the market-unit level, entailing rivalry in one product in multiple locations or multiple products in a single location, or more complex still, multiple products in multiple locations. The most direct impact of these localized interactions is performance (e.g. market share) changes among competitors across the market-units in which the interactions occur. Although, particular strategic actions (e.g. mergers and acquisitions) can affect the performance of MUMM firms more broadly, the impact of most strategic actions is more localized to the particular market units involved.

Mutual forbearance among MUMM firms can also attenuate the relationship between their market-unit level strategic interactions and their firm-level market shares. If a MUMM firm i, for example, undertakes an aggressive strategic action in market-unit P_1, its rivals in P_1 may counter in market-unit P_2. And gain in firm i's market share resulting from its action in P_1 may thus be offset by a loss of market share in P_2 (Baum & Korn, 1996; 1999; Edwards, 1955; McGrath et al., 1998). Thus, even though there have been changes in i's market share in both P_1 and P_2, there may be no overall change in firm i's market share across all market-units – that is at the corporate level.

These observations suggest that the relationship between MUMM firms' strategic actions will have a more systematic impact on firm performance at the market-unit level, than at the firm level. Consequently, we examine the strategic action-performance linkage for MUMM firms at the market-unit level (Baum & Korn, 1999). This focuses our attention on strategic interactions among MUMM firms *within* market-units, and facilitates understanding the role of market-unit attributes on the action-performance linkage from MUMM firms.

Range of Action Impact
A second and related theoretical challenge lies in specifying the range of market-unit actions' impact. D'Aveni (1994) suggests that, while focused on one or a few market-units, hypercompetitive strategic actions are often directed at more than one rival and, consequently, influence more than one competitor. Strategic groups researchers (e.g. Hunt, 1972; Porter, 1980) suggest similarly that firms' strategic actions are more likely to be targeted at rival members of the same strategic group, and that the impact of these actions, although not necessarily restricted only to these firms, is felt with greater force among them.

For MUMM firms, the market-unit is the arena in which all competing firms meet (Baum & Korn, 1996), and to which, as we noted above, the impacts of most strategic actions are localized. A MUMM firm's strategic actions in a market-unit can, however, affect many, or possibly all, firms competing in the market-unit. For example, fare reductions and route entries by airlines on a given route were noticed by and countered by many or all other airlines serving the route (Baum & Korn, 1996; Gimeno, 1999). Similarly, rivalry among MUMM hotels at one location led to price collusion among all hotels at that location (Fernández & Marín, 1998). These ideas and evidence suggest that MUMM firms' strategic actions in a market-unit will affect the market-unit performance of firms' undertaking the actions and all their competitors in the market-unit in which the actions occurred.

Hypercompetitive Strategic Interactions and MUMM Firm Performance

A fundamental insights of the hypercompetition perspective is that it is not just a firm's own strategic actions that determine its success, but the effectiveness of its strategic actions vis-à-vis those of its competitors. "There are no absolutes in strategy. A company's competitive position and the sustainability of its advantage are related to the moves of its competitors ... [The] movement by competitors also affects the *sustainability* of a given strategy" (D'Aveni, 1994, p. 227, italics in original). An example illustrates this insight. The fact that a basketball team has been scoring 100 points per game is not a particularly strong predictor of the team's performance in a particular game. However, this information becomes highly predictive and useful when we know that its next opponent has been scoring 120 points per game. The fact that the opponent has been scoring an average of 20 points more per game is an indication of how disadvantaged the team may be facing the opponent. Firms' absolute level of strategic action may thus have less predictive power than its strategic actions relative to other firms in the market-unit. How a firm fares in strategic *interaction* matters most – the success or failure of a firm's strategic actions depends on the responses (or non-responses) of its competitors (Chen & Miller, 1994).

The level of *market-unit rivalry* thus defines the rules of competition in a market-unit. Discontinuous patterns of market-unit rivalry can disrupt causal linkages between MUMM firms' strategic actions and performance and render useless firms' strategists' mental model of competition (Bogner & Barr, 2000; Weick, 1995). The effectiveness of current strategic actions is undermined as originally novel moves and countermoves become mundane and previously unpredictable repertoires of moves become easily anticipated. In hypercompetition, this disruptive process is the norm, rather than exception. Persistent market-unit disruption requires constant surveillance, interpretation andinitiative, and may even alter key determinants of performance (e.g. innovation vs. efficiency), and thus the nature of the strategic action-performance linkage.

HYPOTHESES

The concept of hypercompetition centers on the dynamic nature of firms' strategic interactions. Although there are other barometers of hypercompetition, the dynamism of hypercompetitive strategic actions is captured well by the aggressiveness and the intricacy of these actions (D'Aveni, 1994). To reflect the aggressiveness and intricacy of strategic actions, we consider the impact of strategic actions on MUMM firms' market-unit performance along two dimensions – number of strategic actions and strategic action simplicity. Our model of the market-unit strategic action-performance linkage for MUMM firms is summarized in Fig. 1.

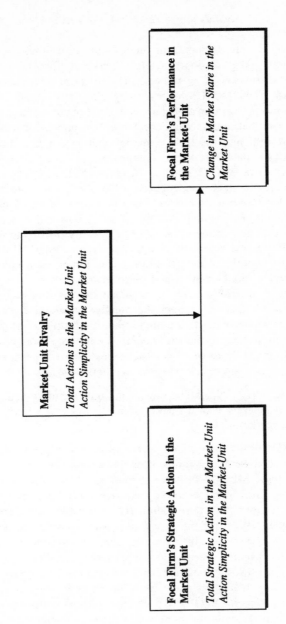

Fig. 1. Linking Multiunit-Multimarket Firms' Strategic Actions and Performance.

Number of Strategic Actions in a Market-Unit

In their quest to out-compete their rivals, firms must engage in a series of continuous and escalating strategic actions to disrupt the market-unit status quo. Market disruption is a prerequisite for earning abnormal economic rents (Jacobson, 1992). MUMM firms engaging in a greater number of strategic actions in a market-unit signal a higher level of competitive intensity and aggressiveness in that market-unit. The larger the number of total strategic actions a MUMM firm undertakes in a market-unit in a given time period, the more frequently it demonstrates its competitive posture (D'Aveni, 1994), its determination to defend its position (Chen & Miller, 1994), and its capacity for preemption (Nault & Vandenbosch, 1996). Frequent strategic actions also signal firms' development of greater speed and competence at engaging in strategic actions (Kim & Kogut, 1996), which lower cost and increase the effectiveness of their actions (Young et al., 1996). Thus, by disrupting the market-unit (and responding to the actions of others) more frequently, MUMM firms signal their strategic intent, build their disruptive capabilities, and improve their likelihood of achieving higher market-unit performance.

Research provides some indirect support for this argument. Young et al. (1996) found that the greater the number of strategic actions undertaken by computer software firms, the higher their performance. Roberts (1999) showed that the propensity to launch innovative new drugs was positively related U.S. pharmaceutical firms' profit persistence and long-run profit rates. Based on these arguments and empirical evidence, we hypothesize:

> *Hypothesis 1 (H1)*: The greater the number of strategic actions a MUMM firm undertakes in a market-unit the greater its market share increase in that market-unit.

A MUMM firm's market-unit performance also depends on its *relative* aggressiveness compared to competitors in the market-unit. In hypercompetitive market-units, MUMM firms often find themselves in 'market share races' in which the firms attempts to outpace each other by carrying out more frequent strategic actions (D'Aveni, 1994). By undertaking more strategic actions than its competitors, a firm puts itself in a better position to act first on changing market-unit conditions in ways that favor it vis-à-vis its competitors, as well as making it more difficult for competitors to keep pace. Supporting this idea, Ferrier et al. (1999) found that market leaders generating fewer strategic actions compared to their challengers were more likely to suffer market share losses. Relatedly, Richardson (1996), found that fashion apparel firms more responsive to new market trends and more successful in implementing process innovations than their competitors achieved superior performance. Expanding this line of empirical investigation, we apply the concept of relative aggressiveness at the market-unit level for MUMM firms. Thus, we hypothesize:

> *Hypothesis 2 (H2)*: The greater the number of strategic actions a MUMM firm undertakes in a market-unit vis-à-vis others competing in the market-unit, the greater its market share increase in that market-unit.

Simplicity of Strategic Actions in a Market-Unit

The simplicity of strategic actions refers to the extent to which a firm carries out a narrow range of similar strategic actions, as opposed to a broad range of diverse strategic actions (Ferrier et al., 1999; Miller & Chen, 1996a). One way for a MUMM firm to achieve competitive advantage in a hypercompetitive market-unit is to adopt a broad repertoire of strategic actions that enables it to surprise its competitors in that market-unit (D'Aveni, 1994). In contrast to the competitive opportunities available to firms that generate a broad range of strategic actions, firms making use of a limited scope of strategic actions may exploit a narrow opportunity set (Grimm & Smith, 1997). Indeed, in Schumpeter's (1934) conceptualization of competition, competitiveness is the ability to carry out a range of strategic actions to achieve substantial performance in the market place. Contemporary dynamic capabilities perspectives suggest, similarly, that for a firm to gain competitive advantage, it must participate in an ongoing process of industry restructuring by searching for new core competencies and ways of delivering services that change industry rules (Hamel & Prahalad, 1994, p. 283; Teece et al., 1997). Supporting these ideas, Miller and Chen (1996a) found that the simplicity of U.S. airlines' strategic actions had a significant negative effect on their passenger operating revenues. Given the foregoing arguments and evidence, we hypothesize:

> *Hypothesis 3 (H3)*: The greater the simplicity of strategic actions a MUMM firm undertakes in a market-unit the greater its market share decline in that market-unit.

We again expect that effect of the MUMM firms' strategic actions simplicity on its market-unit performance will depend on the action simplicity of its rivals actions in that market unit. A MUMM firm's ability to acquire an abnormal economic rent depends on whether it can discover new profit opportunities in the marketplace (Jacobson, 1992). Consequently, MUMM firms in hypercompetitive market-units must continually outmaneuver their competitors by executing new types of strategic actions (D'Aveni, 1994). The likelihood that a MUMM firm will discover a new profit opportunity is conditioned by the simplicity of its strategic actions relative to those of its competitors in a market-unit. At one extreme, if all MUMM firms competing in a market-unit rely on a single strategic action (e.g. price cutting), then they all exploit a limited set of opportunities. Any firm in the market-unit that broadens its range of strategic actions increases its chances of discovering new, untapped opportunities in the market-unit. At the other extreme, if all MUMM firms in a market-unit engage in a broad range of strategic actions, then they all attempt to explore a wide range of possible opportunities. Any firm that narrows its range of strategic actions in such a market-unit will thus lower its chances of discovering novel untapped opportunities – along with its potential performance.

The nature of hypercompetitive rivalries also suggests that no replicable strategy, or core competence, will allow MUMM firms to earn long-run abnormal profits, since the return on easy-to-implement strategies dissipates quickly. In hypercompetition, because competitive change frequently cannot be predicted ex ante, but only responded to more or less efficiently ex post, economic rents are derived from the capability for implementing complex, adaptive behaviors that undermine competitors' advantages (Volberda, 1996). Consequently, the more complicated a MUMM firm's set of strategic actions vis-à-vis its rivals, the more difficulty the firm's rivals have either replicating or countering the firm's actions because they are unable to understand or discern the motivation behind its actions. And, even if rivals correctly decipher and unravel the implications of the firm's actions, they must then design and implement an appropriate response. The uncertainty a MUMM firm creates for its rivals in a market-unit by engaging in more complex, multifaceted strategic actions suggests that MUMM firms capable of such bundling will enjoy superior market unit performance. Therefore, we hypothesize:

Hypothesis 4 (H4): The greater the simplicity of strategic actions a MUMM firm undertakes in a market-unit vis-à-vis others competing in the market-unit, the greater its market share decline in that market-unit.

METHODS

Sample: Canadian General Insurance Industry

The data for this study contain information on 232 general insurance companies actively operating in Canada between 1993–1998, including 78 federally registered Canadian insurers, 93 federally registered foreign insurers, and 61 provincially registered insurers. General insurers, also called property and casualty insurers, sell any type of insurance with the exception of health and life insurance. The data were provided by Trac Insurance Services Ltd. (TIS), the major independent Canadian insurance industry rating agency. TIS obtains its data directly from annual statements filed by insurers with the Office of the Superintendent of Financial Institutions Canada (OSFI). A cross-check with data available from the OSFI, provincial regulators (e.g. Financial Services Commission of Ontario) and Stone & Cox Ltd. (a publisher of information on the Canadian insurance industry) indicated that the Trac data covered over 95% of general insurers operating in Canada during the study period. Firms not included in the data were either inactive or very small insurers.

During the study period, the Canadian insurance industry experienced a wave of consolidations. In 1996 alone, there were 14 mergers among Canadian firms and seven among international insurers with a significant presence in Canada (Christie, 1997). Reflecting this, the percentage of all Canadian premiums written by the 10 largest insurers jumped from 31% in 1991 to 52% in 1998. The accelerating consolidation was sparked by the combination of industry fragmentation and a climate of intense competition in a slow-growing market (Bain, 1998; Canadian Insurance Congress, 1995; Christie, 1997). Consolidation notwithstanding, rivalry among general insurers remained intense as a result of excessive surplus industry capacity. At the end of 1993, the leverage rate of general insurers stood at 2.5 : 1, producing $28 billion of capacity against only $14.8 billion of net premiums written (Cudlipp, 1999; Praskey, 1994). The reduction of this 'surplus surplus,' although eagerly anticipated by industry practitioners, had not materialized by 1998 (Cudlipp, 1999), with the market share leader, CGU Group Canada Ltd., still writing only 8.76% of all premiums. Rivalry was also promoted by the increasing prominence of innovative niche players (Christie, 1997), and by the passing of the 1991 *Insurance Companies Act of Canada*, which allowed commercial banks to expand into the general insurance arena for the first time.

Our data contain a breakdown of written insurance policy premiums from 16 product lines across (the then) 12 provinces and territories of Canada. The 16 product lines represent different categories of insurance as defined by the *Insurance Companies Act*: property-personal, property-commercial, aircraft, automobile, boiler and machinery, credit, fidelity, hail, legal expense, liability, mortgage, surety, title, marine, accident and sickness, and reinsurance. Thus, in total there are 193 (i.e. $16 \times 12 = 192$, plus an "outside Canada" category) market-units in the Canadian general insurance industry.

Strategic Action Data
Following Ferrier et al. (1999, pp. 377–378), we require strategic actions to be observable by different industry stakeholders, including customers, competitors,

and industry regulators (Ogden & Watson, 1999). Consequently, we identified firms' strategic actions by searching for reports of their strategic initiatives in major industry and general media outlets. Using the sample firms' names as keywords, we searched three sources for news reports during 1993–1997:

(1) *Canadian Business and Current Affairs*, which includes full text of 141 Canadian trade and business periodicals (including *Canadian Underwriter*, one of two major Canadian insurance industry trade journals, and the *Financial Post*, a major Canadian business newspaper).
(2) *The Globe and Mail*, a major Canadian national daily newspaper which has a significant business section.
(3) *Canadian Insurance*, the second major Canadian insurance industry trade journal.

Our search yielded nearly 8,000 articles and abstracts. Strategic actions were coded from these articles into the following eight categories: (1) major new pricing actions, (2) new marketing and promotional actions, (3) new products, (4) new capacity additions, (5) new legal actions, (6) new signaling actions, (7) new M&As for the purpose of increasing capacity, and (8) new M&As for the purpose of acquiring access to new products. Our coding scheme is consistent with Ferrier et al. (1999) and Young et al. (1996), but adds the two final M&A categories. To enhance the reliability in our data coding, we coded the strategic actions separately and compared our coding derived from a sample of 2,715 articles. Our inter-rater reliability was 0.78. Our disagreements were discussed until we had reached consensus. We then read and coded the remaining articles and abstracts. Strategic actions were recorded at the market-unit level. When the article did not mention a specific market-unit or market-units that an action targeted, the action was regarded as targeting all market-units in which the firm had sold premiums in the year before the action year. Examples for each type of strategic action are given in Table 1.

Sensitivity Analysis
Although used previously, the method we used to code strategic actions may result in a selection bias in our strategic action variables. Of course, not every strategic action undertaken by firms in our sample would be reported in the media, and those that are not might impact firm performance in our analysis. Although the exact nature of this bias (if any) is unknown, we attempted to gain some insight into its direction by comparing sample firms for which strategic actions were reported in the media, with those for which no strategic actions were reported. Firms whose actions received media attention had significantly greater total assets, wrote more premiums, and generated larger

investment, before tax, and after tax incomes (all $p < 0.01$, two-tailed). Thus, while smaller firms may actually have undertaken fewer strategic actions, their actions may also have been systematically under-reported in the media, and so are underrepresented in our data.

There are two ways to examine the extent of this potential sample selection bias. One is to randomly select a subsample from the firms whose actions were reported by the media and compare estimates from the random subsample with those from the full sample. A second is to select a subsample of firms based on some characteristic that appears to be related to the selection bias – the 30 largest in terms of total assets, for example – and compare estimates from this subsample with those from the full sample. Since our measurement appears to be systematically biased according to size, we employed the second approach. Specifically, we conducted sensitivity analyses for subsamples of the 30 and 120 largest firms in terms of total assets. Below, we report and compare these subsample estimates to estimates for the full sample.

Dependent Variable and Model[1]

The dependent variable in our study, $ChangeMS_{ik,t+1}$, is the change in the market share of firm i in market-unit k between years t and $t + 1$. $ChangeMS_{ik}$ was calculated as:

$$Change\ MS_{ik} = \frac{WrittenPremium_{ik,t+1}}{\sum_f WrittenPremium_{fk,\,t+1}} - \frac{WrittenPremium_{ik,\,t}}{\sum_f WrittenPremium_{fk,\,t}} \quad (1)$$

where $WrittenPremium_{ik,\,t+1}$ and $WrittenPremium_{ik,\,t}$ are the values of premiums written by firm i in years t and $t + 1$ in market-unit k. We use change in market share as our measure of market-unit performance because it is the most direct measure of success of strategic market behaviors.

We perform our analysis using hierarchical linear modeling (HLM) (Bryk & Raudenbush, 1992; Bryk, Raudenbush & Congdon, 1994). The fundamental conceptual logic of HLM is that an actor's performance is influenced by the

---

[1] In the following sections, several conventions are adopted. A firm is referred to as f, where $f = 1, 2, \ldots, 232$. Firm f may be an "active" or a "non-active" firm. The "active" firm is denoted as firm i (or firm j). The market-unit in which the action occurred is referred to as k, where $k = 1, 2, \ldots, 193$. The types of strategic actions are denoted $p = 1, 2, \ldots, 8$. Year is given by $t = 1993, 1994, \ldots, 1998$.

Table 1. Definitions and Examples of Strategic Actions.[a]

Types of Actions	Definition	Example of Competitive Actions
New pricing action	Set a new price level	Canadian General Insurance Co. had reported the largest rate cut at 7.07%.
New marketing action	Established new broker channel, promoted a new company image, advertisement, sponsored sports or other activities, etc.	Peace Hills General Insurance Company set up a marketing representative in Manitoba.
New product action	Introduced new product or *stopped selling an existing product*	1. Pafco Insurance Co. Ltd. of Toronto introduced a home warranty insurance program, at no additional cost, a one-year home warranty insurance policy with mortgages or principal residences not covered under provincial warranty plans. 2. Pafco Insurance Co. Ltd stopped offering residential policies.
New capacity action	Adopted new technology, more efficient business practice; increased capital, etc.	1. Kingsway Insurance had a new public offering 2. Pafco insurance Co. (Toronto, Ontario) received a $3m capital infusion after a complex restructuring of parent company Pembridge Capital Inc. by controlling shareholder Gornitzki Thompson and Little (Toronto), a merchant banking group. 3. The Portage La Prairie Mutual Insurance in Portage La Prairie, Manitoba, created a specialized invoicing system based on Dynamics C/S+ applications from Great Plains Software of Fargo, N.D.
New legal action	Litigated, joined a collective action to lobby, etc.	1. Allstate Insurance Company filed a lawsuit against Project Langchow. 2. Canadian Direct Insurance Inc. took the Insurance Corp. of B.C. to court, claiming the government monopoly was driving up auto body rates to try to reduce competition.
New signaling action	Sent a message of an intended competitive actionpes of Actions	Canadian Direct Insurance Inc. said it would enter Alberta in 1997

Table 1. Continued.

Types of Actions	Definition	Example of Competitive Actions
New M & A[b] for new product	Insurer acquired or merged with another insurer involved in dissimilar market-units	1. Canadian General Insurance Company took over Constitution Insurance's special risk and other insurance portfolios in 1993. 2. The Canadian branch of General Reinsurance Corp. took over a significant portion of Pembridge's reinsurance business.
New M & A for new capacity	Insurer acquired or merged with another insurer involved in similar market-units	London Guarantee Insurance Co. bought Toronto-based Motion Picture Guarantors Ltd. and its sister company in Quebec, Cinegarantie Ltee, for an undisclosed price. The company, which operated under the name Motion Picture Bond Co., was expected to use the new equity capital to expand its international operations into areas such as animation and multimedia.

[a] Strategic actions taking place in one or more market-units. [b] Merger and acquisition

social context in which the performance is embedded. For example, a high school student's grade is not only affected by her personal characteristics, such as intelligence, but also by the social context in which she studies (e.g. the characteristics of the school where she is a student) (Bryk & Raudenbush, 1992). Statistically, inattention to the effect of social context produces inefficient estimation by introducing correlated bias into the results (Bryk & Raudenbush, 1992).

HLM can be used as a two-level approach. For our study, the 'level 1' model estimates of intercept and slope parameters represent effects of within-market-unit independent variables on $ChangeMS_{ik}$. Thus, the level 1 model is similar to a general regression model. In the 'level 2' model, the intercept and slope parameters from the level 1 model are used as dependent variables and regressed on between-market-units variables (Hofmann, 1997). To test our hypotheses, we used the following level 1 and 2 model specifications:

Level 1

$$ChangeMS_{ik} = \beta_0 + \beta_1\ TotalAction_{ik} + \beta_2\ ActionSimplicity_{ik} + \beta_3\ MarketImportance_{ik} + \beta_4 LogSize_i + e_{ik} \qquad (2)$$

Level 2

$$\beta_0 = \gamma_{00} + \gamma_{01} \; TotalAction_k + \gamma_{02} \; ActionSimplicity_k + \\ \gamma_{03} \; MarketImportance_k + \gamma_{04} \; LogSize_k + u_{00} \tag{3}$$

$$\beta_1 = \gamma_{10} + \gamma_{11} \; (TotalAction_k)^{-1} + u_{10} \tag{4}$$

$$\beta_2 = \gamma_{20} + \gamma_{21} \; (ActionSimplicity_k)^{-1} + u_{20} \tag{5}$$

$$\beta_3 = \gamma_{30} + u_{30} \tag{6}$$

$$\beta_4 = \gamma_{40} + u_{40} \tag{7}$$

where $TotalAction_{ik}$ and $ActionSimplicity_{ik}$ are the independent variables at level 1, $(TotalAction_k)^{-1}$ and $(ActionSimplicity_k)^{-1}$ are the independent variables at level 2, and $TotalAction_k$, $ActionSimplicity_k$, $MarketImportance_{ikt}$, $MarketImportance_k$, $LogAsset_{ik}$ and $LogAsset_k$ are control variables. For the analysis, all independent and control variables were measured at the start of the year in the in which the market share change occurred.

Independent Variables

TotalAction.
For level 1, total action is the total number of strategic actions, across all eight types (see Table 1), adopted by firm i in market-unit k in year t:

$$TotalAction_{ik} = \sum_{p=1}^{8} Action_{ikp} \tag{8}$$

where $Action_{ikp}$ is firm i's number of strategic actions in category p in market-unit k in year t. At level 2, it is the total number of strategic actions adopted by all the firms that sold policies in market-unit k in year t:

$$TotalAction_{ik} = \sum_{i} \sum_{p=1}^{8} Action_{ikp} \tag{9}$$

The main effect of $TotalAction_{ik}$ predicted by H_1 is tested with γ_{10} in Eq. 4. In Eq. 4, the impact of firm i's own actions, $TotalAction_{ik}$, on change in its market share is conditioned on $TotalAction_k$, which represents the context in which the actions of firm i took place. To test H_2, we estimate the effect of the inverse of $TotalAction_k$, which is represented by γ_{11} in Eq. 4. $TotalAction_k$ is inverted because H_2 predicts that a firm's market share in a market-unit increases when $TotalAction_{ik}$ increases and $TotalAction_k$ decreases.

ActionSimplicity

Following past research (e.g. Ferrier et al., 1999), we operationalize firm i's action simplicity in market-unit k by using the equivalence of the Herfindal index (Montgomery, 1985):

$$ActionSimplicity_{ik} = \sum_{p=1}^{8} \left[Action_{ikp} / \sum_{p=1}^{8} Action_{ikp} \right]^2 \tag{10}$$

$ActionSimplicity_{ik}$ measures, for the level 1 model, the extent of *within* firm action simplicity. The *higher* the score, the simpler firm i's actions. For level 2, action simplicity measures *across* firm diversity of strategic actions launched by firms operating in market-unit k:

$$ActionSimplicity_{k} = \sum_{p=1}^{8} \left[(\sum Action_{ikp}) / (\sum_{i} \sum_{p=1}^{8} Action_{ikp}) \right]^2 \tag{11}$$

The main effect of $ActionSimplicity_{ik}$ on changes in market share predicted by H_3 is estimated as γ_{20} in Eq. 5. To test H_4 we again estimate the inverse of $ActionSimplicity_{k}$, which represents the context in which the simplicity of firm i's actions is nested, and is represented by γ_{21} in Eq. 5.

Control Variables

Market Unit Rivalry

Interfirm rivalry may affect firm performance. The strategic actions of all firms in a market-unit may create and modify the environments of these competing firms. Consequently, we control for the effects of rivalry in a particular market-unit on firms' performance that market-unit. Specifically, we include main effects for $TotalAction_{k}$ and $ActionSimplicity_{k}$ (defined above) in Eq. 3.

Market Unit Importance

Individual market-units may vary in their importance to particular (or all) MUMM firms and this may affect market share changes. One determinant of market-unit importance is the percentage of a firm's (all firms') revenues derived from a given market-unit. MUMM firms may be more aggressive in efforts to strengthen or defend their positions in markets from which they derive more revenues, and the intensity of competition more generally may be fiercer in market-units with more revenue at stake. We control for the importance of a market-unit with two variables:

$$MarketImportance_{ik} = Premium_{ik} / (\sum_{k=1}^{193} Premium_{ik}) \tag{12}$$

Table 2. Means, Standard Deviations, and Bivariate Correlations for Variables.

Level 1[a]

	Mean	S.D.	1	2	3	4
1. ChangeMS$_{ik}$	0.0038	0.054				
2. TotalAction$_{ik}$	2.5455	2.123	−0.012			
3. ActionSimplicity$_{ik}$	0.7318	0.280	0.026	−0.638		
4. MarketImportance$_{ik}$	0.0404	0.128	−0.011	0.078	−0.022	
5. LogAsset$_{ik}$	12.8563	1.439	−0.069	0.190	−0.218	0.016

[a] Level 1 includes 6944 firm-market-unit-years.

Level 2[b]

	Mean	S.D.	1	2	3
1. TotalAction$_k$	74.352	329.4			
2. ActionSimplicity$_k$	0.269	0.057	0.135		
3. MarketImportance$_k$	0.193	0.286	−0.022	−0.202	
4. LogAsset$_k$	17.672	0.105	−0.021	−0.081	−0.281

[b] Level 2 includes 406 market units during 1993–1998.

$$MarketImportance_k = \sum_f Premium_{fk} / (\sum_{k=1f}^{193} Premium_{fk}) \qquad (13)$$

where $Premium_{ik}$ is the value of firm i's premiums sold in market-unit k in year t. $MarketImportance_{ik}$, which measures the importance of market-unit k for firm i, enters Eq. 2. $MarketImportance_k$, which measures the market importance of market-unit k for all firms active in that market-unit in year t enters Eq. 3.

Firm Size
It is also possible that MUMM firms' market share changes depend on their sizes. Large firms in particular may find it more difficult than small ones to gain market share because the high shares they have already attained makes further increases are more difficult to achieve. Large firms may also by less likely to lose share than small firms, however. Therefore, at level 1 (Eq. 2), we control for the natural log of firm i's total assets in year t. And, at level 2, (Eq. 3), we control for the natural log of the total assets of all sample firms in year t.

Table 2 presents means, standard deviations and bivariate correlations for our independent and control variables. Most correlations are moderate, and so will not bias coefficient estimates. Although not posing a serious estimation problem, moderate multicollinearity may introduce a conservative bias to tests of significance for specific coefficients by inflating standard errors for the collinear variables (Kennedy, 1992). Therefore, following Bryk and Raudenbush (1992), we test the significance of groups of variables by comparing nested regression models instead of relying only on significance tests for individual coefficients.

RESULTS

Preliminary Analysis

Following procedures recommended by Bryk and Raudenbush (1992), before testing our hypotheses, we used a model of one-way ANOVA with random effects, in which there are no level 1 and level 2 predictors, and estimates from all three samples (i.e. 30 largest firms, 120 largest firms and all firms) indicated that there was significant cross market-unit variation ($p < 0.001$). A two-level analysis is thus preferred for testing our hypotheses than simple OLS. We then entered only level 1 independent and control variables, and found significant variation across market-units for each level-1 variable (i.e. the slopes in level 1). These estimates are reported as Model 1 in Table 3. Next, in Model 2, we entered each level 2 variable to capture these variances across market-units. When all level 1 and level 2 predictors were included none of the residuals for the level 2 equations (i.e. u_{10}, u_{20}, u_{30}, and u_{40} in Eqs. 4–7) were significant. Only the residual u_{00} for Eq. 3 was significant ($p < 0.001$). These residuals represent the difference between the fitted value of the parameter based on the market-unit level measures and the empirical estimate based on both within- and between-market-unit information. The non-significance of the residuals indicates that the level-2 predictors have captured well the variation across market-units. Therefore, we set u_{10}, u_{20}, u_{30}, and u_{40} to zero for our analyses. Notably, setting these terms to zero renders our model equivalent to an OLS regression with heterogeneous error terms across different market-units. Nevertheless, the application of HLM is a prudent practice because it can test and correct for situations in which one or more of the level 2 residuals is nonzero, while White's method (White, 1980) and its variants cannot. Following Bryk and Raudenbush's (1992) we used the deviance statistic to compare the fitness of Models 1 and 2: the *greater* the deviance, the poorer the fit. As reported in Table 3, the change in the deviance statistic between Models 1 and 2 (2.08, 2 *df*) was not significant, indicating that Model 2 is not a significant improvement over Model 1.

Table 3. Hierarchical Linear Models of Change in MUMM Firms' Market-Unit Market Share.

Variable	Model 1 All Firms	Model 2 All Firms	Model 3 All Firms	Model 4 30 Largest Firms	Model 5 120 Largest Firms
Intercept (γ_{00})	0.0001898**	0.001640*	0.001640**	0.0001628*	0.001663***
	(0.000725)	(0.000694)	(0.000694)	(0.000864)	(0.000680)
Control variables					
Market Importance$_{ik}$ (γ_{30})	-0.002164	-0.002419†	-0.002394	-0.002262	-0.002615
	(0.006498)	(0.006495)	(0.006491)	(0.009153)	(0.006371)
LogAsset$_{ik}$ (γ_{40})	-0.003046**	-0.002998***	-0.002971***	0.004270**	0.000525
	(0.000461)	(0.000473)	(0.000474)	(0.001509)	(0.000652)
TotalAction$_k$ (γ_{01})	0.000005***	0.000005***	0.000005***	0.000005***	0.000004***
	(0.000001)	(0.000001)	(0.000001)	(0.000001)	(0.000001)
ActionSimplicity$_k$ (γ_{02})	-0.008082	-0.008165	-0.008162	0.001370	-0.008500
	(0.013215)	(0.013193)	(0.013182)	(0.015647)	(0.012802)
MarketImportance$_k$ (γ_{03})	0.004099†	0.004102†	0.004102†	0.004596†	0.002847
	(0.002739)	(0.002739)	(0.002737)	(0.003302)	(0.002672)
LogAsset$_k$ (γ_{04})	0.009304†	0.009378†	0.009376†	0.016260*	0.001211
	(0.006902)	(0.006886)	(0.006880)	(0.008519)	(0.006923)
Hypotheses					
TotalAction$_{ik}$ (γ_{10}) **H1**		**0.000490**	**0.001218****	**0.000401**	**0.000844***
		(0.000416)	**(0.000515)**	(0.000645)	**(0.000481)**
ActionSimplicity$_{ik}$ (γ_{20}) **H3**		0.004321†	0.004523†	0.008508**	0.006550**
		(0.003097)	(0.003115)	(0.003732)	(0.002949)
TotalAction$_{ik}$ × (1/TotalAction$_k$) (γ_{11}) **H2**			**0.076001****	-0.016652	0.037545
			(0.030189)	(0.039990)	(0.028369)
ActionSimplicity$_{ik}$ × (1/ActionSimplicity$_k$) (γ_{21}) **H4**		**-0.005714****	**-0.013107*****	**-0.006088****	
			(0.002930)	**(0.003623)**	**(0.002755)**
d.f. of β_0	401	401	401	401	401
Reliability of β_0	0.005	0.005	0.005	0.008	0.049
χ^2 of β_0	242.497	242.490	242.846	197.198	268.982
Number of Estimated Parameters	9	11	13	13	13
Deviance	-21008.22	-21010.30	-21022.20	-11975.56	-20630.42?
∇ Deviance		2.08 (2 *df*)	11.9 (2 *df*) ***		

†$p < 0.10$; *$p < 0.05$; **$p < 0.01$; ***$p < 0.001$, one-tailed test

Hypothesis Testing

Table 3 presents the results of hypothesis testing. Models 3, 4 and 5 in Table 3 report coefficients for the full sample, and the two subsamples, respectively. Model 3, in which we entered all four theoretical variables for the full sample, provided a significant improvement over Model 2 (11.9, $df = 2$, $p < 0.001$). Below, we detailed our analysis results for our hypotheses testing.

Total Strategic Actions

In Model 3, the significant positive coefficient for $TotalAction_{ik}$ (γ_{10}), supports H_1 ($p < 0.01$), which predicted that firms' total number of strategic actions in a market-unit would increase their market shares more in that market unit. The coefficient for γ_{11} is also significant and positive ($p < 0.01$), providing strong support for H_2. This means that firms engaging in more strategic actions in a market-unit relative to their competitors in the market-unit experienced greater market share increases in that market-unit. Thus, MUMM firms in the Canadian general insurance industry that engaged in greater absolute (H_1) and relative (H_2) numbers of strategic actions experienced larger increases in their market shares. And, these effects are of a substantial magnitude. For each additional action in a market-unit, a firm increased it's market share in that unit by more than one-tenth of 1% (i.e. $1*0.0012 = 0.12\%$), a sizeable increase given that in 1998, the largest firm had an average market-unit share of less than 9%. A firm engaging in 10% more strategic actions than its competitors in a market-unit increased it's market share in that unit by more than three-quarters of 1% (i.e..$1*0.076 = 0.76\%$).

Also notable is the significant, positive main effect for $TotalAction_k$ (γ_{01}) – the total strategic actions of all the firms in market-unit k. Consistent with the idea that hypercompetitive rivalry serves to expand markets (D'Aveni, 1994), this coefficient indicates firms' market share increases were larger in market-units experiencing a greater intensity of competition.

Action Simplicity

Contrary to H3, which predicted that engaging in a limited range of strategic actions in a market-unit would lower firms' market share in the market-unit, the coefficient for $ActionSimplicity_{ik}$ (γ_{20}) is positive and marginally significant ($p < 0.10$). Supporting H_4, however, the coefficient for the interaction term, $ActionSimplicity_{ik} \times (1/ActionSimplicity_k)$ (γ_{21}) is negative and significant as predicted ($p < 0.01$). Taken together, these two results suggest an interesting tension not captured in our original theoretical arguments. Although firms benefited from engaging in more complex strategic actions than their competitors in a market-unit, their market-share performance suffered from the complexity. Thus, as firms struggle to outwit and avoid being transparent to one another in the race for market share, they also engage in strategies whose complexity increasingly interferes with their effectiveness. Eventually, the escalating complexity may overwhelm the benefit of outwitting competitors, perhaps ultimately even causing firms with complex strategic actions to fall prey to firms challenging them with simpler ones. A 100% decrease in a firm's strategic action simplicity in a market-unit, for example, leads to an improvement of almost half a% of market share in that market-unit (i.e. $1*0.0045 = 0.045\%$). In contrast, when a firm increase its action complexity in a market-unit vis-à-vis its rivals by 10% only, the firm can gain more than half a percent market share in the market-unit ($0.1*0.0057 = 0.57\%$).

Sensitivity analysis
Models 4 and 5 show that our findings for the full sample (Model 3) are broadly consistent with those for the two subsamples. In addition to reducing concerns that our theoretical findings for the full sample are biased by our approach to identifying firms' strategic actions, this comparability also reinforces our view that the range of firms' strategic actions in a market-unit is all other firms competing in the market-unit.

Although broadly consistent, an interesting pattern emerges across the different subsamples of firms. The size of the coefficient for the number of strategic actions (*Total Action*$_{ik}$) increases with the number of the firms sampled, suggesting that larger firms may have to launch a greater number of strategic actions to enhance their market-unit performance. Indeed, among the largest firms, neither the absolute nor the relative number of strategic actions affects performance. The coefficients suggest in contrast, that the effects of action simplicity (both main and interactive) on market-unit performance is more consequential for larger than smaller firms. Taken together, the sensitivity analysis indicates that smaller firms benefit more than large firms from acting frequently (both absolutely and relatively), while large firms benefit more than small firms from acting complexly vis-à-vis their competitors in a market-unit – but also suffer more greatly from the difficulty of doing so.

DISCUSSION AND CONCLUSIONS

As hypercompetition spreads, academics and practitioners are becoming increasingly interested in the linkage between hypercompetitive strategic actions and firm performance. Although the nature of this linkage is central to strategy management research, there are few empirical studies on this topic. Among the few studies that have examined this relationship, researchers have either studied the relationship between competitive activity and firm-level outcomes (e.g. Miller & Chen, 1996b; Young et al., 1996), or limited the scope of their analysis to rivalry among a large firms (Ferrier et al., 1999). In contrast, we focused on the linkage between MUMM firms' strategic actions and their performance at the market-unit level. We also carefully considered the problem of level of analysis incongruence (Klein, Dansereau & Hall, 1994; Gimeno & Jeong, this volume) and range of strategic action impact, both of which, while often overlooked, are basic to understanding competition among MUMM firms.

Drawing on the concept of hypercompetitive rivalry from the new Schumpeterian school (D'Aveni, 1994; Jacobson, 1992; Schumpeter, 1934), we hypothesized that firms' market performance is influenced both by the characteristics of its own strategic actions, and the characteristics of its strategic actions vis-à-vis the firms with which it is competing. Our study contributes to research on the action-performance linkage in three ways. First, we tested two major constructs of strategic action – total number of actions, and action simplicity – simultaneously. Second, we conditioned the performance effects of firms' strategic actions on the actions of their competitors. And, finally, we made use of HLM techniques, which permitted us to address the level of analysis and range of impact issues explicitly in our empirical analysis. Our study thus begins to expose some of the key theoretical and empirical linkages between MUMM firms' strategic actions and market-unit performance.

Our finding that the number of strategic action firms' launched in a market-unit improved their market-unit performance in that market-unit reinforces past research on the relationship between firms' strategic actions and firm-level performance (e.g. Roberts, 1999; Young et al., 1996). Insurers undertaking more frequent strategic actions in a market-unit – both absolutely and relative to their competitors in the market unit – signaled their resolve to improve and defend their position in the market-unit, helping create an advantage for them in the market-unit. Our sensitivity analysis also revealed that small insurers benefit more than large firms from undertaking frequent strategic actions.

Our action simplicity findings warrant a more detailed discussion. Contradictory to our prediction (H_3), simpler strategic actions in a market-unit resulted in greater the share increases in that market-unit. One explanation for this finding is that Canadian insurers benefited by repeatedly exploiting strategic actions that they had honed through experiences of the past (Cyert & March, 1963; March, 1991). When firms attempt more complex and unpredictable strategic actions, they must often do so without the benefit of experience. And, so given their greater novelty and more exploratory nature, complex strategic actions may have more uncertain immediate benefits. Thus Canadian insurers may be better off focusing on and exploiting strategic actions that seem to have worked in the past. That said, supporting our prediction (H_4), our findings also indicate that firms whose actions were simpler than those of their rivals compromised their performance. Combined, these results indicate that Canadian insurers must trade off the difficulty of engaging in complex strategic actions against the possibility of either being too transparent to their competitors, or outwitted by them.

Notably, our findings are consistent with Buckley's (1968. p. 495) law of requisite variety: "the variety within a system must be at least as great as the environmental variety against which it is attempting to regulate itself. Put more succinctly, only variety can regulate variety." Thus, the complexity of Canadian insurers strategic actions must match its rivals' strategic action variety, but yet remains simple enough to reap the benefits of experiential learning. An overly simple pattern of strategic action renders the focal firm susceptible to the pitfall of becoming too focused on a single theme, activity, or issue at the expense of other alternatives (Miller, 1993). A pattern that is too complex may scatter firms' attention and resources in too many directions, and rob them of the benefits of experience.

Our study points to several directions for future research. The nature of our data did not permit us to operationalize an important dimension of strategic action – speed and timing (Chen & MacMillan, 1992). Considering speed and timing alongside the number and simplicity of actions would enrich our initial effort to link MUMM firms' strategic action and performance. Reinforcing earlier research suggesting that large and small firms compete in different ways (Chen & Hambrick, 1995), our sensitivity analysis suggests that large and small firms may need to compete in different ways. Understanding nature and implications of these differences in greater detail may offer new insights into the nature of hypercompetitive rivalry among MUMM firms and how large and small firms can compete more effectively. Perhaps the most important extension of our work, however, is to combine our focus on strategic action with ideas on multimarket contact and mutual forbearance. As many of the papers in this volume attest, multimarket contact and mutual forbearance are central concepts in the literature of multimarket firms. Careful elaboration of the interrelationships among these important theoretical constructs will surely be fundamental to the development of a full theory of the competitive dynamics of MUMM firms.

ACKNOWLEDGMENT

The authors wish to thank Joel Baker and Terri Vaillancourt from Trac Insurance Services Ltd., and John D. Wyndham and David McGibney from Stone & Cox Limited, for their assistance in data collection. The authors thank Terry Amburgey, Tony Calabrese, and Martin Evans whose comments improved arlier drafts of the paper. Additionally, the authors are also grateful for the suggestions provided by the two editors, Joel Baum and Henrich Greve.

REFERENCES

Andrews, K. R. (1971). *The Concept of Corporate Strategy.* Homewood, IL: Irwin.

Bain, J. S. (1951). Relation of profit rate to industry concentration: American manufacturing, 1936–1940. *Quarterly Journal of Economics, 65,* 293–324.

Bain, T. (1998). The information source. *Canadian Insurance, 103,* 26–28.

Baum, J. A. C., & Korn, H. J. (1996). Competitive dynamics of interfirm rivalry. *Academy of Management Journal, 39,* 255–291.

Baum, J. A. C., & Korn, H. J. (1999). Dynamics of dyadic competitive interaction. *Strategic Management Journal, 20,* 251–278.

Bogner, W. C., & Barr, P. S. (2000). Making sense in hypercompetitive environments: A cognitive explanation for the persistence of high velocity competition. *Organization Science, 11,* 212–226.

Bryk, A. S., Raudenbush, S. W., & Congdon, R. T. (1994). *Hierarchical linear modeling with the HLM/2L and HLM/3L programs.* Chicago: Scientific Software, International.

Bryk, A. S., & Raudenbush, S. W. (1992). *Hierarchical linear models: applications and data analysis methods.* Newbury Park: Sage Publications.

Buckley, W. (1968). Society as a complex adaptive system. In: W. Buckley (Ed.), *Modern System Research for the Behavioral Scientist* (pp. 490–513). Chicago: Aldine.

Canadian Insurance Congress (1995). Distribution forces. *Canadian Insurance, 100,* 29–31.

Caves, R. E., & Porter, M. E. (1977). From entry barriers to mobility barriers. *Quarterly Journal of Economics, 91,* 421–437.

Chen, M.-J., & Hambrick, D. C. (1995). Speed, stealth, and selective attack: How small firms differ from large firms in competitive behavior. *Academy of Management Journal, 38,* 453–482.

Chen, M.-J., & MacMillan, I. (1992). Non-response and delayed response to competitive moves. *Academy of Management Journal, 35,* 539–570.

Chen, M.-J., & Miller, D. (1994). Competitive attack, retaliation and performance: An expectancy-valence framework. *Strategic Management Journal, 15,* 85–102.

Christie, J., (1997). Tracking the trends. *Canadian Insurance, 102,* 41–43.

Cudlipp, G. (1999). Canadian property and casulty industry statistics. *Canadian Insurance, 104,* 20–22.

Cyert, R. M., & March, J. G. (1963). *A Behavioral Theory of the Firm.* Englewood Cliffs, N. J.: Prentice-Hall.

D'Aveni, R. (1994). *Hypercompetition: Managing the Dynamics of Strategic Maneuvering.* New York: Free Press.

Edwards, C. D. (1955). Conglomerate bigness as a source of power. In: G. Stigler (Ed.), *Business Concentration and Price Policy* (pp. 331–352). Princeton, N. J.: Princeton University Press.

Fernández, N., & Marín, P. L. (1998). Market power and multimarket contact: Some evidence from the Spanish hotel industry. *Journal of Industrial Economics*, *46*, 301–316.

Ferrier, W. J., Smith, K. G., & Grimm, C. M. (1999). The role of competitive action in market share erosion and industry dethronement: A study of industry leaders and challengers. *Academy of Management Journal*, *42*, 372–388.

Gimeno, J. (1999). Reciprocal threats in multimarket rivalry: Staking out 'spheres of influence in the U.S. airline industry'. *Strategic Management Journal*, *20*, 101–128.

Gimeno, J, & Jeong, E. (2001). Multimarket contact: Meaning and measurement at multiple levels of analysis. In: J. A. C. Baum & H. R. Greve (Eds), *Multiunit Organization and Multimarket Strategy: Advances in Strategic Management*, Vol. 18, (pp. 359–410). Oxford U.K.: JAI Press.

Gluck, F. W. (1986). Strategic management: An overview. In: J. R. Gardner, R. Rachlin & H. W. A. Sweeny (Eds), *Handbook of Strategic Planning* (pp. 1–36). New York, NY: John Wiley & Sons.

Grimm, C. M., & Smith, K. G. (1997). *Strategy as Action: Industry Rivalry and Coordination*. Cincinnati: South-Western College Publishing.

Hamel, G., & Prahalad, C. K. (1994). *Competing for the Future*. Boston, MA: Harvard Business School Press.

Hofmann, D. A. (1997). An introduction to the logic and rationale of hierarchical linear models. *Journal of Management*, *23*, 723–744.

Hunt, M. S. (1972). *Competition in the major home appliance industry, 1960–1970*. Unpublished doctoral dissertation, Harvard University.

Jacobson, R. (1992). The "Austrian" School of strategy. *Academy of Management Review*, *17*, 782–807.

Karnani, A., & Wernerfelt, B. (1985). Multiple point competition. *Strategic Management Journal*, *6*, 87–96.

Kennedy, P. (1992). *A Guide to Econometrics* (3rd ed.). Cambridge, Mass.: MIT Press.

Kim, D.-J., & Kogut, B. (1996). Technological platforms and diversification. *Organization Science*, *7*, 283–301.

Kirzner, I. M. (1997). Entrepreneurial discovery and the competitive market process: An Austrian approach. *Journal of Economic Literature*, *35*, 60–85.

Klein, K. J., Dansereau, F., & Hall, R. J. (1994). Levels issues in theory development, data collection, and analysis. *Academy of Management Review*, *19*, 195–229.

March, J. G. (1991). Exploration and exploitation in organizational learning. *Organization Science*, *2*, 71–87.

McGrath, R. G., Chen, M.-J., & Macmillan, I. C. (1998). Multimarket maneuvering in uncertain spheres of influence: Resource diversion strategies. *Academy of Management Review*, *23*, 724–740.

Miller, D. (1993). The architecture of simplicity. *Academy of Management Review*, *18*, 116–138.

Miller, D., & Chen, M.-J. (1994). Sources and consequences of competitive inertia: A study of the U.S. airline industry. *Administrative Science Quarterly*, *39*, 1–23.

Miller, D., & Chen, M.-J. (1996a). The simplicity of competitive repertoires: An empirical analysis. *Strategic Management Journal*, *17*, 419–439.

Miller, D., & Chen, M.-J. (1996b). Sources and consequences of competitive inertia: A study of the U.S. airline industry. *Administrative Science Quarterly*, *39*, 1–23.

Montgomery, C. A. (1985). Product-market diversification and market power. *Academy of Management Journal*, *28*, 789–797.

Nault, B. R., & Vandenbosch, M. B. (1996). Eating your own lunch: Protection through preemption. *Organization Science*, 7, 342–358.

Nelson, R. R., & Winter, S. G., (1982). *An Evolutionary Theory of Economic Change*. Cambridge, MA: Harvard University Press.

Ogden, S., & Watson, R. (1999). Corporate performance and stakeholder management: Balancing shareholder and customers interests in the U.K. privatized water industry. *Academy of Management Journal*, 42, 526–538.

Porter, M. E. (1980). *Competitive Strategy*. New York: Free Press.

Praskey, S. (1994). Highlights from Halifax. *Canadian Insurance*, 99, 24.

Richardson, J. (1996). Vertical integration and rapid response in fashion apparel. *Organization Science*, 7, 400–411.

Roberts, P. W. (1999). Product innovation, product-market competition and persistent profitability in the U.S. pharmaceutical industry. *Strategic Management Journal*, 20, 655–670.

Schumpeter, J. A. (1934). *The Theory of Economic Development*. Cambridge, MA: Harvard University Press.

Steiner, G. (1979). *Strategic Planning*. New York, NY: Free Press.

Stone & Cox (varied years). *Provincial Results*. Toronto: Stone & Cox Limited.

Teece, D. J., Pisano, G., & Shuen, A. (1997). Dynamic capabilities and strategic management. *Strategic Management Journal*, 18, 509–533.

Volberda, H. W. (1996). Toward the flexible form: How to remain vital in hypercompetitive environments. *Organization Science*, 7, 359–374.

Weick, K. E. (1995). *Sensemaking in Organizations*. Thousand Oaks, CA: Sage Publications.

White, H. (1980). A heteroscedasticity-consistent covariance matrix estimator and a direct test for heteroscedasticity. *Econometrica*, 48, 817–838.

Young, G., Smith, K. G., & Grimm, C. M. (1996). "Austrian" and industrial organization perspectives on firm-level competitive activity and performance. *Organization Science*, 7, 243–254.

MULTIMARKET CONTACT: MEANING AND MEASUREMENT AT MULTIPLE LEVELS OF ANALYSIS

Javier Gimeno and Eui Jeong

ABSTRACT

The growing literature on multimarket contact and mutual forbearance in management and economics has produced an inflation of multimarket contact measures. The lack of validation of these multiple measures has hindered the accumulation of consistent knowledge and comparison of empirical findings. This paper investigates the measurement of the multimarket contact concept. Specifically, we review the existing measures of multimarket contact, identify the main differences among them, and evaluate their reliability and discriminant and predictive validity at multiple levels of analysis, both cross-sectionally and longitudinally. The results indicate substantial differences in the reliability and discriminant validity of these measures. Predictive validity depends critically on the level of measurement and on whether longitudinal or cross-sectional correlations are considered.

Multiunit Organization and Multimarket Strategy, Volume 18, pages 357–408.
ISBN: 0-7623-0721-8

INTRODUCTION

Research on the competitive consequences of multimarket contact has blossomed recently, both in economics (e.g. Bernheim & Whinston, 1990; Evans & Kessides, 1994; Feinberg, 1985; Scott, 1982, 1989, 1991) and in management (e.g. Baum & Korn, 1996, 1999; Boeker, Goodstein, Stephen & Murmann, 1997; Chen, 1996; Gimeno & Woo, 1996, 1999; Gimeno, 1999). Yet, a lack of attention to the measurement and construct validity of multimarket contact is apparent from any review of extant empirical research. Many researchers have created their own measures of multimarket contact, and seldom adopt measures developed by others. This inflation may not be entirely a bad sign. For instance, different measures may be better adapted to different research questions (e.g. Hofer, 1983). Diverse measures may also be useful for theory development. However, multiple measures are useful only if they are adequately validated (Venkatraman & Grant, 1986). In this respect, the problem is not the inflation of measures of multimarket contact, but their lack of validation.

This paper is concerned with the validation of existing measures of multimarket contact. As such, the paper belongs to the measurement stream of research on multimarket competition rather than the substantive stream (Venkatraman & Grant, 1986). The measurement stream of research focuses on the relationships between the results obtained from the operationalization and the underlying theoretical concepts (Schwab, 1980). In contrast, the substantive stream focuses on the nature of theoretical relationships between independent and dependent variables. We believe that the measurement stream of research on multimarket contact will help the accumulation of knowledge in the substantive stream.[1] More generally, this paper heeds recent calls for expanded emphasis on construct measurement in strategic management (Venkatraman & Grant, 1986; Hoskisson, Hitt, Johnson & Moesel, 1993; Boyd & Reuning-Elliott, 1998).

The goal of this paper is twofold. First, we seek to identify the important theoretical considerations involved in selecting one measure over another. Based on the literature review, we identified two specific dimensions of discrepancy among authors: (a) the level of measurement of multimarket contact, and (b) the scaling or weighting in the construction of multimarket contact measures. Recognition of these differences will enhance consistency of measurement in this area of research.

Second, we empirically compare multiple measures available in the literature and assess their reliability and validity. The empirical validation of these measures is carried out using data from the U.S. domestic airline industry between 1986 and 1995. The reliability and validity of the measures is assessed at multiple levels of analysis, using both cross-sectional and longitudinal data.

This empirical evaluation of existing measures has implications for the measurement of multimarket contact in future research.

MULTIMARKET CONTACT

Multimarket contact occurs when firms encounter the same rivals in multiple markets. An equivalent concept, multipoint competition, has been defined as "a situation when firms compete against each other simultaneously in several markets" (Karnani & Wernerfelt, 1985: 87). In its most basic definition, multimarket contact simply reflects whether two or more firms are positioned in the same multiple markets, and the degree of their overlap. An advantage of this definition of multimarket contact is that it is simple, general, and independent from its expected theoretical associations with other concepts. However, the generality of the definition makes it difficult for researchers to construct a 'definite' measure of multimarket contact that is acceptable across theoretical perspectives. Indeed, in most empirical research, multimarket contact measures have been constructed to test specific theoretical associations: most commonly, the mutual forbearance hypothesis (Edwards, 1955; Bernheim & Whinston, 1990).

The concept of multimarket contact emerged in association with the mutual forbearance hypothesis (Edwards, 1995), which surfaced during the 1950s–1970s as an extension to single-market oligopoly theories (Solomon, 1970; Adams, 1974; Areeda & Turner, 1979). Oligopoly theory suggests that the intensity of rivalry in a market is negatively related to the concentration in the market, since concentration facilitates the recognition of competitive interdependence among market participants, and facilitates tacit collusion. This perspective is known as the *horizontal interdependence* hypothesis (Adams, 1974). In contrast, multimarket competition theorists argue that *extended interdependence* among incumbents should be considered. Extended interdependence reflects whether participants compete in other fronts, and perceive their relationship in an extended or multimarket way (Areeda & Turner, 1979). With extended interdependence, firms considering a market-specific attack may recognize the possibility of retaliatory responses at other points of contact, and may therefore forbear from initiating the attack.

The mutual forbearance hypothesis is not the only theoretical perspective associated with the multimarket contact construct. The mutual awareness that results from multimarket contact may influence firms to use each other as benchmarks or reference points, and thus enhance inter-organizational mimicry among multipoint competitors. Multimarket contact among firms may influence the mimicry of the market scope of competitors. For instance, commuter airlines with moderate multimarket contact with other competing airlines tended to enter the markets of those competitors (Baum & Korn, 1999). Global integrated circuit manufacturers were more likely to open a sales office in a foreign country if the incumbents in that country also sold products in the firms' home markets (Gimeno, Loree & Beal, 1999). Multimarket contact may also affect the diffusion of other strategic choices. For instance, multimarket contacts influenced the diffusion of the abandonment of the 'easy listening' radio format in the U.S. radio industry (Greve, 1995). And multimarket contact may affect the diffusion of knowledge. For instance, multimarket contact across the product and innovation markets positively influenced a firm's citations of the patents of another firm in the chemicals industry (Scott, this volume). In sum, multimarket contact may influence inter-firm diffusion and mimicry of strategies and knowledge through market observation, in addition to inter-firm competitive interactions.

Researchers have conceptualized and measured multimarket contact in different ways. In particular, measures differ fundamentally along two dimensions: (a) the level of measurement and analysis of multimarket contact, and (b) the appropriate scaling and weighting of multimarket contact.

Levels of Measurement and Analysis.

Given economists' original interest in extended interdependence as a predictor of market rivalry and market performance, it is not surprising that most empirical studies carried out in economics have focused on the effect of multimarket contact on some aggregate measure of market rivalry or market performance. Accordingly, these researchers developed measures that capture the level of multimarket contact among all incumbents in a market, as a characteristic of the market. We refer to this level of analysis as the *market* level.

In contrast, management scholars have been less concerned than IO economists or antitrust scholars about the intensity of market-level competition, and more interested on the patterns of inter-firm competitive activity (Baum & Korn, 1996, 1999; Chen, 1996; Gimeno & Woo, 1996, 1999; Li & Chuang, this volume). This different emphasis has resulted in different levels of analysis. Management researchers have studied the effect of multimarket contact on competitive decisions of firms within specific markets, such as pricing decisions (Gimeno & Woo, 1996, 1999; Gimeno, 1999), competitive actions and responses (Young, Smith & Grimm, 1997), or market entry and exit decisions (Barnett, 1993; Baum & Korn, 1996; Boeker et al., 1997). When the focus has been on the competitive activity of firms within specific markets, researchers have adopted what we refer to as the *firm-in-market* level of analysis, and have developed measures that capture the multimarket contacts of a firm in a market with the remaining participants in that market.[2]

Alternatively, other management researchers have been interested in the overall level of competitive activity between pairs of firms across all their markets (Chen, 1996; Baum & Korn, 1999). Accordingly, they sought measures of multimarket contact that capture the level of contact between two firms across all possible markets. We refer to this level as the *dyad* level of analysis.

As Baum & Korn (1999: 251–252) have argued, multimarket contact is "*not* an aggregate property of industries, markets, or firms; it is a property of the *relationship* between two firm," each pair of competitors has different levels of multimarket contact. The dyad level is probably the most natural level of measurement to capture multimarket contact. The dyad level may also be the most appropriate level of analysis for relating multimarket contact to competitive actions that are dyadic in nature (i.e. actions that are targeted against an specific rival and are not market-specific, such as promotional attacks or legal actions against a rival), or to other dyadic variables, such as strategic alliances, resource similarity, etc.

One problem with dyad level measures of multimarket contact is that most of the variables associated with it are measured at different levels. Many competitive actions (market entry, market exit, pricing or capacity decision, etc), interactions and outcomes, are localized within specific products and market contexts (Nayyar, 1993), and may not be obviously targeted against a specific rival. In those cases, the actions may be targeted against one or all of the market incumbents, and it is difficult to assign the actions to a specific dyad. For instance, if Southwest enters a set of markets where both American and Continental compete, should these entry moves be considered a dyadic competitive attack targeted against American, Continental, or both? Unless the researcher can specifically identify that the moves were targeted against one rival but not the other incumbents (perhaps by tracking press releases that capture the intent of the attacker), the aggregation of firm-in-market level actions to the dyad level may lead to overestimation of competitive activity. The same moves would be simultaneously interpreted as competitive actions in two different dyads, Southwest-American and Southwest-Continental. Moreover, the competitive actions in the Southwest-American dyad may in fact be attacks of Southwest to Continental, or vice versa. So, while the dyad level may be a more natural level for measuring multimarket contact among firms, it is a less natural and more problematic level for aggregating market-specific competitive actions.

When competitive activity occurs at the firm-in-market level, the natural level of analysis for evaluating these competitive actions is the firm-in-market level of analysis, although the market level may also capture the aggregate competitive activity in the market. The countervailing disadvantage is that firm-in-market or market levels of measurement of multimarket contact aggregate (usually by averaging, sometimes by summing) multimarket contacts among multiple incumbents in that market, and therefore blur details about individual dyadic contacts. For instance, if a potential entrant to a market with two incumbents has high multimarket contact with one incumbent, but low multimarket contact with the other, the aggregation process would make this situation indistinguishable from a situation where the potential entrant had moderate multimarket contact with both incumbents. Yet, these situations may lead to quite different consequences, particularly if multimarket contact has nonlinear effects.[3]

A firm-in-market level measure of multimarket contact aggregates the dyad level multimarket contact measures of a focal firm with its competitors in a focal market. Since a firm faces different rivals in different markets, this measure varies across firms and markets. This measure can be easily associated with firm-in-market competitive actions or outcomes, such as price levels, changes in product offering, market entry, market exit, market share, performance in the market, etc (Barnett, 1993; Baum & Korn, 1996; Gimeno & Woo, 1996, 1999; Gimeno, 1999).

From the standpoint of IO economics, rivalry is mainly a characteristic of the market context. If the market is relatively homogeneous (a requirement for the determination of the boundaries of the market as a theoretical entity), firms within the same market cannot face radically different levels of rivalry, since rivalry would spill over to all firms in a similar fashion. Accordingly, researchers from an economics perspective have conceptualized multimarket contact as a characteristic of the market. Empirically, this is achieved either by aggregating the multimarket contacts of all of the dyads in the market (Evans & Kessides, 1994), or by evaluating some representative dyads (Heggestad & Rhoades, 1978; Scott, 1982; Mester, 1987; Hughes & Oughton, 1993).

The theoretical implications of the distinction between market level and firm-in-market level conceptualizations of multimarket contact are intriguing. For instance, assume a market with four firms (A, B, C, D) such that firms B, C, and D have very extensive multimarket contact with each other, but firm A has minimal contact with the rest. A firm-in-market level measure of multimarket contact would aggregate the multimarket contact of the AB, AC, and AD dyads, and would lead to the conclusion that firm A has negligible multimarket contact with the other incumbents. A market level measure of multimarket contact would aggregate multimarket contacts among all dyads (AB, AC, AD, BC, BD, and CD) and, since half of them have high multimarket contact, would lead to the conclusion that the market is characterized by moderate multimarket contact. The two views can be reconciled by recognizing that the market level measure aggregates multimarket contacts between the firm and other incumbents (AB,

AC, and AD; similar to the firm-in-market operationalizations) as well as among the other incumbents (BC, BD, and CD).

The theoretical distinction between the measures then hinges on the question: "Is the level of multimarket contact among other market incumbents (B, C, D) an important consideration in determining the competitive behavior of the focal firm (firm A)?" The market-level conceptualization of multimarket contact assumes that if contacts among other incumbents are high, then the forbearance among those rivals will create a collusive umbrella that will allow firm A to behave less competitive as well. If contacts among those incumbents are low, their rivalry will force firm A to behave competitively too. Thus, multimarket contacts between the focal firm and the other incumbents, and among the other incumbents, have parallel effects on firm behavior and may be aggregated. On the other hand, the firm-in-market conceptualization is silent about the effects of multimarket contacts among the other incumbents. Indeed, it is quite possible that multimarket contact among other incumbents (at least at very high levels) may encourage competitors with low firm-in-market multimarket contact to behave aggressively (Haveman & Nonnemaker, 2000). This line of inquiry is likely to lead to insightful findings about how multimarket contacts aggregate among heterogeneous firms.

In conclusion, while the dyad level of measurement of multimarket contact is the most natural level for that relational variable, the need to align analyses with the level of the dependent variables may change the level of analysis, and require the aggregation of multimarket contacts at different levels (market level, firm-in-market level). Data availability may therefore drive the choice of level of analysis. For instance, if the only available dependent variables were at the market level (e.g. average market prices), statistical analysis would also have to be carried at the market level, even if firm-in-market measures were more appropriate theoretically. The opposite may not be true; analysis at the firm-in-market level can be carried out using market level measures of multimarket contact as independent variables (Evans & Kessides, 1994).

Table 1 summarizes the major measures of multimarket contact used in the literature and their respective levels of analysis. In the following sections, we compare these measures and test their reliability and validity.

Measurement of MMC Across Levels

In this paper, we offer a method to compare multimarket contact measures developed for different levels. All the levels of analysis used in the literature (market, dyad, firm-in-market) can be construed as aggregations of a more basic level of analysis: the *dyad-in-market* level. This level of analysis would describe the level of multimarket contact outside the focal market between two firms

Table 1. Summary of Multimarket Measures Used in this Study.

Level	Notation	Authors	Dependent variables	Market	Major Findings Effects of MMC on DV	Remarks
Dyad-in-market level	MMC_{ijm}	Scott (1982)	Operating income/Sales (Firm)	Manufacturing product	$\otimes$ high (low) concentration: positive (negative) effect	– Randomly choose 2 firms in each market – a representative dyad – Focal market is *not* included
		Chen (1996)	Interfirm rivalry	Airline route	N/A	– MMC value is *asymmetric* – Weights: proportion of a focal firm's revenues from route & position of rival in the route.
Dyad level	MMC_{ij}	Baum & Korn (1999)	Rate of market entry and exit	Airline route	Inverted-U relationship	– MMC value is symmetric – Centrality of a route against route networks is considered
Firm-in-market level	MMC_{im}	Baum & Korn (1996)	Rate of market entry and exit	Airline route	$\otimes$ spheres of influence: negative effect concentration: no effect	– Focal market is included
		Gimeno & Woo (1996)	Yield (dollar per mile)	Airline route	$\otimes$ Positive effect on yield (i.e., decreases rivalry)	– Potential entrants are included – Focal market is *not* included

Table 1. Continued.

Feinberg (1985)	Firm's weighted average PCM	Manufacturing product	Positive effect on PCM	- "Sales-at-risk" of the focal firm at a contact is considered - Focal market is *not* included
Boeker, et al. (1997)	Market exit	Hospital services	Negative effect	- Focal market is included
Evans & Kessides (1994)	Log of average price	Airline route	Positive effect on price	- Focal market is included - Pure count measure & revenue-weighted measure
Jans & Rosenbaum (1996)	Price	Regional cement markets	Negative effect (pure count measure) Positive effect (M/S-, HHI-based measures)	- Focal market is *not* included Three different measures
Singal (1996)	Yield change	Airline route	Positive effect on yield	- Hybrid measure - Focal market is *not* included
Market-level MMC_m Hughes & Oughton (1993)	Industry PCM	Manufacturing	Positive effect on PCM	- Only 5 largest firms are included - Focal market is *not* included
Feinberg (1985)	Industry's weighted average PCM	Manufacturing product	Positive effect on industry PCM	- "Sales-at-risk" is considered - Weighted by the total sales of an industry (i.e. market)

Note: $\otimes$ moderator effect.

(*i* and *j*) that encounter each other in a focal market m, and would therefore be subscripted as *ijm*. Although not previously used in empirical research, this level of analysis shares the positive attributes of dyad, market and firm-in-market measures. Similar to the dyad measures, it focuses on the relational characteristics between two firms. Yet, similar to the market and firm-in-market level, it specifies the market context of the dyad, and therefore can be used to explain market-specific competitive behavior.

From a set of dyad-in-market (ijm) measures of multimarket contact, it is straightforward to generate dyad (ij) measures (by looking at the total overlap in all markets, rather than just the markets outside the focal market), as well as firm-in-market (im) measures (by aggregating among focal market rivals), and market (m) measures (by aggregating across dyads within the market). The distinctions are further explained below.

Dyad-in-market level measurement (MMC_{ijm}) This level of measurement captures the degree of multimarket contact outside the focal market between two firms (i and j) which are present in focal market m. This measure captures the number of markets (sometimes referred to as contact markets) in which i and j meet outside focal market m. This count may be weighted by some additional factor. Scott's (1982) purposive multimarket contact measure is an example of a dyad-in-market measure, although he used a representative dyad as a proxy for market-level multimarket contact. Given the difficulty of obtaining dependent variables at this level, the dyad-in-market level of analysis has not been used in empirical research on multimarket contact.

Dyad level measurement (MMC_{ij}) Dyad-level measurements capture the overall degree of multimarket contact between two firms (i and j) across all the markets where both firms are present. Therefore, no distinction is made between the focal market and the other (contact) markets. This level of measurement is often concerned with dyadic competitive behavior between two interdependent firms. Examples of this level of measurement include Chen's (1996) and Baum & Korn's (1999) measures.

Firm-in-market level measurement (MMC_{im}) Firm-in-market level measures capture the overall degree of multimarket contact between a focal firm and its focal-market competitors. Therefore, these measures aggregate the dyad-in-market measures of multimarket contact by taking the average, or weighted average, of the multimarket contact of the focal firm with each of the competitors in the focal market. Examples of this level of measurement are common in the management literature on multimarket competition (Barnett, 1993; Baum & Korn, 1996; Boeker, et al., 1997; Gimeno & Woo, 1996, 1999).

Market-level measurement (MMC_m) Market-level measures capture the overall degree of multimarket contact among the firms serving a focal market m. These measures have been mainly used in industrial organization economics (Feinberg, 1985; Hughes & Oughton, 1993; Evans & Kessides, 1994; Jans & Rosenbaum, 1996; Singal, 1996). Although most market-level measures aggregate the multimarket contacts among all the dyads in the focal market, some measures use the multimarket contact of a few representative dyads to reflect market-level multimarket contact. For instance, Scott (1982) used a randomly selected dyad in the market as a proxy for market-level multimarket contact, and Mester (1987) used the multimarket contact among the three leading firms in a market.

The Scaling of Multimarket Contact

Measures of multimarket contact also differ on their scaling and weighting of the multiple contacts. Early research assumed that the count of the number of contacts was enough to capture the level of multimarket contact. Scott (1982) challenged that assumption by asking "how much contact is a lot?" and argued that the focus of inquiry should be whether the level of multimarket contact is greater than that expected by chance contacts among multimarket firms.

In a similar line, other authors argued that the overall count of multimarket contact is not as informative as the ratio of multimarket contact markets to the total markets served by the firms (Baum & Korn, 1996, 1999; Boeker et al., 1997). Since firms active in many markets are more likely to have high multimarket contact purely by chance, the ratio corrects for the possibility of random multimarket contact. In addition, since limits in managerial attention exist regardless of the size of the firm, the amount of attention time a rival receives from a firm may be more strongly related to the relative multimarket contact than to the absolute number of contacts. Therefore, one point of contact among firms present in few markets is more saliently perceived than one point of contact among firms present in many markets.

Researchers have also argued that contacts should be weighted by the importance of the market position of the firms in the contact markets. Within that view, researchers differ about whether multimarket contacts should be weighted by the sales or market share of the focal firm in the contact markets (Feinberg, 1985; Singal, 1996), the market share of the rivals in the contact markets (Chen, 1996), or the shares of both firms (Singal, 1996). Gimeno (1999) partitioned an overall count of multimarket contact according to the positional interests of the rivals in the contact markets. He used three alternative proxies for positional interests: market dependence (percent of revenues), market dominance (market share), and resource centrality (the resource-based advantage of the firm in the market). Baum and Korn (1999) used the centrality of the markets (i.e. airline routes) in the firms' networks (airline route networks) to capture the significance of those markets for both firms in the dyad. Other researchers have argued that the size of the contact markets influences the magnitude of the contact, and therefore the forbearance effect. This view implies that contacts should be weighted by the size of the markets (Singal, 1996).

Overall, the issue of scaling and weighting multimarket contacts is still unresolved. The scaling factors and weights make theoretical sense according to the logic of mutual forbearance, and there is some consensus about the type of scales and weights that are appropriate. For instance, there is general concern about multimarket contacts being large just by random contacts, which has led many researchers to use measures of multimarket contact relative to the scope of the firms. Researchers also agree that some contacts may be more important or salient than others, although they differ on how to capture that importance in an empirical weight.

The use of different scales and weights can alter the distribution of the measures substantially, leading to situations where the weighted variables have low or negative correlation with other weighted or non-weighted measures. For instance, if the weights are inversely correlated with the count of multimarket contacts (as would happen, for instance, with weights such as the inverse of the number of markets served, or the percent of revenues from the market), weighted measures may be weakly or negatively correlated with non-weighted measures.

Scales and weights often bring theoretical assumptions about what contacts are more consequential. Yet, those assumptions should logically depend on the theoretical logic of the study, and may not be generalizable. Weights that capture the forbearance potential of multimarket contacts may be different from weights that capture the knowledge diffusion potential of the same contacts. It is unlikely that a set of weights will serve for all the theoretical applications of multimarket contact. Perhaps a more conservative goal is to understand how the choice of different weights modifies the distribution of variables.

Other Measurement Differences

Measures also differ in the way they aggregate multimarket contacts across levels. For instance, firm-in-market measures aggregate multimarket contacts with multiple rivals. Market-level measures aggregate multimarket contacts of multiple dyads within the market. Although most researchers have used simple averages to aggregate across levels, others have used weighted averages, sums, or weighted sums. Some others have used representative rivals or representative dyads instead of the full set. Different approaches to aggregation may influence results. For instance, aggregation methods that use the sum (rather than the average) of multimarket contacts across rivals or dyads tend to produce measures that are highly correlated with the number of incumbents in the market. This issue bears on the discriminant validity of measures.

Second, measures differ in whether the contact in the focal markets is included or excluded from multimarket contact measures at the dyad-in-market, firm-in-market and market levels. By definition, firms in the focal market always have a contact. If the contacts are weighted, the inclusion or exclusion of the focal market may have material influence in the distribution of the measure. From the economics view of extended interdependence, multimarket contact illustrates how contacts outside the focal market influence conduct in the focal market. Accordingly, many researchers have preferred to exclude the focal market contact from the measures to avoid muddled causality. Scott's (1982) dyad-in-market measure explicitly excludes the contact between the firms in the focal market. Among firm-in-market measures of multimarket contact, Gimeno and Woo's (1996) and Feinberg's (1985) measures exclude contacts in the focal market, whereas Baum and Korn's (1996) and Boeker et al.'s (1997) include them. Among market-level measures, all but Evans and Kessides' (1994) measures exclude focal market contacts in constructing multimarket contact measures.

Third, choices about weighting factors imply that multimarket contact may be a symmetric or asymmetric relationship. For instance, if a measure weights contacts by the inverse of the number of markets served by the focal firm, or by the percentage of revenues obtained by the focal firm in the contact market, the measure is inherently asymmetric. Measures that focus on pure counts, or that are equally weighted by both the focal firm and the rival's characteristics, are symmetric. Symmetric measures are not necessarily better. Chen (1996) argued that competitive relationships are inherently asymmetric, because of the asymmetric perceptions due to size and focus differences. However, asymmetric measures can lead to radically different measurement of multimarket contact for firms with objectively the same numbers of contacts; their use should be carefully grounded in theory.

REVIEW OF MULTIMARKET CONTACT MEASURES

Dyad-in-market Measures

Basic Count

In its most basic conceptualization, multimarket contact describes the count or number of markets in which some firms compete against each other. Indeed, the first measures of multimarket contact used in the literature were count measures of multimarket contact, although aggregated at the market or firm-in-market levels. Simple count measures of dyad-in-market multimarket contact, which capture the number of contacts between two firms outside the focal market, are often used as an intermediate step to create other aggregated measures. Dummy variables such as I_{jn} indicate whether a firm j is present in market n. Dummies for the firms in the focal market (I_{im} and I_{jm}) are inserted so that the measure equals zero if either firm is not present in the focal market. The dyad-in-market measure is:

$$M_{ijm} = I_{im} \cdot I_{jm} \cdot \sum_{n \neq m} I_{in} \cdot I_{jn}$$

The extension of this measure to the dyad level evaluates the number of contacts in all possible markets. For instance, Parker & Röller (1997) addressed collusion in duopoly markets in the mobile telephone industry (where regulation only allows two incumbents per market), and used M_{ij} to capture multimarket contact between the incumbents.

$$M_{ij} = \sum_{n} I_{in} \cdot I_{jn}.$$

Probabilistic Measure

In his study on the impact of multimarket contact on economic performance using line-of-business data of 437 U.S. large manufacturing firms in 1974, Scott (1982) challenged prior emphasis on count measures of multimarket contact.[4] He proposed measures that explicitly control for the probability that some degree of multimarket contact may be expected due to probabilistic overlap, even if firms enter markets at random. Scott (1982) presented two symmetric measures: *PMMC* and *ADEV*. Both measures describe how unlikely it is that the observed number of multimarket contacts between two firms may be due to random overlap. Under the null hypothesis of random diversification, the number of multimarket contacts should follow a hypergeometric distribution. If firms i and j compete respectively in n_i and n_j markets of N possible markets, and if they overlap in M_{ijm} markets outside the focal market, the PMMC measure captures the probability that ($M_{ijm} - 1$) or fewer contacts would have occurred by chance. High *PMMC* indicates that multimarket contact is greater than random, which may imply purposeful multimarket contact.

$$PMMC_{ijm} = I_{jm} \cdot I_{im} \cdot \sum_{f=0}^{M_{ijm}-1} P(f)$$

$$\text{where } P(f) = \frac{\dbinom{n_j-1}{f}\dbinom{N-n_j}{n_i-1-f}}{\dbinom{N-1}{n_i-1}}, \text{ for } n_j \geq n_i.$$

Scott (1982) used the dyad-in-market measure for a randomly-selected dyad as a proxy for market-level multimarket contact, and Mester (1987) extended the measure to three firms. In addition, Scott (1982) defined *ADEV*, a z-score equivalent, as the standardized difference between the actual number of contacts and the mean of the distribution under the null hypothesis of random diversification. The mean and variance of the distribution of multimarket contact under random diversification are:

$$E(M_{ijm}) = \frac{(n_i-1) \cdot (n_j-1)}{N-1} \text{ and } \sigma^2(M_{ijm}) \frac{(n_i-1) \cdot (n_j-1) \cdot (N-n_j) \cdot (N-n_i)}{(N-1)^2 \cdot (N-2)}$$

and the measure of ADEV is

$$ADEV_{ijm} = \frac{M_{ijm} - E(M_{ijm})}{\sigma(M_{ijm})}.$$

Dyad Measures

Chen (1996)
Chen (1996: 118) defined *market commonality* as "the degree of presence that a competitor manifests in the markets where it overlaps with a focal firm." This market commonality is a function of two factors: (1) the strategic importance for the focal firm of each of the markets shared with a competitor (captured by the

percentage of the focal firm's sales obtained in the market), and (2) the competitor's market position in these markets (captured by the competitor's market share in the market). Essentially, this measure is a weighted average of a rival's market share in the markets occupied by the focal firm, with weights based on percentage of the focal firm sales. Chen (1996) used units (passengers) rather than revenues to calculate market shares and percentages of sales. The measure ranges from 0 to 1, and is asymmetric (i.e. $MktComm_{ij} \neq MktComm_{ji}$). In the formula, P_{in} represents the number of passengers served by the focal firm i in the market n, P_i captures the total number of passengers served by the focal firm i, and P_n is the total number of passengers in the market n.

$$MktComm_{ij} = \sum_n \left(\frac{P_{in}}{P_i} \right) \left(\frac{P_{jn}}{P_n} \right).$$

Baum and Korn (1999)
Baum and Korn (1999) presented another dyad-level measure that captures the potential for mutual forbearance between focal firm i and competitor j as the sum of centrality-weighted proportions of jointly occupied markets. Implemented in the commuter airline industry sample, this measure uses route centrality as an indicator of the significance of a city-pair market for a firm. Route centrality (C_{in}) is defined as the proportion of airline i's city-pair routes that connect with a focal city-pair route n. Centrality for each firm is summed up across all markets where both firms are present, and divided by the sum of the markets served by the firms. The measure takes the value of zero when firms have a single contact. The measure is symmetric (i.e. $MMC_{ij} = MMC_{ji}$).

$$MMC(B \& K'99)_{ij} = \frac{\sum_n (C_{in} \cdot (I_{in} \cdot I_{jn})) + \sum_n (C_{jn} \cdot (I_{in} \cdot I_{jn}))}{\sum_n I_{in} + \sum_n I_{jn}} =$$

$$= \frac{\sum_n ((C_{in} + C_{jn}) \cdot (I_{in} \cdot I_{jn}))}{\sum_n I_{in} + \sum_n I_{jn}}, \text{ for } \forall \sum_n (I_{in} \cdot I_{jn}) = M_{ij} > 1, \ 0 \text{ otherwise.}$$

Firm-by-market Measures

Basic Count
The simplest measure of firm-in-market multimarket contact involves the average of multimarket contact counts with rivals in a focal market. This

measure ranges from zero to the number of markets served by the focal firm outside the focal market. For instance, Gimeno and Woo (1999) and Gimeno (1999) used this measure as a point of departure for more elaborate analysis.

$$\text{MMC(count)}_{im} = I_{im} \cdot \frac{\displaystyle\sum_{j \neq i} I_{jm} \cdot \left(\sum_{n \neq m} I_{in} \cdot I_{jn} \right)}{\displaystyle\sum_{j \neq i} I_{jm}} = I_{im} \cdot \frac{\displaystyle\sum_{j \neq i} I_{jm} \cdot M_{ijm}}{\displaystyle\sum_{j \neq i} I_{jm}} .$$

Gimeno & Woo (1996)
Unlike other measures that only take into account contacts with other market incumbents, Gimeno and Woo (1996) included potential entrants in the definition of focal market competitors. In their airline industry study, a firm was defined as a potential entrant if it was present in both endpoints of a city-pair route, but it did not serve the route. They also considered potential multimarket contacts, where a focal firm was a potential entrant into a competitor's market. This measure captures the focal firm i's average number of (actual and potential) multimarket contacts with focal-market competitors (actual and likely potential) in market m. This measure may be difficult to create in an industry where likely potential entrants are difficult to identify. Using a dummy variable T_{jn} to represent presence of firm j as a potential entrant to market n, this measure is

$$\text{MMC(G \& W'96)}_{im} = I_{im} \cdot \frac{\displaystyle\sum_{j \neq i} (I_{jm} + T_{jm}) \cdot \left(\sum_{n \neq m} (I_{in} + T_{in}) \cdot I_{jn} \right)}{\displaystyle\sum_{j \neq i} (I_{jm} + T_{jm})} .$$

Feinberg (1985)
Feinberg's (1985) measure, known as "sales-at-risk", has been adopted by several other authors (e.g. Alexander, 1985). This measure derives from the argument that the inducement for a focal firm to "forbear" in the focal market is proportional to the sales volume that the focal firm has "at risk" in the contact markets (S_{in}), and therefore should be used to weight the contacts. The measure is atypical in that it aggregates multimarket contacts among rivals using a sum, rather than the average. The measure is therefore likely to be correlated with the number of rivals in the focal market.

$$\text{SAR}_{im} = I_{im} \cdot \sum_{j \neq i} I_{jm} \cdot \left(\sum_{n \neq m} I_{in} \cdot I_{jn} \cdot S_{in} \right) .$$

Baum and Korn (1996)

Baum and Korn's (1996) measure was developed to study market entry and exit by firms. In contrast to other firm-in-market measures, presence of a focal firm in a focal market (I_{im}) is not required a priori. Their measure is similar to other firm-in-market count measures with the exceptions that: (a) the measure is divided by the number of markets served by the focal firm, and (b) only multimarket competitors are considered in both the numerator and denominator (two firms should meet at least in two markets to be considered multimarket competitors). The measure is thus not affected by the presence of single-market competitors in the focal market. The measure reflects the average multimarket contact with multimarket competitors present in the focal market, where multimarket contact is defined as the proportion of markets in which the focal firm meets with the multimarket competitors.

$$
\text{MMC(B \& K'96)}_{im} = \frac{\displaystyle\sum_{j \neq i} B_{ij} \cdot I_{jm} \cdot \left(\frac{\displaystyle\sum_n I_{in} \cdot I_{jn}}{\displaystyle\sum_n I_{in}} \right)}{\displaystyle\sum_{j \neq i} B_{ij} \cdot I_{jm}} = \frac{\displaystyle\sum_{j \neq i} B_{ij} \cdot I_{jm} \cdot \left(\frac{M_{ij}}{\displaystyle\sum_n I_{in}} \right)}{\displaystyle\sum_{j \neq i} B_{ij} \cdot I_{jm}},
$$

where $B_{ij} = 1$ if $\displaystyle\sum_n (D_{in} \cdot D_{jn}) = M_{ij} > 1$, 0 otherwise.

Boeker, Goodstein, Stephen, and Murmann (1997)

In their study on the impact of multimarket competition on service market exit using 286 hospitals in California between 1980 and 1986, Boeker, et al. (1997) presented another firm-in-market measure. This measure is almost identical to Baum and Korn's (1996) except that Boeker, et al.'s (1997) measure counts multimarket contacts with all focal-market competitors, including single-market competitors. The measure reflects the average percentage of multimarket overlap with focal market rivals.

$$
\text{MMC(BGSM)}_{im} = I_{im} \cdot \frac{\displaystyle\sum_{j \neq i} I_{jm} \cdot \left(\frac{\displaystyle\sum_n I_{in} \cdot I_{jn}}{\displaystyle\sum_n I_{in}} \right)}{\displaystyle\sum_{j \neq i} I_{jm}} = I_{im} \cdot \frac{\displaystyle\sum_{j \neq i} I_{jm} \cdot \left(\frac{M_{ij}}{\displaystyle\sum_n I_{in}} \right)}{\displaystyle\sum_{j \neq i} I_{jm}}.
$$

Market-level Measures

Basic Count

The first measures of multimarket contact proposed in the literature were market-level multimarket count measures (Heggestad & Rhoades, 1978; Whitehead, 1978). Early measures calculated the average number of multimarket contacts among a subset of dominant firms in the focal market (Heggestad & Rhoades, 1978; Whitehead, 1978; Rhoades & Heggestad, 1985; Sandler, 1988). More recently, the measure has been calculated by averaging the multimarket contacts of all the dyads in the market (Evans & Kessides, 1994). Evans and Kessides' (1994) measure calculates the average count of multimarket contact (including contacts in the focal market) among all dyads in a focal market.[5]

$$\text{MMC(E \& K)}_m = \frac{\sum_i \sum_{j>i} I_{im} \cdot I_{jm} \cdot \left(\sum_n I_{in} \cdot I_{jn} \right)}{N_m(N_m-1)/2} = \frac{\sum_i \sum_{j>i} I_{im} \cdot I_{jm} \cdot M_{ijm}}{N_m(N_m-1)/2}, \text{ where } N_m = \sum_k I_{km}.$$

Other researchers have modified this count measure by excluding the number of contacts in the focal market. The first measure presented by Jans and Rosenbaum (1996) is identical to the previous measure by Evans and Kessides (1994) except that it excludes focal market contacts.[6]

$$\text{MMC(count)}_m = \frac{\sum_i \sum_{j>i} I_{im} \cdot I_{jm} \cdot \left(\sum_{n \neq m} I_{in} \cdot I_{jn} \right)}{N_m(N_m-1)/2} = \frac{\sum_i \sum_{j>i} I_{im} \cdot I_{jm} \cdot M_{ijm}}{N_m(N_m-1)/2}, \text{ where } N_m = \sum_k I_{km}.$$

Evans & Kessides (1994)

In addition to the count measure described above, Evans and Kessides (1994) constructed another measure of multimarket contact based on revenue contact. This market-level variable is defined as the average revenue multimarket contact among dyads in a market (a U.S. airline city-pair market), where the revenue multimarket contact is calculated as the sum across all markets of the product of the percentages of revenues obtained by both firms in the contact markets. Using S_{in} to represent revenues of firm i in market n, and S_i to represent total sales by firm i, the measure is written as

$$\text{RMMC(E \& K)}_m = \frac{\sum\limits_i \sum\limits_{j>i} I_{im} \cdot I_{jm} \cdot \left(\sum\limits_n \frac{S_{in}}{S_i} \cdot \frac{S_{jn}}{S_j} \right)}{N_m(N_m-1)/2}, \text{ where } N_m = \sum\limits_k I_{km}.$$

Hughes and Oughton (1993)

Hughes and Oughton (1993) presented another market-level multimarket contact measure with several interesting features. First, the measure weights the number of multimarket contacts between a dyad by the sum of the employment shares of both firms in the focal market (where E_{jm} represents the number of employees of firm j in market m, and E_m represents the total number of employees in market m). To our knowledge, this is the first published measure of multimarket contact to weight multimarket contact by the focal-market positions of the firms. Second, the measure aggregates dyads by calculating the sum, rather than the average, of multimarket contacts across dyads. Although the original measure by Hughes and Oughton (1993) was only calculated for the dominant five firms in the industry, the measure can be generalized to any number of incumbents. In fact, the number of incumbents can equal the number of incumbents in the market, although this may have the disadvantage of making the measure highly correlated to the number of incumbents in the market.[7]

$$\text{MMC(H \& O)}_m = \sum\limits_i \sum\limits_{j>i} I_{im} \cdot I_{jm} \cdot \left(\frac{E_{im} + E_{jm}}{E_m} \right) \cdot \sum\limits_{n \neq m} (I_{in} \cdot I_{jn})$$

$$= \sum\limits_i \sum\limits_{j>i} I_{im} \cdot I_{jm} \cdot \left(\frac{E_{im} + E_{jm}}{E_m} \right) \cdot M_{ijm}.$$

Feinberg (1985)

Feinberg (1985) extended his "sales-at-risk" measure to the market level. This measure aggregates "sales-at-risk" firm-in-market measures of multimarket contact by summing the contacts of all the focal-market incumbents, and dividing by the total sales in the focal market. This measure therefore controls for the relative size of the focal market relative to the contact markets.

$$\text{SAR}_m = \frac{\sum\limits_i I_{im} \cdot \sum\limits_{j \neq i} I_{jm} \cdot \sum\limits_{n \neq m} (I_{in} \cdot I_{jn}) \cdot S_{in}}{\sum\limits_i S_{im}} = \frac{\sum\limits_i \text{SAR}_{im}}{\sum\limits_i S_{im}}.$$

Singal (1996)

In his study on the impact of U.S. airline mergers on airfares, Singal (1996) developed the most comprehensive and complex measure to date. He incorporated several critical weights previously discussed in the literature. The importance of the contact for the dyad is:

(a) inversely related to the number of dyads in the market: $N_m(N_m-1)/2$, where N_m is the number of firms in the market,
(b) directly related to the joint presence of the dyad in the market (measured by the sum of market shares),
(c) directly related to the asymmetry of market shares of the dyad (measured by the root of the ratio of higher to lower market shares) (Bernheim & Whinston, 1990), and
(d) directly related to the size of the market (measured by the root of the percentage industry revenues from the market).

These weights lead to the following expanded measurement of a point of market contact:

$$MC(Singal)_{ijm} = I_{im} \cdot I_{jm} \cdot \frac{(MS_{im} + MS_{jm})\sqrt{MS_{im}/MS_{jm}}}{N_m(N_m-1)/2} \cdot \sqrt{\frac{R_m \times 100}{R_{total}}}, \text{ for } MS_{im} \geq Ms_{jm}.$$

Two firms in a focal market will have high multimarket contact when the sum of the market contacts outside the focal market is high. Singal (1996) argues that market-level multimarket contact should reflect the aggregate effects of the multimarket contact of all the dyads in the focal market. However, multimarket contact for different dyads would have market-level effects proportional to the amount of focal-market contact for the dyad. Accordingly, Singal's (1996) measure weights the multimarket contact (outside the focal market) of each dyad by the focal-market contact of the dyad.

$$MMC(Singal)_m = \sum_i \sum_{j>i} MC(Singal)_{ijm} \cdot \sum_{n \neq m} MC(Singal)_{ijn}.$$

Extending Existing Multimarket Contact Measures Across Levels

In order to facilitate comparisons of existing measures, and to evaluate reliability and validity at different levels of measurement, we extended existing measures to other levels of measurement for which they were not originally designed.

While this extension involved the risk of misinterpreting the intents of prior researchers (for which we apologize in advance), it allowed direct comparison of measures originally designed for different levels, and helped identify the best performing measures across multiple levels. Appendix B presents the full set of multimarket contact measures extended across multiple levels of measurement. Measures with an asterisk indicate that they are in the form proposed and tested by the original authors.

RELIABILITY AND VALIDITY ASSESSMENT

We were concerned with assessing consistency and validity of multimarket contact measures. Validity refers to the crucial relationship between a construct and its indicators (Carmines & Zeller, 1979), and generally relates to the extent that the measurement captures what it is supposed to capture. Reliability, on the other hand, reflects the consistency among measures. Although reliability is sometimes discussed distinctly from validity, here we followed Venkatraman and Grant (1986) and Bagozzi (1980) in treating reliability as one of the components of validity, internal consistency. The empirical part of the study assessed the validity of the multimarket contact measures in multiple ways: content validity, internal consistency (unidimensionality and reliability), discriminant validity, and predictive validity.

The Empirical Context

We assessed the reliability and validity of the multimarket contact measures in the context of the U.S. domestic airline industry. The motivation for this choice was both theoretical and practical. Compared with other industries, the airline industry offered clear market definitions, which is critical for research on multimarket contact (Singal, 1996). Second, there was great variance in the amount of multimarket contact, regardless of how multimarket contact was defined. Some dyads competed over hundreds of markets, whereas others did not compete at all. Third, high quality secondary data was available from reliable government agencies. Fourth, airline industry data had been widely used in prior empirical research on multimarket contact (e.g. Sandler, 1988; Chen, 1996; Evans & Kessides, 1994; Baum & Korn, 1996, 1999; Gimeno & Woo, 1996, 1999; Gimeno, 1999; Singal, 1996; Smith & Wilson, 1995), which facilitated replication of measures and comparison with previous results.

Data Source

The data used in this study covered U.S. airlines' scheduled passenger operations in domestic city-pair markets for the fourth quarters of 1986 to 1995. Our data sets reflected the positions of 59 airlines across 3,120 city-pair markets over 10 years. For detailed description of the data source, please see Gimeno & Woo (1996, 1999). In order to study multiple levels of analysis, we created three data sets at the dyad, firm-in-market, and market level, respectively. All the data sets were unbalanced panels of data. Each data set contained distinct information about multimarket contact and other variables at the relevant level.

The dyad data set comprised eleven multimarket contact measures at the dyad level, three variables related to the combined size of the firms in the dyad (average markets served by the dyad, average revenues of the dyad, average passengers of the dyad), and three variables tentatively associated with mutual forbearance (Baum & Korn, 1999). These variables were the rate of entry of a focal firm into rivals' markets (calculated as the number of next-year entries by the focal firm into markets where the rival was present), rate of exit (the number of next-year exits by the focal firm from markets where both the focal firm and the rival were present), and net entry (the number of next-year entries minus the number of next-year exits, relative to the current number of markets of overlap). Industry-wide exits were not considered to be market exits. The data set contained information on 1,415 dyads, and a total number of 4,285 observations.

The firm-in-market data set comprised eleven measures of multimarket contact at that level, three variables capturing the size of the firm (number of markets served, total revenues, total passengers), the number of focal-market incumbents, and two variables tentatively related to mutual forbearance. These variables were the firm-in-market yield (average price of tickets divided by distance traveled), and a dummy variable reflecting market exit in the following year. Observations of monopoly markets were removed from the set. The data set contained observations from 15,875 firms-in-market combinations, and a total of 85,757 observations.

The market-level data set comprised twelve multimarket contacts measures, three aggregate measures of size of the market incumbents (average number of markets served, average total revenues, average total passengers), the number of incumbents in a market, and two variables tentatively related to mutual forbearance outcomes. These variables were the average yield in the market (passenger-weighted average of firm-in-market yields), and the rate of market exit (ratio of next-year market exits to current market incumbents). As before, monopoly markets were eliminated from the data set. The data set contained information on 3,120 markets, for a total of 25,510 observations.

Empirical Analysis

We took advantage of the panel characteristics of our data in evaluating the reliability and validity of the measures. The distinction between cross-sectional and longitudinal variations in multimarket contact measures is important. Casual observation suggests that longitudinal studies have been more consistent than cross-sectional studies in finding evidence of forbearance.

For each data set at a different level of analysis, we created two subsidiary data sets that focused on the longitudinal and cross-sectional covariance of the measures and variables. Building on the econometrics of panel data analysis, we transformed each data set into a within-unit of analysis data set that captured longitudinal variations of variables within a given unit of analysis, and a between-unit of analysis data set that captured the cross-sectional variation between units of analysis. The within-unit data set was constructed by "absorbing" the effects of the unit of analysis, which was equivalent to taking the differences of the variables with respect to the unit-specific means (Greene, 1997; Searle, 1971). This was equivalent to including fixed effects dummies for each unit of analysis. The between-unit data set was constructed by taking the means of each variable across time for each unit of analysis. For instance, at the dyad level of analysis, an observation of the new data reflected the average of the variables across all years for a given dyad. Correlations in the within-unit data set reflected longitudinal correlations among variables; correlations in the between-unit data set reflect cross-sectional correlations among variables. Since cross-sectional correlations between units may reflect the spurious effect of unobserved heterogeneity, within-unit correlations have stronger causality implications than between-unit correlations, although they may be inaccurate for variables with negligible longitudinal variation.

We used correlation analysis as an analytical method, and we present zero-order (Pearson) and partial correlations for relevant variables in the tables. This method of assessing reliability and validity, while simplistic, was appropriate for understanding basic relationships among the measures and variables in question. More elaborate analytical tools, such as structural equation modeling, failed to display sufficient model fit in the confirmatory factor analysis. Tables 2, 3 and 4 report basic statistics and correlation coefficients of the multimarket contact measures for three levels of analysis. Tables 5, 6 and 7 present statistics assessing the reliability, discriminant validity and predictive validity of the measures. For all the measures in the tables, raw, within-unit and between-unit statistics are presented.

Table 2. Descriptive Statistics and Correlations: Dyad Level.

Variable	Data type	N	Mean	Std Dev	Skewness	1	2	3	4	5	6	7	8	9	10
1. M_{ij}	Raw	4,285	61.05	167.07	3.70	0.97									
	Within	4,285		38.86	-2.73	0.91									
	Between	1,415		102.61	5.83	0.97									
2. MMC (G&W'96)$_{ij}$	Raw	4,285	109.90	273.81	3.21	0.87	0.79								
	Within	4,285		55.47	-2.60	0.86	0.72								
	Between	1,415		171.57	5.08	0.88	0.80								
3. MMC (H&O)$_{ij}$	Raw	4,285	14,586.65	68,910.87	8.76	0.92	0.89	0.78							
	Within	4,285		27,000.09	-0.62	0.68	0.66	0.56							
	Between	1,415		38,051.71	12.28	0.93	0.89	0.80							
4. SAR$_{ij}$	Raw	4,285	8.33E+07	2.19E+08	3.97	0.28	0.28	0.22	0.25						
	Within	4,285		6.59E+07	-1.74	0.18	0.18	0.13	0.14						
	Between	1,415		1.32E+08	5.85	0.23	0.24	0.18	0.22						
5. MktComm$_{ij}$	Raw	4,285	2.33E-02	5.66E-02	5.44	0.30	0.30	0.22	0.30	0.50					
	Within	4,285		1.83E-02	1.55	0.24	0.23	0.15	0.22	0.23					
	Between	1,415		4.93E-02	6.01	0.19	0.19	0.14	0.20	0.34					
6. MMC (B&K'99)$_{ij}$	Raw	4,285	6.94E-03	2.19E-02	11.18	-0.02	-0.03	-0.01	0.00	0.44	0.67				
	Within	4,285		4.56E-03	11.60	0.02	0.02	0.01	0.04	0.24	0.16				
	Between	1,415		2.34E-02	12.79	-0.01	-0.02	-0.01	0.02	0.30	0.63				
7. RMMC (E&K)$_{ij}$	Raw	4,285	2.84E-03	1.46E-02	12.45	0.30	0.27	0.21	0.32	0.42	0.35	0.25			
	Within	4,285		2.42E-03	-0.73	0.19	0.16	0.12	0.15	0.21	0.21	0.19			
	Between	1,415		1.78E-02	13.3	0.25	0.22	0.16	0.29	0.42	0.34	0.28			
8. PMMC$_{ij}$	Raw	4,285	0.32	0.43	0.76	0.48	0.51	0.36	0.43	0.66	0.36	0.17	0.53		
	Within	4,285		0.17	0.58	0.28	0.31	0.19	0.21	0.34	0.22	0.10	0.43		
	Between	1,415		0.39	0.93	0.40	0.42	0.29	0.36	0.72	0.31	0.16	0.53		
9. MMC (B&K'96)$_{ij}$	Raw	4,285	0.13	0.23	2.00	0.42	0.44	0.31	0.37	0.70	0.31	0.22	0.54	0.88	
	Within	4,285		0.08	-0.88	0.31	0.33	0.21	0.23	0.49	0.18	0.18	0.50	0.72	
	Between	1,415		0.20	2.63	0.34	0.36	0.25	0.31	0.72	0.26	0.21	0.54	0.89	
10. MMC (BGSM)$_{ij}$	Raw	4,285	0.15	0.25	1.90	0.16	0.16	0.11	0.15	0.28	0.25	0.13	0.25	0.25	0.22
	Within	4,285		0.07	-0.46	0.08	0.07	0.06	0.07	0.09	0.03	0.01	0.05	0.08	0.12
	Between	1,415		0.22	2.53	0.21	0.22	0.13	0.22	0.36	0.32	0.15	0.37	0.32	0.28
11. MMC (Singal)$_{ij}$	Raw	4,285	44.04	90.11	4.84										
	Within	4,285		56.31	3.26										
	Between	1,415		62.33	4.70										

Table 3. Descriptive Statistics and Correlations: Firm-in-market Level.

Variable	Data type	N	Mean	Std Dev	Skewness	1	2	3	4	5	6	7	8	9	10
1. MMC (count)$_{im}$	Raw	85,757	553.28	260.40	0.28	0.25									
	Within	85,757		126.19	-0.25	2.69									
	Between	15,875		246.56	0.02	-0.28									
2. MMC (G&W'96)$_{im}$	Raw	85,757	813.77	292.33	-0.34	0.66	0.81								
	Within	85,757		142.32	-0.36	1.47	0.72								
	Between	15,875		291.96	-0.64	0.32	0.87								
3. MMC (H&O)$_{im}$	Raw	85,757	728.84	415.13	0.89	1.75	0.76	0.61							
	Within	85,757		209.39	-0.11	3.97	0.66	0.55							
	Between	15,875		357.64	0.57	0.86	0.84	0.71							
4. SAR$_{im}$	Raw	85,757	1.93E+09	1.51E+09	1.39	2.19	0.41	0.36	0.60						
	Within	85,757		7.21E+08	-0.12	3.32	0.36	0.44	0.60						
	Between	15,875		1.29E+09	1.19	1.42	0.52	0.45	0.64						
5. MktComm$_{im}$	Raw	85,757	6.91E-02	2.86E-02	2.92	35.37	0.33	0.10	0.18	-0.02					
	Within	85,757		1.60E-02	0.94	17.35	0.59	0.30	0.31	0.14					
	Between	15,875		2.71E-02	2.51	20.28	0.20	-0.01	0.12	-0.06					
6. MMC (B&K'99)$_{im}$	Raw	85,757	2.56E-02	9.32E-03	14.37	466.02	0.48	0.38	0.38	0.27	0.53				
	Within	85,757		4.03E-03	11.46	876.14	0.58	0.40	0.39	0.30	0.53				
	Between	15,875		8.93E-03	14.48	518.11	0.51	0.45	0.44	0.31	0.40				
7. RMMC (E&K)$_{im}$	Raw	85,757	1.92E-03	4.27E-03	32.99	1,280.18	-0.07	-0.12	-0.05	0.00	0.41	0.70			
	Within	85,757		1.19E-03	38.71	4,605.33	-0.03	-0.07	-0.03	-0.04	0.14	0.38			
	Between	15,875		3.78E-03	30.20	1,111.65	-0.09	-0.14	-0.07	0.00	0.41	0.64			
8. PMMC$_{im}$	Raw	85,757	0.68	0.30	-0.67	-0.45	0.19	0.00	0.13	0.08	0.42	0.35	0.15		
	Within	85,757		0.17	-0.05	2.67	0.21	0.00	0.08	0.03	0.32	0.34	0.14		
	Between	15,875		0.27	-0.57	-0.48	0.14	-0.04	0.12	0.06	0.46	0.33	0.17		
9. MMC (B&K'96)$_{im}$	Raw	85,757	0.45	0.13	0.06	0.46	0.36	0.19	0.19	-0.04	0.69	0.32	0.10	0.35	
	Within	85,757		0.08	-0.27	2.28	0.81	0.52	0.47	0.28	0.75	0.57	0.00	0.26	
	Between	15,875		0.12	0.05	0.78	0.18	0.03	0.10	-0.13	0.71	0.21	0.13	0.44	
10. MMC (BGSM)$_{im}$	Raw	85,757	0.45	0.13	0.06	0.43	0.36	0.20	0.19	-0.04	0.69	0.32	0.09	0.36	1.00
	Within	85,757		0.07	-0.25	2.07	0.81	0.52	0.47	0.28	0.76	0.57	0.00	0.26	1.00
	Between	15,875		0.12	0.05	0.73	0.19	0.04	0.10	-0.12	0.71	0.21	0.13	0.44	0.99
11. MMC (Singal)$_{im}$	Raw	85,757	10.53	20.10	12.00	336.47	-0.04	-0.08	-0.03	-0.15	0.04	-0.02	0.06	-0.01	-0.05	-0.05
	Within	85,757		12.34	10.38	516.89	0.16	0.12	0.04	-0.06	0.08	0.05	-0.06	0.06	0.12	0.12
	Between	15,875		17.70	8.92	146.21	-0.09	-0.12	-0.07	-0.18	0.02	-0.03	0.08	-0.04	-0.12	-0.11

Table 4. Descriptive Statistics and Correlations: Market Level.

Variable		N	Mean	Std Dev	Skewness	1	2	3	4	5	6	7	8	9	10	11
1. MMC (E&K)$_m$	Raw	25,510	566.41	259.21	0.43											
	Within	25,510		173.54	0.00											
	Between	3,120		204.18	-0.09											
2. MMC (count)$_m$	Raw	25,510	565.41	259.21	0.43	1.00										
	Within	25,510		173.54	0.00	1.00										
	Between	3,120		204.18	-0.09	1.00										
3. MMC (G&W'96)$_m$	Raw	25,510	826.27	273.65	0.19	0.83	0.83									
	Within	25,510		185.41	-0.23	0.82	0.82									
	Between	3,120		213.32	-0.28	0.85	0.85									
4. MMC (H&O)$_m$	Raw	25,510	1,241.38	775.58	0.70	0.36	0.36	0.30								
	Within	25,510		444.20	-0.05	0.44	0.44	0.48								
	Between	3,120		650.40	0.58	0.38	0.38	0.24								
5. SAR$_m$	Raw	25,510	6,114.28	6,960.77	2.50	0.23	0.23	0.30	0.36							
	Within	25,510		4,144.05	1.35	0.16	0.16	0.20	0.58							
	Between	3,120		5,525.83	1.65	0.31	0.31	0.38	0.29							
6. MktComm$_m$	Raw	25,510	7.24E-02	2.70E-02	3.40	0.47	0.47	0.23	0.08	0.06						
	Within	25,510		1.63E-02	0.70	0.51	0.51	0.29	0.17	0.06						
	Between	3,120		2.36E-02	4.46	0.41	0.41	0.15	0.04	0.06						
7. MMC (B&K'99)$_m$	Raw	25,510	2.60E-02	1.09E-02	17.29	0.35	0.35	0.24	0.14	0.11	0.65					
	Within	25,510		5.58E-03	14.22	0.51	0.51	0.37	0.26	0.11	0.55					
	Between	3,120		1.20E-02	21.65	0.21	0.21	0.11	0.07	0.09	0.64					
8. RMMC (E&K)$_m$	Raw	25,510	1.96E-03	5.36E-03	27.81	-0.09	-0.09	-0.15	-0.04	-0.02	0.51	0.78				
	Within	25,510		1.77E-03	21.41	-0.08	-0.08	-0.14	-0.07	-0.01	0.30	0.46				
	Between	3,120		5.46E-03	24.64	-0.11	-0.11	-0.18	-0.05	-0.03	0.59	0.84				
9. PMMC$_m$	Raw	25,510	0.69	0.29	-0.84	0.18	0.18	-0.04	0.01	0.03	0.45	0.28	0.12			
	Within	25,510		0.20	-0.18	0.13	0.13	-0.08	0.03	0.06	0.42	0.31	0.17			
	Between	3,120		0.22	-0.74	0.19	0.19	-0.04	0.05	0.06	0.47	0.24	0.12			
10. MMC (B&K'96)$_m$	Raw	25,510	0.46	0.10	-0.49	0.87	0.87	0.66	0.31	0.22	0.66	0.51	0.11	0.47		
	Within	25,510		0.06	-0.38	0.86	0.86	0.66	0.39	0.13	0.70	0.61	0.09	0.40		
	Between	3,120		0.08	-0.72	0.87	0.87	0.65	0.31	0.29	0.62	0.39	0.13	0.50		
11. MMC (BGSM)$_m$	Raw	25,510	0.46	0.10	-0.48	0.87	0.87	0.66	0.31	0.22	0.66	0.51	0.11	0.47	1.00	
	Within	25,510		0.06	-0.38	0.86	0.86	0.66	0.39	0.13	0.70	0.61	0.09	0.40	1.00	
	Between	3,120		0.08	-0.69	0.87	0.87	0.65	0.31	0.29	0.62	0.39	0.12	0.50	1.00	
12. MMC (Singal)$_m$	Raw	25,510	18.23	27.04	8.49	-0.11	-0.11	-0.17	-0.10	-0.33	0.03	-0.03	0.07	-0.02	-0.13	-0.13
	Within	25,510		17.21	9.28	0.15	0.15	0.14	-0.04	-0.08	0.04	0.02	-0.09	0.04	0.12	0.12
	Between	3,120		22.41	5.49	-0.31	-0.31	-0.39	-0.15	-0.46	0.00	0.00	0.14	-0.08	-0.30	-0.30

Table 5. Reliability, Dicrimination Validity and Predictve Validity: Dyad Level.

Overall MMC Score		RELIABILITY DISCRIMINANT VALIDITY		PREDICTIVE VALIDITY					
		Cronbach's Alpha	Zero-order correlations: Size Score	Rate of entry		Correlations: Rate of exit		Net Entry	
				Zero	Partial	Zero	Partial	Zero	Partial
Overall MMC Score	Raw	0.87	0.63	0.20	0.02	−0.09	−0.07	−0.07	−0.06
	Within	0.78	0.51	−0.06	−0.03	0.01	0.02	−0.17	−0.10
	Between	0.86	0.56	0.20	0.04	−0.10	−0.08	−0.03	−0.06

Individual Measures		Correlation with the remaining total	Contribution to Alpha	Zero-order correlations: Size Score	Rate of entry		Correlations: Rate of exit		Net Entry	
					Zero	Partial	Zero	Partial	Zero	Partial
M_{ij}	Raw	0.72	0.02	0.67	0.22	0.12	−0.07	−0.02	−0.08	−0.06
	Within	0.69	0.05	0.55	−0.06	−0.03	0.03	0.03	−0.12	−0.02
	Between	0.69	0.02	0.55	0.17	0.07	−0.10	−0.06	−0.06	−0.11
MMC (G&W'96)$_{ij}$	Raw	0.70	0.02	0.68	0.21	0.09	−0.06	0.00	−0.07	−0.06
	Within	0.65	0.04	0.57	−0.04	−0.01	0.04	0.04	−0.13	−0.02
	Between	0.67	0.02	0.57	0.16	0.04	−0.09	−0.05	−0.05	−0.11
MMC (H&O)$_{ij}$	Raw	0.59	0.01	0.51	0.15	0.06	−0.06	−0.01	−0.05	−0.03
	Within	0.53	0.03	0.39	−0.04	−0.01	0.01	0.00	−0.03	0.05
	Between	0.56	0.01	0.41	0.11	0.04	−0.06	−0.02	−0.04	−0.08
SAR$_{ij}$	Raw	0.68	0.02	0.66	0.22	0.12	−0.09	−0.04	−0.08	−0.07
	Within	0.53	0.03	0.59	−0.09	−0.06	0.02	0.02	−0.10	0.01
	Between	0.66	0.02	0.56	0.19	0.09	−0.12	−0.09	−0.07	−0.12
*MktComm$_{ij}$ [b]	**Raw**	**0.61**	**0.01**	**0.31**	**0.03**	**−0.10**	**−0.04**	**−0.04**	**0.02**	**0.03**
	Within	**0.39**	**0.01**	**0.17**	**−0.02**	**−0.01**	**−0.05**	**−0.03**	**−0.03**	**−0.01**
	Between	**0.58**	**0.01**	**0.30**	**0.06**	**−0.05**	**−0.01**	**0.00**	**0.06**	**0.05**

Table 5. Continued.

MMC (B&K'99)_ij −0.06		Raw	0.53	0.01	0.15	0.15	0.08	−0.05	−0.08	−0.06
	Within	**0.32**	**0.00**	**0.16**	**−0.03**	**−0.02**	**0.01**	**0.03**	**−0.12**	**−0.12**
	Between	**0.44**	**0.00**	**0.05**	**0.17**	**0.13**	**−0.06**	**−0.12**	**−0.06**	**−0.05**
RMMC (E&K)_ij	Raw	0.26	−0.01	−0.05	0.10	0.09	−0.06	−0.09	−0.03	−0.02
	Within	0.16	−0.01	0.01	0.00	0.01	−0.01	0.00	−0.02	−0.02
	Between	0.25	−0.01	−0.04	0.25	0.27	−0.07	−0.10	−0.04	0.00
PMMC_ij	Raw	0.51	0.01	0.30	0.24	0.13	−0.06	−0.07	−0.11	−0.11
	Within	0.38	0.01	0.08	−0.04	−0.03	0.05	0.05	−0.18	−0.17
	Between	0.52	0.01	0.31	0.25	0.13	−0.11	−0.11	−0.10	−0.08
MMC (B&K'96)_ij	Raw	0.71	0.02	0.49	0.04	−0.16	0.01	0.03	−0.02	−0.01
	Within	0.51	0.03	0.23	−0.01	0.00	0.06	0.06	−0.19	−0.15
	Between	0.69	0.02	0.44	0.01	−0.18	0.03	0.04	0.09	0.07
MMC (BGSM)_ij	Raw	0.68	0.02	0.46	0.01	−0.20	−0.03	−0.02	0.02	0.02
	Within	0.59	0.03	0.24	−0.02	0.00	−0.02	−0.02	−0.12	−0.07
	Between	0.65	0.02	0.40	−0.01	−0.20	0.00	0.00	0.09	0.07
MMC (Singal)_ij	Raw	0.28	−0.01	0.36	0.09	−0.04	−0.08	−0.07	−0.04	−0.03
	Within	0.11	−0.02	0.15	−0.03	−0.01	−0.09	−0.09	−0.05	−0.03
	Between	0.39	0.00	0.43	0.14	0.00	−0.09	−0.08	−0.03	−0.05
Size Score[a]	Raw				0.24		−0.09		−0.05	
	Within				−0.06		0.01		−0.18	
	Between				0.22		−0.12		0.05	

[a] Cronbach's alphas for Size Score for Raw, Within, and Between data are 0.98, 0.86, and 0.98, respectively.
[b] Measures with '*' are original ones suggested in previous research at the dyad level of analysis.

Table 6. Reliability, Discriminant Validity and Predictive Validity: Firm-in-market Level.

Overall MMC Score		RELIABILITY	DISCRIMINANT VALIDITY		PREDICTIVE VALIDITY			
			Zero-order correlations:		Correlations:			
					Yield		Exit	
		Cronbach's Alpha	Size Score	Number of Incumbents	Zero	Partial	Zero	Partial
Overall MMC Score	Raw	0.82	0.45	-0.16	0.01	-0.09	-0.06	-0.03
	Within	0.87	0.50	-0.15	0.27	0.16	0.02	0.02
	Between	0.80	0.47	-0.17	-0.02	-0.14	-0.15	-0.10

Individual Measures		Correlation with the remaining total	Contribution to Alpha	Zero-order correlations:		Correlations:			
						Yield		Exit	
				Size Score	Number of Incumbents	Zero	Partial	Zero	Partial
*MMC(count)_im [b]	**Raw**	**0.75**	**0.04**	**0.75**	**-0.24**	**0.10**	**-0.07**	**-0.07**	**-0.02**
	Within	**0.87**	**0.03**	**0.59**	**-0.23**	**0.27**	**0.14**	**0.01**	**0.00**
	Between	**0.72**	**0.04**	**0.81**	**-0.24**	**0.06**	**-0.13**	**-0.13**	**-0.04**
*MMC (G&W'96)_im	**Raw**	**0.51**	**0.02**	**0.68**	**-0.26**	**0.15**	**0.01**	**-0.02**	**0.04**
	Within	**0.60**	**0.01**	**0.65**	**-0.12**	**0.34**	**0.22**	**0.02**	**0.02**
	Between	**0.50**	**0.02**	**0.75**	**-0.28**	**0.10**	**-0.07**	**-0.06**	**0.06**
MMC (H&O)_im	Raw	0.59	0.02	0.64	0.08	-0.03	-0.09	-0.14	-0.13
	Within	0.60	0.01	0.51	0.21	0.20	0.10	-0.02	-0.03
	Between	0.63	0.03	0.73	-0.01	-0.05	-0.16	-0.23	-0.22
*SAR_im	**Raw**	**0.29**	**0.00**	**0.56**	**0.54**	**-0.15**	**-0.08**	**-0.03**	**0.01**
	Within	**0.37**	**0.00**	**0.49**	**0.46**	**0.23**	**0.18**	**0.04**	**0.04**
	Between	**0.32**	**0.00**	**0.64**	**0.46**	**-0.18**	**-0.13**	**-0.08**	**-0.02**
MktComm_im	Raw	0.59	0.02	-0.07	-0.21	-0.02	-0.08	-0.01	-0.02
	Within	0.65	0.02	0.08	-0.21	0.12	0.09	0.03	0.03
	Between	0.52	0.02	-0.14	-0.18	-0.03	-0.09	-0.06	-0.08

Table 6. Continued.

IMMC (B&K'99)$_{im}$	Raw	0.67	0.03	0.28	-0.13	0.01	-0.07	-0.03	-0.01
	Within	0.68	0.02	0.27	-0.14	0.18	0.11	0.02	0.02
	Between	0.67	0.04	0.34	-0.16	0.00	-0.09	-0.10	-0.05
RMMC (E&K)$_{im}$	Raw	0.18	-0.01	-0.09	0.01	-0.01	0.00	0.00	-0.01
	Within	0.05	-0.02	-0.08	0.01	-0.04	-0.01	0.00	0.00
	Between	0.18	-0.01	-0.11	0.03	0.00	0.01	-0.01	-0.03
PMMC$_{im}$	Raw	0.34	0.00	0.01	-0.08	-0.08	-0.11	-0.05	-0.05
	Within	0.26	-0.01	0.04	-0.10	-0.03	-0.05	0.00	0.00
	Between	0.35	0.01	-0.06	-0.07	-0.06	-0.09	-0.12	-0.13
*MMC (B&K'96)$_{im}$	**Raw**	**0.55**	**0.02**	**-0.21**	**-0.19**	**-0.05**	**-0.09**	**0.02**	**0.00**
	Within	**0.82**	**0.03**	**0.25**	**-0.25**	**0.23**	**0.16**	**0.03**	**0.03**
	Between	**0.44**	**0.01**	**-0.31**	**-0.13**	**-0.11**	**-0.16**	**-0.01**	**-0.05**
*MMC (BGSM)$_{im}$	**Raw**	**0.55**	**0.02**	**-0.21**	**-0.19**	**-0.05**	**-0.10**	**0.02**	**0.00**
	Within	**0.83**	**0.03**	**0.25**	**-0.25**	**0.23**	**0.16**	**0.03**	**0.03**
	Between	**0.45**	**0.02**	**-0.31**	**-0.13**	**-0.11**	**-0.16**	**-0.02**	**-0.06**
MMC (Singal)$_{im}$	Raw	-0.05	-0.03	0.01	-0.20	0.13	0.07	-0.02	-0.02
	Within	0.11	-0.02	0.17	-0.27	0.06	0.01	0.01	0.01
	Between	-0.11	-0.03	-0.03	-0.21	0.16	0.10	-0.05	-0.05
Size Score[a]	Raw					0.13		-0.08	
	Within					0.27		0.01	
	Between					0.11		-0.12	
Number of Incumbents	Raw					-0.31		0.01	
	Within					-0.07		0.00	
	Between					-0.35		0.04	

[a] Cronbach's alphas for Size Score for Raw, Within, and Between data are 0.96, 0.85, and 0.97, respectively.

[b] Measures with '*' are original ones used in previous empirical research at the firm-in-market level of analysis.

Table 7. Reliability, Discriminate Validity and Predictive Validity: Market Level.

Overall MMC Score		RELIABILITY	DISCRIMINANT VALIDITY		REDICTIVE VALIDITY			
		Cronbach's Alpha	Zero-order correlations:		Correlations:			
			Size Score	Number of Incumbents	Market Average Yield		Rate of Exit	
					Zero	Partial	Zero	Partial
Overall MMC Score	Raw	0.83	0.67	-0.08	-0.03	-0.10	-0.04	-0.03
	Within	0.85	0.71	-0.08	0.33	0.02	0.01	-0.02
	Between	0.81	0.64	-0.02	-0.18	-0.10	-0.18	-0.09

Individual Measures		RELIABILITY		DISCRIMINANT VALIDITY		REDICTIVE VALIDITY			
		Correlation with the remaining total	Contribution to Alpha	Zero-order correlations		Correlations:			
				Size Score	Number of Incumbents	Market Average Yield		Rate of Exit	
						Zero	Partial	Zero	Partial
*MMC(count)$_m$[b]	Raw	0.79	0.04	0.88	-0.21	0.05	-0.08	-0.06	-0.06
	Within	0.82	0.03	0.88	-0.24	0.38	-0.03	-0.03	-0.05
	Between	0.76	0.04	0.90	-0.13	-0.11	-0.01	-0.14	0.00
*MMC(E&K)$_m$	Raw	0.79	0.04	0.88	-0.21	0.05	-0.08	-0.06	-0.06
	Within	0.82	0.03	0.88	-0.24	0.38	-0.03	-0.03	-0.05
	Between	0.76	0.04	0.90	-0.13	-0.11	-0.01	-0.14	0.00
MMC(G&W'96)$_m$	Raw	0.56	0.02	0.82	-0.23	0.12	0.07	-0.01	0.04
	Within	0.63	0.02	0.85	-0.15	0.45	0.15	0.02	0.02
	Between	0.52	0.02	0.81	-0.21	-0.03	0.06	-0.09	0.04
*MMC(H&O)$_m$	Raw	0.31	0.00	0.37	0.74	-0.26	-0.12	0.03	-0.01
	Within	0.44	0.01	0.47	0.58	0.22	0.07	0.21	0.01
	Between	0.29	0.00	0.38	0.81	-0.42	-0.15	-0.27	-0.03
*SAR$_m$	Raw	0.20	-0.01	0.23	0.18	-0.10	-0.06	0.10	0.10
	Within	0.19	-0.01	0.19	0.52	0.06	-0.01	0.21	0.06
	Between	0.24	-0.01	0.31	0.10	-0.19	-0.11	-0.10	-0.01

Table 7. Continued.

MktComm$_m$	Raw	0.66	0.03	0.30	-0.21	-0.01	-0.09	-0.09	-0.07
	Within	0.64	0.02	0.34	-0.19	0.12	-0.04	-0.09	-0.06
	Between	0.65	0.03	0.22	-0.19	-0.03	-0.07	-0.11	-0.13
MMC (B&K'99)$_m$	Raw	0.60	0.02	0.19	-0.10	-0.02	-0.05	-0.03	-0.02
	Within	0.64	0.02	0.34	-0.12	0.16	0.00	-0.03	-0.01
	Between	0.50	0.02	0.03	-0.06	-0.03	-0.06	-0.06	-0.07
*RMMC (E&K)$_m$	**Raw**	**0.19**	**-0.01**	**-0.18**	**0.00**	**-0.01**	**-0.01**	**0.00**	**0.00**
	Within	**0.09**	**-0.02**	**-0.17**	**0.01**	**-0.07**	**0.01**	**0.00**	**0.01**
	Between	**0.22**	**0.01**	**-0.22**	**-0.01**	**0.01**	**-0.04**	**-0.02**	**-0.06**
*PMMC$_m$	**Raw**	**0.31**	**0.00**	**-0.05**	**-0.08**	**-0.10**	**-0.13**	**-0.06**	**-0.06**
	Within	**0.26**	**-0.01**	**-0.09**	**-0.10**	**-0.07**	**-0.04**	**-0.05**	**-0.01**
	Between	**0.34**	**0.00**	**-0.06**	**-0.05**	**-0.13**	**-0.17**	**-0.11**	**-0.14**
MMC (B&K'96)$_m$	Raw	0.89	0.05	0.70	-0.20	0.01	-0.10	-0.08	-0.07
	Within	0.90	0.04	0.70	-0.23	0.34	0.04	-0.05	-0.05
	Between	0.89	0.05	0.70	-0.13	-0.13	-0.09	-0.16	-0.08
MMC (BGSM)$_m$	Raw	0.89	0.05	0.70	-0.20	0.01	-0.11	-0.08	-0.07
	Within	0.90	0.04	0.70	-0.23	0.34	0.04	-0.06	-0.05
	Between	0.89	0.05	0.70	-0.13	-0.13	-0.09	-0.16	-0.08
*MMC (Singal)$_m$	**Raw**	**-0.14**	**-0.03**	**-0.06**	**-0.02**	**0.07**	**0.07**	**0.01**	**0.01**
	Within	**0.08**	**-0.02**	**0.19**	**-0.22**	**0.10**	**0.01**	**-0.02**	**0.03**
	Between	**-0.30**	**-0.05**	**-0.28**	**0.02**	**0.09**	**0.06**	**0.09**	**0.04**
Size Score[a]	Raw					0.08		-0.03	
	Within					0.45		0.01	
	Between					-0.14		-0.18	
Number of Incumbents	Raw					-0.30		0.06	
	Within					-0.11		0.28	
	Between					-0.36		-0.21	

[a] Cronbach's alphas for Size Score for Raw, Within, and Between data are 0.96, 0.96, and 0.98, respectively.
[b] Measures with '*' are original ones used in previous empirical research at the market level of analysis.

Content Validity

Content validity refers to the extent to which empirical measurement reflects a specific domain of content. However, due to its qualitative nature (Bollen, 1989; Nunnally, 1978), there are no definitive criteria to evaluate content validity. Are the weights theoretically appropriate? Should multimarket contact capture information not only about the number of contacts, but also about the position of firms in those markets, market characteristics, and firm characteristics? Beyond what point do these weights transform the measure of multimarket contact enough to be considered a measure of a different construct? Are the weights that are theoretically appropriate for measuring the forbearance potential of multimarket contacts the same as those measuring the knowledge diffusion potential of the same concepts? Obviously, this is a subjective issue, and researchers have not reached consensus. Given the lack of a widely accepted universe of content to be captured by the multimarket contact measures, the question of validity must rely on other dimensions of the validity of the construct (Cronbach & Meehl, 1955).

Internal Consistency

Reliability
Reliability refers to the absence of measurement error in cluster scores, and can be evaluated from the correlations among the different indicators.[8] Overall, the reliability of multimarket contact measures was generally appropriate regardless of levels of measurement. Coefficients of Cronbach's α ranged from 0.82 to 0.87 for raw measures, which were above the recommended level 0.7 (Nunnally, 1978). Since different levels of analysis used different number of multimarket contact measures and Cronbach's α tends to increase with the number of items, the Cronbach's α coefficients should not be compared across levels.

Table 5 presents the reliability assessment for the dyad-level data set. Among the three α coefficients, the coefficient from raw data was the highest (alpha = 0.87). Reliability among dyad measures was greater in cross-sectional data (alpha = 0.86) than in longitudinal data (alpha = 0.78). That is, the multiple measures agreed more in determining which dyad had greater multimarket contact than in determining whether multimarket contact for a given dyad was increasing or decreasing.

Among the dyad measures, Singal's (1996) measure [MMC(Singal)] and Evans & Kessides's (1994) revenue-based measure [RMMC(E&K)] were least reliable. The respective correlation coefficients of these two measures with the overall multimarket contact score (the sum of all measures) were relatively low. The column 'Correlation with the remaining total' in Tables 5 to 7 represents the correlation between individual measures and the sum of the remaining (standardized) variables. The column 'Contribution to Alpha' represents the difference of Cronbach's coefficient α when the measure in question is added after the other measures. A measure with a "Contribution to Alpha" below zero indicates that the measure did not increase the overall Cronbach's coefficient α when the measure was added to the other measures. The lack of reliability of Evans & Kessides' (1994) revenue-based measure [RMMC(E&K)] may have been due to its weighting contacts by the product of the percentage of revenues, so that the sum of the weights varies inversely with the number of markets served by the firms.[9] The two measures that were originally designed as dyad level measures [MktComm, MMC(B&K'99)], although reliable, did not stand out as being more reliable than the others.

Table 6 shows that, unlike dyad level measures, firm-in-market level measures showed greater reliability in longitudinal settings (alpha = 0.87) than in cross-sectional settings (alpha = 0.80) or in raw data (alpha = 0.82). Therefore, longitudinal changes in the measures were more reliable than cross-sectional levels of the measures. Two measures in particular [MMC(B&K'96), MMC(BGSM)] were substantially more reliable in the within-unit analysis than in the between-unit analysis. As before, Evans & Kessides's (1994) revenue multimarket contact measure [RMMC(E&K)] and Singal's (1996) measure [MMC(Singal)] had low reliability. In addition, Feinberg's (1985) firm-in-market measure [SAR] and Scott's (1982) measures [PMMC] had low correlations with the rest. Among the original firm-in-market measures, all but Feinberg's (1985) seemed reasonably reliable.

Table 7 presents reliability analysis at the market level measurement. Similar to the firm-in-market level, this level of measurement showed higher overall reliability longitudinally (alpha = 0.85) than cross-sectionally (alpha = 0.81). Measures with low correlations with the rest included RMMC(E&K), MMC(Singal), SAR, PMMC, and MMC(H&O). Among the original market-level measures, only MMC(E&K) and MMC(count) were substantially reliable. The remaining original market-level measures – MMC(H&O), RMMC(E&K), PMCC and MMC(Singal) – had correlations with the remaining measures below 0.5.

In summary, across all levels of measurement, we observed that some measures displayed low correlations with the remaining measures in the set, e.g. RMMC(E&K) and MMC(Singal). These variables shared little common variance with the others, and their variance was highly idiosyncratic. The simple count measures performed very well across all three levels in terms of reliability. While they lacked the elaborate weighting scheme of other measures, they captured well the main dimension of commonality among the measures. This is not surprising, since most measures begin with a count of multimarket contact, which is then transformed through scaling or weighting.

Unidimensionality

We carried several exploratory factor analyses (with principal components factors and both orthogonal and oblique rotation) to test whether the various multimarket measures loaded into one or more factors that explain their common variance. Using the Kaiser criterion, these exploratory analyses suggested three factors across all levels. However, only one measure loaded strongly into the third factor, which explained less than 10% of variance. Accordingly, we also considered models with two factor solutions, with orthogonal and oblique rotations. Regardless of rotation methods, the results were consistent across levels.

Among the two factor solutions, one factor reflected measures that have an upper limit that is varying among firms, usually a function of the number of markets served by the firms. We refer to these measures as being in *absolute scale*, and the measures included MMC(E&K), MMC(count), MMC(G&W'96), MMC(H&O), and SAR. The other factor reflected measures that have been forced to a well-understood distribution with lower and upper limits (usually, 0 to 1) by the application of scales or weights such as dividing by the number of markets served or weighting contact by the percentage of revenues. We refer to these measures as being *relative scale*, and such measures included MktComm, MMC(B&K'99), RMMC(E&K), PMMC, MMC(B&K'96) and MMC(BGSM). MMC(Singal) did not load well on either factor. As we compared the results of these exploratory factor analyses across levels, we found some interesting contrasts. For instance, MMC(B&K'96) and MMC(BGSM) loaded highly on both factors at the market level of measurement, but not so at other levels of measurement.[10] In sum, we didn't find unidimensionality among existing multimarket contact measures.

Discriminant Validity

Discriminant validity refers to how much a construct differs from other constructs. To assess the discriminant validity of multimarket contact measures, we selected several variables that were not part of the nomological network of multimarket contact, but were related to multimarket contact. Those variables were size-related variables and the number of competing firms in a market. Size was chosen because large firms active in many markets were more likely to meet other firms in multiple markets (e.g. Scott, 1982). The number of incumbents was chosen at the firm-in-market and market levels because multimarket contact measures at those levels are aggregates of contacts among market incumbents.

At the dyad level (Table 5), the correlations between the overall score of multimarket contact (sum of standardized measures) and the size score (sum of three standardized measures of average dyad size) ranged between 0.51 (within) to 0.63 (raw data). These correlations were larger than many of the correlations among measures of multimarket contact (Table 2). Discriminant validity seemed particularly problematic among measures representing multimarket contact counts in absolute scale [M, MMC(G&W'96), MMC(H&O) and SAR]. Multimarket contact measures in relative scale [MktComm, MMC(B&K'99), RMMC(E&K), PMMC, MMC(B&K'96), MMC(BGSM)] were less correlated to size, and therefore had better discriminant validity. Count measures, while more reliable, have lower discriminant validity.

For the firm-in-market level of analysis (Table 6), the correlations between the multimarket contact score and the size score ranged between 0.45 and .50, and was the lowest among the three levels of analysis. At the market level of analysis (Table 7), the correlations with size reached between 0.64 and 0.71, the highest among the three levels. Some individual measures had correlations with the size score above 0.80. The findings indicated that the firm-in-market level of analysis allowed better separation between the constructs of multimarket contact and size, whereas the market level of analysis afforded the least separation. Generally, measures of multimarket contact on absolute scales [that is, MMC(E&K), MMC(count), MMC(G&W'96), and less so, MMC(H&O) and SAR] had much lower discriminant validity. Therefore, researchers using these measures should be careful to include statistical controls for firm size or number of markets served in order to avoid spurious correlations. Discriminant validity with respect to the number of incumbents was generally high (i.e. correlations between measures of multimarket contact and the number of incumbents were low), although some measures that were constructed as sums of multimarket contacts across rivals displayed low discriminant validity (e.g. SAR and MMC(H&O)).

In sum, the results at the three levels of analysis showed that the overall discriminant validity of multimarket contact was low with respect to size, but high with respect to number of market incumbents. Depending on their construction and the level of analysis, some measures showed high correlation at one level but low correlation at a different level (e.g. SAR showed high correlation with size at the firm-in-market level, but low correlation at the market level).

Predictive Validity

Predictive validity involves the degree to which predictions from a theoretical network are confirmed. Here we assessed predictive validity using correlational relationships between multimarket contact measures and several variables reflecting mutual forbearance. Previous results indicated that some measures suffered from low discriminant validity with respect to size or number of incumbents. Since these variables may also have been causally linked to the dependent variables, we used partial correlations (in addition to zero-order or Pearson correlations) to evaluate the predictive validity of the measures. These partial correlations controlled for the effects of size and the number of incumbents on the relevant dependent variables. More variables could have been controlled to avoid possible spurious correlations. However, our goal here was not to build a well-fitting predictive model for mutual forbearance, but to compare the predictive validity of multiple measures of multimarket contact. The comparisons were simpler and more intuitive if the set of partialled out variables was kept small and consistent across models.

At the dyad level (Table 5), we chose three dependent variables: rate of entry, rate of exit, and net entry. We expected multimarket contact to be negatively related to all three variables. Entry into another firm's markets could be understood as an aggressive move (attack), and therefore low levels of entry might reflect mutual forbearance. Exit may be the result of intense rivalry, and therefore low levels of exit might reflect mutual forbearance. Mutual forbearance may also be associated with lower levels of net entry (entry minus exit) (Baum & Korn, 1999).

The correlations between the overall multimarket contact score and the dependent variables provided mixed results regarding predictive validity at the dyad level. Multimarket contact had strong positive zero-order correlations with rates of entry in the raw and between-dyad data sets ($r = 0.20$), and mildly negative ones in the within-dyad data ($r = -0.06$). The partial correlations with rate of entry were low, reflecting little predictive validity. Perhaps a curvilinear model would have explained this relationship better (Baum & Korn, 1999). The zero-order and partial correlations with rate of exit had greater predictive validity. Using the raw data and the between-dyad data, we found that dyads with high multimarket contact tended have lower exit rates from each other's markets (effects ranging between -0.07 and -0.10). However, longitudinally, we did not find evidence in the within-dyad data that exit rates decreases as multimarket contact increased over time. Finally, with respect to net entry, we found consistently negative zero-order and partial correlations. Interestingly, within-dyad partial correlations were more strongly negative ($r = -0.10$) than between-dyad partial correlations ($r = -0.06$). Therefore, dyads with higher multimarket contact had lower net entry, and net entry decreased if dyads increase their multimarket contact over time.

With respect to individual measures, the results were mixed: while some measures mirrored the results for the overall multimarket contact score, others differed substantially. MktComm, MMC(B&K'96) and MMC(BGSM) had stronger between-dyad negative partial correlations with net entry, but weaker negative (or positive) partial correlations with net exit. The original dyad measures, MktComm and MMC(B&K'99) showed results consistent with the overall MMC score. MMC(Singal) was the only measure in the set with negative raw, within-dyad and between-dyad partial correlations with all three dependent variables, although the magnitude of these correlations was often very low.

At the firm-in-market level of analysis (Table 6), we expected positive correlations with yields (indicating higher prices, or less aggressive pricing behavior) and negative correlations with exit. The zero-order correlation between the overall multimarket contact score and yield was low ($r = 0.01$), yet the within-unit (longitudinal) correlation was substantial ($r = 0.27$). Although firm-in-market combinations with high multimarket contact did not have higher yields than others with low multimarket contact, yields tended to increase if firm-in-market multimarket contact increased for a firm-in-market unit over time. After controlling for the effects of size and number of incumbents, the within-unit correlation remained meaningful ($r = 0.16$), but the between-unit correlation turned negative ($r = -0.14$). So, after correcting for size and incumbents, firm-in-market units with higher multimarket contact tended to have lower yields, yet the yields of those units would increase longitudinally with increased multimarket contact. This paradoxical result may explain why prior cross-sectional research on the price effects of multimarket contact has found inconsistent evidence about forbearance (e.g. Rhoades & Heggestad, 1985), yet longitudinal research – specially using fixed effects – has found support for the theory.

Regarding firm-in-market exit, the expected negative correlations only materialized for the raw and between-unit data sets. In contrast with yield, firm-in-market exit had little within-unit longitudinal variation. Indeed, many firms never exited the markets. The between-unit results indicated that firm-in-market units with more multimarket contact were less likely to exit ($r = -0.10$), yet the within-unit results indicated that the likelihood of exit marginally increased if multimarket contact augmented over time. Variables that had been used at the firm-in-market level [MMC(count), MMC(G&W'96), SAR, MMC(B&K'96) and MMC(BGSM)] displayed correlations with yield that were consistent with those of the overall score (positive within-unit correlations, negative between-unit correlations), but their correlations with exit were less consistent. The measure MMC(Singal) had between-unit partial correlations with both firm-in-market yield and exit that were consistent with theory ($r = 0.10$ and $r = -0.05$, respectively), but the within-unit correlations were weak in both cases.

Finally, at the market level of analysis (Table 7), we calculated the correlations of market-level multimarket contact with average market yield and market-level exit rate. The results closely mirrored the findings at the firm-in-market level. The overall multimarket contact score had a negative between-market

correlation with market yield (r = −0.18), and a positive within-market correlation
with market yield (r=0.33). However, given the low discriminant validity between
the multimarket contact score and the size score at the market-level, the partial
correlations with yield were reduced to −0.10 between-market correlation and
0.02 within-market correlation. The low discriminant validity of the multimarket
contact score also compromised its predictive validity with respect to market yield.
With respect to market-level rate of exit, however, the findings were more consistent than at the firm-in-market level. All three partial correlations were negative,
although the within-market partial correlation was very small (r = −0.02), possibly
due to the limited longitudinal variation on market-level rate of exit.

Against expectations, most individual measures had negative between-
market and within-market partial correlations with market yield, although
MMC(G&W'96) and MMC(Singal) had positive partial correlations with market
yield both longitudinally and cross-sectionally. The correlations of individual
measures with market-level exit rate were more consistent with previous findings
at other levels of analysis. Markets with high multimarket contact showed lower
market-level exit rates, although the exit rate did not necessarily decrease longitudinally as the level of multimarket contact in the market increased over time.

CONCLUSIONS AND RECOMMENDATIONS

Our analysis of reliability and validity of multimarket contact allowed us to
draw several conclusions about the validity of current measures of multimarket
contact, and to advance recommendations for future research. Of course, our
recommendations are constrained by the data used in the study, and we
encourage replication of this measurement analysis with other data sources.
Moreover, our intent is not to single out individual measures for criticism or
praise, but to provide an assessment of the underlying issues and trade-offs
involved in the choice of a multimarket contact measure.

First, there is clearly no consensus about the appropriate content of
multimarket contact measures. Multimarket contact is sometimes measured as
a pure count of the contacts among firms, sometimes as a count of contacts
weighted by their importance, and sometimes as a count of contacts weighted
by their contribution to mutual forbearance. The inflation of weights has
hindered the comparison of results across studies, since empirical results may
reflect different substantive relationships or different measurement weights.
Parsimony and generalizability in the use of weights may increase the comparability of research studies. Data-specific or context-specific weights impede
replication. As an initial step, we encourage proponents of weighted measures

to also analyze their data using unweighted measures and seriously consider whether the weighted measures have greater discriminant and predictive validity than the unweighted measures.

Second, in order to advance research on multimarket competition beyond forbearance effects, future research should conceptually and explicitly separate the constructs of "multimarket contact" and "forbearance potential". While the constructs are causally related, they are not equivalent. In addition to the extent of multimarket contact, forbearance potential may be due to other factors such as concentration, market share or growth in the contact markets, relative position of competitors in contact markets, etc. In our opinion, Singal's (1996) multi-market contact measure actually represents a measure of forbearance potential. This would explain its low reliability vis-à-vis other measures of multimarket contact, and its relatively high predictive validity in the forbearance-related hypotheses. Distinguishing between multimarket contact and forbearance potential allows researchers to explicitly test moderator hypotheses about the effects of multimarket contacts, rather than including those in the construction of the measure. Work by Fernandez and Marin (1998), Gimeno (1994, 1999) and Gimeno and Woo (1999) illustrate how moderator tests can be used for testing differences in the forbearance consequences of multimarket contacts.

Third, existing measures of multimarket contact exhibit adequate reliability (with some exceptions), but lack unidimensionality. Two sets of measures emerge from exploratory factor analysis. The first set reflects multimarket contact measures with absolute scales, whereas the second set includes measures of multimarket contact relative to the size or scope of the firms. In fact, measure of absolute-scale multimarket contact and relative-scale multimarket contact are rather internally consistent. Future research should carefully consider whether an absolute or relative multimarket contact measure fits their theoretical model. Absolute-scale measures may be better for capturing the absolute magnitude of economic retaliation opportunities, whereas relative-scale measures may be better for capturing the managerial perceptions of overlap.

Fourth, discriminant validity with respect to firm size is generally low, and is even lower for some multimarket contact measures in absolute scale. So when size is likely to have a direct effect on the dependent variable, the use of absolute-scale multimarket contact measures without statistical control for size is likely to lead to spurious results. In that situation, it is advisable to use either relative-scale multimarket contact measures (to take out the size component of the measure) or absolute-scale measures together with a statistical control for size effects. Unless multicolinearity prevents the use of size as a predictor, it may be desirable to explicitly control for size so that size may have its own direct causal effect on the dependent variable.

Fifth, level of measurement and analysis (dyad, firm-in-market, and market) matters substantially in determining the predictive validity of multimarket contact measures. As the comparison of the firm-in-market and market level analyses shows, some correlations can be substantially changed by aggregation. Given that there is still no consensus about the appropriate level of analysis, it is perhaps best to select the most disaggregated level of analysis available, and then empirically determine whether a higher level of aggregation is more appropriate. For instance, if the analysis is carried at the firm-in-market level of analysis, it is relatively straightforward to determine whether firm-in-market level or market level multimarket contact have greater predictive validity. Future research would benefit from developing proxies for mutual forbearance at the dyad-in-market level, since this is the most disaggregated level, and would allow researchers to determine which of the three levels of analysis currently in use is best for studying multimarket contact. Of course, the right level of analysis may again depend on the theoretical question asked.

Sixth, in addition to level of measurement, the temporal structure of the data and analysis (i.e. whether it is cross-sectional or longitudinal) is likely to seriously influence results. Our findings suggest that some correlations between variables can switch polarity depending on whether we are considering cross-sectional analysis (comparison among multiple units) or longitudinal/panel analysis (correlations of temporal changes within units). For researchers considering continuous dependent variables, panel data models such as the ones used by Evans and Kessides (1994), Gimeno and Woo (1996, 1999), and Gimeno (1999) can facilitate controlling for unobserved heterogeneity through fixed or random effects.

Although research in multimarket organizations and multimarket competition has grown exponentially over the last few years, the growth potential of this topic is still uncapped. It is hard to think of an industry context that cannot be studied from a multiunit or multimarket perspective. The single-market models of neoclassical economics fail to describe the fundamentally multi-unit/multimarket nature of today's businesses landscape. We expect to see extension of multimarket competition research in international contexts and in high technology contexts. More research on the boundary conditions for mutual forbearance is also required. In addition, researchers have just begun to study the antecedents of multimarket contact and other non-forbearance consequences, such as market-based knowledge diffusion and mimicry. Yet, in order to build that exciting line of research on rigorous ground, careful attention to measurement issues is necessary. By opening discussion and examination of the measures of multimarket contact, this paper indirectly contributes to the ongoing substantive development of multiunit/multimarket research.

ACKNOWLEDGMENTS

We are grateful to the editors Joel Baum and Henrich Greve for their substantive comments and editorial guidance on the previous versions of the paper. And we also thank Metin Sengul and Tieying Yu for comments on a previous draft.

NOTES

1. For more extensive review of the theoretical and empirical literature on multi-market contact or multimarket competition, please see Baum and Korn (1999) and Jayachandran, Gimeno and Varadarajan (1999).

2. The terms market-unit and firm-market have also been used to described this level of analysis.

3. This may explain the difference in results between Baum and Korn (1996) and Baum and Korn (1999). At the firm-in-market level of analysis, Baum and Korn (1996) found a negative linear effect of multimarket contact on entry and exit. Yet, at the dyad level of analysis, Baum and Korn (1999) found an inverted U-shaped relationship between multimarket contact and entry and exit. It is possible that the aggregation of dyadic contacts implicit in the firm-in-market analysis in the first paper concealed the nonlinear relationship of multimarket contact found in the second (Baum & Korn, 1999: 274).

4. The paper by Scott (this volume) expands this measure to include contacts in both product and innovation markets.

5. The denominator in the formula is the number of possible non-ordered pairs of firms in the market.

6. The other two measures presented by Jans and Rosenbaum (1996), but not shown here, are: (1) average market share in non-home contact markets that represents the magnitude of presence of pair of firms in those markets; and (2) average Herfindahl index in non-home markets that captures the level of concentration in those contact markets. These two measures are not shown here because we believe these two do not measure the extent of multimarket contact but rather the characteristics of those contact markets.

7. Due to the unavailability of the information about the number of employees in a certain market, we used the number of passengers instead. Hughes and Oughton (1993: 221) offer a "numbers equivalent" interpretation of the index. However as they pointed out, the interpretation assumes that firms in a market are of equal size.

8. In our specific context, the correlations between the measures may indicate reliability or convergent validity. Convergent validity refers to high agreement between multiple attempts to measure the same construct with different methods. If we think of the multiple multimarket contact measures as multiple indicators of a common underlying construct (multimarket contact), then high correlations among those indicators would indicate high reliability. If we think of these measures as alternative single-item constructs, then high correlations would indicate high convergent validity. Although the evidence of inter-measure correlations is discussed in the section of reliability, the same evidence could be brought forward to evaluate the convergent validity of the measures.

9. For instance, if two firms with 10 equally sized units perfectly overlap, their multimarket contact only adds up to 10*(0.1)2 = 0.1. If they had 100 equally sized units with perfect overlap, the measure goes down to 0.01.

10. Results from these exploratory factor analyses are available upon request from the authors.

REFERENCES

Adams, W. J. (1974). Market structure and corporate power: The horizontal dominance hypothesis reconsidered. *Columbia Law Review*, *74*, 1276–1297.

Alexander, D. L. (1985). An empirical test of the mutual forbearance hypothesis: The case of bank holding companies. *Southern Economic Journal*, *52*, 122–140.

Areeda, P., & Turner, D. (1979). Conglomerate mergers: Extended interdependence and effects on interindustry competition as grounds for condemnation. *University of Pennsylvania Law Review*, *127*, 1982–1103.

Bagozzi, R. P. (1980). *Causal models in marketing*. New York: Wiley.

Barnett, W. P. (1993). Strategic deterrence among multipoint competitors. *Industrial and Corporate Change*, *2*, 249–278.

Baum, J. A. C., & Korn, H. J. (1996). Competitive dynamics of interfirm rivalry. *Academy of Management Journal*, *39*, 255–291.

Baum, J. A. C., & Korn, H. J. (1999). Dynamics of dyadic competitive interaction. *Strategic Management Journal*, *20*, 251–278.

Bernheim, D., & Whinston, M. D. (1990). Multimarket contact and collusive behavior. *RAND Journal of Economics*, *21*, 1–26.

Boeker, W. J., Goodstein, J., Stephan, & Murmann, J. P. (1997). Competition in a multimarket environment: The case of market exit. *Organization Science*, *8*, 126–142.

Bollen, K. A. (1989). *Structural equations with latent variables*. New York: John Wiley & Sons.

Boyd, B. K., Reuning-Elliott, E. (1998). A measurement model of strategic planning. *Strategic Management Journal*, *19*, 181–192.

Carmines, E. G., & Zeller, R. A. (1979). *Reliability and validity*. Beverly Hills, CA: Sage Publication.

Chen, M. (1996). Competitor analysis and interfirm rivalry: Toward a theoretical integration. *Academy of Management Review*, *21*(1), 100–134.

Cronbach, L. J., & Meehl, P. E. (1955). Construct validity in psychological tests. *Psychological Bulletin*, *52*, 281–302.

Edwards, C. D. (1955). *Conglomerate bigness as a source of power. In Business concentration and price policy* (pp. 331–352). A Conference of the Universities-National Bureau Committee for Economic Research Princeton, NJ: Princeton University Press.

Evans, W. N., & Kessides, I. N. (1994). Living by the "Golden Rule": Multimarket contact in U.S. airline industry. *Quarterly Journal of Economics*, *109*, 341–366.

Feinberg, R. M. (1985). "Sales-at-Risk": A test of the mutual forbearance theory of conglomerate behavior. *Journal of Business*, *58*, 225–241.

Fernandez, N., & Marin, P. L. (1998). Market Power and Multimarket Contact: Some Evidence from the Spanish Hotel Industry. *Journal of Industrial Economics*, *46*, 3, 301–315.

Gimeno, J. (1994). *Multipoint competition, market rivalry and firm performance: A test of the mutual forbearance hypothesis in the U.S. airline industry, 1984–1988*. Unpublished Ph.D. dissertation, Purdue University.

Gimeno, J. (1999). Reciprocal threats in multimarket rivalry: Staking out 'spheres of influence' in the U.S. airline industry. *Strategic Management Journal, 20,* 101–128.

Gimeno, J., & Woo, C. Y. (1996). Hypercompetition in a multimarket environment: The role of strategic similarity and multimarket contact in competitive de-escalation. *Organization Science, 7,* 322–341.

Gimeno, J., & Woo, C. Y. (1999). Multimarket contact, economies of scope and firm performance. *Academy of Management Journal, 42,* 239–259.

Gimeno, J., Loree, D., & Beal, B. D. (1999). *The dynamics of global expansion: A system-level approach.* Working Paper, Texas A&M University.

Greene, W. H. (1997). *Econometric analysis.* (3rd ed.). Upper Saddle River, NJ: Prentice-Hall Inc.

Greve, H. R. (1995). Jumping ship: The diffusion of strategy abandonment. *Administrative Science Quarterly, 40,* 444–473.

Haveman, H. A., & Nonnemaker, L. (2000). Competition in multiple geographic markets: The impact on growth and market entry. *Administrative Science Quarterly, 45,* 232–267.

Heggestad, A. A., & Rhoades, S. A. (1978). Multimarket interdependence and local market competition in banking. *Review of Economics and Statistics, 60,* 523–532.

Hofer, C. W. (1983). ROVA: A new measure for assessing organizational performance. In: R. Lamb (Ed.). *Advances in Strategic Management,* Vol. 2. (pp. 43–44). New York: JAI Press.

Hoskisson, R. E., Hitt, M. A., Johnson, R. A., & Moesel, D. D. (1993). Construct validity of an objective (entropy) categorical measure of diversification strategy. S*trategic Management Journal, 14,* 215–235.

Hughes, K. & Oughton, C. (1993). Diversification, multi-market contact and profitability. *Economica, 60,* 203–224.

Jans, I., & Rosenbaum, D. I. (1996). Multimarket contact and pricing: Evidence from the U.S. cement industry. *International Journal of Industrial Organization, 15,* 391–412.

Jayachandran, S., Gimeno, J., & Varadarajan, P. R. (1999). The theory of multimarket competition: A synthesis and implications for marketing strategy. *Journal of Marketing, 63*(3), 49–66.

Karnani, A., & Wernerfelt, B. (1985). Multiple point competition. *Strategic Management Journal, 6,* 87–96.

Li, S. X., & Chuang, Y. (2001). Racing for market share: Hypercompetition and the performance of multiunit-multimarket firms. In: J. A. C. Baum & H. R. Greve (Eds.), *Multiunit Organization and Multimarket Strategy*; Advances in strategic management, 18, (pp. 331–357). Oxford, U.K.: JAI Press.

Mester, L. J. (1987). Multiple market contact between savings and loan. *Journal of Money, Credit, and Banking, 19,* 538–549.

Nayyar, P. R. (1993). On the measurement of competitive strategy: Evidence from a large multi-product U.S. firm. *Academy of Management Journal. 36,* 1652–1669.

Nunnally, J. C. (1978). *Psychometric theory.* (2nd ed.). New York: McGraw-Hill.

Parker, P. M., & Roller, L. (1997). Collusion conduct in duopolies: Multimarket contact and cross-ownership in the mobile telephone industry. *RAND Journal of Economics, 28,* 304–322.

Rhoades, S. A., & Heggestad, A. A. (1985). Multimarket interdependence and performance in banking: Two tests. *The Antitrust Bulletin, 30,* 975–995.

Sandler, R. D. (1988). Market share instability in commercial airline markets and the impact of deregulation. *Journal of Industrial Economics,* (36), 327–335.

Schwab, D. P. (1980). Construct validity in organizational behavior. In: B. M. Staw and L. L. Cummings (Eds). *Research in Organizational Behavior.* Vol. 2 (pp. 2–43). Greenwich, CT: JAI Press.

Scott, J. T. (1982). Multimarket contact and economic performance. *Review of Economics and Statistics, 64*, 368–375.

Scott, J. T. (1989). Purposive diversification as a motive for merger. *International Journal of Industrial Organization, 7*, 35–47.

Scott, J. T. (1991). Multimarket contact among diversified oligopolists. *International Journal of Industrial Organization, 9*, 225–238.

Scott, J. T. (2001). Designing multimarket-contact hypothesis tests: Patent citations and multimarket contact in the chemicals industry. In: J. A. C. Baum & H. R. Greve (Eds), *Multiunit Organization and Multimarket Strategy*; Advances in strategic management, Vol. 18: (pp. 175–203). Oxford, U.K.: JAI Press.

Searle, S. R. (1971). *Linear models.* New York, NY: John Wiley & Sons.

Singal, V. (1996). Airline mergers and multimarket contact. *Managerial and Decision Economics, 17*, 559–574.

Smith, F. L., & Wilson, R. L. (1995). The predictive validity of the Karnani and Wernerfelt model of multipoint competition. *Strategic Management Journal, 16*, 143–160.

Solomon, E. H. (1970). Bank merger policy and problems: A linkage theory of oligopoly. *Journal of Money, Credit, and Banking, 2*, 323–336.

Venkatraman, N. & Grant, J. H. (1986). Construct measurement in organizational strategy research: A critique and proposal. *Academy of Management Review, 11*, 71–87.

Whitehead, D. D. III. (1978). *An empirical test of the linked oligopoly theory: An analysis of Florida holding companies. Proceedings of a conference on bank structure and competition* (pp. 119–140). Federal Reserve Bank of Chicago, Chicago, IL: Federal Reserve Bank of Chicago.

Young, G., Smith, K. G., & Grimm, C. M. (1997). "Austrian" and industrial organization perspectives on firm–level competitive activity and performance. *Organization Science. 7*, 243–254.

APPENDIX A

List of measures of multimarket contact and their extensions to multiple levels.

Notes:

(1) Measures with * indicate that these measures were originally designed and/or used in prior research. Other measures were created by disaggregating or aggregating the originally designed measures.

(2) Except for some notations that are specifically used for the measures concerned, we don't provide explanations for the notations that are common across the measures. Common notations are as follows.

Notation	Meaning
i, j	Firms. Usually i refers to a focal firm and j a competing firm.
n, m	Markets. Usually m refers to a focal market.
I_{im}	If firm i is present at a focal market m, then coded 1, otherwise 0.
I_{jm}	If firm j is present at a focal market m, then coded 1, otherwise 0.
I_{in}	If firm i is present at market n, then coded 1, otherwise 0.
I_{jn}	If firm j is present at market n, then coded 1, otherwise 0.
N_m	Total number of firms at a focal market m.
N	Total number of markets.
n_i, n_j	Number of markets served by firm i, j, respectively.
MMC_{ijm}	Degree of multimarket contact between two firms (i and j), that are present in a focal market m, *outside* the focal market (Dyad-in-market level).
MMC_{ij}	Overall degree of multimarket contact between two firms (i and j) across *all* the markets where both firms are present (Dyad level).
MMC_{im}	Overall degree of multimarket contact between a focal firm and its focal-market competitors (Firm-in-market level).
MMC_m	Overall degree of multimarket contact among the firms serving a focal market m (Market level).

Scott (1982)

$$PMMC_{ijm} = I_{im} \cdot I_{im} \cdot \sum_{f=0}^{M_{ijm}-1} \frac{\binom{n_j-1}{f}\binom{N-n_j}{n_i-1-f}}{\binom{N-1}{n_i-1}}, \text{ for } n_j \geq n_i.$$

$$PMMC_{ij} = \sum_{f=0}^{M_{ij}-1} \frac{\binom{n_j}{f}\binom{N-n_j}{n_i-f}}{\binom{N}{n_i}}, \text{ for } n_j \geq n_i.$$

$$PMMC_{im} = \frac{\sum_{j \neq i} PMMC_{ijm}}{N_m - 1}.$$

$$PMMC_m = \frac{\sum_{i} PMMC_{im}}{N_m}.$$

where M_{ijm}: see **Count** below

Chen (1996)

$$*MktComm_{ij} = \sum_{n} \left(\frac{P_{in}}{P_i}\right)\left(\frac{P_{jn}}{P_n}\right)$$

$$MktComm_{ijm} = I_{im} \cdot I_{jm} \cdot MktComm_{ij} \cdot$$

$$MktComm_{im} = \frac{\sum_{j \neq i} MktComm_{ijm}}{N_m - 1}.$$

$$MktComm_m = \frac{\sum_{i} MktComm_{im}}{N_m}.$$

where, P_{in} : total number of passengers served by airline i at market n

P_i: total number of passenges served by airline i

P_n: total number of passengers at market n

Baum & Korn (1999)

$$* \ MMC(\text{B \& K'99})_{ij} = \frac{\sum_n ((C_{in} + C_{jn}) \cdot (I_{in} \cdot I_{jn}))}{\sum_n I_{in} + \sum_n I_{jn}}, \ \text{for} \ \forall \sum_n (I_{in} \cdot I_{jn}) = M_{ij} > 1, \ 0 \ \text{otherwise.}$$

$$MMC(\text{B \& K'99})_{ijm} = I_{im} \cdot I_{jm} \cdot MMC(\text{B \& K'99})_{ij}.$$

$$MMC(\text{B \& K'99})_{im} = \frac{\sum_{j \neq i} MMC(\text{B \& K'99})_{ijm}}{N_m - 1}.$$

$$MMC(\text{B \& K'99})_m = \frac{\sum_i MMC(\text{B \& K'99})_{im}}{N_m}.$$

Where, C_{in}: the proportion of airline i's city-pair routes connecting with city-pair route n.

Count

$$M_{ijm} = I_{im} \cdot I_{jm} \cdot \sum_{n \neq m} I_{in} \cdot I_{jn}.$$

$$M_{ij} = \sum_n I_{in} \cdot I_{jn}.$$

$$MMC(\text{count})_{im} = \frac{\sum_{j \neq i} M_{ijm}}{N_m - 1}.$$

$$MMC(\text{count})_m = \frac{\sum_i MMC(\text{count})_{im}}{N_m}.$$

Gimeno and Woo (1996)

$$\text{MMC}_{\text{(G \& W'96)}_{ijm}} = I_{im} \cdot \left(I_{jm} + T_{jm}\right) \sum_{n \neq m} \left(I_{in} + T_{in}\right) \cdot I_{jn}.$$

$$\text{MMC}_{\text{(G \& W'96)}_{ij}} = \sum_{n} \left(I_{in} + T_{in}\right) \cdot I_{jn}.$$

$${}^{*}\text{MMC}_{\text{(G \& W'96)}_{im}} = \frac{\displaystyle\sum_{j \neq i} \text{MMC}_{\text{(G \& W'96)}_{ijm}}}{\displaystyle\sum_{j \neq i} \left(I_{jm} + T_{jm}\right)}.$$

$$\text{MMC}_{\text{(G \& W'96)}_{m}} = \frac{\displaystyle\sum_{i} \text{MMC(G\&W'96)}_{im}}{N_{m}}.$$

where T_{in} equals 1 if airline i is a potential entrant to city-pair market n, otherwise 0.

Feinberg (1985)

$$\text{SAR}_{ijm} = I_{im} \cdot I_{jm} \sum_{n \neq m} I_{in} \cdot I_{jn} \cdot S_{in}.$$

$$\text{SAR}_{ij} = \sum_{n} I_{in} \cdot I_{jn} \cdot S_{in}.$$

$${}^{*}\text{SAR}_{im} = \sum_{j \neq i} \text{SAR}_{ijm}.$$

$${}^{*}\text{SAR} = \frac{\displaystyle\sum_{i} \text{SAR}_{im}}{\displaystyle\sum_{i} S_{im}}.$$

where, S_{in} : sales of firm i from market n

Boeker et al. (1997)

$$\text{MMC(BGSM)}_{ij} = \frac{\displaystyle\sum_{n} I_{in} \cdot I_{jn}}{\displaystyle\sum_{n} I_{in}}.$$

$$\text{MMC(BGSM)}_{ijm} = I_{im} \cdot I_{jm} \cdot \text{MMC(BGSM)}_{ij}.$$

$${}^{*}\text{MMC(BGSM)}_{im} = \frac{\displaystyle\sum_{j \neq i} \text{MMC(BGSM)}_{ijm}}{N_{m} - 1}.$$

$$\text{MMC(BGSM)}_{m} = \frac{\displaystyle\sum_{i} \text{MMC(BGSM)}_{im}}{N_{m}}.$$

Baum & Korn (1996)

$$\text{MMC(B \& K'96)}_{ij} = \frac{\sum_n I_{in} \cdot I_{jn}}{\sum_n I_{in}} .$$

$$\text{MMC(B \& K'96)}_{ijm} = I_{im} \cdot I_{jm} \cdot \text{MMC(B \& K'96)}_{ij}.$$

$$* \text{MMC(B \& K'96)}_{im} \frac{\sum_{j \neq i} B_{ij} \cdot \text{MMC(B \& K'96)}_{ijm}}{\sum_{j \neq i} B_{ij} \cdot I_{jm}}, \text{ where } B_{ij} = 1 \text{ if } \sum_n (I_{in} \cdot I_{jn}) = M_{ij} > 1, \text{ 0 otherwise.}$$

$$\text{MMC(B \& K'96)}_m = \frac{\sum_i \text{MMC(B \& K'96)}_{im}}{N_m} .$$

Evans & Kessides (1994): count

$$M_{ij} = \sum_n I_{in} \cdot I_{jn}.$$

$$\text{MMC(E \& K)}_{ijm} = I_{im} \cdot I_{jm} \cdot \sum_n I_{in} \cdot I_{jn}.$$

$$\text{MMC(E \& K)}_{im} = \frac{\sum_{j \neq i} \text{MMC(E \& K)}_{ijm}}{N_m - 1} .$$

$$*\text{MMC(E \& K)}_m = \frac{\sum_i \text{MMC(E \& K)}_{im}}{N_m} .$$

Evans & Kessides (1994): revenue

$$\text{RMMC(E \& K)}_{ij} = \sum_n \frac{S_{in}}{S_i} \cdot \frac{S_{jn}}{S_j} .$$

$$\text{RMMC(E \& K)}_{ijm} = I_{im} \cdot I_{jm} \cdot \text{RMMC(E \& K)}_{ij} .$$

$$\text{RMMC(E \& K)}_{im} = \frac{\sum_{j \neq i} \text{RMMC(E \& K)}_{ijm}}{N_m - 1} .$$

$$*\text{RMMC(E \& K)}_m = \frac{\sum_i \text{RMMC(E \& K)}_{im}}{N_m} .$$

where, S_{in}: sales of airline i from city-pair market n,
$\quad\quad$ S_i: total sales of airline i.

Hughes and Oughton (1993)

$$\text{MMC}^{(\text{H \& O})}_{ijm} = I_{im} \cdot I_{jm} \cdot \left(\frac{E_{im} + E_{jm}}{E_m} \right) \sum_{n \neq m} (I_{in} \cdot I_{jn}).$$

$$\text{MMC}^{(\text{H \& O})}_{ij} = \sum_m \text{MMC}^{(\text{H \& O})}_{ijm}.$$

$$\text{MMC}^{(\text{H \& O})}_{im} = \sum_{j \neq i} \text{MMC}^{(\text{H \& O})}_{ijm}.$$

$$*\text{MMC}^{(\text{H \& O})}_{m} = \sum_i \sum_{j > i} \text{MMC}^{(\text{H \& O})}_{ijm}.$$

where, E_{im} : number of employees of firm i working in industry m.

Singal (1996)

$$\text{MC}^{(\text{Singal})}_{ijm} = I_{im} \cdot I_{jm} \cdot \frac{(MS_{im} + MS_{jm}) \sqrt{MS_{im}/MS_{jm}}}{N_m(N_m - 1)/2} \cdot \frac{\sqrt{R_m \times 100}}{R_{total}}$$
$$\text{, for } MS_{im} \geq MS_{jm}.$$

$$\text{MMC}^{(\text{Singal})}_{ij} = \sum_n \text{MC}^{(\text{Singal})}_{ijn}.$$

$$\text{MMC}^{(\text{Singal})}_{ijm} = \text{MC}^{(\text{Singal})}_{ijm} \cdot \sum_{n \neq m} \text{MMC}^{(\text{Singal})}_{ijn}.$$

$$\text{MC}^{(\text{Singal})}_{im} = \sum_{j \neq i} \text{MMC}^{(\text{Singal})}_{ijm}.$$

$$*\text{MC}^{(\text{Singal})}_{m} = \sum_i \sum_{j > 1} \text{MMC}^{(\text{Singal})}_{ijm}.$$

where, MS_{im} : market share of airline i in the market m,
$\quad\quad$ R_m : revenue-per-mile (RPM) in market m,
$\quad\quad$ R_{total} : total revenue-per-mile (RPM) across all markets.